TO MY NAVY FRIEND [illegible]

THE WORLDS GREATEST J-3 PILOT

BES WISHES

[illegible]

WG

On The Edge

(an autobiography)

by

Major Bill L. Disbrow
(USAF Retired)

Winlock Galey
Book Publishers to the Public

On the Edge
(an autobiography)
by
Major Bill L. Disbrow
(USAF Retired)

Published by
Winlock Galey
Book Publishers to the Public
26135 Murrieta Road
Sun City, Ca 92585-9462
www.winlockgaley.com

ISBN 1-890461-33-4

Library of Congress Control Number: 20059206

Price: $34.95

Contents

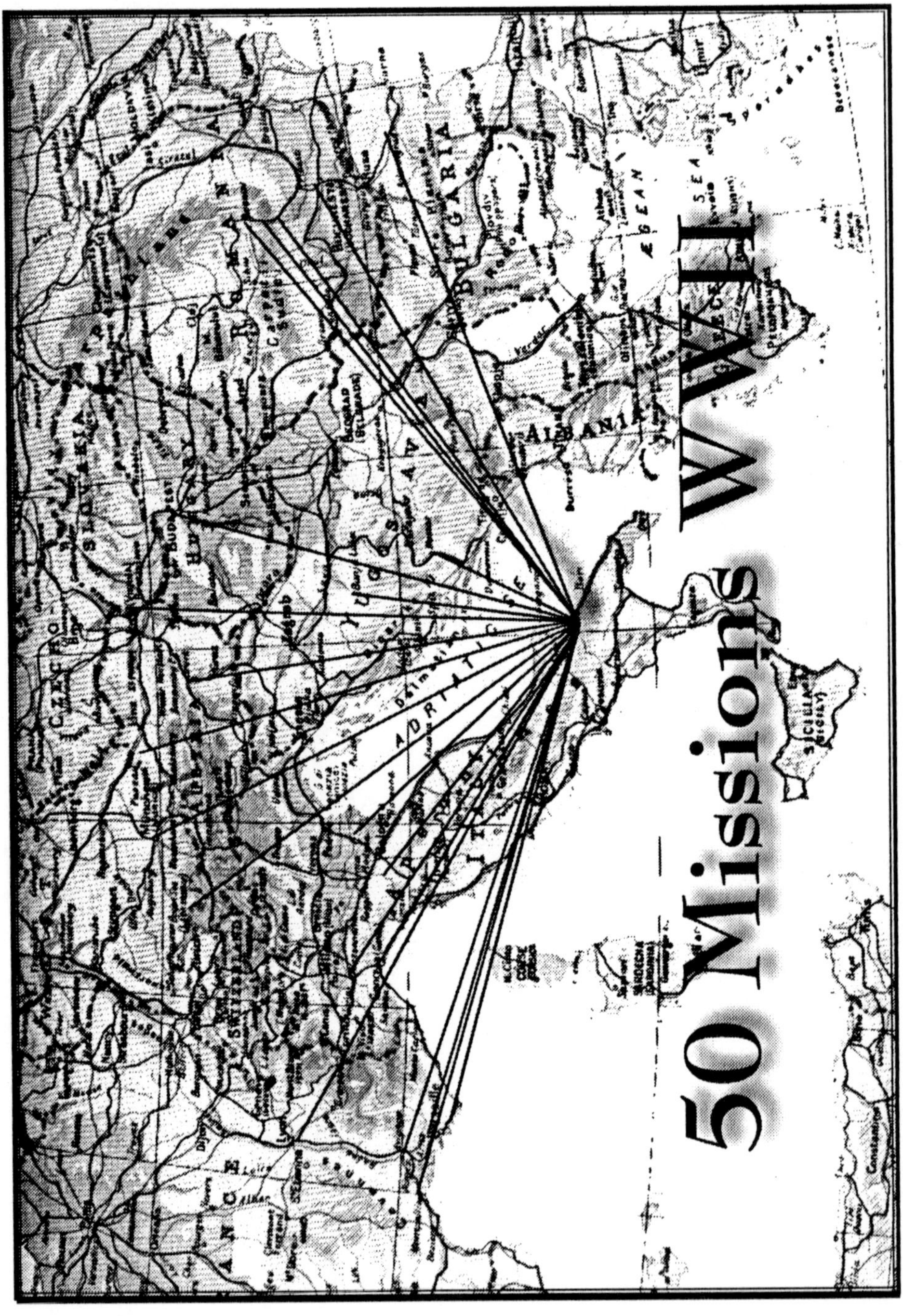
50 Missions WWII
ALBANIA
BULGARIA

DEDICATION

I dedicate this book to my wonderful family, friends, and my wonderful dance partner "Pirry" Petrich who got me dancing again and to our Lord Jesus Christ who made everything possible by letting me live so long.

On The Edge

I WAS BORN

I was born on the 23 Sept 1915, at 2:30 AM, at 560 33rd street, Oakland, California. My fathers name was Louis Nash Disbrow (AKA Luis Gomez) and my Mothers maiden name was Audrey Hitchcock. My father was born in Colima, Mexico, on the 6 Dec 1891; my mother was born in Piedmont, California, on the 22 Feb 1898. She was 16 years old when she had me.

Bill Disbrow and his mother Audrey in Santa Cruz, California, 1918

My Mother and my Father met when my Father was demonstrating a new automobile to her father, Cecil Hitchcock. I don't know how long they knew each other before they eloped. My aunt was the instigator of the plot and they were married on 24

Bill Disbrow and his dog at Fort Bragg, 1918

Jan 1914.

At about 6 months old my folks moved to a little town in Mendocino County, California. The town was named after the county. This town was a logging center. My Father was an auto mechanic by trade and was working on their rolling stock. After about six months we moved again, to the town of Fort Bragg, Ca. which was about 20 miles north of Mendocino, on the Pacific Coast. We were now about 150 miles north of San Francisco. This would be in early 1917.

In Fort Bragg my Father worked for the Redwood Lumber Company as an auto mechanic. I remember him building an automobile that would run on the narrow gauge railroad. This railroad would run out to the camps they had for the loggers. The car was made from an old Locomobile touring car, a very powerful car in its day. It would pull a flat car full of employees out to the logging camp and back. This was a lot cheaper than running a loco-motive back and forth.

During this time we lived in many different houses. I can only remember a few but I do remember that all the streets were dirt or gravel. The only place I could roller skate was at the grammar school where they had sidewalks. Of course I would see how fast I could go which resulted in many skinned knees. I got my first roller skates when I was 5 years old.

Fort Bragg was a great place for hunting and fishing. My father would take me hunting and fishing all the time. When I was 5 years old he bought me a .22 cal. Stevens single shot rifle to take hunting with him. When I was 4 years old I used to go fishing by myself to the Nojo River and catch "shiners" and bring them home in a can and let them swim around in the kitchen sink. My mother would feed us tuna and say it was the fish I caught. One day I caught a 12 inch trout and a man gave 10 cents for it. That was a fortune; I could buy two ice cream cones for that amount.

It seemed that my Mother worried more about me when I got to be a teenager than she did when I was in Fort Bragg. Of course it was a small town and everyone knew me.

I had a brother named Keith, who was born on the 15 Mar 1920 at the Fabiola Hospital, in Oakland, California. My mother thought she would get better care there and would be close to her family who lived in Oakland, since there was no hospital in Fort Bragg. When she got home I started school in the first grade. I was 5 years old at that time. I liked school and was quite smart for my age since my dear mother had taught me so well when she was home. I knew my ABC's, could read a little, and could tell time. I would raise my hand on every question the teacher asked the class. I would be put in the second grade early so I would not become bored.

During this time, 1920, my father opened his own garage named "DISBROWS GARAGE". One day a "Barnstormer" named "Spike"

My mother, Audrey Disbrow in the WWI Curtiss JN-4 "Jenny" in which I had my first airplane ride with my father in 1920 at Fort Bragg, California

Eldrige came into the garage to have his gas tank repaired on his old JN-4 "Jenny." He had been giving rides at a price when the gas tank sprung a leak. Since my Dad had the only garage in town at the time he volunteered to fix it for him. For doing many more favors for "Spike" he gave my Dad and me a ride in his airplane. This would be my first ride in the air. After that I would live and breathe airplanes for the rest of my life. I was going to be a military pilot in the US Army Air Corps. I was very fortunate to do this and became a combat pilot in the US Army Air Corps, which later became the US Army Air Force then the USAF.

After that ride in that old "Jenny" every thing I did was about airplanes. Unfortunately, one day my Father and me were watching the aircraft fly at the airfield, I noticed that a few more aircraft had arrived at the airfield and were taking off to fly formation. They all got off OK and joined up but as they came across the field two ran together, with one spinning in and bursting into flames right in front of me. It did not seem to bother me much but it sure bothered my Father, who was trying to get close enough to pull the pilots from the flames. It was impossible since it was an inferno and very hot. (This would not be my last mid-air collision I would see in my flying career.)

Spike Eldridge who gave me and my father the flight in the Jenny

My father always wanted to be a pilot and

My father, Louis Disbrow in his 1920 Model "T" Racer,
Fort Bragg, CA 1921

go off to WW1 but my Mother would not let him go since she had me and did not want him going off to war. He would in 1925, join the 381st Reserve Squadron in San Francisco after we left Fort Bragg.

They had started a racetrack at Mendocino to drum up a little excitement in the area. It was a flat dirt track. So of course my Dad had to build a racecar and go racing. This would be in the 20's. It was a Model "T" Ford with only a couple of bucket seats and a gas tank behind on a stripped chassis. He called his creation "Baby Lincoln". He had quite a time racing and had his share of spills and chills and later would get involved with the Lincoln Dealer and drive a Frontenac Ford for him at the Cotati Board Speedway, at Cotati, California. I was never told how well he did in his racing but he was going to a lot of races around California.

I guess I was about seven years old when we left Fort Bragg and "DISBROWS GARAGE", Dec. 1922. There were some financial problems with the bank where my Dad had the loan on his garage. It seemed one of the key personnel had embezzled a goodly amount of money from the bank and "skipped", leaving the bank in the red and they had to call in all the loans to cover their loses. That finished my Dad's business.

The Disbrows: My brother Keith, My dad, Louis and Me
Fort Bragg, Ca 1921

We moved back to Oakland, Ca. to 558-58th Street, next door to my grandfather Cecil Edward Allen Hitchcock! He owned this duplex, so it was very convenient for my folks. Grandfather Hitchcock was my mother's father who owned the Hitchcock Detective and Patrol Service in Oakland and had his business in the Lurie bldg. at 12th and Broadway.

I was enrolled in the Washington Grammar School on Shattuck Avenue and 60th street. I started in the 3rd grade but they put me in the 4th grade due to the good tutoring by my Mother. By this time it was Jan 1923 and my father got a job with the Doble Steam Company. It was located in Emeryville, Ca. not too far from our house. He was to be a test driver and assembly engineer.

We moved again to 1140 Allston Way, Berkeley, Ca. where I had to change schools again and I was enrolled in Columbus grammar school. After a short stay here we moved again to 1818 Curtis Street Berkeley and had to change schools and I was enrolled in Franklin Grammar School on San Pablo Avenue near University Avenue

Here at Franklin I became a Junior Traffic Policeman. I would stop traffic on busy San Pablo Avenue before school, lunchtime, and after school, so the children could cross the street safely. This was in the sixth grade in 1926. Being a Junior Policeman gave me the privileges of riding the streetcar free and get into the movie theaters free in Berkeley. All I had to do was show my badge.

During this time I proceeded to catch all the childhood diseases. They included mumps, measles, chicken pox, small pox, and scarlet fever. It seems I had the family quarantined most of the time. My dear Mother seemed to be immune to everything. She never caught any of the sickness I brought home, but my Father caught the mumps, so we were quarantined again. My Mother did not believe in vaccinations so I caught everything.

During this time, 1927, my Father started to work for the Hertz Drive-Ur-Self Company in San Francisco. We still lived on Curtis Street and it was a record. We had lived in one place for 3 years. The Doble Steam Company went broke due to the mismanagement of the stock sales. It was a shame since it was such a wonderful car and so advanced for its point in time. My Dad would put on demonstrations of the cars out- standing

My father Louis Disbrow testing a Doble Steam Car 1924

abilities. One of which was to be at a standing start at the bottom of the steepest and longest hill in Berkeley, Marin Avenue. He would ease the power to the car and go over the top at 45mph. No other car could even come close to that in 1924 or later. Another feat was to go in a large circle near Lake Merritt in Oakland. He would go as fast in reverse as he did in his forward speed just before the tires would break loose to the amazement of the onlookers, my dad also tested the car for top speed at Muroc dry lake at speeds over 100mph to prove that the car would not explode like the Stanley Steamer at that speed. The Doble had a steam regulator on it to prevent this.

These cars were built in Emeryville, California and the Murphy Body Company built the bodies in Pasadena, Ca. My Dad would drive a car down and bring a finished car back. One of his favorite stories was the one he used to tell about Abner Doble, who was the owner of the company. He was riding in the back seat of a Doble Phaeton touring car coming back from Pasadena. It was late at night and they were coming up the old highway on the west side of the San Joaquin Valley. Mr. Doble was riding in the back seat and my Dad and another employee were in the front with my Dad driving. Mr. Doble had been dozing in the back seat and woke up with the sensation of going quite fast. He asked my Father, "Louie how fast are we going?" My Dad looked down at the speedometer and said, "90". Mr. Doble retorted. "What's holding you back?"

My Father hated to leave his job. We even owned one of the demonstrator chassis. We were going to get one of the touring bodies to put on it but my

Bill Disbrow 1924, Kieth Disbrow

Father sold it when he got an offer he could not refuse.

Before my Dad sold the Doble we used to go the auto races on Sunday at the San Jose Speedway. We liked going to the races with him in our Doble. It would attract lots of attention. Going home after the races was a "bear". The road to Oakland and Berkeley was a "two-laner" and it was packed with all the Sunday traffic. In the 1920's it was a Sunday ritual to go for a drive out of the city so everybody was coming home at the time the races were over. It was like 5 o' clock traffic in Los Angeles on the freeway today. The Doble had so much acceleration that my Dad would see an opening to pass and would go by about 5 cars before they knew what was happening and get back into line before the oncoming traffic would get there. He did this for quite a while until a police officer pulled us over for cutting in. When he saw what kind of a car it was he got so interested in it and asking questions about its performance that he did not write my Dad a ticket.

While living at Curtis Street for a time I finally became old enough to join the Boy Scouts. I never got passed Tenderfoot because we moved again and I did not get a chance to join another troop. While I was in troop 20 we went to many local Jamborees. Our troop seemed to specialize in first aid and I being the smallest one in the troop I was always the patient. They would cover me with artificial blood and bandage me up with a lot of splints for good measure. I did get a chance to go on many hikes and to the Berkeley Scout Camp in the hills. I also got to go to Mt. Diablo scout camp and to Stevens Creek camp ground where I learned to swim. These were weekend overnighters. I became the troops champion fire builder but it seemed that every time I participated I would get poison oak. I found out that my wood gatherers were getting poison oak in with the other firewood. My Mother finally went to the University of California and got me a serum to take. After that I never caught poison ask again.

At Franklin grammar school I made my first appearance on the stage. Thanks to our special teacher Miss Bell. She was the one that taught Spanish dancing and I have been dancing ever since. She had all the Spanish costumes for the whole troupe and we played the castanets. We appeared in most of the schools in Berkeley.

I was a good marble shooter in grammar school. I was so good that I won every bodies' marbles. They complained to their teachers and I had to give them all back. From then on I played mostly around my home.

At Curtis Street I made a life long friend with Allen Shattuck. He lived next door to me and we were the same age. He had a twin sister named Eleanor and a brother named Gordon, who was the oldest. His parents were very nice and we became fast friends. Even after I moved away I seemed to always find Al and renew our friendship. This lasted for over 20 years, even after I came back from being a combat pilot in WWII.

It seemed that Al had a nervous breakdown when he was a young man and never quite got over it. He died quite young under circumstances that were a bit foggy to me after finding his brother to get the information on Al's demise.

I also had another good friend while I was at Curtis Street. He lived across the street from me and his name was George Tallone. His family was Italian from the "Old Country". They still made their own wine like they did in Italy. They also made all the Old Italian food, which was great, even down to the making of their own bread sticks. I sure liked having lunch with George. They would even serve wine with our lunch, which was their custom.

George and I used to write stories for a little newspaper that we published ourselves. I would write the stories and George would illustrate it with cartoons. This was my first attempt to writing anything. I then wrote a few stories for the Children's Section in the Oakland Tribune. I won a few prizes for this effort. I kept in touch with George for many years until I went by his house one day after WWII and found his mother all alone. Her husband had died and George had gone to New York City to study to become an opera singer. That was the last I had heard of George and I never got back to see his mother again.

During our stay at Curtis Street my grandfather Hitchcock and my grandmother bought a big ranch, 150 acres, near Concord, Ca. on the Cowell road. They used to take me out there on weekends in their new 1926 Studebaker Roadster. All our families would get together at the ranch house for Thanksgiving and Christmas. This became a tradition until my grandfather passed away in 1938 with my grandmother passing away shortly after that. The ranch was divided up between the heirs; instead of waiting and selling it all in one big piece to a land developer for much more money than each one realized when they sold their share piecemeal.

I rode horseback on an old plow horse my grandfather had on the ranch. It was my first ride on a horse such as it was. I also had a job trapping gophers in his orchard and grape vineyard. I got 25 cents a head. I did quite well in the short time I was on the job. Every time I went out to the ranch my grandfather had something to keep me busy and out of trouble. The next job that I remember was picking up nails. It seemed that in days gone by that there had been a lot of construction going on through the years and they were not too careful on dropping nails around the big dirt parking area. The nails did not do the tires on the cars and trucks any good when they drove over them and got a flat tire. I was about 11 years old then. I had devised a method so that I could pick up a lot of nails quickly and not break my back having to stoop all day.

I looked around and found an old magnet from a model "T" flywheel. I tied it to a piece of string and proceeded to drag it through the dirt in the yard and had all the nails picked up in a jiffy. That was one of my early brainstorms to beat the system. My grandfather was surprised on that one I forgot how much he was paying me for each nail I picked up. He was always thinking up some job to keep me busy. I was always thinking of things to amuse myself in my free time. One day I built myself a sled and waxed the runners good. There was a big hill in back of barn that was covered with wild oats. I took my sled to the top of the hill and proceeded to slide down it. I went so fast that I was getting airborne. I always had this quest for speed and being always on the ragged edge. When my mother wondered where I was, she came looking for me just as I was going down the hill for about the fourth time and almost a had "stroke", as I got airborne half way down the hill. Well she ended that for that day but I would attack that hill regularly when nobody was looking.

I remember one event at the ranch that happened after a big rainstorm. There was a creek that ran through the ranch. It was usually dry but now was a raging torrent. My brother, Keith, who was about 5 years old at the time and me were going out to look at the water rushing under a bridge. Of course the instructions from father was don't go near the water or get wet. The water in the creek must have been at least 2 feet deep under the bridge. My brother Keith and I went out on the road where the creek went under the bridge to watch the rushing water. I wasn't looking at Keith and when I turned around Keith was throwing rocks into the water on the edge of the bridge, standing on some rocks. Before I could say anything as a warning he slipped as the rocks gave way and fell down the embankment into the raging water. In a flash I jumped in and pulled him to safety. Nether one of us could swim at the time.

Of course we had on our Sunday best clothes on. I was little afraid to go home after the warning we had gotten to not go near the water or get wet. Well when we got home we looked like couple of drowned rats. Before I could explain anything my father walloped us both, he had a short fuse for disobedience, much to the consternation of my

Grandparents. After I stopped crying I explained the whole thing as to what had happened and that I had probably saved my brothers life. My father was very sorry that he was so fast in punishing us and loved us very much.

My grandfather had bought a movie camera for use in his detective business. It was the top of the line in its day, a Bell and Howell 70D 16mm, just like the newsmen used. One day while visiting the ranch, he brought it out and took pictures of our family. I was showing off the glider I built and was throwing it into the air. He was quite proud of his new camera, and was practicing on how to use it.

Some years later I bought a Univex single 8mm movie camera for 10 dollars and took many pictures with it, which I later showed to my grandfather. He was amazed that I had taken such good pictures with my little cheap camera. He brought out his pictures and showed them to me, which were very poor in technique and exposure; I was 20 years old at the time. When he died in 1938 he left his whole outfit to me. It consisted of his camera, camera case, projector, screen and accessories. I was the only grandson that got anything directly from grandfather. I guess I was his favorite since there were 9 grandchildren in all.

We moved from Curtis Street in 1927. I had graduated from Franklin grammar school in 1927 and now was going to go to Burbank Junior High School at University Avenue and Curtis Street, in Berkeley. We moved to 1421 Francisco Street. It now was about 10 blocks further than it was before we moved.

I now became interested in building model airplanes and gliders. I joined a model airplane club at a department store in Berkeley, called Roos Brothers. We would meet every Saturday morning and got our instructions from a young man how to build these models and gliders. I loved it since it was "down my alley". I would now learn how airplanes fly. I was always building things I would go to the Library and check out the books on "How to Build Things". I built coasters and went coasting all through the Berkely Hills and down through the University of California grounds All the time seeing how fast I could go. I had no brakes so the only way to stop was to "spin out". I even used to put tin can headlights on them with a candle as my light.

I forgot to mention one trip with my father to Lovelock, Nevada. This was in 1926 during school vacation. He was then working for the Hertz-Drive-Ur-Self Company in San Francisco. It seemed the district Presidents son was coming out to California from Detroit, Michigan, to see his father, Mr. Begley. He was driving an old Franklin air-cooled car at the time. The car gave out at Lovelock so my Dad got the job to go get the car and get it safely back to San Francisco. The company had an old "Daytona"1924 Paige touring car that they used at times for a tow truck. We loaded all the necessary equipment aboard to tow the Franklin back to San Francisco. Young Begley had taken the train to San Francisco. We all got in the Paige, Dad, young Begley and me and off we started for Lovelock, Nevada.

We made Reno OK, but on the way we picked up an old hitchhiker at Truckee. They had just graveled and oiled the road from Truckee to Reno and my Dad was no slow driver. I was riding in the front seat with my father and Don Begley. The hitchhiker was in the back seat. The old Paige was touring car with no top or rear fenders. Well when we got to Reno the old fellow was covered with oil, sprayed from the rear tires. He got out at Reno and I didn't blame him.

In those days roads were not too good or marked very well. Well we left Reno for Lovelock, taking a short cut that followed the railroad through Carson Sink, which in those days was a big dry lake. Don was driving with me in the front seat with him; my Dad was in the back seat taking a short nap since he had been driving all this time and we were on the road very early in the morning. All of a sudden I smelled something like it was getting hot. We were going 80 mph at the time through this dry lake was as smooth as glass. It was late in the afternoon but still warm out. I looked at the temperature gauge and it was pegged on HOT! By the way, this particular car had held all the speed records at Daytona Beach for stock cars in 1924 with speeds over 100 mph. I turned around and hollered at my Dad and woke him up and told him the car was red hot. He immediately told Don to stop. The car was red hot and out of water in the middle of this desert. Well after a long time of letting the engine cool down, my Dad spotted a railroad watering tank in the distance. This was used to put water in the locomotive on the railroad. We drove over and Don climbed up on the tank and turned the water on and we filled up the radiator on the old Paige. We were very lucky since we were off the beaten path and in those days traffic was very sparse. We made it to Lovelock after dark guided by the lights of the town.

The next day after checking the car over my Dad hooked the tow bar on the old Franklin and proceeded to tow it to San Francisco, with Don at the wheel of the Franklin.

On the way back we stopped near Truckee to get a little sleep. I could not sleep so I proceeded to see if I could catch some Chipmunks. My Dad woke up to all the noise of me running after the Chipmunks and them barking so loud. I would chase them up a small pine tree and shake them off and would be after them again. What energy!

We were off again to San Francisco with the Franklin in tow. Everything went smoothly until just out of Sacramento when the tow bar broke. I was dozing a bit and looked back and there was no car back there. I quickly asked my Dad what happened to the Franklin. He could not believe he had lost the Franklin. Of course we were going quite fast, 60 mph, even for this day in age and my Dad hadn't checked his rear view mirror for a short time.

We turned around and after about five miles here came the Franklin. It was hitting on about three cylinders but was coming our way. Dad fixed the tow bar and away we went again. We made it back to San Francisco safe and sound after that. I don't remember much after that because I finally fell asleep until we got home. What a great trip. It was the first time I had been out of California.

At Francisco Street I built my first radio, a crystal set. Of course everybody was amazed, having radio waves coming out of a cigar box. I found the plans in a book or magazine and proceeded to build it. My Mom thought I was spoofing her until the thing worked. Later my folks bought one of the first Majestic console radios. This was like owning a "Rolls Royce" in the radio field.

In the meantime my Dad had joined the 381st Reserve Squadron and went to Rockwell Field, San Diego, California, for his two weeks encampment. Here he would learn to fly the JN-4, "Jenny" and the DH-4. He then would go out to Crissy Field in San Francisco to get his flying time in and attend his meetings once a month. This was the old US Army Air Corps. His CO was Major Burdette E. Palmer, who in later years gave me a recommendation to enlist in the US Army Air Corps as a flying Cadet.

At Francisco Street I was always busy so I started my first theater with my Magic Lantern I had gotten for Christmas. It would project any picture on the screen that you would put in the holder. The only thing wrong, it would project everything backwards. To remedy this I would cut out all the writing and would print it backwards. This way it would come out right and you could read it. I would cut out all the Sunday comics and cut out the writing and print it backwards so the kids could read it. Every Saturday I would have a show for all the children on the block. I would charge one cent a piece for admission. I was about 12 years old then.

While attending Burbank Jr. High I was a member of the Glee Club. We used to sing at the Rivoli Theater on San Pablo Avenue near University Avenue. We also sang at the Berkeley High School and other places in the area. Of course all the proud parents would be there. That is where I got my start in singing which came in handy in later years.

I guess my Father got tired of commuting to San Francisco and since my Aunt Mae Gratton and family had moved to San Francisco we would move there too. So we moved to 516 Victoria Street sometime in June 1929. This place was in a rather nice area of the Ingleside Terrace. The trouble was that the only JR. High School I could go to was Everett Jr. High School. This was located almost all the way to downtown San Francisco. Ingleside was on the other side of Twin Peaks in a new suburb. I guess I was about 7 miles or better from school by streetcar, which I would ride every day for 5 cents each way. Sometimes my Dad would take me to school on his way to work.

I did quite well at Everett and was the second graduating class from this beautiful new school. They don't build schools like this any more. It was a pleasure to attend. It had an auditorium big enough to seat 2000 people with a beautiful stage and big velvet curtains. It also had twin movie projectors, just like a regular movie theater. They would show educational pictures at times.

Children of today would not understand the discipline then. No one was allowed out of the classroom at any time, except in an emergency. You could hear a pin drop in the classroom. The only time you spoke was when you were spoken to, or raised your hand. Students were very respectful to their teachers.

One day the Vice principal came in to get me for an interview on which high school I would like to attend. As we were going out the door to the hallway he spotted a boy riding a bicycle down the hall toward us. The boy did not see the VP as he went back in the classroom and got a big yard stick with the brass ends on it. As the boy approached us the VP leaped out of the room and hit the boy across the back and knocked him off the bike. With that he got another wallop across the rump. The VP then told him to get to his office immediately. When we got there the boy was waiting. I don't know what happened to him but he probably got expelled after his parents came to school.

I graduated from Everett Jr. High School in December 1929. I wanted to go to Polytechnic High School because it was the only high school that taught Aeronautics. Since I was trying to prepare myself to be a pilot in the US Army Air Corps, I figured any course pertinent to being a pilot I had to take. So when I got my paper stating which high school I was to attend after graduation it stated that I was to attend Balboa High school in the Mission district. It was closer than Polytechnic HS to my house. It was a brand new school and only went to the 11th grade. It also did not offer any aeronautics class. I told my father that I was not going to school unless I went to Polytechnic. My Dad got an interview with superintendent of schools and after me staying out of school for a week; I was allowed to attend "Poly".

THE TEEN YEARS

Going to school at "Poly" was the best time in my life. I thoroughly enjoyed it. I also had enjoyed Everett Jr. High. In fact, in the four years of schooling I was never late or absent. My curriculum consisted of courses to qualify me to enter the University of California at Berkeley. This was considered the best University on the west coast at the time. I took 3 years of English, 3 years of math, including algebra, geometry, trigonometry, plus advanced algebra. Also 3 years of engineering drafting, history, civics. 2 years of science, including, physics and aeronautics. I also took geography and 2 years of Latin, (Ugh).

I became a member of the Poly Aero Club and eventually became president. I was a member of the 130-pound basketball team, also the pitcher for the 130-pound baseball team. I won my letter for sports, the block "P". I wanted to play football but my mother would not let me play since I had bands on my teeth, which cost $500 to straighten them. Also I only weighed 120 lbs. at the time. My cousin Dick Gratton went to school with me at Poly and played football. He was 6'3" and weighed 180 lbs. when he was 17 years old. We were both the same age. He made all-city halfback and was the star of the Poly football team. He and I used to play a lot of "Sand Lot" football.

We used to have Friday dances at the school gym, which I attended regularly. My dear mother taught me how to dance when I was 9 years old. I used to dance when I was in Jr. High school. It made me quite popular with the girls since I could dance so well. Dancing was to be one of my best attributes as the years passed by. Dancing was always "in" when I wanted to make a good impression.

During those years at High School I was pursuing my goal to be a military pilot. I joined the Junior Birdmen of America. This organization promoted aviation by having members participate in model airplane building and having contests in model flying. I won many of these contests along with the contests put on by the city of San Francisco. These contests were held in the San Francisco Armory, which was great for indoor flying since it was so big. This was on Valencia Street. They also had outdoor contests at the Funston playground in the Marina District and some at the

Mom, Keith and me in the snow above Placerville 1927

San Francisco Airport. I was fortunate to win many of these contests which I received many ribbons and medals. I still have one of the silver medals and one gold medal. I showed the dentist who was straightening my teeth my silver medal and he insisted in engraving my name on the back with his dentist drill. I still have the medal with his engraving on the back.

Later while I was going to San Mateo Jr. College, I was the California State Champion for hand-launched gliders. This got me a gold medal from the Junior Birdmen of America. It was a coincidence that Major Burdette E. Palmer had become the head of the organization which was sponsored by the San Francisco Examiner a Hearst Newspaper.

I later, after graduation from "Poly", organized my own 99th squadron and was the Commander. I had appeared on the local Hearst radio station for an interview on the ambitions toward being a pilot in the U.S. Army Air Corps and what drove me to this decision.

During my senior year at poly I was quite active in student entertainment and student affairs. My Cousin Dick Gratton became student body president. I was designated to organize the senior "Jinx". This was a tradition for the entertainment of the whole student body by the graduating senior class. My theme was football since we were graduating at the end of football season. This would be in December 1932.

I wrote the script for the stage show and the lyrics to one of the songs taken from "You Got to Be a Football Player", also lyrics from the "Sweetheart of Sigma Chi". It was a big success from the consensus of student opinions.

We also had "Dress-up Day". All the seniors were allowed to come to school dressed in any type of costume for the whole day. I of course put on my Dad's flying suit, which was black with white letters on the back that read, 381st SS. The SS stood for Service Squadron. I also wore a white helmet and goggles as a military pilot. I even painted on a black moustache, which seemed to be the trademark of a dashing pilot. When I was old enough I grew that moustache and have had it ever since. Of course everyone had their cameras to take pictures of most of the "troops" which I still have in my old photo album.

I forgot to mention that I had my first real "girl friend" when we moved to Victoria Street. Her name was Martha Ward and she lived one house from me, which was practically next door. She was 14 and I was 13 years old. She went to Commerce High School while I went to Polytechnic. She worked in the office so I got to go to their school dances, which was taboo for any outsiders to do. We went steady until we moved away to a new home at 822 45th Avenue, in the Richmond district. It was the depression and my father lost his job as Vice President of maintenance for the Hertz-drive-ur-self Company. I attended the senior prom with another girl, Alice Sullivan. We had lived at Victoria Street for two and one half years, a record.

While we lived at Victoria Street I started a movie theater in our basement, which was as big as the upstairs floor plan of the house. I called it the "Diamond Theater" and made an electric sign with "Diamond Theater" on it and fixed it with lights that blinked and hung it over our garage door. My parents bought me a 35mm hand cranked projector, which I immediately converted it into an electric motor drive with an old electric motor I had acquired. I used to have movies every Saturday and all the kids in the neighborhood would attend. I think I charged 5 cents admission. All the mothers on the block knew where their children were on Saturday. I got my films downtown at the film dealers. I could buy old films and short subjects very reasonable then, in 35mm.

After I tired of the "Diamond Theater", I started a model airplane club. Of course most of my members came from the children that had attended my shows. Most of the models at the start were solid scale models of the popular aircraft of the day. The Curtiss Hawk, Curtiss Falcon, The Spirit Of Saint Louis, Ryan, etc. I became quite proficient in building these models and started to enter them in the local contests. I won a few ribbons to start with, but then I started building flying scale models. I was not too successful at the start but gradually got better. Some of the members of my club entered their models in these contests, which created quite a bit of interest. It seemed that the best builders soon moved away and the club broke up. I still built models for myself and still entered the contests whenever I could.

About this time I got the "bug" to build a full size man carrying secondary glider. I drew the plans in my drafting class at High School. I bought my wood at the local lumberyard and started making my wing ribs. The design I took from an aircraft design book. I think it was a type of Gottingen airfoil. It would have a 20-foot wing spread. I finished the wing but never finished the whole glider, since we had to move to a new

Louis & Keith and out 1930 Hertz Car

area where my father took over a garage, on Cabrillo Street. I had it in my fathers garage for a while when someone wanted it for a display in a local school, so I gave it to them. That was the end of my glider project; I had no money to finish it. I did learn a lot about making wing ribs and wing spars. I later figured out my lift and was surprised to learn that I had to get up too much speed to have left the ground for the wing area. A glider was supposed to fly at half the speed I had calculated.

Before we moved from Victoria Street, I started building coasters to run down the hills around our area. San Francisco being built on hills our area was no exception. We had lots of coasting area. The street, beyond .our house, was quite steep and one could get up lots of speed by the length of how high you wanted to start. Of course I always had to try for the maximum, always on the edge. I found out that if the coaster was not built with a very low center of gravity, it would tip over on the high speed turn you had to make at the bottom of the hill. So I designed my coaster with a very low center of gravity so I was able to make the 90 degree turn at the bottom of our hill. We would station a person at the bottom to warn us if any automobiles were coming. When we got the "all clear" sign away we would go. It was quite a thrill for a boy of 13 years old as we got to some good speeds. I later went back to my old house in 1993, 61 years later. Our hill was now full of houses. It even seemed steeper than it did as a boy. It was a wonder how I survived coming down there and did not bust my butt.

I learned to drive my uncles Model "T" Ford when I was nine years old. My uncle Edwin Hitchcock taught me when I would go out to my grandfather's ranch in Concord, California. I finally got my drivers license when I turned 14 years old. With all the driving of coasters and the model "T" Ford along with my father's good instruction paid off. We were living at Victoria Street at the time. This was going to the big event in my life, getting my drivers license. I took my test in downtown San Francisco. The DMV was at Market Street and Van Ness Avenue. My Dad had taught me right and I had no trouble passing my driving test, the first time out. I took my test in our 1924 Wills St, Claire Roadster. It had an old "crash box" of a transmission and you had to double clutch to make good shifts without crashing the gears. Transmissions did not have "synchronizers" in those days.

We also had a Hertz car. The Yellow Cab Company produced this car for Hertz-Drive-Urself Company for rental purposes. My father was to become the VP of maintenance for this company, with its headquarters at the Bell Garage in downtown San Francisco.

Well the depression finally caught up with us and my Dad lost his fine job with Hertz. I think his salary at the time, was a big $400 per month. It was quite a shock for the family. We had to move since we could not afford to pay the big rent money on our house ($50 per month) at Victoria Street. I could hardly believe it. Here I had planned to go to the University of California at Berkeley after I graduated from Poly now we had nothing and I would have to go to work if I could find a job, which was very scarce even for a grown man, much less for a high school graduate.

We moved from Victoria Street in June 1932 to 822-45th Avenue in the Richmond district where my Dad acquired a garage at 47th and Cabrillo Streets. Of course it would be named "Disbrow's Garage". I worked there after school for my Dad and use to keep it open on weekends when my Mom and Dad would take a break and go away for the weekend. My brother Keith would go with them since he was only 11 years old at the time.

I learned a lot about auto mechanics from my father during this time. A trade, no one could ever take away from me. It would come in very handy in my later years. In fact I could build an automobile from scratch in my adult years.

While working at my father's garage I built my brother Keith a coaster, since we were surrounded with steep hills, which was ideal for coasting. I built it like a midget racer. Keith sat inside of it and it was only 3 inches off the ground. The center of gravity was so low it would spin out before it would tip over on high speed corners.

We used to have races down "Cliff House Hill" at the beach, which was close by and ended going down the great highway at the beach. I was interested how fast my brother was going down the hill one day, and ran along side of him with our "Wills" and watched the speedometer get up to 45mph, which amazed me. With all the rest of the children catching on to coaster building we had some great races. Finally one of the newsreel companies came out and took pictures of us all racing down the hill. I am sure that this was the "brain child" for the "Soap Box Derby" that, in later years for the children to race their coasters and compete in the finals at Akron, Ohio. Here they would win scholarships to universities. Chevrolet sponsored these races, and they are still going on to this day. It was great practice for learning to drive a car.

It seems that speed was in our blood. We inherited it from my Dad. I used to take the Wills out on the Beach Highway on Tuesday nights and race the "Hot Rods" from the RPM Club. I was 16 years old at the time. The Wills would peg the speedometer at 85mph, which was fast for a 1924 automobile in 1932 for a stock car. I figured I was going faster than 85mph since my Dad had put different camshafts in the engine when he overhauled it, which made it, go faster.

I graduated from "Poly" in December 1932. Things were not going to well with the garage business. People did not have any money to fix their car much less to buy a new one. It was hard to collect your money after we did the work on someone's old "clunker" I guess my folks were having a hard time of it. We moved again to a smaller place from 822-45th Avenue to a little house on 43rd avenue. My Dad lost the garage and my mother developed bronchial pneumonia. I remember that the only heat we had in the house was on old kerosene portable heater. The doctor recommended that she should get out of the very damp climate of San Francisco. So we moved again to a house in Redwood City in January 1933, to 450 Vera Street. I had graduated from High School by this time. I knew things were really tough. There was no money for me to go to school, my Dad was out of a job and was going out each day trying to find one, and I could not get one either. Fortunately the little money we did have came from my folks cashing in my fathers insurance policy. I helped out by planting a garden in our back yard to at least have some fresh vegetables for our subsistence.

During the day, when I did not have anything to do I would listen to the radio to all the popular tunes of the day and memorize them. Then I would sing along with the bands playing the music on the radio. Finally one day I saw an ad in the newspaper for amateur entertainers to appear on the local radio station in San Francisco. I applied for the show and got on. This was my debut as a singer. I had never sung solo before much less on a radio station. The song I sang was a hit tune of the day called, "Sweetie Pie", which was a "Pinky Tomlin" song that he sang in one of his movies.

Well that broke the ice and gave me the confidence, which I needed. From that time on I entered every amateur contest I could find.

In the meantime I met a new girl in the neighborhood, Vera Lee, who liked me to sing to her. She became my new steady date. She lived only a few blocks from our house which very convenient, since I could walk over to her house. She went to school at Sequoia High School, which also was within walking distance. We would attend all the dances and school functions together.

My father finally got a job with the Auburn Car Dealer in Palo Alto. This allowed me to start back to school at San Mateo Jr. College in San Mateo. I had stayed out a whole six month semester. I enrolled in August 1933. I hitchhiked back and forth from Redwood City to San Mateo everyday and carried a brown bag lunch that my dear mother packed for me. It was about a 20 mile round trip per day. This way I kept our expenses to the minimum. By the way, in this day Jr. College was free, the only things you had to buy were your books. I built model airplanes for display for a model airplane store to pay for my books. There would be notices on the bulletin boards advertising used books for sale, which you could buy quite reasonable. At this time I was appearing on many amateur programs and winning a little money to help with my expenses. I was also singing with the college dance band at our Wednesday lunch dances and anything special that came along on Friday night dances. I wasn't getting paid anything but I was getting a lot of good experience, and the audience seemed to like me with the applause I would always get. I met a girl in the college auditorium one day who was playing the piano. She was great. I asked her to play a few tunes that I was practicing on for the band. She played like a professional. She could play in any key I wanted to sing in and could play any song I new. We became fasts friends and at lunchtime we would meet there and I would practice all my songs. She would tell me the key to sing in which made it easy for the band to play in my key. This made the singing easy.

I wasn't too good a student the first year in college. After staying out of school for so long it was hard to get down to studying very hard after graduating from High School. I guess I was having to good of a time with my extra curricular duties. I also went out for the football team. This was a goal that eluded me in high school, because of the bands on my teeth. This was my first semester and football took up quite a bit of my time. I was fortunate to make the team and play a few minutes of every game. I played quarterback in the single wing formation. This before the "T" formation came into practice. I played both defensive and offensive back, which was the case in those days.

When spring rolled around I went out for the track team as a pole-vaulter. We used the old bamboo poles wrapped with tape in those days. I managed a best jump of 11' 6". By the standards of today that was terrible but it wasn't too bad when the worlds record was 14' and most of the jumps were around 12'6". I think I placed fourth most of the time.

May 1934 arrived and we were out for summer vacation. There wasn't too much to do since money was still very scarce. I had to do things that did not cost too much money. I was always thinking of things to do anyway. I would build model airplanes of the popular aircraft of the day, or trying to build an electric car out of one my Dad's old starter motors. Even building a boat out of an old piece of canvas I had found which was big enough to cover the hull. It was about 10' long and I painted the canvas to make it waterproof and my dear mother made the sails out of old sheets. I did sail it out in Redwood City harbor while my mother watched in amazement with my brother with me. We didn't even have life jackets on and we were not very good swimmers. People were not very safety conscious in those days. The Lord must have protected us for not being aware of the danger we were in.

One day just after vacation started I was over at my girlfriend's house, Vera Lee, and her girlfriend was there. She was telling us how she hated to move but had to. Her father was a contractor and he had a contract to build a dog racetrack at Bedford, Ohio, a suburb of Cleveland, Ohio. He had already left the day before and told his wife to get some one to drive her out to Bedford with their two children, a boy and an older girl of 16 years. He could not come back and get her since he would be too busy with the new contract. The wife could not drive very well if at all and the daughter who was 16 was in the same boat. So I said that I would drive them out. On asking my mother and father if I could go they were all in favor of it since I had never been farther than Lovelock, Nevada, with my dad. That night I went over to see the girl's mother and told her that I would drive them out just to see the 1934 Worlds Fair in Chicago.

I was in luck; they had a brand new 1934 DeSoto sedan, which was quite a luxurious automobile for its day. We left Redwood City and headed for Salt Lake City. This must have been around the end of May 1934. As we were driving along old Highway 30, I noticed that the car was hard to keep it going straight down the road. It had a bad tendency to want to wander. I told the lady I would like to stop and have the front end checked at the next town, which was Winnemucca, Nevada. We stopped at a garage and had the front end checked, and he found out that the front axle did not have enough caster. After shimming up the axle it steered great and did not wear me out trying to keep it on the road. I was thankful for all the things my dad had taught me about automobiles to know when something is not right and know how to fix it. It would have been a real chore to drive that car all the way across country the way it was.

We made Salt Lake City and stayed over night. The next day we visited the Mormon temple square and went through the museum and Tabernacle. It was a new experience for me. The only thing I new about the Mormons in those days they had a lot of wives. In the Tabernacle they gave a demonstration of the good acoustics in the building, which was made of entirely of wood even to the nails. There was not a metal nail in the whole building. One of the members rubbed his hand together while up on the stage and it sounded like he was rubbing sandpaper together. Then he dropped a pin and it sounded like he had dropped a ten penny nail. It was amazing. Little did I ever dream that some day I would become a member of The Church of Jesus Christ of Latter-day Saints the only true church in the world today with a living prophet at its head who takes his direction directly from the Lord Jesus Christ through revelation. They did not have a visitor's center like they have today. Over the years I have been back and forth to Salt Lake City visiting "General Conference" with Ezra Taft Benson presiding, as well as Gordon B. Hinkley, our current President of the Church. I think we stayed about two days so we could see the Great Salt Lake and the town. We then left for Omaha, Nebraska with a stop about half way.

When we got to Omaha, the lady had friends there and we stayed 3 or

4 days. This was a nice leisurely trip. I saw "heat lightning" for the first time and it was quite spectacular. It was caused by the heat of the plains making the hot air rise up fast and to cool rapidly at altitude, causing it to condense and forming these big cumulus clouds. The air inside was very unstable causing the lighting. Of course the Midwest is noted for thunderstorms in the summer months.

After visiting for 3 or 4 days we left for Collinsville, Illinois. Here we visited more relatives and friends. Collinsville is just across the Mississippi River from St. Louis, Mo. I remember it was very hot and "muggy" and they did not have any air conditioning in the old hotel we stayed in.

We went fishing for blue gills and snapping turtles at a lake near Collinsville and had a big picnic with all the friends and relatives. It seemed like everyday they had a big spread. I met some of the cousins, female, and went dancing and drinking 32 ounces of beer in the big schooners they served for only ten cents!

After staying about a week or so we headed for Bedford, Ohio. We arrived in Bedford without any trouble. The DeSoto ran great all the way after having the front end fixed. We had a hotel waiting for us that Mrs. Edward's husband had reserved for us. I stayed a few days and met a young fellow who was singing with a local band. I think I took Mrs. Edward's daughter to a dance to hear him sing. When I was ready to go home Mrs. Edward gave me ten dollars for driving them to Bedford and I started to Chicago to see the Worlds Fair, after I got all my gear together.

I got on the main road and started to hitchhike. I guess it took me a couple of days to get to Chicago. My Mom told me to always go to the YMCA for a room in any big city. It was always clean and cheap, so that is what I did. It only cost me a dollar a day, which was great since I was on a tight budget. I had to get back to San Francisco on the 10 dollars I had and it was 2000 miles away and I had only 11 days to make it before I had to go back to college.

I got up very early so I would be the first one to get into the Worlds Fair. I got breakfast at a nice café next to the YMCA. It consisted of bacon and eggs, toast, coffee, and hash browns for 25 cents! That was a bargain even in those days.

I got to the fair before they opened just like I had planned. I think the admission for me was 50 cents. I wanted to see as much as I could of the fair in one day and started with all the big exhibits first. General Motors, Ford, Hupmobile (where I took a driving test and got a diploma for being an outstanding driver in a new Hupmobile), General Electric had a big exhibit, also. There were many more, which I tried to see. They also had a midway with all the games of chance and sideshows.

I was watching and listening to the "Barker" for the Sally Rand Show when Sally came out on the stage. The "Barker" told me to hold onto one of her veils while she did a little dance and on cue to pull on it. When I pulled the veil off it revealed a very scanty costume to lure all the "suckers" into the show. Since I had cooperated with the "Barker" I got in free. This helped me with my budget.

I finally saw everything I could, that was free. I had been there since 8am and it was now 12pm as they closed up and everybody had to go home. As I was crossing the bridge that went over the railroad tracks it was a beautiful sight seeing the lights of the skyline of Chicago. Then I realized that that I had a total of $4.95 in my pocket and I had 11 days to get back Home and go back to college.

The next day I got up bright and early and had my 25 cent breakfast again. I began asking the directions to the nearest Studebaker Dealer. During the depression Studebaker was caravanning their cars from South Bend, Indiana, to all parts of the USA, especially to the West Coast. They would advertise for drivers at no pay to drive a car and tow another behind. This would allow them to get two cars out for the price of one (half of the cost of putting them on a freight car). It was also faster if they did not run into any mechanical problems. They could sell them cheaper than their competitors.

After enquiring at the local Studebaker Dealer how to get to drive one of theses cars I was told I would have to go back to South Bend to the factory drive-a-way. Off I went back to South Bend immediately.

I didn't have as much luck going back to South Bend as I did coming out from Bedford. It seemed I got on the wrong numbered highway and this was not used very much. I did a lot of walking carrying my old suitcase. It began to get very heavy and after a while I thought I would never get a ride. It was getting late in the afternoon and up came a big thunderstorm.

I was out in the open and no place to get any protection from the storm, when I spotted a large culvert underneath the road I was traveling on. I got down in it; it must have been 10 feet in diameter and was dry inside with sand and rocks. I knew I was taking a chance if the drainage ditch started to fill up with water but I was so tired by this time I cared less. I picked out a spot and went to sleep.

The next day I got a ride to an old motel about 5 miles from South Bend. Here I told the owner of my plan to drive a caravan car home from South Bend. He said that he would take me in the morning since he was going in to South Bend.

In the morning I got my ride with him into South Bend. As we approached the outskirts of South Bend I spotted a long line of Studebakers parked along the opposite side of the highway. The first car had a painted sign on the windshield, OAKLAND, CALIFORNIA. The fellow who gave me my ride had hardly stopped the car before I was out and thanked him.

I ran across the highway with my suitcase and asked who was in charge. I was informed that the guy in the straw hat was the boss. I ran over to him and explained that I would like to drive one of the cars since my home was in Oakland, California. I also told him I had just driven some people from California to Bedford, Ohio, and had a current California driver's license. I had references from the people I had driven to Bedford, and a real good one from my grandfather. I found out that I was the only one in the caravan with a California driver's license. I was immediately assigned to car #6. What a relief. Then he told me I had to have $5.00 'for insurance but waived that since I only had four dollars by this time to eat on.

We left within the hour after I got there and drove to Kankakee, Illinois. One hundred and five cars left South Bend. It was quite a caravan. Some were going to San Diego, Los Angeles, and the rest to Oakland.

It seemed we stopped in all the small towns so we would not snarl traffic, I suppose. We finally hit Oklahoma City then into Gallup, New Mexico. By this time my money was about gone when I picked up a girl who was hitchhiking at Gallup. I guess none of the other drivers wanted to pick her up due to the interstate law of transporting strange females across state lines. Me being only 18 years old I was under age so it did not apply to me. Well I drove her all the way to Modesto, California. When

I stopped and asked her where she was going I told her this was her lucky day I was going to Oakland. My luck was still holding out also, since she bought my meals all the way to Modesto, where she left.

After dropping the girl off at Modesto it was a short distance to Oakland and home. Upon arriving at Oakland and dropping the cars off at the dealer I made a collect call to my home and was told that the number had been disconnected. I then called my Aunt Mae Gratton and found that my Mon, Dad, and my Brother Keith had moved to 219 Dolores Street in San Francisco, from Redwood City, California, where we lived when I left for Bedford.

During the time I was traveling cross- country with the caravan a letter for me with $35 in it was following me. It seems my grandmother Hitchcock found out that I was hitchhiking all over the place and had given my mother money for a bus ticket to get me home. She had sent it to Bedford, Ohio, because I had written to her where we would be but I left before the letter got there. I left a forwarding address at the post office to send it back home. Then when I got the ride in the caravan and found out the route we were taking, I wrote and told her to send it to Gallup, New Mexico. Well I never got the letter since it was sent general delivery and we got there on a Sunday and the post office was closed. So the letter was waiting for me when I got home. The money came in real handy to buy books for the new semester.

I got home on a Friday night and was greeted with much enthusiasm and love. We stayed up very late as I related all my experiences on my trip. I think I took the 5 cent ferry from Oakland to San Francisco and the 5 cent streetcar home. I think the head of the caravan gave me a dollar so I could get home, since I was broke. After all the excitement wore off I remembered that I had to go back to college on Monday and this was Friday.

It took me a month to settle down to the routine of going to school and studying. I had been traveling for two months and seeing a lot of the US that I had not seen before. It was quite an experience for an 18 year old in those days and the responsibility of getting the Edwards to their destination safely.

While I was gone my Uncle Edwin Hitchcock and my Father got in a deal to buy a big ranch (8000 acres) in the west side hills near Westley, California. It seems my Dad had put up his Hertz car for part of the money to obtain the ranch. He still had his Wills St. Claire roadster for transportation. My Uncle was in the real estate business and was a "wheeler and dealer". Somehow he made a few trades and ended up with this ranch with a $25,000 mortgage against it. This was during the depression when property wasn't worth very much because of the mortgages on them with very little hard cash money around. Everybody was making trades to try to get out from under their heavy mortgages and realize some cash in the bargain. So my Dad and my Uncle were in the ranching business.

My folks had moved to San Francisco from Redwood City to be closer to the ranch and my Uncle's wife, Marie who lived in Berkeley. I think Marie was the only one working at the time, while my Dad and my Uncle Edwin were down at the ranch trying to make it livable. It seems it was practically abandoned at the time.

In the interim of me trying to go to college and my folks trying to get the ranch going, I was boarded out to friends. First, with the Morrison's, who lived in Belmont, California and then with the Olson's who lived in San Francisco. It was neat with the Morrison's because I was only about 5 miles from College but when I moved to San Francisco I was 20 miles from College. I stayed with the Morrison's for a semester and my last semester with Olson's. The Olson's lived at 618 Oak Street in a flat. I had to sleep on the sofa since the place was small and they had two small children and a nephew living with them.

While I was staying with the Olson's (Jan 35 to Jun 35) I had to get up at 6am and walk about 6 blocks to catch a street car that would take me out to the end of the line on Mission Street in Daly City. There I would get out on the highway and hitchhike 18 miles to college in San Mateo. After school I would reverse the procedure. I was never late or absent for my two years in college, even though I hitched hiked every day for two whole years. I needed this education to become a Flying Cadet and I was determined to make it.

I was still singing in the meantime to keep myself in spending money. I kept looking at the ads in the paper for amateur contestants. I sang on Radio stations, KGO, KFRC, and tried out for a radio program, which I did not make. It seems I had to sing with only a guitar accompanist and I could not hear myself in the soundless environment of the studio, which did not allow for any echo of the sound for me to hear myself. Also the guitar player was only playing cords when I was use to a piano playing the complete melody or a full orchestra as my background. It was a good experience for me.

During Easter Vacation I decided to hitchhike down to the ranch to see my folks. I had no way of contacting them to let them know I was coming. It was a spur of the moment thing. They had no telephone and the nearest mail was nine miles away and I would beat any letter I sent to them.

I took the five-cent ferry across the bay from San Francisco to Oakland Then I took the 5-cent streetcar to the end of the line where I could hitchhike on the main highway to Tracy, California. Here I would take the Westside Highway to the town of Westley, California. The ranch was 9 miles into the hills from Westley.

This time it did not work out that way. I got a ride on a coal truck going to Modesto. The driver asked me if I wanted to make 50 cents an hour unloading the sacks of coal he was hauling. Since I could use the money, I agreed. So I went to Modesto and helped to unload 11 tons of coal. After this he had another job for me if I wanted it, loading 11 ton of "Green Hides" out of a slaughter house in the same town. Not knowing what "Green Hides" where I did not know what I was getting into, but soon found out. I was given a yellow waterproof apron to keep the blood and water from getting on me but no gloves to protect my hands from the rock salt that cover the hides. Well between these two jobs I made a total of $3.00 for 6 hours of the hardest work I had ever done. The eleven- ton of green hides was an experience. I could hardly lift them up to the high bed of the truck, so I would bump them with my knee for the added height. I never want to do that again.

By the time I got through loading the green hides it was dark. The truck driver dropped me off at the junction of the road that went to Westley from Modesto. I walked quite a ways since this road was seldom traveled doing the day much less at night. I was so tired by this time I was looking for a haystack along side of the road to sleep in. I finally found one and lay down and went to sleep. It must have been 10pm by this time and I fell asleep at once.

In the morning I was up with the sun and back on the road. As I was walking a fellow came along and gave me a ride to Westley and the road to the ranch. There was no traffic on this road at all and I started walking to the ranch, which was 9 miles away. I walked all the way to the mountains, which was about 7 miles. I walked about one mile into the mountains when I saw a cloud of dust coming out of the hills and recognized my Dad's Wills St. Claire roadster coming down the hill my way. Was I glad to see him since the temperature was about 90 degrees in the shade and no shade...

My Dad could hardly believe his eyes to see me walking toward the ranch. There being no way to contact them they had no idea I was coming. Fortunately Dad was going to Westley to check their mail, I had been in luck.

The ranch was quite primitive after me living in the city all my life. It had no running water, outside privy, and a large washtub to take a bath in, or else go up to the watering trough in cold water. The ranch was big, 8000 acres! This land included a lot of mountains, including Mt. Oso, which had a lookout station on the summit. How I wish we had this property today. It was so large that if you accidentally shot a stranger he was trespassing on our property.

After Easter Vacation at the ranch in Ingram Canyon, my Dad gave me a ride into Westley. I was lucky. I got a ride directly to San Francisco.

I finally graduated from San Mateo JC, in May 1935 with an AA degree in Mechanical Engineering. My folks were there to see me get my diploma. After which we were on our way to the ranch. The ranch was like a storybook of the old wild-west. There was the old ranch house with its large screened in front porch the full length of the house. It had one large room as you came in the front door, which served as the living room, dining room, and kitchen, with a large pantry at one end. The three bedrooms were directly off this room. It was more fun sleeping out on the front porch when it was warm. It had a big old wood stove for cooking and heat. It had a sink and a few cabinets, if I remember right. Outside there was big old barn and a big "B" corral with a chute on one side for the dipping or vaccinating the cattle. It was a typical old western ranch. It seemed to me to be in another world.

My folks and my uncle Edwin had befriended all the neighbors in the surrounding ranches. When it was branding time it was the old west. Everyone came to help and when it was over there was a big barbeque, beer and "Bronc" riding was in the offing. It seems that they would go out on the range and find a horse that had not been ridden in some time and bring him in and all the brave cowboys would put in a dollar a piece and the winner for the best ride would take all. There was a lot whooping it up as the riders got bucked off. There were a lot of sore rears and such after this contest but with all the beer, etc., it made it worthwhile, I guess. Of course all the cowboys looked like they just stepped out of the pages of the stories of the "Old West". It was awe inspiring to a young man who had just come from the big city. They had on their Justin high- healed boots, spurs, chaps, and their ten- gallon hats with their Levis it was quite picturesque.

We had 500 head of Hereford cattle that paid $1.00 a head for grazing rights, plus 3000 head of sheep for the same price. It was something to see the sheepherders, who were Basque, driving all the sheep with their sheep dogs. All they had to do was whistle and wave their arms which way they wanted the sheep to go. The dogs were worth their weight in gold.

While I was at the ranch I learned to ride a cow horse. Typically they put me on a broken "wild mustang" called Red Horse. He was a typical Indian pony with a wild look in his eye, short ears, and a Roman nose. He wasn't very big but oh was he tough! He belonged to Harry Lawley, who owned 3000 acres adjoining our property. After riding about a mile or so on this little "mustang" I was really broken in. I had to stand up to eat my dinner my rear end was so sore. Of course everybody was laughing at me but I would eventually learn to ride Red Horse.

Harry used to let me ride Red quite often. My brother Keith had his own horse so we all would ride together. I had a lot of respect for Red horse. Being a wild mustang, at one time, he was quite unpredictable. His favorite trick on the first ride in the morning was to buck, no matter who was on him. Harry always told me first, not to cinch him up too tight in the morning for the first ride, second, always face him when you are getting on. Look him straight in the eye because when your foot hit the stirrup he was gone. Facing him you would be automatically thrown up into the saddle and away you would go. Of course he would buck on the first ride in the morning. I would immediately rein him into a tight turn and after a few jumps he would behave decent for the rest of the day. He tried many times but never bucked me off. I was lucky.

My brother, Keith used to ride his old horse to school every day, 9 miles each way and was a real cowboy. One day he let me take his horse up to the watering trough to let him drink. The watering trough was about ¼ of a mile from the house. I was riding him bareback. As I was coming back I was running the old horse quite fast, as I went by the ranch house I waved to my mother and as I approached the barn my brother opened the barn door. Well the old cow horse made a square corner to go into the barn and I kept going straight and landed with a thud on my rear. I couldn't move for 5 minutes. My mother thought I was dead and came running but I was just stunned. I did not do that again with this old cow pony.

Living on a ranch of this size was a real experience for a young man who was a city boy. It was a great life in the outdoors. We went hunting for deer, quail, and cotton tail. Not just for the pleasure but for our food. Wild life was plentiful and we used it to our advantage.

I was always on the lookout for rattlesnakes. There were plenty of them here on the ranch. I remember riding my brothers horse one day along a dirt road with a high bank on one side, about my eye level. When I came around a bend in the road I saw this big black snake staring me in the eye. Before I could identify it, it was gone in the flash of the 410 shotgun I was carrying. The poor snake did not have a chance. I later found out that it was a gopher snake that was a good snake, harmless and beneficial to the environment. From them on I was more cautious at what I was shooting. I did exterminate a lot of the rattlers while we on the ranch. I became very familiar and accustomed to their traits and habitats. I was no longer afraid of them but had a lot of respect for them.

I remember when my Dad and Mom were going to town with me in the rumble seat of the Wills St. Claire. We came around a bend in the road and there was a big rattler in the middle of the road. I jumped out of the car as my Dad stopped the car. As usual I had my 410 shotgun with me. I walked over to the old rattler with my Mom screaming at me that I was going to get bit. I was poking the snake with the barrel of the gun to make him curl up so I could get a good shot. By this time my Mom was going into hysterics so I shot its head off. I kept the skin for ages for a band for my hat band on my Stetson. By the way a rattler can only strike the length of his body, when he is coiled up.

My Dad in order to bring in a little extra money to survive in those days got a job at the little garage in Westley. I had this Indian "Pony" motorcycle I had fixed myself. I had ground the valves and put new piston rings in it but did not put new bearing in the lower end. Well it froze up on me one day before I left San Francisco. I had one of my friend's tow me home with his motorcycle from Belmont. We had hauled the Indian down to the ranch since the engine was still frozen-up; I finally "bugged" my Father to fix it for me. I had painted it and it looked real nice. After he fixed it for me I had much faster transportation than a horse. In fact I had met a girl friend from the San Antonio Valley, which was about 20 miles over a dirt road from our place. This road was a 4X4 jeep road in those days. My girl friends Father, Mr. Gerber, owned 6000 acres in this valley, which was back of Mt. Hamilton. I would ride up to see her and go to the dances in the little red school house. It was real old fashioned hoe down music, with a fiddle, banjo, and a piano. We would have a blast. I would stay three or four days and we would go horseback riding. At mealtime I never saw so much food. They fed everybody at once. All their cowboys and family sat down to a huge table. I was never a big eater so they kept passing me food until I was stuffed. It was just like you see in the old western movies. This was a big cattle ranch, The Gerber Ranch. My girl friend was, Irene Gerber. After we lost our ranch and moved to Patterson, California, she would come down and visit me for a weekend.

Well after becoming a "cowboy" my folks and my Uncle Edwin and his wife Marie, lost the ranch. It seemed that President Roosevelt was over ruled on the Frazier-Lempke Act, which was declared unconstitutional by Congress. This act would have given the rancher and farmers loans at low interest rates so they could save their properties from foreclosure. It sounds familiar today as I write this. All that was owed on the ranch was $25,000. Of course it was a fortune in that day in age. So we had to move to Patterson, California, which was about 10 miles south of Westley. It was a nice little house two bedrooms and one bath. I shared a room with my brother Keith.

My Dad got a job at the Ford dealer in town and I got a job at the Cox Ranch nearby, raking hay with a team of horses! On my first day going to work on my Indian motorcycle I got hit by a pickup truck as I was approaching a railroad crossing. It was about 6am in the morning and the sun was in the eyes of the driver coming in the opposite direction and he did not see me. He hit me broadside and threw me 20 feet threw the air and I hit with a thud. The clutch pedal had gone through the side of my foot and broke my arch and my knees were full of gravel as well as skinned hands since I landed on all fours.

They carted me off in the pickup to Dr. Allen's office in Patterson. The Doctor set my foot and gave me a Tetanus shot. When my mother heard of this she was in a state of shock since my Dad was sent home with pneumonia. Doctor Allen who set my foot could not put a cast on it until the wound healed up, so I had to stay in bed most of the time so the bones would set properly.

The insurance company was there immediately. My Mother insisted that I sign the papers to settle for $150! She was afraid we would not get

Our ranch, (8,000 acres) Ingram Canyon, Wesley, Ca 1935

Bill Disbrow on Titus Ranch 1935

any money at all since I did not have any license on the motorcycle as yet. I told her that it did not make any difference, but she insisted. So we got $150 for three months on crutches and with a cast on my foot almost to my knee. I guess we needed the money, although this was a company owned truck that hit me and we should have gotten more. That's how it was in those days. This was in May 1936 and I had until the 1 October to heal so I could go to Crissy Field in San Francisco and take my test to be an Aviation Cadet in the Army Air Corps.

My brother Keith was going to Patterson High School at this time and was on the basketball team. I was his avid rooter every time they played a game, since I could not do much else while I was on crutches. Also I kept trying to whistle with my fingers. I was getting hoarse shouting while I was in the rooting section. One night while trying to whistle it finally happened. I about deafened myself along with the people sitting next to me. This was very gratifying since I had been trying for months to do this. To this day you can hear me two blocks away. This is how I called my children when they were growing up. They always knew Dad's whistle and would come a running.

I startled my Mother one day by borrowing a friend's motorcycle and road by the house where she could see me with the cast on my foot. I told her I was seeing if I could still ride. She took a dim view of this. I was always on the edge.

One day Harry Lawley came down to see me. Of course it was boring for me hobbling around on those crutches. He asked my Mother if I could go up to his ranch and give me a little change in scenery. Off I went raring to ride my old friend, "Orphan Boy". I had not been on a horse since we left the ranch and I had not seen "Orphan Boy" for two months.

As we approached Harry's ranch I told him to stop his pick up. The road overlooked his horse corral. I rolled the window down on the pickup and gave my best whinny. "Orphan" came running out of the barn and saw me and whinnied right back to me. He was a great horse but Harry said that I had spoiled him. He was a very large pet to me and the horse knew it.

The first thing we did the next day was to go out and poison squirrels. I having the cast still on my foot, Harry saddled up "Orphan" and helped me up in the saddle and away we went. I had a big sack of poison grain, which I hooked on the saddle horn so it was easy for me to reach. I would find a squirrel hole and grab a handful of grain and try to throw it as close to the hole as possible.

Well, we were doing just find when "Orphan" decided he did not want to go to the left of the tree that was in our way. I kept reining him left but he would go right. Harry made me get off and proceed to wallop "Orphan" along side of the head. I felt so sorry for the old horse but when Harry got on him he went to the left side of the tree like he was supposed to in the first place. I don't know what got into him but he might have seen something he did not like so he decided he would go right with me instead of left. I felt so sorry for him I petted him and told him I was so sorry I got him into trouble.

"Orphan" was a very smart horse. I remember riding him in some very steep country rounding up strays. Harry was with me and so was my brother Keith. We were on our own searching for strays. I could hear them going through the brush in the distance but could not see them. I was on a very steep trail on the side of a ridge, which had loose rock on it and "Orphan" slipped and fell with me trying to get my foot out of the stirrup. He dragged me to the bottom of the ravine, which was about 25 feet deep. As we stopped "Orphan" got up and just stood there as I was trying to get my right foot extricated from the stirrup. "Orphan" didn't move a muscle until I got my foot out. I did not have cowboy boots on so my foot went right through the stirrup when we fell. I never road again until I had a pair of cowboy boots with undershot heels.

"Orphan" was particular who got on him without permission. I had my friend from San Francisco visiting at Harry's ranch one weekend. "Orphan was wandering around the area until I called him over to meet my friend. He wanted to ride "Orphan" bareback. I told him he would have to get permission from Harry. There was a bank along side of where "Orphan" was standing. It was just high enough to step off on to the back of the horse. I told him he better not get on him. He got on him anyhow. Well "Orphan" took two jumps and bucked him off, then stood there looking down at my friend as to say, "What are you doing down there? you should listen when someone says not to get on me". I just stood there and laughed.

Many years later Harry wanted to give "Orphan" to me for just paying his feed bill. Harry was on his way to Midway Island and I was in San Francisco with no place to keep him. I loved that old horse and I knew he loved me. I could get on him any which way I wanted to but don't let anyone else try it.

During the time I was waiting for my arch to heal I also was waiting to get my call to Crissy Field to take my physical examination to qualify to be a flying cadet in the U.S. Army Air Corps. I was really sweating it out since I would be 20 years old the 23 Sept. 1935, and my appointment to take my physical was the first week in October! I finally got my cast off 3 weeks before I was scheduled to go Crissy Field at the Presidio in San Francisco.

I was still limping a little when I reported to Crissy Field. My Father drove me up from Patterson and was as anxious for me as I was. When we walked into the dispensary, where the examinations were to be given, there were 36 people waiting there for the same thing,

Well I passed all my tests in the morning and when we came back after lunch I found only 3 people left. By the time all my tests were over I found that I was the only one left. I took the rest of my tests and the Flight Surgeon, who must have been at least 6'6" tall, said that I was the ideal fighter pilot. With that he said, "Let's take your blood pressure". He wrapped the blood pressure tube around my arm. I had never had my blood pressure taken. As the thing started to tighten up on my arm I could feel my heart start to race. With that, he looked at me surprised like, and said, "You're dead". My blood pressure had shot up to 160 over 80. I was so excited and apprehensive after all these years preparing for this moment and now I was going to "blow it". The Doc said that he knew I was excited but relax and come back tomorrow.

My Dad could not believe it but we had to come back the next day. I got my blood pressure down to 140. The Doc said come back in a week and he would take it again.

My Dad and I went back home, to Patterson, California. I went back to my old Doctor Allen, who treated me for my broken arch. My Dad told him the story about me having too high a blood pressure I was so excited. The Doctor gave me some pills to calm me down and to take them just before I was going to get my recheck the following week.

Well the week went by and my Dad took me back to Crissy Field again. In the meantime I took the pills the Doctor had given me. We went in to see the Flight Surgeon again and when he took my blood pressure it came down to 130. He then told the corporal who was in the office to take it and I got it down to 125. I thought I had passed but the Doctor said that he knew I was excited and the blood pressure machine made me apprehensive but he could not take the chance of me going to Randolph Field, Texas, and have me do the same thing all over again. It would be a reflection on him. With that he said, "Try the Navy"!

It was quite a disappointment after all the years I had prepared for this day, to be a pilot in the Army Air Corps, and I "blew It". I knew my Father was as disappointed as I was. We went back home to share the disappointment with the rest of the family and friends. My dream was shattered.

It wouldn't be too long before I would leave home and relieve my folks of the burden of supporting me. I would go up to the big city of San

Francisco to seek my fortune, (Ha)!

Before leaving I started to sing again. I thought I could make a little money for my "stake". I won a lot of amateur programs and won everything from groceries to cash. I finally won the Graven-Ingels Bread Company sponsored contest at the theater in Modesto. My Brother Keith went with me as my rooting section. There were ten people in on the program. Of all things I was first on the program! I always hated to be first but this was it. I had to be good enough so they would not forget me by the time all the acts got finished. I sang "Take Me Back to My Boots and Saddles". This song was very popular at this time. My accompanist was just a piano, but he was an excellent player and made it sound like a whole orchestra. At the end we all came out on the stage to receive our final applause, I knew I got more applause and the applause meter that they used verified my ears when I won. I won $25, a fortune in those days. By the way I was dressed in my cowboy outfit, Stetson, chaps, shirt, boots, and spurs, etc, the whole bit. Years later I would wear the same outfit for my western movie I made in the hills around Millbrae, California.

After saving a little money and saying goodbye to all the family, I took off for San Francisco. It was a shame I never went back to retake the test. I could have taken it every three months until I passed it. Maybe it was fate. If I would have made it I would have been stationed in the Philippines or Hawaii, when WWII started. Very few fighter pilots survived the first days of the war. I would have graduated in class 36A, if I had made it. The Lord works in strange ways.

So I went to San Francisco to find a job. Any job since it was still the depression and hard to find a job. I went to an employment agency on seeing an ad in the newspaper. In those days you had to pay the agency for finding you a job. Now the company that hires you has to pay the fee.

I got a job riding a three-wheeled motorcycle as delivery boy for a Sherry's Liquor store. It was a chain in San Francisco. They had three or four stores in the San Francisco area. I worked out of the Larkin Street store. I would also help out the other stores when they got too busy. Here I was riding a motorcycle as a delivery boy with a college education. I wasn't proud it was an accomplishment just to get a job, back then.

I had never ridden a three-wheeler before. The cycle was leased from

Al Thomason, the Indian Dealer at Van Ness and Market Streets. I went down to pick it on my first day on the job and Al asked me if I had ever ridden a three wheeler before. "Of course", I replied. With that I cranked up and very nonchalantly rode off into the traffic on Van Ness Avenue. It was quite an experience when I went to shift out of first gear. You have to have a very positive hold of the handlebars since it will wobble with you if you don't. I know they were all watching me as I tried to control the" beast" going all over the street.

By the end of the workday I had finally mastered the "beast". When I took the cycle back at the end of the day, Al said that after watching me he knew I had never ridden a three-wheeler before but was pleased I had made it through the day without any mishap. I then became well acquainted with all the people who worked there as well as all the riders who hung out there.

Before I got my job I had to find a temporary place to live. I had an old friend, Alan Shattuck, who lived in San Francisco at the time so I bunked with him and his mother until I got my job. I had known Al since we were 10 years old when we lived next door to him in Berkeley on Curtis Street. I would cross Al's path many times during his life on this earth. Al died rather young and under strange circumstances.

My new job paid $60 per month plus any tips I would get. Seven days a week 12 hours a day. No days off!

Al worked for the Bank Of America and wanted to try and get me a job in the bank but I knew I would not like being confined in a bank after being out in the open most of my life. So I liked riding the motorcycle out in the traffic all day. I gave very fast service and I bought myself a pair of riding boots and breeches plus a leather jacket with a motorcycle cap. I even wore a tie. I knew the manager of the store was impressed. My first paycheck was used up but very frugally. I did my shopping at an Army-Navy store on Market Street, which had many bargains, especially if you did your shopping first thing Monday morning. The manager was Jewish and would not let you out of the store if you were his first customer of the week, without buying something. You could really get a bargain.

I forgot to mention that Al had a twin sister, Eleanor, and an older brother, Gordon. Eleanor worked for the Emporium Department Store on Market Street and Gordon worked for the American Can Company. The family had moved to San Francisco, after their father died at Berkeley.

I finally found a room in an old converted mansion for $10 per month! I was always writing home and keeping abreast of my life in the big City. My Mom became worried about the conditions I was living in so her and my Aunt Mae came to San Francisco to check things out. When they saw the place where I was living they immediately set out to find me a nicer place. I admit it was not the best place in town but for $10 a month it was in my budget. Of course my Mom and Aunt Mae found me a much nicer place with better surroundings at 1492 Pacific Street. It was only $12 a month and was only three blocks from where I was working. It was very convenient and the price was right. I figured my rent should not be over 25% of my income and I was well within that.

I soon made enough money to buy myself another motorcycle. It was an Indian "101" Scout, and it was a "stroker". It had a special flywheel that gave the engine a longer stroke and it was over bored to give the engine more cubic inches than the original 45 cu. in. This made the Indian quite fast. I joined a motorcycle club with my friends so I could go on rides with them and go to their meetings, etc.

I worked for Sherry's Liquor Store for about six months riding the 3 wheeler, delivering liquor. I then got a promotion to assistant manager. I now would work 12 hours a day but got two days off a month, so I had much more time to go riding with my "Buddies". I did not make any more money; since I was not getting the tips I used get from deliveries. But I now had an inside job and met a lot of people and had much more responsibility. I had just turned 21 years old, which made me eligible to sell liquor.

I was doing real well with my job and I was making a living wage for that time. In fact my Mother and Father and brother were not doing very well. My Father was out of a job and no one was working and my brother was going to Patterson High School. I began sending them $5.00 every paycheck. I bought a meal ticket at the local café for $5.00, which would last me almost a month. Gas for my Indian was only 15 cents a gallon or less. My room was $12.00 per month. I was making $85.00 per month and I managed very well even paying for my new Indian Daytona Scout of $25.00 per month in 1936, money seemed to last much better than it does today, 2003. It took so much less to have a good time. Life was much simpler. Of course I was very frugal throughout my life. It paid off with money management and to differentiate between wants and needs Later in life my family always had their needs.

I forgot to mention how I got my new, 1935 Indian Daytona Scout. I would park my old Indian Motorcycle at Al Thomason's and get on the three-wheeler for Sherry's Liquor Store and when the day was through I would ride the three wheeler back and ride my motorcycle home. One day when I was off I rode by Al Thomason. All the riders used to hang around the motorcycle shop when they were off from work and did not have anything else to do on Saturdays. They just stood around and shot the "breeze". Al called me in and said, "Bill, you need a new "cycle" and I have just the motorcycle for you". I said, I don't think I can afford it" At that he showed me this beautiful piece of machinery, a 1935, 45 cubic inch Indian Daytona Scout!

The Indian Motorcycle Company sent this Motorcycle to Oakland Speedway, California, for the National Motorcycle Championships. They did not have a chance to test it before they sent it out for the races. As a result at speeds of 100mph the valves began to float and hit the head due to the racing camshafts they had put in the engine. So their entry was out of the race early. Al Thomason, the Indian Dealer in San Francisco obtained it from the factory to sell since they did not want to haul it back to the factory back East. Al then sold it to a girl rider. Who, on her first ride got confused with the controls and the clutch operation and went through a plate glass window of the plumbing shop next door. Al took the motorcycle back and there it was for me to buy. When he said that the motorcycle would only cost me $425 with $25 per month payments, it was within my budget now especially when I was offered $100 for my old Indian by one of my fellow riders. I sure was proud of my new machine. It sure could go for a 45 cu. in. When I got to be real sure of myself I began to race it and compete in all the events at the rallies. We would have runs to all the different places and events. I belonged to the "Lou Cazzaza Riders" club, which later changed the name to the "Pacific Motorcycle Club". I became the road captain of the club and led the club to all the events.

I worked for Sherry's Liquor Store for about a year. During this time I worked from delivery boy to Assistant manager. One day I was 5 minutes late getting back to work (due the big crowd in the little café where I had my meal ticket). It just happened that the big boss was checking out the store with Mr. Landi, the manager of the store who was a great guy. The boss asked me what time I was supposed to be back from lunch and said that I didn't care "whether school kept, or not." This made me quite angry, since I hadn't missed a day of work in over a year and was never late. Paying me $80 per month for 12 hours a day with only 2 days off per month!

I began inquiring through all my rider friends and contacts about riding jobs and found that J.E. French Co. was looking for a rider for their pickup and delivery service in their service department. They were the Dodge and Plymouth dealer for the San Francisco area. I also found out that they paid $4.75 per hour for a 5 day week with Saturdays and Sundays off!

I immediately went for an interview and got the job. I quit Sherry's Liquor store on a Friday and went to work on my new job the following Monday. I gave Sherry's two weeks notice and didn't lose a days work. This was the only way to do it when you have obligations to meet. The beauty of the new job that was the same distance to work as before but I could ride my motor to work to a special parking place at the shop and when I was through work I could hop on my motor and blast off to where ever I wanted to go. Plus I had all my weekends off. I also got 2 weeks vacation.

I had to join the Garage Employees Union to keep my job. I did not believe in Unions but San Francisco was a very strong Union city, so I joined. The dues were two dollars per month, which I could afford, especially getting a raise in pay of more than $50 per month. I was in "Tall Cotton".

There were a couple of other riders that worked at the same job as me. One was Bob Leavitt and his Brother. Bob had ridden the delivery cycle before he went to tune up school and now was the tune up mechanic in the service department. He was about my age. His Brother was a service salesman. Their father had been the Willys Dealer in San Francisco and he committed suicide after being charged with embezzlement from the company.

Bob Leavitt had a special built Indian pony, 30.50 cubic inch displacement engine bored and stroked to give it almost 45 cubic inch; it could really go for a small bike. We became friends and went to a lot of the

Bill Disbrow on his 1935 Indian Daytona Scout 1937

races and events together.

One of the big Motorcycle events of the year was the Hollister Gypsy Tour. It was sponsored by the AMA and had championship races and other events. Our club was preparing to go since it was on a weekend. I was all set to go since I had become a member of the AMA, The America Motorcycle Association, so I was eligible in any of their sanctioned events.

Our club had 20 riders and their wives or girlfriends. I was single but had no trouble getting a girlfriend. In fact girls were my downfall but that is another story. My mother said that I took after my Father. We had a great time at the races and events at Hollister and got there and home safe and sound. It was quite an experience to see about 5000 motorcycles lined up on the main street of town. Of course, it got bigger every year until the really bad element invaded the motorcycle world, the Hell's Angels, the Axe Men, etc. They started a big riot about 10 years after I stopped going. It was featured on the cover of "Life Magazine".

I attended all the runs around Northern California and the local areas. Our club got to be quite well known. We eventually painted all our motors the same color, black and white. We all dressed the same with black riding breeches with a competition white and black sweater and the club name on the back, with our emblem on the front. We all wore white caps. We looked real "sharp". For the 1938 Hollister run I installed lights in all the wheels of the member's bikes for our drill team. We would give a demonstration at night for one of the events at Hollister. The club got a big trophy for putting on such a good display. I was the leader of the drill team with our club flag on a chrome standard fastened to my front forks with a light on top and blue and red lights in all the wheels of the bikes. We did this at night at the ballpark with all the lights off. It was quite impressive. It must have taken me two months to make all the brass rings and make all the insulators that went on the hub of each wheel both front and rear.

It was on one of our runs that I met my first wife, Florence Abad. We dated a lot and she began riding with me on a lot of the runs. In the meantime, I bought a model A Ford roadster with 16inch wheels on it for $50 so we could go out in the rain and fog and not freeze to death.

One night while we were driving in the Model A Ford, we were hit head on by a drunken driver, while driving through Golden Gate Park. I tried to avoid him by going to the shoulder but he followed me and hit me head on. The impact threw me out of the car and I remember seeing the two cars rare up, as I hit the pavement. The car that hit us was a Graham, which was much heavier than my Ford. Both cars were totaled. Fortunately it happened about 50 yards from the emergency clinic in Golden Gate Park. I looked bad I was bleeding from the mouth where my face hit the steering wheel. I had such a tight grip on the steering wheel that I bent the steering

The Daytona Scout after it's new paint job 1937

column against the dash, when we hit. I also broke a few ribs to boot with bruises and contusions on the rest of my body. We did not have shatterproof glass in those days and the windshield exploded. Florence was the one who was really hurt. She had a broken neck! She had a little scratch on her face where a piece of the windshield had cut it and she had a broken collarbone and a concussion. They put a cast on her from her neck to her waist.

Well we sued for $20,000 but it seems that the driver of the Graham was a son of the Supervisor for the City of San Francisco who had a lot of friends in high places, especially lawyers. We got a lawyer who was well

Keith Disbrow's Indian "101" Scount 1930 Model 1939

known for winning cases. What we didn't know, he was a good friend of the defendant. The case dragged on so long that Florence and I were married. I guess it took about a year and we settled out of court for a net of $1600. Today we would have gotten well over $100,000 for the seriousness of the injuries, and knowing of the after effects as one grows older. It knocked all my front teeth loose, broke some of my ribs, and demolished my Ford.

We were married on the 12 February 1938 at a little church in the Potrero district in San Francisco. It was near Florence's mother's house. Florence had graduated from Balboa High School. She was 18 years old at the time we were married and I was 21, actually too young. Instead of getting married I should have gone back and tried to get in the Army Air Corps again.

We moved from my apartment house to a little bigger place until we could find something better. I was still working for J.E. French Company and our place was real handy. I borrowed a car from one of my friends where I worked and we drove to Yosemite National Park for our honeymoon.

About 6 months after we were married I got laid off from J.F. French Company, isn't that always the way. I was lucky; I went to work for the Oldsmobile Dealer, W.A. McFarlane, which was just a block down the street. I held this job for about 3 months when they went broke and closed their doors. At this time things were bad in San Francisco. With my contacts I found another job with James F. Waters, the DeSoto and Plymouth Dealer as the car pickup and delivery rider on the three-wheeler. It was another 2 blocks down Van Ness Avenue, still nice and handy. In the interim, I worked for United Motors for a short time and then a friend of mine, who was in our motorcycle club, talked me to going into the Italian grocery business in North Beach. He was an Italian named Angelo Carnevale. Well that did not last very long since I could not talk Italian and he was keeping his job at Dean Whitter, the stock brokerage house. I worked days and he worked nights.

After this experience I then did go to work for Waters. It was a good job riding the three-wheeler and picking up and delivering mostly new cars. One of our members of motorcycle club was the service manager for Les Vogel the Chevrolet Dealer at Van Ness and Market Streets. He wanted me to come and work for him in the same type of job. It was hard to actually to get a good three-wheeler rider. You had to know the city and be fast and careful. I had a very good record. He offered me all kinds of things but they sure did not plan out the way he said they would, after leaving a real good job at J.F. Waters. I would work overtime almost every day and he would not pay me, which he had promised. I finally had to bring the Union in to get my money.

The Union was very good to me. I was surprised. They told me to quit my job and that they would get me another job. I would be off work for just a month before they had a new job for me. It would be the first time I ever drew Unemployment money. This helped out. We only had to pay rent and food. We had moved to a flat at, 333 Page Street, I think. This was not far from Van Ness Avenue where I was working at my new job at Don Lee

Cadillac. I would be running their automobile elevator taking the cars to the different shops for repair and bring them down again for the customers, when they were finished. I worked there for about a month and the Union got me a permanent job at J.W. McAllister, the Chrysler-Plymouth Dealer as a floor boy. Don Lee wanted me to stay there permanently but did not inform the Union of their intentions so I went to McAllister's.

McAllister's was a good job and nice people to work for. My job was to keep the cars flowing through the service department to all the different floors in the building for repair. It also had an elevator but I did not run this one. I also did odd service jobs for the service salesmen, i.e., adjusting headlights, replace dash lights, replace batteries, etc. This was usually free work for the customers. They just paid for the parts. I met a very good friend there, Bob Lively, he was the wheel aligner and his wheel aligning rack was next to my headlight adjusting station. We played softball together the whole time I was employed at MacAllisters. We became very good friends and used to go to their house for dinner and poker at least once a month. Bob died a few years back and I did not know it until I sent them a copy of the "Bronco Kid" the movie we all made at Millbrae, south of San Francisco.

Since we got a little money from our accident, we bought another nice Model A Ford roadster, for $120. It had a new paint job, black, with yellow 16" wire wheels. It had two spares, one in each front fender, and with a trunk on the back and a rumble seat. We would drive down to see my family in Patterson about once every 2 months. I later traded it off for a beautiful 1936 Ford V8 convertible coupe with 15,000 miles on it for $450. I wish I had it now; it was a classic I would keep this car for 14 years.

While we were living at 333 Page Street my brother Keith was killed with another boy coming home from a motorcycle club meeting in Modesto. They were riding double on Buddy Avila's Harley. It was night and they missed a turn coming home to Patterson from Modesto. It seems they missed this turn that wasn't that bad. It could be taken at 60mph without any trouble. They ran up on a small bank and went into a big wheat field and would have been all right except for a cable holding up an old hog tight fence. The cable caught under the handlebars as they went by and broke an old 6X6 the cable was fastened to. When the 6X6 snapped off it hit both riders in the head and broke both their necks! They were both killed instantly. It was a freak accident. The motorcycle shop came, got the motorcycle and rode it off to the shop. It wasn't hurt a bit. Years later I met a friend of Keith's that was in his class at Patterson High School, and he thought they might have run into some ground fog which would come up suddenly on this road. This could be the cause of them missing the corner.

This was a tremendous blow to my parents. Keith was 5 years younger than me and was just 18 years old ready to graduate from high school. We were a very close family and loved one another very much. Keith worked for our Dad in his garage at Crows Landing after school and when ever my Dad needed help. My Dad appreciated Keith's help very much since Dad operated the garage by himself. Keith was going to be a Navy flier but never got the chance. His very good friend, Arnie Ingerbritsen, who was in many of Keith's classes at Patterson High School, went on to be a P-38 fighter pilot in the US Army Air Corps. I would meet Arnie at Itazuke AB, Japan, in 1959, while I was stationed there as the deputy commander of the 68th Fighter Interceptor Squadron. I was flying the F-86D.and the F-102. Arnie got out of the service after the war and went into Civil Service and was a troubleshooter for some of the electronic equipment, which was installed in the aircraft in Japan. He had seen my name on one of the base locaters and gave me a call at work. We had a nice reunion while we had him to dinner. His folks owned a dairy in Patterson.

The thing that hurt the most was that I had bought Keith his motorcycle. It was a 1929 Indian Scout and the reason he was not riding his own motorcycle that night my father had ordered a new "Knobby" tire for the rear wheel of his motorcycle and it did not come in time. So he rode with his friend Buddy Avila. What a shame and what a waste of two young people. I know the Lord is taking good care of him. Keith was a very good person and brother and we all loved him very much. He was killed in May 1938.

I had also bought a front drive Model "T" Roadster and towed it to Patterson with the help of my friend Al Shattuck; we towed it with my other Ford Model "T" Roadster. What a time we had. Patterson was about 110 miles from San Francisco. I could not take it across on the Ferry from San Francisco to Oakland so we had to drive down the peninsula to

Dumbarton Bridge, which was south of San Francisco. We had to take the Mission San Jose cut-off, which wandered through the hills to Livermore. I could hardly make it up some of the hills pulling it with my other "T". After much patience we finally made it safe and sound.

This Model "T" was a real racer. Always looking for more speed and this car had it. It had a Rajo head, dual magnetos, gear driven water pump, twin Winfield SR carburetors, and many other modifications to make it go. It was originally built in the Polytechnic High School somewhere in the Los Angeles area. The engine had been turned around so it could drive the front drive. The steering wheel was on the right side instead of on the left. It seemed the design did not suit the steering being on the left side. It could go 113mph, which was flying in a Model "T" in those days. It was the scourge of Patterson until I got Keith his Motorcycle. My Dad and Keith finally took the front drive off and made a rear wheel drive out of it, since the bearings and the U-joints were not available anymore. My Dad and Keith used to race the train that ran down the west side of the valley and right through Patterson, Crows Landing, Gustine, Los Banos, to Los Angeles. We were going to build a car for the Indianapolis 500 until my brother was killed. It was a shock but did not deter the quest for speed.

During this time I also acquired a midget racer with an aluminum body and a Harley-Davidson engine in it. I think I traded it off for my first Model "A" Ford Roadster. I could not pass up a bargain and usually made out quite well by trading or reselling it.

After losing Keith I got a steady job at McAllister's and settled down quite a bit. I had sold my beautiful Indian "Daytona" 45, after I hit a car broadside. I was going home for lunch on Franklin Street in San Francisco, when this fellow in a Plymouth sedan made an illegal left turn in front of me and I hit him just behind his front wheel. I hit him so hard that it bent his frame and bent my front forks 90 degrees from normal. I had such a tight hold on the handlebars that it did not even budge me off the motor. I had sore arms for a week. I figured Florence and my Mother did not need the stress of me riding my motor any longer. I then turned my talents to amateur movie making. My Grandfather Hitchcock died and left me his beautiful Bell and Howell Movie outfit which consisted of a B&H 70D camera, projector, screen, case, etc. He used it in his detective business,

The Hitchcock Detective and Patrol Agency, in Oakland, California. This was actually a very professional piece of equipment. I had to make real movies now no making faces at the camera. They had to be productions.

Florence and I joined the Sherman Clay Camera Club. In the meantime I met another good friend that would be in most of my productions, Dudley Key. Dud had a motor too, and belonged to our Motorcycle Club. In fact we had been friends before I stopped riding. We met a lot of nice people who were professional people who used their movie hobby to give them a diversion from the usual hustle and bustle of the everyday work. One such couple was the Hones. He was a lawyer with his brothers in one of the big buildings in the financial district. We became very good friends and used to go to their nice home in the Marina District.

Work at McAllister's was great and after meeting Bob Lively, Lee Green, Walt Riggs, Vince Onorato, and many others including Pete Taylorson, the Service manager, I felt right at home. I went to work for McAllisters 1938. We had a great time playing on the softball team, which McAllisters sponsored. We even had nice uniforms. Bob Lively played first base or catcher. I started in the outfield but was brought in to play third base, the "Hot Corner". I played the whole time I worked for McAllisters. Bob and I were great friends and always kept in touch even after I left McAllisters until Bob died years later.

After being a floor boy for about a year I was promoted to Apprentice Mechanic. I was placed in the new car accessory department. Here I would install new accessories on the new car that the customer ordered. I also did specialty work for anyone that brought his car in and wanted something special installed on his car, like horns, spot- lights, etc. My specially was installing new seat covers. I could do it faster than a full fledged mechanic and they were paying me less as an apprentice mechanic, 83 cents an hour. I could make the company much more money on the job I did, and they liked that. I had a journeyman in the same department that showed me all the tricks of the trade on all the installations. I learned quickly since I had a lot experience working for my Father and had a lot of mechanical insight. In fact one day the journeyman told me to slow down. I guess I was showing him up unintentionally.

In the meantime, Florence and I moved to a bigger flat at 415 Page

Street, about two blocks from our old place. Our friend, Dud Key moved in with us while he was looking for a place of his own after moving out of his folk's house in the Richmond District.

Since I now owned a very nice 16mm Bell and Howell movie camera we joined the Sherman Clay Camera Club on Kearny Street in Downtown Can Francisco. I think Dud key was a member so we joined, I wanted to make real movies and being a member of the club gave me a lot of people to talk to concerning this. I also had an outlet to show my movies.

My first attempt was called the "life guard" which was shot at a lake on the Peninsula near Palo Alto. I used Flo and her brother's girlfriend and her brother, Bud Abad. It was shot on a 100 foot roll of black and white film. I made the movie title out of alphabet soup letters. It didn't turn out too badly in fact it gave me some good ideas for my next productions.

The next one was a real production. I wanted to make a mystery thriller. So I started to write the scenario, using many of the mysteries I had seen ("The Cat and the Canary", with Bob Hope, "The Bat" and many others). First I had to write the story and then the scenario.

I used to take a bag lunch to work and eat it in my car, which was parked across the street from MacAllisters, so it was in plain view from the windows of the building. I would quickly eat my lunch so I could write my story. It was called "the Curse Of The Cobra". It took about three months to write the story and the scenario. During this time some of the workers were watching me and were wondering what I was doing. When I told them that I was writing a scenario for a movie they thought I was kidding them.

After getting the scenario finished I now had to cast my picture, also find a suitable place to shoot the production. I drew most of my cast from the people in our movie club. My friend Steve Jetters was my leading man. He was not a member of the club but worked for the Bear Photo Company and could get my 16mm film wholesale for me. He rode a three wheeler for the company, picking up and delivering film for processing. He would always stop at Sherry's Liquor Store where I worked at the time to see me, since it was on his route. Since I had to pay for everything myself it helped me defray some of the expenses by Steve getting my film wholesale.

The Hones were both cast in the movie since they so graciously let me use their beautiful two-story home in the Marina District to shoot the picture. The picture was shot on Agfa Super-Pan Film. This was the fastest black and white film for this period of time, Weston 100, in 1939. Each roll was processed for me at the Agfa Laboratory. I would tell them what type of scene I shot and they would process the film to the affect I wanted, since some of the scenes were shot under adverse lighting conditions. I would take each processed roll of film and edit it right away as we went along. I tried to shoot in the right sequence so editing would be easier. As it was the finished film would have over 1000 splices in it and ran for 45 minutes at 16 frames per second. It took a year to finish it until it was shown at the Hones home as a big premier showing. The picture was in black and white and silent with titles since I did not have sound.

The night of the big premier of the "Curse of the Cobra", at the Hones home was a big success. There must have been at least 40 people there plus the cast. We had champagne, flashing lights outside into the sky by some of the cars that had spot lights on them. We also had one of the cast members, Bob Vaughn, play eerie music for the background as the picture was being projected. Bob shot the movie in 8mm also. Bob was an excellent pianist, which added the professional touch. The evening was a huge success. It was worth all the effort for a years work. Everyone was totally surprised how professional the picture turned out, since most of the people were members of the movie club and never attempted such a production. It was a real movie.

I eventually entered the movie in the Home Movie Magazine National Contest and won Honorable Mention with 3 stars. I made a negative copy of the movie from the master print many years later when I was stationed near Tokyo, Japan. I now have it transferred to a VCR tape but it lost some of its effect after all the years in the can. It was shot in 1939 and I had it printed in 1949.

The cast consisted of Florence Disbrow, my wife at the time. Bud Abad, her brother, Dolly Hone and her husband, Steve Jetter, Dudley Key, Florence Balzerini, Bob Vaughn; I was the director, producer editor, cameraman, etc.

With the success of this movie I made a lot of short features and wrote and directed more, winning a lot of prizes for my effort. But I was anxious to start another production. I had always wanted to do a western, so I started writing again at lunch time in my car. I finally finished it and got most of my cast from the people at McAlisters that I worked with.

I had to find a good location with horses ready available for rent. I found that area around Millbrae, California, was just right. It had a riding stable real handy with the right price, 60 cents per hour. My actors had to rent their own horses in order to be in the picture. The hills around Millbrae were vacant, no houses or any civilization at all. We used 21 actors, 18 horses, and shot up 400 rounds of movie ammunition. The manager of the riding stable loaned me beautiful silver and gold mounted saddle and trappings, worth over $500. Who would do that now? People were much more trusting and honorable in those days.

The picture was shot on location on weekends. After we would get through we would stop at a local bar for refreshments on the way home. We were still dressed in our cowboy outfits, guns and all (The Hollywood Cowboys). We would have a roaring time in the bar discussing the parts everyone was playing. It took three months of weekends to finish the movie. We got to be well known at the bar as we stopped there all the while we were shooting at Millbrae. They could not believe that we were making an amateur western when we first stopped there.

In the meantime, Germany had marched into Poland, Czechoslovakia, and England was about to go to war against Germany. My Mother told me that during the last war, WWI that all jobs not in the war business slowed down because everybody was working for the war effort. My Father had already sold his garage at Crows landing and got a job as engine inspector at McClellan Field in Sacramento, California. They had bought a new home in Del Paso Heights, not far from McClellan Field. They talked me into applying for a job there, also, which I did. Florence did not like the idea of leaving San Francisco since her folks were there. I got the job and got more money than I was making before, so the move was worthwhile. We also bought a new home in North Sacramento for $2900. It had two bedrooms; all tile bathroom, tiled sink in the kitchen, and hardwood floors. It had a large living room that served also as a dining area. I think I paid $500 down. Prices sure have changed since then.

Before I was accepted for my new job at McClellan I had a preview of the

Bill Disbrow as the "Bronco Kid" 1940

"Bronco Kid" that I finally finished. I was the "Star" as the "Bronco Kid", cameraman, director, producer, and editor, just like Orson Wells, Ha. It was a silent picture and had titles but was filmed in color. Kodachrome was just out so it was quite unique for an amateur movie to be in color. We had the preview at the IOF hall in San Francisco. The cast for the "Bronco Kid", consisted of, Florence Disbrow, Bob Lively, Lee Green, Bob Lively's brother, Lee Greens wife, Jim Low, Wayne Carr, and Paul Costello as my side kick. I can't remember the names of the others but they all worked with me at McAllisters. I find now that most of them are dead, in the year 2002. The cast had sold tickets for our big preview. I think I almost broke even for the cost of the production. I also showed the "Curse of the Cobra" and all the short subjects I had produced.

By the time I left McAllisters, I was making 83 cents an hour. The new job paid $1640 per year to start, much more than I was making. I said, "Good bye" to all the workers at McAllisters and moved to 2601-17th Street, Sacramento, California, to our new house. My folks lived in Del Paso Heights on 3618 Jasmine Street, which was only a few miles away.

When I reported to McClellan Field, they put me in Plant Maintenance, when I had applied for Junior Aircraft Electrician. I didn't mind since I had a good job. In Plant Maintenance I did heavy wiring for a while as a helper and learned a lot about electricity. I had a good back ground for it since I had taken Physics when I was in school. I even learned to rewind armatures for electric motors from a fellow worker. He was a very good friend, "Shorty" Miolenze. I finally became the "trouble shooter" for the whole depot. I remember one night, when I was on the swing shift, I got a call that they had a P-38 aircraft hanging from the traveling crane in the big hanger and they could not get the crane to move up or down or move at all. It was holding up the whole production line. I had to climb up the side of the hanger to get to the electrical circuits and found that it had popped a circuit breaker. I reset the circuit breaker and everything was back to normal with a big shout from the workers.

I remember changing light bulbs in another big hanger. It was about 100 feet high to the top of it. The lights were hung on a long extension that hooked in the ceiling girders. There was no way up there but to climb up the side of the hanger on the girders. I strapped all the stuff I had to have to do the job to myself. I then climbed up the side of the hanger and changed about 5 light bulbs. The hard part of the job was unhooking and lifting the long extension pipe that held the fixture and the light bulb in it. I did this about three times and then they decided to get a professional steeplejack to do the job and they used scaffolding! They also had to pay them much more than they paid me. When I visit McClellan now and look up at the light bulbs I replaced, I can't believe I climbed up there as a young man. I was fearless, always on the edge.

There was an opening in the instrument repair department, which was a better job than I had so I transferred jobs. I also got a raise in doing so. After being there for about 6 months I was eating my breakfast on a Sunday morning and listening to the radio, they broke into the program and said that the Japanese had just bombed Pearl Harbor, Hawaii, 7 Dec. 1941. Of course, I could hardly believe it and now I could I get into the US Army Air Corps. I was married and they were not taking married men at the time. In the meantime England was in the war against Hitler and we were supplying with all the war materials. Also the Canadian RAF was taking foreign enlistments for pilots, of course I applied. I went to the Fairmont Hotel in San Francisco for my interview with my pictures for my application. I waited about two months when President Roosevelt cut off all foreign enlistments and lifted the ban on married men for pilot training. I was down to the recruiting office immediately. I took my entrance examinations at that station in Sacramento and made the highest score they ever had to date.

THE MILITARY YEARS

I could not believe who was the recruiting officer for the flying cadets at Sacramento. It was none other than Major Burdette E. Palmer, who had given me one of my recommendations for flying cadets in 1935! He did not recognize me at first; I now was 7 years older and had a trim moustache. I had his letter from 1935 on top of the other recommendations I had gotten the first time I had applied for cadets. He read the letter that he had written in 1935 and was startled. He looked up at me from his desk and said, "Is that you Bill?" We shook hands and renewed our old acquaintances. He showed the letter to his secretary and asked her if she thought that the recommendation was good enough. Then he explained how it happened to have a 1935 date on it. Major Palmer suggested that I get new recommendations, which I already had with me.

I was eventually called to take my physical at Mather Field, and I passed everything OK. When the Doc put the blood pressure tester on my arm, of course my blood pressure jumped up again, since I was so excited to be getting a second chance. I told the doctor what had happened before 7 years ago and I wanted to get in on this second try. He made me lay down for about 15 minutes and took it again and it was normal! I was in! I could hardly believe it. After all of these years I had been wasting. By this time I was 26 years old and the age limit was 26 1/2. I was sworn into the U.S. Army Reserve on the 31st of July 1942, one day before I was over the age limit. Then the time dragged on as I waited for my call to active duty. A lot of my friends had applied also and they were sweating it out as well. My Dad was very happy for me, and very proud. My mother and wife had mixed emotions, since I would most likely go to war.

At last I received my call to report to Santa Ana Army Air Base to active duty on the 29th of Jan. 1943. After all the years of waiting I was finally in the Army Air Corps to be trained as a pilot. I did not give it a thought that I would not make it. I just knew I could fly.

After many tears and goodbyes I was off to Santa Ana Air Base, California, for Pre-flight training. I was assigned to a squadron with a serial number 19069814, and started my indoctrination as an Aviation Cadet. It was quite an experience, marching, learning the movements, military courtesy, discipline, and getting classified. Everyone that became an Aviation Cadet did not become a pilot automatically. Everyone had to go through a battery of tests to classify you either as a pilot, navigator, or Bombardier. I was very fortunate to have qualified for all three so had my first choice as a pilot. A movie was made of the Cadets going through training during this time. It was called, "I Wanted Wings," it was written by Bernie Lay. It really showed what we had to go through.

It took three months of ground school, military courtesy, warfare, etc., before we were sent to primary flying school. During the three months of Pre-flight, we were restricted to the base for the first 6 weeks as underclassmen. Then we got Saturdays off and had to be back at the base for the Sunday Parade. A few of the troops fainted while standing at attention in the hot sun. You were supposed to be eliminated if this happened but I didn't know anyone that was. I found that if I did not lock my knees while standing at attention it did not bother me, after a big night in Hollywood dancing the night before. We used to take the big red train from Newport Beach to Los Angeles, then the street car to Hollywood. Nobody was allowed to have a car while at Santa Ana. I was a poker player and everyone wanted to play. It was quite easy to win since my Father had taught me the fine points of the game. He had been a poker player in Fort Bragg many years ago and lost a lot and won it all back by never staying in a stud hand with less than a 10 in the hole or a pair to start with. It was against regulations to gamble so we never had any money showing on the table. We played with chips. White was 5 cents, red 10 cents, and blue 25 cents. I got KP "Mess Management", twice for getting caught. I got the "China Clipper", the dishwasher, which wasn't too bad.

In pre-flight we had to learn all about poisoned gasses and went through the gas chamber and had to take off our gas masks to experience how tear gas affects you. We also learned to identify the gasses by smell. It was a very good indoctrination to military life.

We finally got orders to primary flying schools. Some went to Oxnard, Ontario, some to Texas. I was sent to Ryan Field, Hemet, California. Here I was to fly the Ryan PT-22., A low wing monoplane. Some of the other schools had the Stearman, PT-17, a biplane. I was very happy to be still in California and close to home.

Primary was a lot different than pre-flight. Here you were constantly harassed by the upper classmen like before but now you had to learn to fly at the same time. The first day pre-flight they marched us out to the flight line to watch the cadets shoot landings. A cadet "lost it" on landing and flipped on his back. It was quite a shock to everybody as we watched the whole thing. The Tactical Officer in charge stated that this was no way to land the airplane. The pilot was lucky and walked away unhurt. The old saying is "any landing you walk away from is a good landing".

I though I could always fly without any trouble. On my first ride I took the airplane off with no trouble. I had been practicing on the rudder control machine and was quite good at it. My instructor was showing me the area also the fine points of the use of stick and rudder. His name was "Shorty" Townsend, as we approached the airport for a landing he wanted me to follow him through the landing by putting my hand on the stick and my feet on the rudder pedals. As we were coming down the final approach the ground was coming up very fast. I was a little apprehensive about being able to land the plane on the first try. The P-22 was a hot little aircraft for its day and came down the final at 80 mph. Things began to happen very rapidly at this speed. You have to make sure that you make the aircraft go where you want it to go or you are in trouble. After about five tries I finally got the perspective with the help of my instructor. After seeing the accident on the first day at Primary I was very attentive at what my instructor was telling me and learned quite quickly.

Of course I took my flying very seriously since this was my second time around and only chance since I now was overage In fact I would go to the rudder trainer every chance I got to practice so my reactions were becoming very fast. This rudder control keeps you out of trouble when you are flying a "tail dragger".

We did not get much time off at primary but more than at pre-flight. In the meantime my folks brought down my 1936 Ford V8 convertible coupe and also my wife Florence. We had a nice weekend visit and I had to get back to the base. I hadn't seen my folks or my wife in quite a while. Now I had transportation to take my friends into Hollywood since I won all their money playing poker. After a week of discipline and flying we could let off a lot of steam.

I proceeded better than average in my flying and my ground school. They had a spot-landing contest between all the cadets. The instructor selected one of his best students to participate. My instructor had selected me out of the 4 students he had and I won the contest and a case of beer for my instructor. I was ready to solo in 6 hours but regulation made 8 hours mandatory for solo flights.

We learned navigation, radio procedure, aerobatics, etc. After almost three months at primary we were ready for Basic Training if we passed all our check rides. I had no trouble passing my checks. Some people could not fly and "washed out". It was a fact that 50% of the class would be "washed out" by the time we graduated from Advanced Flying School.

I got my orders to basic flying school at Merced Army Air Base at Merced, California. Here I would be flying the BT-13 Vultee "Vibrator", an all- metal low wing monoplane with a 450hp P&W engine on it. It was quite a change from a PT-22 with a 100hp Kinner to a plane with 450hp. The biggest change was going from a civilian instructor to a military instructor. I happen to draw a little 2nd Lt., named Wells, who thought he was God. I just could not do anything right for him. He would cuss me constantly with horrible language no matter what I did. One day after a trying ride I got out of the plane and he told me I had to relax up there while I was flying. With that I let go at him and told him nobody could relax with him using such horrible language as he cussed at me. I walked a way without saluting, which was a "no no". That night I wrote home to my folks and Florence that I might be "washed out". I felt so bad, here I had gotten this far and knew I could fly as well as any cadet in the class and to have an uncouth instructor like I got would ruin my whole career. This was my last chance to be a military pilot and I "blew it".

The next day I got the surprise of my life. I had a new instructor! He was a disgruntled fighter pilot, who had been sent to instruct by the Army Air Corps. I had no trouble flying with him. We did mostly aerobatics and formation flying. I became quite proficient in the BT-13. After I soloed I went up and proceed to spin it. Nobody told me not to. I climbed to 10,000 feet and did a one turn spin and it came out real nice I then climbed back up and did a two turn spin and it came out all right. I climbed back up to 10,000 feet and did a three turn spin, whoa it wasn't coming out!

Let's do that again, into the spin opposite rudder and pop the stick forward (I really popped it) and it immediately came out. I looked at my altimeter and I was 3000 feet! I had lost count on how many turns I made but it was plenty, about least 10. I found that spinning the PT-22 it came out real easy, it didn't take the real positive pop on the stick like the BT-13 did to bring it out of the spin.

I went back to 10,000 feet and did a five- turn spin and came right out using my new found technique. I new now, that I had really learned to fly the airplane. I had 65 spins before anybody had 20. One day after doing my first spin I told my instructor what happened. He almost had a heart attach. I was supposed to have my instructor check me out on the spin characteristics of the BT-13, before I spun it solo!

We went up and I did a 5 turn spin for him coming out right on the reference point which pleased him very much. I was already for my check ride. Now whenever they gave me a check ride I would give them a 5 turn spin and come right out on the point. I would have no further trouble flying the BT-13 since now I had a lot of confidence in myself.

On our cross-country flying both day and night I had an advantage over most of the other cadets, since I had lived in the San Joaquin valley at Patterson, California. I had driven up and down it for many years. I knew all the rivers and other prominent land marks. Of course the Sierras were on one side of the valley with the west coast range on the other. It was quite hard to get lost.

Basic training was not as restrictive as it was in primary. We used to have dances on Saturday nights. The local girls would come in and give the cadets a break. I would pick out the best dancer and proceeded to have a ball. Florence was working and could not get off the same time as I did so we did not see much of one another for quite awhile.

One incident at Merced "frosted me". I was barracks chief for the weekly inspection. It was a white glove type and I had checked everything, I thought, until the Tact Officer opened the window and found cigarette burns outside on the windowsill! I did not notice it since it was cold and I did not open the window. None of the cadets in my room smoked so it must have been there a long time. I had to walk tours for this discrepancy after duty hours. I made sure that I opened the window after that when I was barracks chief.

After mastering the flying of the BT-13 and passing all my check rides, which took three months, I was transferred to Advanced Flying Training School at Stockton Army Air Base, at Stockton, California. I now was on my last lap to becoming a pilot in the U.S. Army Air Corps.

My desire, of course, was to fly the P-38 fighter plane, even before Tony Lavier gave a flying demonstration in the aircraft at Merced, Ca. So when I got my orders to Stockton AAB I thought I was going to twin-engine fighter school. I found out later it was for twin –engine but not for fighters, much to my consternation.

At Stockton we flew the AT-17, the Cessna "Bobcat", or the "Bamboo Bomber". It was made out of wood and fabric. It was checked out in three flights and was on my own from there on out. I seemed that there was a shortage of instructors at the time so they flew cadets with cadets since it was a four place aircraft, but only as co-pilots. In between they would give a periodic check ride with a regular instructor to see how you were doing.

Advance Flying Training was very easy for me compared to the rest of the training of the past. I did a lot of cross-country flying day and night. I was assigned new instructors to check them out for flying in the San Joaquin Valley so they would not get lost... Most of the new instructors were from out of state and it was their first time to California, I would take them up and show them all the important check points, such as the San Joaquin river, Highway 99, the Sierra Nevada Mountains to the east and the Coast Range to the west. It was hard to get lost if you noted these landmarks. It made it easy for me since I had taken my Basic training in the San Joaquin Valley at Merced. I showed them all the airports available for emergency landings. Cross-countries were easy for me since I was so familiar with the area.

We had a little more time off than we had before in the past and my wife Florence could come down to see me once in a while since she had to work most week-ends when I got off. She worked for Sears and had odd hours, which made it bad for us. I guess it was hard for her not to see me very much but maybe it was what she wanted since she was not very "passionate". In fact, she was glad she did not have to see me very much because I was always the "tiger". I always wanted to be the model husband and be true to her but that ruined me.

Most of my classmates stayed with me all through cadet training. That is alphabetically C to F. The military likes to characterize by the alphabet. We were wondering what would be our assignment when we graduated in 43K class on the 5 Dec 1943. I had started my training on 29 Jan 1943 and would graduate 5 Dec 1943, which was about a year of training and I would have a total of 277 flying hours. I would also have a white instrument card, which made me a rated instrument pilot. I remember flying into a fog bank that we got periodically, and doing actual instrument flying. I would make a 180 degree turn and come back out. It was not legal but I always cleared myself before I went in, so there would not be any other aircraft in the area. My co-pilot would keep an eye open for any other aircraft that might be in the area by mistake. It gave a flying cadet much confidence. It paid off after I got into combat.

Graduation Day was coming up and we got our $299 uniform allowance. The vendors put on a big show so we could pick out what we wanted. In those days we had lots of choices for our uniforms. We could have "pink" pants with pink shirt, tan shirt, dark green shirt, tan tie, "pink" tie, green tie, with a green blouse. You set this off with a pair of tan shoes, which were usually Justin Jodhpurs. I forgot the socks, which came in the same colors as the ties. There was no doubt in anybodies mind what you were. It was a very distinctive uniform. We were all very proud of it, everything was tailored to your physique even our shirts, which made you look real trim. I weighed only 140 pounds of sheer muscle (Ha! Ha!) when I graduated from cadets, which made my uniform fit real well.

I bought the 50 mission type cap instead of the old Army felt job. To get that 50 mission look I took out the grommet and put paper clips on the side where the head set would go so it would put that crease in the hat. By graduation day I hoped it would look good.

Graduation Day was the high point in my life. My Dad and Mother and my wife Florence were there. As we lined up to march to the graduation proceedings we were all in our new uniforms and me with my new "50 mission" look. I immediately caught the eye of the Tact Officer, who shouted, "The fellow that looks like Clark Gable, take that crease out of that hat!" I took it off and pushed the crease out but the moment we started to march it was back in. With the grommet out of the hat the creases were there to stay. I had the best looking hat in the in the outfit.

After graduation my Father pinned on my new silver wings and Florence pinned on my new gold bars as a new Second Lieutenant. After that due to the custom of the service, I would give the first enlisted man who saluted me a dollar. I think all the new 2nd Lts. had a silver dollar in their pocket for that first salute as an Officer. My new serial number would be 0760597, as an Officer.

After a wonderful leave I had orders to report to Hammer Field, Fresno, California. I was shocked. It was to fly B-24s, what a revolting development. I reported and got a chance to sit in the monster. I told them by regulation I was too small to fly the monster, but to no avail. I was assigned to Muroc Army Air Base, California for RTU (replacement training unit). The only good thing about the whole affair was that I had taken all my training in California my home state.

When I got to Muroc I again complained about having to fly the B-24, this time to the C.O. of our squadron especially when I found out that I was assigned as a co-pilot. When I went in to see him with my complaint, with my pilot, he told me I had two choices fly the aircraft or get court-martialed. That made it easy, I flew it.

Being assigned as a co-pilot frosted me no end. If I had to fly this monster I wanted to be the driver. I told my pilot that if I had to fly this thing I would make every other landing. He was a 2nd Lt. like me so I guess it startled him so he agreed. So I made every other landing and if he forgot I would remind him by grabbing the controls and informing him that it was my landing.

At Muroc AAB, we went through ground school as well as flying. I learned the systems on the B-24 as well as aircraft identification, which I became quite good. I could identify 25 aircraft at speeds exceeding 1/50 of a second, one at a time. I even learned how to drop the bombs with the super secret Norden bombsight. I use to fly the bomb dropping machine with my bombardier, Lt. Harry McCracken, and I would beat him a few times I would get a chance to drop the bombs from the B-24 in actual practice on the bombing range, and did quite well. We had quite a few night flights and flew mock bombing missions. We acquired a lot of knowledge in a very short time. I got to Muroc AAB, on the 5 Jan 1944 and left for overseas 5 April 1944. There were ten members in our crew and we trained together during this time. We had a tail gunner, two waist gunners, a ball turret gunner, a top turret gunner and a nose gunner, pilot, co-pilot, navigator, and a bombardier.

After 135 hours of flying time in the B-24 for me, we got our orders on the 30 March 1944, to go overseas. We took the train from Muroc to Hamilton Field, California, near San Francisco where we would pick up our new aircraft, a B-24, and to fly it to an unknown destination.

I forgot to mention that I had my 1936 Ford convertible with me at Muroc. When we had time off I would take some of the crew into Hollywood and Vine Streets, about every week-end. Gas was rationed at the time and the octane rating was not very good, so the crew chief on our airplane would save up the gas he would drain out of the tanks on the B-24, which was 100 Octane. On receiving my orders I had to take my car back to Sacramento to my wife. They would not let you take you own transportation to the new station. So I had to drive the Ford to Sacramento leave the car with my wife and take the train back to Muroc! Get on the train again and go back to Hamilton Field. What a waste of time. I guess they thought we would go AWOL or something.

We arrived at Hamilton Field and I discovered I had lost my new Officers I.D. It took a week to get a new one and you could not leave the base without one. I had a few I.D. pictures left from getting my first I.D. Card in my wallet. Always the innovator I borrowed a friends I.D. and slipped one of my pictures over his, which was in a plastic folder. It worked perfectly and I got off the base. I got a chance to visit all my old friends in San Francisco and go to the Officers only dance at the Terrace Plunge at the Fairmont Hotel. This was held quite often for all the armed services Officers. It was quite an affair with everyone in his or her respective uniforms. The atmosphere was terrific. I took an old friend, Dolly Hone, with me. She was a good dancer and was quite attractive. Florence could not come down from Sacramento since she was still working for Sears. She new all the people I was visiting. She missed a lot of fun.

Finally the day came and our aircraft was ready to go. We had our secret orders and were ready to take off for parts unknown. Pilot, ROBERT R. WIGLEY, Co-Pilot, Lt. BILL L. DISBROW, Navigator, JOSEPH J. LUKASHEVICH, Bombardier, HARRY McCRACKEN, Radioman, Herbert B. Cornell, Engineer, John Merfeld, Tail gunner, Robert L. Caldwell, Ball gunner, Billy J. Finks, Waist Gunners, James E. Weeks and Kenneth J. Vincent. That was our crew.

As we were taxiing out for take-off, "low and behold" Pilot Wigley got too close to another B-24 and hit our wing tip. That made us taxi back to the line to check the damage. That took a couple of days and then we were off again to our first stop, Big Springs, Texas. We landed and got our BOQ, which was a tarpaper shack. We got cleaned up and went to the mess hall and had dinner. After dinner we had a big poker game with another crew that was on the same orders as ours. I was lucky and won $250, which was a good start for our trip with extra spending money, since a 2nd Lt. made only $225 per month including flight pay.

We took off the next day for Macon, Georgia, at Warner Robbins AAB. On the way I got up in the nose turret to see how it felt riding in the turret. I noticed that the ground crew had left the cowling loose on the inboard engine on the left side of the B-24. It was nothing drastic, when we landed the ground crew had it fixed in no time. We were not allowed to fly at night that is why we had to make all these stops. I guess it was a precaution since there was a war going and they wanted to keep track of all the aircraft for identification purposes.

Our next stop was West Palm Beach, Florida. When we got there it was hot and muggy, normal for this part of the country. We stayed here a couple of days or so. While we were waiting for our orders to fly out, I had a beautiful Palm Beach Uniform tailor made for myself with a battle jacket. It was real sharp and fit me perfect. I could afford it since I won the money in

Lt Paul Corbisererio
Muroc AAB 1944

Muroc AAF Training Crew 1944 Jan , B-24A

the poker game. I also stocked up with nylon stockings, lip stick, and perfume, for trading purposes. We were told a pair of nylon stockings was like gold in the areas we were going, which would be South America, Africa, and Europe.

After getting all stocked up we got our orders to take-off and we headed this time for Bourinquen Field, Puerto Rico. Here we landed and got all cleaned up and went to the

Huff, Corb, Disbrow

Officers Club. It was beautiful, on a hill over looking the Caribbean Sea. We had dinner and then we all proceeded to drink up some of their rum, etc. Well both my Navigator and Bombardier got loaded and almost rolled down the lawn into the sea, until I stopped them. There were some big hangovers the next morning when we took-off for British Guiana. We would land out in the jungle near the capital, Georgetown. We were supposed to open our secret orders 2 hours out to our destination. When we finally opened them up we found out that we were assigned to the 455th Bomb Group, 741st Squadron, at Cerignola, Italy. At last we now knew where we were going.

We landed at Atkinson Field about 20 miles up the river from Georgetown, British Guiana. This landing strip was cut right out of the jungle and run by the British giving the US permission to land there during our ferry flights.

Huff, Corb, Disbrow

When we parked the aircraft I noticed a lot of monkeys running through the trees and had all I could do to stop the crew from trying to shoot at them with their "45s". A jeep came out and picked us up and brought us to our barracks. I proceeded to take a shower and put on my new Palm Beach Uniform. I was greeted with whistles and such from the rest of the crew. It was a very sharp uniform.

We had a cute hostess assigned to us to show us around and I finally took her to the base movie that night. She was the prettiest girl on the whole base. She was very exotic looking due to all the mixtures of nationalities she had in her. The rest of the crew could not get over me getting a date with her right off the bat. I guess I wasn't too bad looking myself, in those days,

Lt Wigley & Lt Lukeshevich

especially in my new uniform and the moustache I had grown back the moment I graduated.

At the BX I bought solid gold rolled 2nd Lt. bars for 80 cents! (I wish I had bought more!). I also bought myself a pair of mosquito boots for $6.00, which was all the rage for crews going overseas.

I said, "Goodbye" to our hostess and we were off to our next stop, which would be Belem, Brazil, at the mouth of the Amazon River. On the flight there it was a tremendous sight to see the top of the jungle. It was like a big green carpet below us covering everything. I got in the ball turret and they let me down, what a sensation. It was quite an experience. I rotated the ball around to all the positions, to get the best view. I flew in all the gun positions to get to know what it was like and learned to operate the turrets and guns, just in case I had to.

We were flying at about 6000 feet when we spotted some big thunderstorms ahead. We were not allowed to fly instruments, since the radio ranges were not reliable in this part of the world. We started down and ended up at 500 feet under the stuff and just grazing the jungle. We finally veered to the east and found the coast line of Brazil and followed it to Belem. It was situated on the Amazon Delta, with the river at least a mile across at that point. Did I say a mile? It was more like miles and miles across!

By now it was raining as we landed and it was Wigleys turn to land. We were taking turns landing, just like I said I would. I was getting real proficient in landing this big bird and had a lot of confidence in handling it.

We got our billets and the EM crew headed for town. I stayed home, since I did not want to get my new uniform wet. I found that one of the sports was to throw raw meat into the Amazon and watch the Piranhas boil the water fighting for the meat.

Lt Disbrow

In the morning we were preparing to take off when we found that one of the crew had obtained a monkey while in town the night before. I did not think it was a good idea to have a monkey aboard but we took off anyway.

Landing at Fortalezia, Brazil, we found that this was where we would leave South America for Africa for a non-stop flight across the Atlantic Ocean. Fortalezia is closer to Africa than any other point in South America. Other aircraft flying from Natal would have to land at Ascension Island to refuel to make it to Africa.

We stayed a few days at Fortalezia and roamed around the base. When I went to take my clothes out of my B-4 bag I found that a bottle of Tabu Perfume had broken and had permeated all my clothes with the greatest of odors. My crew went wild with that and kept giving me the wave.

After an incident with the monkey the crew decided to sell it to another crew. I don't know what ever happened to the poor monkey. This was a big load off our minds, since we were ready for that long flight over the Atlantic Ocean and did not want to contend with a sick monkey.

They woke us up at 3AM in the morning for our long flight. We were really loaded with a full fuel load of 2700 gallons of fuel. They topped off the fuel tanks before we taxied out for take-off to make sure we had a full load for the flight.

We took-off with a very heavy aircraft and on climb out for some unknown reason the turbochargers started to "torch", shooting flame past the waist-gunners window. In the meantime our angle of attack was so steep that fuel was over flowing into the bomb bay! All I could think about was being blown out of the sky. Even though it would slow down our climb I pulled the turbochargers levers back and the torching went out much to the relief of crew who could see the fire lighting up the early morning sky.

We slowed our climb down to avoid any reoccurrence from the "turbos". After that everything seemed to go real smoothly until we hit the equatorial front. The equatorial front is a line of thunderstorms that sit out in the middle of the Atlantic Ocean between South America and Africa.

Our Navigator Lt. "Luke" Lukashevich (from Elizabeth, N.J.) was shooting the stars to check our position as we approached the "squall line" of clouds. It looked to me like a fire was raging below the clouds. After checking with Luke, who was in the astrodome, we came to the conclusion that it was the moon rising. What an unusual sight at 11,000 feet of altitude.

After sitting in the co-pilots seat for 11 and half hours without getting out I was ready to land. It seemed that we saw no land. The Navigators ETA (time of arrival) was just about up and no land in sight. We later knew what the trouble was. The West Coast of Africa at Dakar has a continuous haze from the sands of the Sahara Desert being blown by the winds out to sea. So finally with everyone staining his eyes, we saw the airfield. It was right on course, thanks to Luke.

We landed and found the place filled with B-24s and all kinds of other Aircraft. Dakar was the hub for all aircraft coming from the U.S. From here the aircraft went in all directions. To England, Italy, India, etc. It was also the Air Transport Command route to Europe, Africa, and Asia.

After staying a few days at Dakar and having our aircraft inspected, we took-off for Marrakech, Morocco. We got off OK but as we were approaching St. Louis, Spanish Territory, we had one of the engines started to act up just when we were on the edge of the Sahara Desert. We turned back to Dakar. The territory below us was not inviting for an emergency landing. We could get good maintenance at Dakar.

We landed back at Dakar and they found a pigtail or P-lead on one of the magnetos was loose. So we took-off again and made it to Marrakech with me making the landing after flying over the Sultans Palace.

We stayed at Marrakech for a few days until the other crews moved out. I went to town and found all the natives "hustling" all kinds of wares, including swords made in "Brooklyn". Most of them were wearing G.I. barracks bags with two holes cut in the bottom of them for their legs with the drawstring around their waists. Most of the bags still had the G.I. serial numbers on them. I found out later that they brought a very good price.

While there I asked the way to the Sultan's Palace but on reaching it they would not let me in to see the Sultan's harem (Ha).

Leaving Marrakech we headed for Oran, Algeria, over the Atlas Mountains to the Mediterranean Sea. After take-off we proceeded to climb to 10,000 feet to make sure we cleared all the mountains. After leveling off at 10,000 feet, I noticed my pilot, who was flying the aircraft turn on the auto- pilot, which was an old Sperry.A-1. As we proceeded to fly along I noticed that we were getting a few clouds forming underneath us also that my pilot was trimming the aircraft the airplane "nose down" without disengaging the autopilot. This is the wrong procedure. You are supposed to disengage the auto pilot, trim up the aircraft so it flies straight and level "hands off" and then engage the auto pilot.

I was just about to call him on what he was doing when the excessive trim "kicked the auto pilot out and we were in a breath taking vertical with the power on. I immediately grabbed the control wheel and started to pull us out of the dive, while the pilot pulled off the power. It took both of us to pull the B-24 out of the dive plus me rolling back the trim tab. The crew had been napping in the back of the aircraft when the B-24 went into the dive and it threw them up to the top of the aircraft, with all the baggage hitting them and bouncing all over the place. There was a lot of profanity coming over the interphone when it was all over as well as bruises and contusions to the crew. When it was all over I wondered how close we came to hitting the mountains that we had just passed. Needless to say our pilot never did that again.

We landed at Oran without further incident and had the B-24 inspected for any damage or popped rivets from the excessive "Gs" we might have pulled on our recovery from the dive. It was OK after the inspection. After staying over night at Oran we took-off the next morning for Algiers. This was a beautiful trip as we flew along the coast of North Africa along the blue Mediterranean Sea shore. The weather here was just like it was in Southern California. We landed at Maison Blanc airport and were transported to town for our billets. They were in a nice Hotel, in downtown Algiers, for a change. We must have spent over a week here, why I don't know, but it was a pleasure.

Algiers had many nightspots as well as an Allied Officers Club, plus a Red Cross Officers Club. They had many nice Hostesses. Of course I attended them all.

It just happened that Count Basie was playing at the Red Cross Officers Club. What a pleasant surprise. I asked the cutest and best dancer for a dance and we had a ball. In fact she invited me to her apartment for a party she was having for some of the Allied Officers. She lived on the Rue Michele, a beautiful tree lined street in the Algiers hills.

When I got there I found that I was the only American there. Most were French; the hostess was French and English. I guess I made quite an entrance as the only American and the only pilot in my new "pinks and greens" uniform with solid gold bars.

I had a very nice time except for one "Limey" Major telling me the Americans are spoiling all the natives by throwing all their money around and giving excessive tips. It seemed I made more money as a 2nd Lt. On flying status than he did as a Major with 10 years of service.

About midnight the party broke up and I left by myself and started walking back to the hotel. It was about a mile I guess. Algiers at the time was totally blacked out since the war was still going on. I could hardly see and guided myself along the very wide sidewalk with trees that grew in a row down the walk near the curb. As I was grouping my way along somebody grabbed me by the arm. Of course I was startled and started to reach for my G.I. 45 automatic which was in my shoulder holster under my left arm, when a female voice said, "Where are you going big boy?" in broken English. Recovering quickly from my start, I said, "I don't know now". Well she propositioned me all the way to my Hotel but I didn't give in. This was my first night out and I wasn't too secure with the area as yet.

The next night I went to the dance at the Allied Officers Club and met a cut little French girl who was a 2nd Lt. In the French Air Force and was an Air line Hostess. She was now in the military for the duration. She was an excellent dancer and to say the least we had a ball. I saw her home to her apartment and bid her goodnight. I had made a date for the next night. We went to all the available places in Algiers, including one that was the "Underground" a bar and restaurant down in a basement. I ordered champagne, which startled my little French Gal. She thought it was too expensive and we should have ordered beer. I told her nothing was too good for her so we had Champagne. I think the price was equivalent to $3.00 a bottle in francs.

Well after living it up for a week it was time for her to fly back to France. She gave me her address in Paris, which later I would correspond with her. I forgot to mention that she could speak very little English, about as much as I could speak French, which amounted to, merci beaucoup, cheri, goodbye, hello, etc.

I gave her my address and would get many letters from her wanting to marry me after the war was over and come to the United States. How did I know this when the letter was written in French? We had a couple of high school French language students in our squadron that that took turns trying to translate for me.

We finally got our orders to leave Algiers and went out to the airport to pre-flight our B-24 to get ready for take-off the next day. As I was checking the exterior of the rear part of the fuselage I noticed a C-47 making a long base leg for landing and it had a lot smoke coming from the right engine. As it got closer I could see flames shooting from the back of the cowling. As he turned on the final approach it was burning bad. I was hoping that they would make it as the whole crew shouted, "hang in there". As the C-47 touched down the right engine fell off the aircraft and rolled down the runway ahead of the C-47 with the propeller flying off and almost hitting a parked aircraft along the runway. As the big bird slowed down the top hatch came open and some of the crew were trying to get out as fast as they could. As the plane stopped all the hatches flew open and the rest of the crew evacuated the aircraft very fast. The fire crew was there immediately and had the fire under control before it could do any more damage. They were very lucky.

After take-off the next day from Maison Blanc Airport, we flew along the coast of North Africa at about 2000 feet and we had a beautiful view of the Mediterranean Sea and the beaches. We finally landed at Tunis, Tunisia, and checked into our quarters. We stayed a few days and saw a lot of Axis wrecked aircraft along the perimeter of the airport. We were warned to stay away from the area since it might be "booby trapped". There were German Me-109s, FW-190s, Italian Macchis, etc. I would have like to have at least gotten an instrument out of one of them but the risk wasn't worth it. We stayed just long enough to visit the city and get our bearings and were off in a few days to Toronto, Italy. We landed at Toronto after passing near Malta and making sure we knew the password for the day for the fighters that were protecting the area. We could see Mt. Etna as we approached the heel of Italy. It was a good checkpoint.

On landing we were informed that another crew would take over our B-24. We were flown into Cerignola, Italy, to the 455th Bomb Group and were assigned to the 741st Squadron. When we reported to the C.O. who was Maj. Langford, he asked my pilot how his co-pilot was and he told him that I was as good as he was. It was not much of a compliment since I thought I was better than he was. I had made every other landing while we were in training and every other landing on our way from Hamilton Field where we left on 7 April and arrived in Italy 20 April 1944. After we were assigned I never saw my pilot again. I heard later he could not fly formation in combat and was sent home. I don't know if this is true or not but I never saw him again. His name was not on the 455th register either.

After getting our quarters, a G.I. pyramidal tent with a dirt floor in an old olive orchard, we visited some of the more experienced troops to find out what it was like to fly combat. Their experience ran from 25 missions to 42 missions. It was quite interesting to listen to their tales and the "hot targets".

We found the Officers Club, a converted cowshed; our briefing room was an old wine cellar, which was underground and quite large. Our Headquarters was and old farm house. Our runways were PSP (pierced steel planking). We shared dual runways with the 454th Bomb Group, which was on the opposite side of our area. They were on the west and we were on the east with the two runways in the middle. Our airplanes were parked on the "hard stands" where we could taxi out to the taxiways in the proper order for take-off on our missions.

I was assigned to a pilot to get my indoctrination to combat. He had 40 missions and my first mission was to Campina, Rumania. This was the Ploesti area where all the oil refineries were. This was supposed to be an easy target since all the big guns were protecting Ploesti. This was on 6 May 1944. The first thing I noticed was all these black spots ahead of us at our altitude. I thought it was another group of aircraft. I was immediately informed that was "flak" or exploding anti-aircraft shells. They are set to explode at our altitude. Little did I know that this "milk run" (easy target) was one of the hottest targets in Europe. Campina was the home of the Shell Oil Company of Rumania, the dreaded Ploesti area where there was at least 300 heavy guns (88mm) that were called "squirrel shooters". They could shoot you out of the sky at 26,000 like nothing. Well this was my indoctrination to combat! We were issued "flak" vests, which looked like a baseball catcher's chest protector, only it had two sides, one in front and one in back with a hole to put your head through. It was suppose to be bullet proof. It would ward off small pieces of "flak". I also wore a steel helmet over my flying helmet. It made you feel a little more secure than nothing at all.

12 May 44. I went on my second mission with the same pilot to La Specia, in Northern, Italy. I was learning fast. We were flying at 22,000 feet and the "flak" was hot and heavy bouncing off the sides of the airplane. I think we were bombing marshaling yards. We were doing strategic bombing, knocking out their railroad yards and their oil and their bridges, anything to stop the flow of supplies for their war effort. I made it safe and sound on mission number two.

My third mission on the 18 May 1944 was to the dreaded Ploesti oil fields again. We would get our briefing for the day down in the old wine cellar. They would have the map of the day's mission covered up until the briefing officer and the C.O. came in. After the short briefing on who was flying where and with whom, they would take the curtain off of the map, which had a blue string showing our route and destination. Every time it was a trip to Ploesti there would be a big groan from the audience. Everyone knew how rough this mission could be. It seemed that they shot at least one aircraft out of the air each time we went there. We would get a double mission for this raid since it was so dangerous. There were 41 B-24s loaded with 500 pound GP bombs to bomb the refineries at Dacia Romano, Rumania. This time the "flak" took its toll as we lost 3 aircraft and 30 crew members missing in action. We bombed by Pathfinder for the first time (radar) and saw many fires burning in the target area, a good mission but a heavy price to pay. I had survived again, thanks to my dear Lord.

When I wasn't flying missions I was fixing up our tent. I went down to the bomb dump and got a lot of fragmentation bomb boxes and made a wooden floor for our tent. I also made a chest of drawers for my clothes. The other crew members kept saying they would have a nice place after I was shot down. Of course I took a dim view about that remark. I marked my missions on the tent with chalk near my bed after each mission. It sure looked a long way to 50 missions. I had lots of hope and new everyone was praying for me at home.

My 4th mission was on 23 May 44. It was to Nemi, Italy, to help out the 5th Army. We were among the 39 other B-24s that were loaded with 500 GP pound bombs to bomb enemy troop concentration of Germans around Nemi. Light "flak" was seen in the target area but it was not very accurate, thank goodness. Only 26 aircraft dropped their bombed on the target due to cloud cover. All planes returned safely to home base. I made it again. It seemed like a slow process.

I heard about the Red Cross Officers Club at Foggia. They had dancing every Sunday. I made it a point when I was not flying on Sunday to go dancing. I would hitchhike to Foggia, which was about 20 miles from Cerignola. They did not have enough girls to go around for all the pilots that attended, but I managed to dance quite a bit. The girls liked the way I danced and I cut in quite a bit. I got to be a fixture at the Sunday dances. I also would tour the town and take pictures. I had received a 35mm Robot camera from home with colored film, which I was utilizing as much as possible.

One day while I was in Foggia I was told of a place where I could buy a straw mattress for my GI cot. I bought one and proceeded to hitchhike with it. I guess the GIs that picked me up in a 6X6 truck thought I was crazy. A 2nd Lt. Carrying a mattress on his back and hitching a ride. It sure felt good after I got home and put it on my cot.

My 5th mission was on the 27th of May 44, to Montpellier, France. There were 37 B-24s on this raid. It was to an airdrome called Frejorges and we did a good job on it, "Flak" at the target was moderate and accurate was the report. We picked up a few holes, as did 17 other aircraft on the raid. No enemy fighters were seen and the group returned with out any casualties. I made it again but it seemed that the Germans were getting my range. When we landed after our mission, trucks would pick us up to take us to debriefing but before we would go in they would give each of us a shot of whiskey to settle our nerves. When we got into briefing they would ask us questions on the target coverage, fighters in the area, cloud conditions, etc. By the time I got out of debriefing I was half drunk. I would hop in the back of the truck for the ride back to our tent area and lie down on my cot and go into a deep sleep. I would forget everything until one of my crew would wake me up and ask me if I wanted to go eat at the mess hall. I would ask them what they were having for dinner. It would usually be Spam, dehydrated potatoes, and canned fruit salad. I would not eat if it did not sound good.

Since I was not a smoker I would trade my cigarette ration for cheese, almonds, Spumante wine, eggs, and potatoes, plus green olives. My crew would cook me eggs and chips when they had the time. I would do it if they were too busy. They wanted to take good care of their pilot.

My 6th mission on the 28 May 44 was to Genoa, Italy. We were in with 37 other B-24s. The "flak" at the target was moderate and accurate. We picked up holes as well as 14 other aircraft that had holes in them. No enemy fighters were seen, thank goodness and all the planes returned safely.

Our showers were about a mile away and we had to walk to them. By the time you took your shower and walked back to our tent you needed another shower, since it was so dusty on the trail on the way home. I found a couple of five- gallon cans and decided to rig up a shower next to our tent. I rigged one can to an olive tree next to our tent to hold water and another can that I had punched tiny holes in the bottom for our shower spray. I found a piece of canvas, which I put up to give us a little privacy. We heated our water on our GI stove that was fueled with 100 Octane gas! It worked great after I made duck boards to stand on so we would not get all full of mud. Shortly after that they finally built us showers close to our tented area, which made it real nice.

One thing I was sure of that I was not going to get Malaria. I took my Adabrine faithfully and slept under my mosquito netting always. The only thing that bothered me was the ants, which ran up the legs of my cot and ran all over me. I remedied that by putting the legs of my cot in cans of water. With my new mattress, board floor, and chest of drawers I had quite a nice living area.

29 May 44. I was scheduled for an unusual dual mission. One in the morning, my 7th, to Bos Krupa, Yugoslavia and the other one in the after noon to Banja Luka, Yugoslavia, this would be my 8th mission. There were 40 B-24s on the first mission with hardly any opposition and 39 B-24s on the second run. We were bombing German emplacements with

Getting ready for a dawn takeoff to Ploesti

100 pound GP bombs. We were very successful with no losses since we caught them unaware that we were coming. I flew two missions in one day, without any opposition, I liked that.

31 May 44. I was scheduled for my 9th mission. When we got to briefing I noticed the big mission board was covered as usual. Nobody knew where we were going. The Operations Officer got up on the stage with the C.O. Col. Cool. They then took the curtain off the board, which revealed a piece of blue yarn going from our base way up to the dreaded land of Ploesti. There was a big groan from everybody. This would be my third trip to the area. This was the graveyard of the 15th Air force. I said my prayers for the Lord to protect me and away we went.

I said my prayers to the Lord many times over and over again to protect me, which he did. This was the last mission of the month. We had 36 B-24s up for the day to drop 500 pound GP bombs on the Sperantza Oil

Refinery at Ploesti, Rumania. "Flak" at the target was intense and accurate. Twenty-five fighters were seen but they appeared awaiting for stragglers, as they did not press their attacks against the formation, thank goodness. We did lay claim to three enemy fighters destroyed and one probable. All the aircraft returned safely but we had a few holes in us.

It was the end of May 1944 and I had only 9 missions in. I was wondering how long this was going to take. I had been flying as a co-pilot still and I wanted to be the driver! I had flown 9 missions in 25 days. Of course the time in between my missions was getting shorter. We were having the big push to cut off all the fuel we could by bombing all the refineries and storage areas plus all the marshalling yards to stop the Germans from using any of their transportation. I still was going to Foggia to the Sunday dances at the Red Cross Officers Club for my relaxation. I also played baseball and made a lot of pictures in the photo lab on our base. You had to get your rest in because they would wake you up at 4am in the morning. You would get dressed and go to the mess hall to get your

On the way to target Ploesti, July 1944

The B-24 we flew to combat in April 1944

powdered eggs, dehydrated potatoes, and fruit cocktail all on one plate mixed together. It was quite cold at that time of the morning so we would stand around a 50-gallon drum that was burning gasoline, to keep warm before the mess hall opened. Our area was about a half mile from the airstrip and briefing, so they would ride us down in a truck.

On days that I did not go dancing I would go into Cerignola by myself or with one of my crew and tour the area and have eggs and chips for lunch. Then we would shop around for more food by bargaining with our cigarettes. A carton of cigarettes would cost us 50 cents and it would bring $5.00 on the black market. I think I got two cartons a week if I wanted them. They were very good for trading, especially for food. I took many pictures on my day off as well as when I was flying missions. I would pass my camera around to the different crew members to take pictures while we were in the air.

A "Tech Rep", who was a Canadian, wanted me to take his 8mm movie camera and take some pictures on a bombing mission. I took the camera and 4 rolls of colored film and proceeded to make a complete movie of getting us up in the morning to going to breakfast, flying to the target, dropping the bombs, the whole works. I gave the movie back to him to get the film through customs and to send me a copy when I got home. I never saw the rascal again or even heard from him after writing to the address he had given me of his home in Canada. It was a complete documentary of a complete bombing mission. It took me 4 missions to make it.

During the bombing mission to the two targets in one day, Banja Luka and Bos Krupa, Yugoslavia, we had a combat cameraman aboard, as did the B-24 flying our wing. They took pictures of everything that day as well as each other's aircraft. It was a combat film that was later tuned into a newsreel, which I later saw and there was my airplane in the movie. I identified our aircraft by the number on the side. I later got the film after the war

My home away from home in the Olive grove,
Cerignola, Italy 1944

The bombed out YMCA where I would shower every Sunday, June 1944

from the film library and showed it at home. I wish I could have gotten a copy of it for my files. I think it was combat film number 68.

Sometimes when I would get off on a Sunday I would hitchhike to Foggia and take a shower at the bombed out YMCA the showers happened to be in the basement and survived the bombing. After a nice shower I would hit the Red Cross Officers Club and go dancing with all the girls there. Although out numbered 10 to one I always got a lot of dancing in.

2 June 1944. I was scheduled to go back to Misconic, Hungary; this was a double mission, since it was such a tough target. It was after oil again. We had to pass by the Udine Area where a lot of German fighters were based. There were a lot of aircraft in the sky this day, a lot of groups going the same direction. When we got to the target we find it is marshalling yards. Doing strategic bombing keeps the enemy from manufacturing anything; by hitting factories and if they go underground, hit their delivery system, their trains, tracks, bridges, roads, etc

The "flak" is thick as usual but we manage to drop our bombs on the target and get through with minor holes. We are headed back home through the fighter area. They come up and make a few passes at us but jumped "The Tail End Charlie Group" so they let us get through. Good luck today. This is a double mission due to the length of the mission, 6 hours and 35 minutes, and the number of big guns in the area. When I got home I would mark two more bombs on my tent, making it 13!

3 June 1944. Got the day off again. Got a nice clean uniform, sun tan, and went to Foggia to dance at the Red Cross Officers Club. I see more of Foggia and take a shower at the YMCA. It was dark when I started hitchhiking back to Cerignola. I got a ride in a jeep with a Sgt. who turned out to be a mad man at the wheel. Of course everything was blacked out and we were flying down the Appian Way with no lights and blacker than pitch. I thought I had had it. I was glad to get out and walk the half- mile back to our base.

4 June 1944. We were scheduled to bomb industrial targets but they were covered with clouds so we would go to Genoa as our alternate. 36 B-24s loaded with 500 pounders, with the 454th bomb group leading. We were flying a left wing so I got a chance to fly, since it was very hard for the pilot to keep good

Results of war: Poor little children of Foggia, Italy 1944

formation flying cross- cockpit. After they find that I can fly formation quite well in this monster, I get a chance to fly formation whenever we are flying a left wing. We get our share of "flak" and drop our bombs successfully on the target. We get home without any incident. I was sorry that I did not keep a record of the pilots that I flew co-pilot with. I guess I was lucky enough to remember the names of all my crew!

5 June 1944. I can't believe it I get two days off. I borrow a Harley-Davidson motorcycle, which someone had confiscated from a ranger outfit. I proceed to ride to Bari in Southern Italy, which was on the Adriatic coast. As I rode along, the war seems to be in another world. I was feeling detached from everything with the wind in my face. It was like the old days when I would race along the roads on my Indian Motorcycle along the California highways. It had been a long time since I rode one of these things but it was second nature after all the miles I had put on these machines. When I got to Bari I parked the beast and went to the local barbershop and got a haircut I always liked getting haircuts. It made me feel so clean. Just as I was coming out of the barbershop I saw an old Gran Prix Alfa Romero go racing down the street streaming smoke out of the exhaust pipe, before I could crank up the Harley it was gone (I sure would like to have had that car). I stayed overnight with some Army outfit and rode home the next day. It was so great to have such a nice time away from the war for a couple of days. But as I rode into camp my bubble burst. I was back to reality and was scheduled to fly the next day.

7 June 1944. We received news of the invasion of Europe at Normandy and other spots. It was D-day, on June 6, 1944. Our spirits were given a lift as it meant that the war would be shortened. Our target this day was Sestri, Italy. It was a "milk run" and was I glad. Sestri was covered with clouds so we went to Voltri, Italy and dropped our bombs. "Flak" was considered light so we all managed to get home safely. I find that we are getting a few easy targets. I guess it is because the pilots I am flying with are at the end of their tour and ready to go home after a few more missions (am I glad of that). I get to chalk up another mission on my tent. Little do I know what lies in store for me when I get my own aircraft.

8 June 1944. I can't believe it; I got two days off again. I go into Cerignola to take pictures and take my laundry to a family that does a nice

job for me at very reasonable rates. I also trade my cigarette ration for eggs, cheese, potatoes, and sparkling wine. We have a banquet when I get back to the base. My old crew is in a tent nearby, the one I trained in the states with. They cook up the eggs and chips and we live it up with fresh food. What a change. The next day I am off to Foggia for the dance.

10 June 1944. We are on are way to Ferrare, Italy to bomb the factories and marshalling yards. We have 38 B-24s loaded with 1000 pounders. They changed our target and loaded us with fragmentation bombs. We are off to bomb an airfield with these fragmentation bombs. They are the most dangerous bombs of all the bombs that we drop. If you can't drop the bombs on the target you have to salvo them anyplace that is safe and if they hang up in the bomb bay you are in trouble. One of our pilots tried to salvo his load over the Adriatic and just as the load left the bomb bay one of the bombs exploded and they had to ditch it in the Adriatic.

"Flak" at the target isn't too bad as long as I had my 'flak" helmet and "Flak" suit on. I kept my parachute alongside of my seat within easy reach. It is a chest pack with the snap rings to your harness, if you have to use it. This isn't very encouraging if you have to bail out in a hurry, or the aircraft blows up. I promised myself that I would get myself a back-pack parachute, which all the older pilots were wearing. I found out that they were getting them from the "Limeys", (the British) by trading for them. We had a good bomb run and everyone made it home safely. One more bomb marked on my tent.

11 June 1944. This time when we got briefed that old feeling of uncertainty was in the air. When they take the shade off of the map board there is a big groan from all the troops. The target is Giurgiu, Rumania. This mission will take 6 hours and 50 minutes (this is a suburb of Ploesti). It was the refinery for the Standard Oil of Rumania. We will put up 38 B-24s. As we rally into formation there are many groups forming. We all headed for the Ploesti area. The weather is perfect, CAVU. As we approach Rumania we can see smoke ahead. They are trying to obscure the target. When we approach the target the "flak" is intense and pieces are flying off our aircraft. I am saying my prayers as fast as I can for the Lord to protect me again. We lost one aircraft and a crew of 10. One enemy fighter got too close and got shot down. One of the nose gunners made the remark

that at least he got to shoot at the enemy while the pilot and co-pilot just had to sit there and take it. The fighters would come at you at 12 O'clock high and fly right through the whole squadron of aircraft and you would be in a cold sweat and when they were gone you would freeze all the way home. It got to 60 degrees below zero at 26,000 feet! It was another double mission for me and I thanked the Lord again for sparing me as I marked another two bombs on my tent.

12 June 1944. Good news I get the day off after the rough trip to the Ploesti area. I hitchhiked to Foggia for my weekly dance and to take more pictures. I also got a haircut and a manicure. I had a hard time trying to make the manicurist understand me but she wouldn't go to dinner with me. It was taboo for the locals to fraternize with the military. It was late again when I started back to the base and I caught a ride in a Jeep. It was not as "hairy" as the last ride I had in a Jeep, when everything is blacked out and pitch black, you can't see and every once in a while you come up on old farmer in a cart with no lights it would give you a real thrill. I always made it safe and sound and thanked the dear Lord who was watching over me.

13 June 1944. We get to briefing at 0400 and this briefing shows another long mission, this time to Munich, Germany. My first run on Germany, the target is the BMW factory. We put up 33 B-24s loaded with 1000 pound GP bombs, each carrying 10 bombs. The pilot I am flying with had 40 missions and this was a real tough target. It was well defended and the "flak" was heavy and accurate. We lost one aircraft and the crew of 10 men and two members on another aircraft were killed by "flak" with another seriously wounded. I sneaked through again and now had in 20 missions. I was a seasoned combat pilot by this time.

14 June 1944. Good news our crew is going to the Isle of Capri for rest and recuperation. I had been flying with most of my crew that I had trained with. So it made it nice for all of us to get to go to Capri. This would be for 7 days in the Paradise Isle of Italy. We rode in a weapons carrier from our base to Foggia and then over the mountains to Naples. When we got to Naples they put us up on the top floor of the Hotel and there were no elevators working. On the way to Naples we were held up by an accident that had a weapons carrier overturned on the highway. I don't know whether anybody was injured our not but it looked like they could

have I took a colored picture of it for my album.

The first night in Naples we had an air raid. Being on the 7th floor and no elevators working I was not about to run down 7 flights of stairs so I went up on the roof and watched the action. It was quite an experience being on the ground and having all these guns going off and making the air full of tracer bullets. It just happened that on the top of the building next door was an anti-aircraft gun, which was blasting away as fast as it could. I had to hold my hands over my ears the noise was so intense being so close on the roof of our Hotel. It happened to be a lone German reconnaissance aircraft. With all the shooting and noise they missed the aircraft. It lasted about 3 minutes and when it was over it was nice and quite again.

The next afternoon we were on a boat to the Isle of Capri. Naples harbor was littered with sunken ships. We were tied up along side of one. The war had traveled so fast that there was no time to clean up all the debris as yet. We finally got underway and got out of the harbor. It was beautiful looking back at Naples harbor with Mount Vesuvius in the background.

Capri sits out in the Bay of Naples about the same distance from Naples as Catalina, California, is from Wilmington, California. Capri is smaller than Catalina and rockier. We docked our boat in the little harbor of Capri Piccolino. Capri is like a giant rock sticking out of the water with very little land to dock any boat. We drove up a very steep and winding road in a little Italian Fiat Topolino (mouse). I would own one of these little vehicles many years later in Florida. There was only room for two and the baggage. I did not think the little car was going to make it. When we got to the top I was surprised to see so many Hotels and summer homes built on top of the island. The view was magnificent.

For 7 days I had a ball, dancing every night to a big band at one of the nice hotels, swimming, and boating during the day. They even had a small snack bar at the beach for us with good food. We also explored the island, which was steep going in most places but usually had paved trails to everywhere.

A friend and I rented a boat and went sailing around the island. The Captain of our "ship" was a "would be" opera singer like all Italians he sang all the songs he knew. The bottle of wine we supplied him with helped. We landed at the "Blue

Grotto". This is a cave that has a very small opening at high tide but when you get inside the place is quite large. The water is beautifully blue. This is the place to see when anyone visits the area. It was said that in the time of Tiberius' reign there was a tunnel from the cave to the top of the island to Tiberius' castle. It now was plugged up.

I met a very interesting lady while I was at Capri. She was the Countess "Marty" Croissant. She was supposed to own a lot of property in Rome and was vacationing on the Isle of Capri. Her home was quite nice. She wore a ten- carat diamond ring on her finger that was as big as a dime. I made the mistake by asking her if it was real but she got over it. She was an excellent dancer, which was great. She dressed like a Countess. When we would go dancing she wore a strapless evening gown, which was beautiful. Of course I could not be out done and I wore my tailor made Palm Beach suntan uniform. If I say so I we made an outstanding couple. In fact, when we walked into the dance everybody whistled and carried on. They had a live orchestra, which was great and played all the dance tunes. We did this every night until I had to leave. The time passed so quickly, I wasn't ready to go back to war, but I did.

22 June 1944. This mission is to Chiavasea, Italy. I am flying with a pilot who has been a co-pilot for 45 missions so I am not too enthused. We are going to bomb the Germans build up. Fortunately it is not too bad and we don't pickup too many holes. This is more like a "milk run", and I am thankful for that. I am still flying co-pilot and getting tired of not being the driver. I sense that the pilot I am flying with is not to sure of himself and isn't the best of pilots, although I will learn many years later that his pilot was killed on a mission and he had to get him off of the controls and fly the aircraft safely back to the base and got the Silver Star! This experience may have made him hesitant in his flying, who knows, but I did not think too much of his flying. Having 45 missions and still a co-pilot did not impress me.

24 June 1944. The mission is to Craivova, Italy. I am flying with the same pilot and part of my old crew I trained with in the states. We "rally" into formation and the pilot isn't doing too well. We are flying almost "tail end Charlie". We finally got into formation, when on the climb out we encounter a deck of clouds. When in formation and approaching a cloud

layer the aircraft flying wing is supposed to turn 45 degrees from course and fly for one minute and then turn back to the original heading so when you break out of the clouds you are not scattered all over the place and can join up again. All this time we were still climbing to altitude and my pilot became confused upon going into the clouds, he was not quite ready to go on instruments. He turned the aircraft 45 degrees to the right since we were flying a left wing but pulled the nose of the aircraft up too steep for our load. The airspeed started to drop and I put down the flaps to keep us from stalling out and also I was pushing on the control wheel trying to get the nose down and to pickup our airspeed. I was also watching the artificial horizon to see that we were keeping the wings level. We finally got our airspeed back where it was supposed to be as I picked up the flaps while keeping my hand on the wheel so the pilot could not pull up the nose again. We finally broke out of the clouds and joined up with the formation.

We all got joined up again and now I had my eye on the sky ahead. I finally spotted the "flak" in the distance and new that the IP (Initial Point) was near where we would turn on the bomb run. The aircraft must stay as steady as possible so the bombs will drop accurately with the lead ship. This is supposed to be a ten second run. So the Bombardier must lock on the target during these ten seconds and drop the bombs. This is the longest ten seconds in the world or in history. At this time we are very vulnerable. We drop our bombs and rally to the left losing altitude as we turn to confuse the "flak" guns. We have 37 aircraft on this raid and we all make it home safely. Another good mission was over, but I don't have much confidence in my pilot. I asked him, "When was the last time he took instrument training in the Link Trainer"? He said, "He hadn't been in the Link Trainer since he came to combat". The Link Trainer is used for training you on flying instruments. I had been going to the Link Trainer about once a week on my own to keep me sharp. It is a good thing I did because I could fly instruments as well as anyone and probably saved all our lives.

26 June 1944, little did I know that this would be one of my worst missions of all 50 when the Sgt. woke me up out of a sound sleep. It was 4 am and he was giving me a little briefing on the weather to help reduce the shock of waking me up. After breakfast we were off to briefing. When we

got there that feeling was in the air that this was to be a max effort. When they removed the shade on the target map there was the usually big groan from the "troops". This mission would take 6 hours and 10 minutes. The course string went almost to Germany but turned around to a place called Moosebierbaum. It was north of Vienna, Austria and we would fly past Vienna on the east and hit Moosebierbaum on a due west heading and rally due south for home. The target was the Austria Oil Refinery, a big target. We drew aircraft "Swamp Angel" for this flight. I now had most of my old crew aboard. As we all waited for that green flare to be shot off, which would be the sign to crank up and taxi out, the mission was on. We would take off every 30 seconds and rally into formation with the lead ship making big a big round circle and climbing so we could cut him off and get into the formation. When we joined up in formation I could see aircraft in all directions, it is going to be a big raid.

We are flying a left wing so I am doing the flying, which suits me fine. The only stranger aboard is the pilot. We are flying in number 6 position in a flight of 9 B-24s from our squadron, the 741st. We are stepped down in elements of three so we are in the second element on the left wing of number 4 aircraft. We finally spot the "flak" and it is intense, you can walk on it, it is so thick. I am doing evasive action, moving every 20 seconds up and down and in and out making a box. I would fly into the "flak" bursts, as they would bracket me. It took 20 seconds for the shell to get to our altitude, 26,000 feet, so if I moved every 20 seconds into the burst they would shoot where I just left. The "flak" would come up in bursts of four, usually. Everything was going great until we reached the IP I had to stay still for the bomb run. Well during those 10 seconds they got my range and we took an 88mm shell through our right wing just as we dropped our bombs. As we were rallying off the target I could see numerous vapor trails at 12 a clock high at about 35,000 feet altitude. It was the German Luffwaffe out in force with Me-109s and FW-190s and they happened to be Goring's Elite "yellow nosers". There were 150 of them! There were over five groups of B-24s hitting the target, 175 aircraft. The Germans turned and dove on the big formation ten abreast, right through the whole formation with guns blazing using machine guns and cannons, rolling on their backs to protect them from our fire. They had armor plate on the bottom of the aircraft under the pilot's seat.

Well, it was like a war movie with aircraft being hit and burning and exploding, wings coming off, crews bailing out and some not being able to get out. The only trouble was we were the main characters in this movie and it was for real! Our interphone was going wild as the gunners were calling out the fighters. As I was flying a left wing of the element leader I could see he was under attack from fighters as well as a J-88. The JU-88 came up right between the other wingman and me. As I tried to hold my position to get maximum firepower from our guns I looked over and I could see the gunner from the JU-88 shooting directly at me he was so close I could see his goggles on his helmet. He put a lot of holes in us but failed to hit any of our personnel. As he disappeared I noticed our element leader was starting to smoke in his inboard engine on the left side. I then noticed a lot of pieces flying off the aircrafts tail. Our gunners chased off the German but he had done a lot of damage before he left. Their aircraft went into a steep climb right over the top of us and I could see Lt. Harrington, the co-pilot trying to get out of the co-pilots window as we went by, Lt. Harrington was the only survivor I heard later on.

Sgt Baevis, Sgt Caldwell, Sgt Vincent and Sgt Merfield at the Isle of Capri July 1944

I immediately took his position in the formation, when I noticed that the right wingman was on fire. He pulled up and exploded. What a sight. I heard later that everybody survived but I don't think this was correct because our original Navigator, Lt. Lukashevich, and Lt. Harry McCracken our bombardier were aboard that aircraft and I never heard of them again.

During all this time there are aircraft burning all over the sky, with pieces flying off all over the place and many people bailing out with our gunners calling out how many parachutes are seen, after the crew bailed out of their stricken aircraft. As all this was going on I noticed we were all alone except for a lone B-24 about a mile ahead of us who was our squadron leader. In the meantime I noticed a FW-190 coming at us from 12 O'clock high. As he approached us he rolled on his back with his guns firing. Just as I thought he was going to ram us my nose gunner took his wing off inboard of his black cross. I thought he was going to hit us but he went right under our nose and the wing went over the B-24. There were so many fighters buzzing around us it was like a shooting gallery. We were being hit from all sides and the guns were firing continuously. All the dust that had accumulated overhead was falling on me as well as everything else that was loose, as those twin 50s fired over my head.

I then noticed a Me-109 making another head on pass at on us. I knew he was getting our range when his wing guns were firing tracers and I knew his cannon in the nose of his aircraft would be next. The cannon is quite powerful and can put a good hole in you. Sure enough I saw a flash from the nose and it missed my head about 2 feet. I did not know where it hit until the crew said that we had a big hole in the wing and I looked out and saw the 20mm hole and said that it did not look very big to me. They said that I was not looking at the one they were looking at.

Then it happened. A 20mm shell came through the aft section of our B-24 and hit Sgt. Vincent in the rear end as he leaned over to help Sgt. Weeks who got knocked down by a "flak" burst that hit him in the shoulder. The shell bounced off of Sgt. Vincent and luckily did not explode on contact. Instead it went though the aircraft and exploded in the hydraulic tank and blew off the bomb bay doors. Fortunately Sgt. Vincent had on a long "flak" suit, since when the shell hit him it ricocheted off. These two were my waist gunners. Of course all this time the interphone was wild with all the chatter calling out the fighters. The tail turret was firing like mad and also calling fighters. When the hydraulic tank blew up all the hydraulic fluid blew out and covered the ball turret so the gunner could not see. The ball turret gunner was Sgt. Magneson and now he could not see to shoot. The tail gunner was calling out the positions of the fighters directing the ball by directions of the clock, 2 o'clock low, and 10 o'clock low, etc. While this was going on I was making the B-24 do all kinds of tricks for evasive action, skidding it back and forth as well as running the engines up to full power. When I did this the pilot said that I was going to blow up the engines. Now I never use any profanity outside darn, so when

I said to Lt. Gorski our pilot, "to hell with the engines, lets get out of here". My crew was both startled and amused.

With the engines going wide open. I think we were indicating almost 200 mph at 26,000 feet in a shallow dive to catch up with the group ahead of us. There we would have more protection with the additional guns. I noticed that there was not much chatter on the interphone and not much machine gun chatter. It seemed the interphone was shot out between the ball and the tail turret. The tail turret had taken a direct hit from one of the shells from one of the fighters. Fortunately the tail turret had a two-inch bullet-proof glass but it blew out the interphone and now he could not see. We now had the ball inoperative, the two waist gunners down and out of commission. The only guns working were the top turret with Sgt. Merfeld and the nose turret! Now all the fighters were coming in from the rear. I then noticed a ME 109 German fighter just off our right wing. He was so close I could see his goggles and he was looking straight at us. I called it out. I guess the German was thinking what was keeping this B-24 flying I didn't know how many holes we had in us at the time but later I found we had numerous machine gun bullets in us and numerous 20mm cannon holes in us, plus an 88mm through the right wing. The bomb-bay doors blown off and the hydraulic tank blown out with hydraulic fluid all over the aircraft I guess we looked like a mess.

Well, the look the German fighter pilot gave us was his last. Just as I called out the fighter the ball gunner jumped out of the ball turret and grabbed the waist gun and blew him right out of the sky! It was just like a movie when that ME-109 blew up only we were the main characters in this wild air war, and it was for real.

That did it, I finally was catching up to the next group and the fighters had gotten low on fuel or gave up the fight. We were credited with shooting down three enemy fighters and three probable. I think there were only two of us left in our original formation after this raid, the lead ship and me. The unofficial report on the raid was 64 B-24s shot down and 64 German fighters shot down. Not a very good exchange rate.

Now that we had protection and all the engines on the B-24 were still running, it was time take stock of how we were going to stop this old "beast" without any hydraulic system. In the meantime I got a call from the waist that we had a big hole in the wing. I looked out my window and noticed a large hole in the leading edge of the wing about two feet from my head and at the same level. That was close. I called the waist and told them that the hole did not look very big to me. Their reply was that I was not looking at the hole they were looking at, again.

As we approached our home base, Sgt. Merfeld was busy cranking the gear down by hand, since we did not have any hydraulic system. The crew in the waist was taking care of Sgt. Weeks wounds and giving him straight 100% oxygen. Sgt. Vincent was nursing a sore rear end. We shot up red flares to donate we had wounded aboard. In the meantime I was telling the gunners in the waist to attach their parachutes to each side of the airplane on the gun mounts. When I call, pop the chutes and feed them out both sides of the aircraft at the same instant. I finally let Lt. Gorski our pilot; fly the aircraft to make the landing. As we touched down I called to pop the chutes and feed them out. Well it helped but we were still going about 25mph as we approached the end of the runway, which had a drop off of about 100 feet into a creek. About this time Lt. Gorski asked, "What are we going to do?" We were told that you couldn't ground loop a B-24 but I was going to do it anyway. With that I pushed the throttles on the two right engines to full power and gave old B-24 full left rudder at the same time. It worked we came around in about a 100 degree turn as I cut all the switches as we coasted along near the runway we finally ran into a drainage ditch which stopped us. When we stopped we were 90 degrees from our original heading. The ditch altered our course as we dropped into it. Later Sgt. Merfeld thought our nose wheel would collapse. Lucky the ditch was not too deep.

The ambulance raced up to us and got Sgt. Weeks out and put him the ambulance. Sgt. Vincent refused any treatment but had a big bruise on his rear end. We looked at the aircraft and could not believe it. It was so shot up and still got us home. We did not even lose an engine and those P&W R1830 engines kept right on running after a work out at full throttle. I thanked the Lord for protecting me and getting us all back home after saying my prayers a mile a minute during the whole mission, especially when we were under attack. He had answered my prayers and brought us all home in an aircraft that should have been shot down.

We all were awarded the Distinguished Flying Cross for surviving this mission and performing so well under attack. I was also awarded the Air Medal. I would finally receive an Air Medal for every 10 missions that I flew successfully. We were awarded the DFC by Col. Upthegrove who later became a General.

The official report on the Moosebierbaum raid is as follows: The Strategic Air Force dispatched 1165 aircraft comprised of 575 B-24s, 165 B-17s, 144 P-51s, and 46 P-47s, for this raid. The main effort was directed against oil refineries at Budapest and Vienna. In this area the enemy put its most aggressive fighter attacks yet encountered. An enemy effort of 150 to 175 aircraft with large number of twin-engine fighters, chiefly the ME-210s and showing a more willingness to fight. They made every effort to draw off the escorting fighters so to leave the bombers unprotected. "Flak" at the target was intense, very accurate, and heavy.

The 455th Bomb Group was leading the 104th Wing with 161 B-24s from the 454th Group, the 456th and the 459th Group following. In the ensuing battle the wing lost 18 aircraft, all of them to enemy fighters. The

My Crew, Cerignola, Italy, June 1944 B-24J

total initial claims of all Groups were 53 enemy aircraft destroyed, 25 probably destroyed, and 7 damaged. This did not include those shot down by missing aircraft

Our Group sent 38 B-24s loaded with 250 pound bombs to bomb the oil refinery at Moosebierbaum, Austria. The refinery was located just northeast of Vienna, Austria. Our approach was to be from the east with the bomb run on an axis of 250 degrees. To approach this angle, our route took us east of Vienna and made a long slow turn to the left. When the Group neared the IP, the second section of 18 aircraft began a lose position and swung far out to the right on the turn made by the lead section. This spread out the formation and the enemy fighters made the most of it. The Group was attacked head on by twin-engine fighters. They made one pass with approximately 20 enemy aircraft and headed down and away with our escort of fighters in hot pursuit. While the formation of the second section was strung out it was attacked from every angle by approximately 60 twin-engine and 60 single engine fighters, a relentless attack on the bombers. Harried on all sides by the enemy fighters and flying through intense 'flak', the group stubbornly presses on to the target. One of the bombers collided head on with an enemy fighter. Despite its mortal wounds it persisted through the bomb run, dropped its bombs and then plummeted to the ground... Two other aircraft set afire in the attack struggled over the target, released their bombs and then the crews abandoned their airplanes. Of the 36 B-24s that took off, only 26 returned to base and of these, three had severe damage inflicted by enemy fighters and three crew members received severe wounds. The Group Leader, Major Hugh Graff and Major David Thayer, Deputy Leader, Captain David Bellemere, Second Unit Leader, Major Russell Welsh, Second Deputy Leader, 1st Lt. Julio Locatelli, Group Navigator, Captain James Moeller and Group Bombardier, Captain Horner. We were awarded the Presidential Unit Citation for this mission. It was a "humdinger" I was very fortunate to survive this mission and thanked my Lord that I did.

After the mission to Moosebierbaum, Austria, I was fed up being a co-pilot to a co-pilot who in my judgment wasn't as sharp as he should be. So I went to my Squadron Commander, Major Horace Langford, and told him he could ground me if I wasn't going to be the first pilot. I then explained what I thought of my pilot. The next day I had my own airplane, "Organized Confusion", and my old crew I trained with at Muroc. I heard that they had to send Lt. Wigley home. He got a case of the nerves and could not stay in formation on the bomb runs. Ford built our new B24J at the Willow Run plant in Michigan. It was in natural aluminum and was a pretty "Bird".

After a day off we were back in the air on the 28 June 1944, minus Sgt. Weeks, who was still in the Hospital with his wounds healing. We were on our way to Karlovo, Bulgaria, my first mission as 1st pilot in my own aircraft. We were to bomb some marshalling yards and oil storage areas. We were only able to get up 29 aircraft for the mission. We dropped 57 tons of bombs on the target. "Flak" was very light and no enemy were seen, and all aircraft returned safely to the base I was flying "tail end Charley" and as we headed for home I noticed a large city ahead and asked my Bombagator (navigator and Bombardier) Lt. Keagan what town it was. He told me it was Sofia, the capital of Bulgaria and heavy protected by big guns, and we were going right over it. He had no sooner given me the information than the "flak" started and shot the lead ship out of the sky. By this time I was pulling out of formation all by myself as they made a quick right turn toward me. I could not believe that the lead navigator would do such a dumb trick. Major Hugh Graf was the pilot of the lead ship.

I wasn't going to be shot down due to a dumb navigator not checking his course and flying over a heavy defended known "flak" area. When the lead ship got shot out of the sky the group immediately turned toward me just as the gunners called out fighters coming up from 6 O'clock low. I was glad to catch up to my Group just before the fighters jumped us. I tucked into formation very close and with all the guns aimed at the fighters they got discouraged after one pass. We made it home without further incident. Nobody even noticed that I had left the formation but it was a calculated risk and I got away with it. The fighters thought I was a straggler and were going to get me. This was on the 28 June 1944.

29 June 1944. I got a pleasant surprise by being promoted to 1st Lt. and got three days off after I had flown that last mission. So I got in a clean uniform and was off to Foggia to get a shower and go dancing to celebrate my promotion. I went sight seeing and went to Julius Caesar's

old Coliseums in the area. As I was standing near an old archway a P-38 was making a landing and was perfectly framed in the arch and me without my camera for once!

2 July 1944. Today we are slated to bomb Bucharest, Rumania the Shell oil refinery. This is going to be a maximum effort. The 15th Air Force is putting up 1128 aircraft on the mission. 551 B-24s, 161 B-17s, 198 P-51s and 140 P-38s. The 304th Wing sent 149 B-24s to bomb the Shell refinery and of these, 32 B-24s of the 455th Bomb Group dropped 57 tons of bombs on the target. The "flak" was heavy and accurate in the target area, but we came through without any casualties. On take-off and rallying into formation I saw a B-24 crash on take-off, which killed two crewmen and seriously injured another.

I got a little time off before our next mission, which would be on the 2 July 1944. Our target would be the longest ever for us. When we went to briefing this morning there was that uneasiness among the troops. When they took the shade off the target map with the areas of "flak" marked on it, I could see why. The red yarn went all the way up to Odertal, Germany! This mission to Odertal was going to be a long one. I had a new co-pilot to check out, his name was Gibson Cole. He had just arrived and I was going to give him his first ride into combat. I was now giving new pilots their indoctrination to combat flying. This was my 28th mission. I was over half through my combat tour and an old timer now. Our course took us right through all the known enemy fighter areas. This was supposed to be the place that Hitler had moved his Headquarters. Our target was the Odertal Refinery on the border of Poland and Germany. Twenty-seven B-24s dropped 59 tons of bombs on the target. "Flak" was very heavy and accurate in the target area. Fighters were very aggressive and pressed their attacks vigorously. We lost one aircraft to flak but none to the enemy fighters. Ten men were missing in action.

Part of the group got "bounced" by the enemy fighters going to the target with heavy "flak" at the target. We picked up a few holes, nothing serious. Coming back through the Udine area in northern Italy, we were "bounced" again by the fighters. We did our part of driving them off. Still we had no fighter escort until we were on our way back home. They helped out to get rid of the German fighters. We were given a double sortie for this mission since it was so long and dangerous.

I got a little time off again; so did my usual thing as well as get my laundry done; get a shave and a haircut, etc. I would trade my cigarettes for almonds and green olives. I think these kept me alive, since the GI chow was so bad. I made some acquaintances in Cerignola and would be invited to visit now and then. I would even go into the Old Catholic church to view the countryside from the top. It had an outstanding view of the area. I took pictures from this viewpoint. While most of the crews stayed on the base and lay in their "sack", on their days off, I was out every chance I got to see everything I could even went into some of the old "Catacombs". Of course, I was at the Red Cross Officers Club in Foggia dancing every chance I could.

12 July 1944. Our mission today is Miramas, France. It will turn out to be the longest mission yet. 8 hours of flying time. It wasn't too bad but the official report would say: We sent 29 B-24s to bomb the marshalling yards at Miramas, France. The "flak" was very heavy and accurate with almost all the aircraft receiving damage. All planes returned to the base safely. Of course we got our share of holes. We made a good run on the marshalling yards. I did not know it then but found out later that this was the softening up of the area for the southern invasion of France. This would occur on the 12 August 1944.

Since I was now the driver, my crew took very good care of me. After I pre-flighted the aircraft they would wrap me up in a turret cover and let me sleep until the green flare went off in the air to start your engines. Then they would wake me up and bodily lift me up to the bomb bay and I would scramble up to the cockpit, put on my "flak" vest, my parachute, etc. and crank up and away we would go. .

15 July 1944. Today I got a whole weather briefing from the duty Sgt. who has the job of awakening all the crews for their morning mission briefing. In order to lessen the shock of being aroused at 2:30 am in the morning, he would ramble on with the weather report, which helped. He would never divulge where the mission was going, since this was restricted information until you got to briefing.

I got dressed and hurried over to the mess hall, which had not opened yet. All the crews were standing around the flaming 50 gallon drums of gasoline trying to keep warm. When the mess hall finally opened it was the same old stuff, dehydrated eggs, dehydrated potatoes, Spam and fruit cocktail, all on one plate. I immediately lost my appetite but ate the fruit cocktail.

When we got to briefing, the hum was in the air. Sure enough when the chart was uncovered there it was Ploesti! Then they put up the flying order, putting the names of the pilots in the boxes in the positions we would be flying, there I was in the deputy lead spot. That wasn't too bad, so off we went after I got a little more sleep in the turret cover.

I was second off the ground and pulled that old B-24 into formation like a fighter. Pulling it in so tight I got a burble of a high-speed stall, which kind of shook my new co-pilot. He asked, "Was that a high speed stall", I remarked, "That it was". As we were circling I saw a cloud of dust come off the runway as a B-24 was taking off. It seemed the nose wheel collapsed on take off and he did not make it and it killed the bombardier.

We all joined up and were off to Ploesti to get those oil refineries once a gain! As we approached Rumania you could see lots of white smoke in the distance, about 100 miles away, coming from the target area. We were flying at 26,000 feet and the Germans were trying to obscure the target with smoke pots. They were having quite a bit of success until we got to the IP. Then the wind changed and got stronger and the lead bombardier got a glimpse of the target and we were able to drop our bombs immediately. We had lost two aircraft to "flak" with 20 crewmembers missing in action. We had our usual holes in us but made it back safe and sound from another raid on the dreaded Ploesti. This would be another double mission for me.

After leaving the target we could see more black smoke coming from the area. We had set the refinery on fire and it was really boiling the black smoke out and there were intermittent explosions. The smoke generators put out mostly white smoke so we knew we had hit the target, good. Ploesti was one of the heaviest defended targets in all of Europe, with up to 300 big guns, 88mm and 125 mm. They could shoot you out of the air without much trouble, since their guns were radar controlled. To beat this, the waist gunners would throw out "chaff" which was tin foil cut in different lengths to jam the radar. I always reminded the gunners to take it out of the packages so it would scatter, just as we were leaving the target we got a burst and a piece of "flak" hit my "bombergator", Lt. Kegan, in his steel helmet, which put a big lump on his head and gave us all a good scare. It put a good hole in the plexi-glass nose of the B-24.

We lost altitude rapidly and rallied to the southwest and headed for home at high speed. We made it home without much ado. I found out later that we lost two of our B-24s with their crews, missing in action. Fortunately we did not lose any from our group. On the way home I noticed I was getting hot when we got down to low altitude. I always wore a towel around my neck as a muffler to wipe the perspiration off me and keep warm at altitude a lot of the pilots asked me why I wore the towel all the time around my neck instead of a scarf. I told them when the going got too tough I could throw in the towel.

16th July 1944. After the usual briefing from the duty Sgt. we are off to our mission briefing. As if it wasn't enough to Ploesti yesterday, today we are going to another hot target, Muchendorf, Austria. We are to hit the

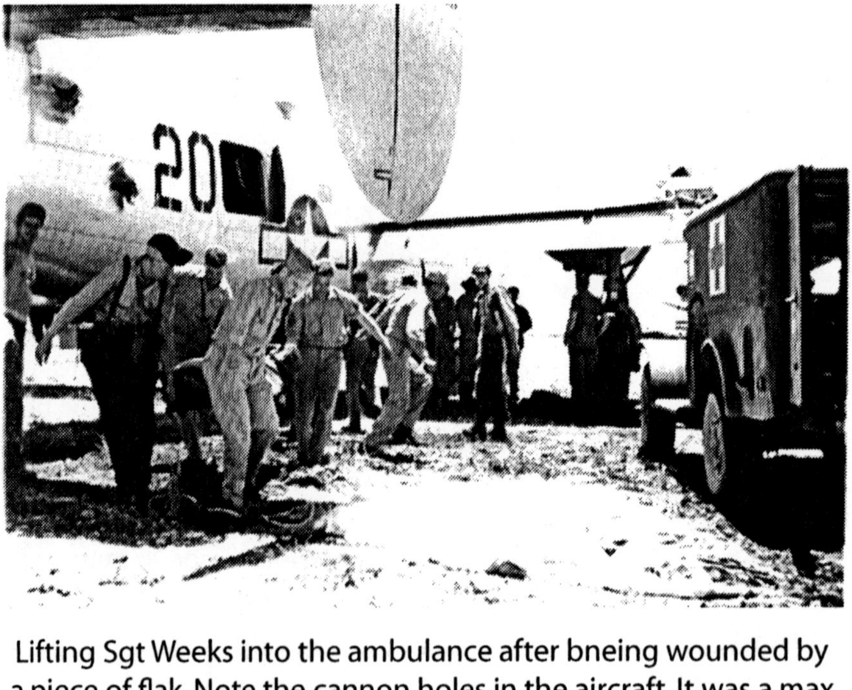

Lifting Sgt Weeks into the ambulance after bneing wounded by a piece of flak. Note the cannon holes in the aircraft. It was a max effort raid on Moosbierbaum, Austria 26 June 1944

I inspect a large hole in the wing caused by a shell from the ground. Moosebierbaum Raid 1944

marshalling yards and the oil storage area. This is another heavy defended area. As we approached, the sky was black with "flak" like Ploesti; you could almost walk on it. I pulled my "flak" helmet down and did my usual evasive action, moving about every 20 seconds until we got to the bomb run, which would be the longest 10 seconds in the world. We dropped our bombs and you could hear the loud explosions from the 'flak" shells and also hear the pieces ricocheting off the aircraft. We dropped our bombs from 26,000 feet with the temperature some where around 50 degrees below zero. All of a sudden I am having hard time breathing. I noticed the red light on for my oxygen supply. I was out of oxygen! A piece of "flak" had cut my oxygen line that supplied the pilot's position. A loud holler to Lt. Kegan over the intercom, that I had no oxygen and to get me a walk around bottle of oxygen quickly. He rushed up from the nose, and plugged me in before I passed out. It was a good feeling to have oxygen again. Under such pressure of flying combat you are using a lot of oxygen at high altitude and it doesn't take long to get Hypoxia if you run out of oxygen.

We rallied off the target and headed for home, when I saw a B-24 dropping out of the formation from another group. There were at least three groups on this raid. I was deputy lead so it was my duty to monitor the fighter channel on the radio. I heard a voice on the radio, with a heavy southern accent, say, "Looks like big friend needs some help down there". He was referring to the B-24 that had dropped out of formation with one engine feathered. The voice continued, "Why don't you go down and help him get home". The other voice came back and said, "why don't you, you're on flight pay". With that I saw two P-51s, Mustangs, from the 99th fighter group drop down and position themselves on both sides of the stricken B-24. The 99th fighter group was the only all black flying outfit in WWII. Their commander was Colonel Benjamin Davis one of the few black West Pointers.

Cannon holes from German fighters
June 1944

We were going quite fast now and passed the B-24 that was in trouble. He had at least some protection with the two P-51s at his side. I hoped he made it home. We made it back safe and sound with a few holes in us but were bounced by a bunch of FW-190s and ME-109s on the way home but they hit the group behind us and left us be.

17 July 1944. I checked the bulletin board and saw that I was scheduled to fly again the next day. That would be three days in a row. This one was to Avignon, France a long mission over Sardinia and into France over the Mediterranean Sea. It was a beautiful day and the visibility was unlimited. Of course there was a lot of water underneath us if you got into trouble. We were to hit the marshalling yards there. There was 37 B-24s in this raid, loaded with 500 pound GP bombs. We were softening up the Germans for the southern invasion of France.

Col. Cool, our Group Commander, was leading the mission of at least three groups of B-24s. "Flak" was very intense and heavy and we picked up our quota of holes. A piece of "flak" had cut one of our spark plug wires and knocked a few cooling fins off one of the cylinders on one of our engines but we did not notice it until we got back home. The engines had twin ignition so it did not make that much difference to the power of the engine.

As we rallied off the target I tucked right under the wing of the lead B-24, when the waist gunner motion me to get in closer. Then I noticed the co-pilot on the lead ship motioning me out. I found out later Col. Cool wanted to know who was flying the aircraft in deputy lead that was staying right in there. From that time on, I always flew deputy lead. I really learned to fly that big monster once I became first pilot.

I was now checking out all the new crews coming into the squadron. They would fly five or six missions with me to get their indoctrination to combat flying then they would get their own aircraft and crew or fly

Sgt. Vincint, Sgt. Beauvis and Lt. disbrow exmaine a hole in our B-24, 26 June 1944, WWII, Italy

missions with other crews. It seemed everybody wanted to fly with me, since I was so lucky. We picked up many holes but we made it back every time while other crews were shot down. We had just lost an aircraft on the mission to Avignon.

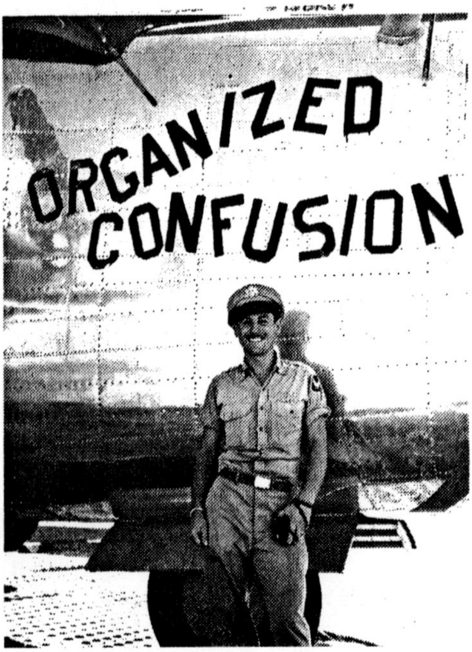

My B-24, Italy 1944

18 July 1944. I got a couple of days off after flying three long and hot missions in a row. Besides they had to patch up all the holes in our aircraft. I wanted to paint all the patches red but the C.O. did not think that was a got idea since it would not do much for the morale of the new "troops" coming into the squadron.

I "sacked" in for the day and the next day I went over to a base near Foggia to see Joe Louis, the heavyweight champion of the world, put on an exhibition match. He had joined the Army and of course they put him special services so he could entertain the troops. He gave up millions of dollars by not defending his championship. I took pictures of him, which I put in my album. After watching the exhibition I went to a concert in Foggia and Jaffa Hefitz put on a great show. He was a great violinist and played every thing from "long haired" music to jazz. In fact when he started out he made the remark to the big crowd that they were going to listen to the "long haired" stuff first then he would take requests. He was great; it was one of the highlights of entertainment while I was over seas. I never saw Bob Hope.

After the show I went to the YMCA and took my shower and went to the Red Cross Officers Club for my dancing. I was a known regular by now and all the girls liked to dance with me. The next day I went to Cerignola and traded for almonds, eggs and potatoes. I visited the catacombs, got my laundry done and got a haircut. By the way, I either walked or hitched a ride with anyone that would give me one. There was no transportation anywhere on a regular schedule.

19 July 1944. The Flight Surgeon wanted me to fly a crew whose pilot wanted to be grounded for the fear of flying. I was supposed to get his reaction as he flew co-pilot with me. We took off and headed for the Isle Of Capri. We had a cameraman aboard. so he could get some pictures of the area with nobody shooting at us. Did we get a surprise as we flew over Naples harbor the Navy let loose with a couple of rounds at us. Boy, anybody can identify a B-24! I made a high speed letdown toward Capri and went across the hotel we stayed in on our R&R, at about 100 feet and then made a sweeping left turn and went through a gap between an little island and Capri in a steep bank to get between them, as I rounded the island I came right over a U.S. Navy Destroyer. I was going so fast we made a big climbing turn and got out of there in a hurry. Then we noticed all the ships

Lt. Bill Disbrow receiving the Distinguished Flying Cross from Col. Upthegrove for the Moosebierbaum raid 28 July 1944

in Naples harbor. This was the invasion fleet for the invasion of Southern France. We were getting all kinds of pictures of this, which was restricted. The co-pilot who I was checking out did not say a word after all these happenings. I gave him back to the Flight Surgeon and told him what happened. I don't know what ever happened to him. I don't know whether I scared him more or amazed him with what a B-24 could do.

Flak 1944 Italy

I did find out later that our buzz job we did on Capri was a good one. A directive came out that there would be no more buzzing of the Isle of Capri or you would be court-martialed Wow! I guess I did a good job.

20 July 1944. Today is another long mission to Fredrickshaven, Germany. We are to bomb the BMW factory that makes the engines for most of the aircraft fighting for Germany. We have no opposition going to the target and I am flying with a new co-pilot. This is his first mission in combat. It so happens I am flying a left wing and it is very hard to fly cross-cockpit in a B-24 and fly good formation by staying in close. We are flying off the lead ship,

As we approached Lake Constance we could see the large dirigible hanger at Fredrickshaven, which is a landmark and the engine shops of the BMW factory. Our IP is out in Lake Constance and we approached the target from the west so we can rally to the right and be on our way home as quickly as we can.

On our briefing we were told that anyone going into Switzerland better have at least two engines out or be in such dire emergency that it is life or death decision, or when the war was over you may be investigated for the dereliction of duty.

New crew just got checked out in combat Italy, July 1944 WWII 455th BG 741st SQDN

I was letting the new co-pilot fly from the co-pilot position after I positioned the aircraft in the right place in the formation off the lead ship. It would take the strain off of me trying to stay in close flying cross-cockpit. Everything was fine as we approached the IP where the "Flak" became heavy and intense. We caught a big burst right close by with that the co-pilot through up both hands to cover his face taking his hands completely off the control wheel. I thought he was hit and grabbed the controls and dropped down so I could see the lead ship and pulled back into position, just as I heard "bombs away". We rallied to the right and headed for home in a fast descending turn, getting out of the "flak" as quickly as possible. I now looked over at the co-pilot who was now looking around and was surprised that we were still flying. He thought for sure we were going to be shot down. I can't remember his name but I have a picture of him.

We made it back home without further incident and nobody went into Switzerland, although when we got that first big blast and then three successive ones I thought for a minute we might be on our way there. There were 37 B-24s on this raid loaded with 500 pound GP bombs. The raid was a success according to the reports. This was my 36th mission; it counted for two since it was so long and the danger of the well-defended target. I now was a seasoned combat pilot and the string of bombs marked on the wall of my tent above my head was growing. I had only 14 more missions to go.

On debriefing I got my 2 ounces of whiskey, which I could not take anymore so I gave it away. I also mentioned the action of my co-pilot under fire at the debriefing and they made a note of it. I also got a surprise; I got two weeks off so I could go to Rome, which we had liberated by this time.

After getting the good news that I had two weeks off to go to Rome, I packed my gear and got a ride to Foggia. There I "bummed" a ride in a B-17 that was going to Naples Airport. I got a place to stay in Naples and the next day I went to see Pompeii and the surrounding area. After spending as much time as was necessary I decided it was time to head for Rome. I got out on the Appian Way out of Naples and hitched a ride on a GI truck, which was one of the "Red Ball Express" jobs. He didn't waste any time. He was on his way to the front lines at Leghorn, Italy.

After about an hour on the road and going as fast as the old 6x6 would go, it started to make little squealing noises at times. Well the driver did not know what it was. He didn't know anything but driving. I told him to slow down and then speed up. I told him it sounded like a universal joint to me. We pulled over off of the road and I instructed him how to check the U-joint and the drive shaft for looseness, and sure enough it was the U-joint on the rear drive shaft. A 6x6 has drive to all the wheels by using two drive shafts in the rear, one from the transfer case to the differential of the front rear axle and another drive shaft from the front rear axle to the rear axle. I asked the GI if he had any tools aboard, since he did not know what to do and was 200 miles from his outfit in Leghorn. He found some tools and I had him disconnect the rear drive shaft completely, since it was the one giving him the trouble. He did not need it, since he still had drive to the first rear axle. He finally got the drive shaft off and threw it in the back of the truck and away we went again without any noise.

Bombs Away!

We finally got to Rome and he asked me if I would like to go to Leghorn with him. I declined and bade him good luck and farewell and thanked him for the lift. Hoping he would make it with out any more trouble.

I checked into the Regina Hotel, which was the same hotel that my Grandfather Hitchcock stayed in 1922! He took my twin uncles with him and my grandmother. It was quite a nice place in its day.

After checking in at the Hotel I proceeded to take in all the sights. I saw the damage we had done. We had hit the marshalling yards and blew the boxcars up on top of the hills, destroyed the entire track, which they were in the process of fixing. I went to Mussolini's Forum, the Coliseum, Victor Emanuel's Tomb, the Vatican, etc. At night I made all the night clubs that were operating and the Red Cross Officers Club. I was fortunate to run into a crew that was up for the weekend from my area in a B-24 so I bummed a ride home with them by air as their co-pilot.

Cooking eggs & Chips for lunch in front of my EMS tent June 1944

When I got back it was the 5 August 1944, and I was scheduled to fly on the 7th of August. In the meantime they had a review to award our crew the DFC, the Distinguished Flying Cross, for our successful raid on Moosebierbaum on the 26 June 1944. I was also awarded another Air Medal. I would end up with three. Every time you won the same medal again they would give you an Oak Leaf Cluster. Col. Upthegrove presented us with our medals.

Well I was ready to fly again after my sojourn in Naples and Rome, so when we got to briefing I was not surprised to see another long mission to Blechammer, Germany. I was flying deputy lead again with another new co-pilot. It seems that the co-pilot I had on the raid to Fredickshaven had turned himself into the Hospital and they didn't find him for days, in fact they had him listed as AWOL.

So off to the target I went with my new co-pilot, which was his first ride into combat. His name was Gibson Cole. He was a good pilot and a big fellow who would be able to fly cross- cockpit if necessary. After he flew with me for his indoctrination he would get his own aircraft and usually his old crew back again.

The "flak" was heavy and accurate. We were bombing the synthetic oil refinery at Glewitz, Germany. This was the longest mission to date, 7 hours and 10 minutes of flying time. We got our usual number of holes with a piece of "flak" bouncing off Lt. Keegan's head, my bombardier. It did not go through his helmet but it gave him a nasty bump on his "noggin". Two other aircraft of the group were severely damaged by "flak". The target was partly obscured with the smoke pots they had going but we managed to make a good run and caused a lot of damage with the 500 pound GP bombs we had aboard. Everyone made it home without further incident. I thanked the Lord again for sparing me.

After we got to our tents from briefing, I told my crew not to wake me up from my nap unless they had something special at the mess hall for dinner. They woke me up and had fixed me eggs and chips. They had traded their cigarettes for all the goodies I liked and had it all prepared for me. What a treat.

I got another couple days off so went sight seeing and dancing, at Foggia. I took my usual shower at the YMCA since it was so dusty going to the showers they built for us at the base. I went to an old Coliseum, which was a small duplicate of the one in Rome. It was in fair shape for the age of it.

10 August 1944. Got my usual briefing from the Duty Sgt. (who woke me up at 2:30 A.M in the morning); he always started my day off right. I would get dressed and head for the mess hall and get my usual powered eggs, etc. Then climb aboard the GI truck and head for briefing.

There was that uneasiness in the air when I got there before the briefing Officer came in. He would give us the "flak" emplacements and the number of big guns and the number of enemy aircraft we might encounter going to the target and on the way home. There was a big groan when he uncovered the map when we saw the red yarn go from our base to Campina, Rumania, and the dreaded Ploesti area! Since I had been there many times before I knew what to expect

We got off the ground OK and were off to Campina. The "flak" when we got there was intense as usual but we managed to make a good run and got a few small holes. This was the Stevea Romano Oil Refinery again. I was beginning to wonder how many times we had to hit this place before we knocked it out completely. I found out later that they were using slave labor to repair it every time we bombed it. This was my sixth trip to the Ploesti area!

I was flying deputy lead again so it wasn't too bad. I was using my evasion action tactics again. If I stood still to long the crew would remind me with a loud "evasive action". As we approached the target they had the smoke pots going but the wind was in our favor so we could see the target. We dropped our bombs and away we went, wading through the intense "flak. Again we made home safely, thanks to my dear Lord. Things were getting short now I only had nine missions to go. After the mission I found I had a day off so went off to Cerignola for eggs and chips.

12 August 1944. Well another day in the life of a bomber combat pilot. After the usual breakfast, UGH! We found that our mission for today was the invasion of southern France! We were supposed to support the invasion forces by bombing the German gun emplacements and soften up the Germans for the landing crafts, gliders, etc., which would be coming in at their positions.

After we became airborne it was a sight to see. As far as the eye could see there were aircraft of all sizes and types. Everybody in the 15th Air Force was in the air, besides the Navy Marines, and the Army. I was later told that there were 11,000 aircraft in the air that day!

As we approached the target and started on the IP Lt. Keegan opened the bomb bay doors and out went our bombs into the water below. We had a malfunction of the system for some reason. Some of the aircraft dropped their bombs off of me thinking the lead ship had some trouble, since I was deputy lead I would receive instructions if the lead ship were having some difficulty.

We didn't do much in the way of supporting the invasion. When we got home I was immediately questioned why we had dropped our bombs early, along with the questioning of Lt. Keegan, my bombardier. Lt. Keegan did not do anything out of the ordinary and gave his explanation of what happened that the bombs were released early for some unknown reason.

When the crew chief and the ground personnel checked the aircraft they found a short in the system caused by a bare wire that had been hit sometime before and caused the short. This made the bombs go out when the bomb bay doors were opened. We were cleared for "goofing up".

13 August 1944. I guess we had to get a second chance to help the invasion because we were now on our way to Avignon, France. We are to bomb a railroad bridge. We had 35 B-24s on this raid with over 82 tons of bombs but we missed the bridge. "Flak" was intense in the target area but we suffered no casualties, just a few holes. A few aircraft got some good damage due to the heavy "flak". Everyone got home safely thanks to the good Lord. Throwing out the "chaff" might have helped. This is the tinfoil cut to different lengths to jam the radar for the big guns that were shooting at us. I always remind the crew to break open the packages before throwing it out. Some of the crews just threw the whole bundle out intact which did no good. This raid on Avignon, France and the invasion we hoped would shorten the war. The allies now had a pincer movement on the Germans, which was taking its toll.

14 August 1944. Well I got 3 days off so off again to take more pictures, dance, etc. Write letters for home to my Mother and Dad, and my wife Florence, who was working for Sears in Sacramento, California.

I left out a mission to Bucharest, Rumania on the 3 July 1944. They messed up my flying record and added it later. It wasn't too bad considering all the other missions I had flown. I am taking the missions directly from my combat flying record.

17 August 1944. After three days off I guess they thought I was ready for another raid on Ploesti, because that is where we are going today. This will be my 7th trip to this dreaded area and I hope it will be my last one. I wonder how long my luck will hold out. I am checking a new pilot who will be my co-pilot. What a target to get his first taste of combat. If I remember right I got my first taste of combat by going to the same area. Our target is the Romano Americano Oil refinery, Ploesti, Rumania. We have thirty B-24s on this raid to start with but 8 returned for some reason or other. I never aborted a mission I figured if that airplane got off the ground I was going regardless.

As we approached the target, the "flak" was so intense that you could walk on it. I did my usual evasive action trick and avoided any big holes but the lead ship took a hit in the left inboard engine as we came off the target after dropping our bombs. He immediately feathered the engine and we began to lose altitude, to pickup his speed. He stayed in the lead all the way home. I guess he did not want to be left behind since the German fighters had come up after us before we got to the bomb run. I wasn't told to take over the lead when we got home and stayed with him until he landed. I told him I was protecting him if we got jumped in the pattern, it had happened before.

After landing we found a few small holes in the leading edge of the wing and a hole in the cowling of one of the engines. Nothing too serious, thank goodness

It seemed I had a good reputation as a good pilot as well as a lucky one. It seemed no matter what happened to us we always made it back home, thanks to the dear Lord watching over me, my crew and answering my prayers, as well as, all the people back home praying for me.

18 August 1944. After Ploesti they gave me two days off to rest and relax with only 5 missions to go. The markings above my bed are many rows of chalk bombs. I am getting a little anxious now. I wrote home that I would like to fly another tour in P-38s with the 1st fighter group, in Foggia, if they would take me. I had met an old classmate from my cadet class, 43K, at the Red Cross Officers Club. He had just arrived in Italy and was to fly P-38s. I told him I had 45 missions in and was about ready to go home and wished him "good luck".

20 August 1944. Our mission today is to Czechoslovakia, to a place named Dubova. We are to hit the oil refinery that is making synthetic oil. We have been hitting their refineries quite regularly. The Germans need this to keep the war going but we were determined to stop their means of continuing to wage war.

We got our briefing on how much "flak" to expect and how many enemy fighters there will be on the way to the target and on the way home and how much fighter cover we will have, if any. I also found out whom my co-pilot is going to be and if we would have any new gunners to check out.

I got down to the aircraft and my crew wraps me in the gun turret cover and I got a little sleep before they "roust" me out when the green flare goes off. They then pick me up bodily and put me into the bomb bay and away we go. We rally into formation and I am flying number two spot in the deputy lead position as usual. We head North through the Udine Area which was where all the German fighters are based to get us on the way to the target and intercept us when we are on the way home. Also to get any stragglers who can't stay up with the formation.

The crew checks out all the guns on the aircraft so that all are working well before we get to the fighter area. Each gunner checks in after his gun check. We will be ready for the Germans if they try anything. We get through the area without any trouble.

We get to the IP and the "flak" is moderate to heavy and we can hear it bouncing off the sides of the aircraft. I pull my "flak" helmet down so far that I can just see. We drop our bombs and rally to the right, which is my side, and start our fast let down. As I mentioned before, this confuses the enemy guns and their gunners. It takes 20 seconds for the shell to reach 26,000 feet so if we keep moving and changing altitude it makes it hard for them to hit us. Also the Germans set the fuses in their shells to explode between 22,000 and 26,000 feet.

We start home and run through the Udine Area again. Up, the German fighters come when we got there but they are driven off from the gun fire of all our aircraft in close formation. They do not seem to be as aggressive as they used to be. We think that their good pilots have been shot down or they have spread them over too large an area to protect Germany.

We make it home without further incident but as we let down from altitude to 2000 feet it becomes quite hot and the perspiration is running down my face and down my back. Fortunately I have my favorite towel around my neck to wipe myself dry. With all the gear on, wool uniform, wool flying suit, leather flying jacket, "Mae west", two pair of socks, GI boots, "flak" jacket, and a back pack parachute, it makes it rather uncomfortable when it gets hot. At 26,000 feet it will be from –40 to –60 degrees below zero. With the aircraft heaters not operating most of the time you have to dress warm. Many a time I have had the front of my chest covered with ice from the condensation freezing from my breath exhalation from my oxygen mask plus ice around my armpits.

21 August 1944. Well I am scheduled to fly again today. I am ready to get this over with. So off we go to the briefing and find it is to a place called Hadu Boszurment, Rumania. I am told this is supposed to be a "milk run".

I am always suspicious when they say that. Going into Rumania I know by experience that the Germans are "squirrel shooters" and can shoot you out of the air if you are unlucky.

We rally into formation as I am in deputy lead again. I pull the my old B-24, "Organized Confusion", into the formation like a fighter and high speed stall it as I pull alongside the lead ship. I have a new co-pilot aboard again; this is his first ride into combat. I guess he was awed on how I got into formation so fast and asked if that was a high speed stall I had just did. I answered that it was. There was little conversation after that.

Today we had no Navigator to check out. Lt. Keegan, my bombardier could do both jobs as well as anybody and we did not need a Navigator. I told my C.O. Major Horace Langford, we could fly without a co-pilot and a Navigator, and they were just excess baggage. He took a dim view of that remark.

We had 30 B-24s on this raid loaded with fragmentation bombs, a very dangerous bomb. They are loaded in clusters on the bomb racks and come apart in the air as they leave the aircraft. Some at times explode accidentally too close to the aircraft if they are not loaded right. This does not do the aircraft any good and sometimes does severe damage.

It seems after we made our run on the target and dropped our bombs one cluster did not leave the bomb bay. It was hung up on one hook on the bomb shackle. Luckily we were now over the Adriatic Sea, when Lt. Keegan noticed it. I did not know what was happening at the time. I did notice that the bomb bay doors were still open and wondered why. They should close after we dropped our bombs. I was informed immediately of our plight and that Lt. Keegan was in the process of trying to release the "frag" cluster from the bomb shackle with a screwdriver. It was hung up on half of the bomb shackle, which was a very dangerous situation. If the cluster was armed it could explode any second! Keegan managed to get it out before anything happened and it dropped harmlessly into the Adriatic. Except for this bit of excitement, the mission was a "milk run" we landed OK with this being my 47th mission with only three to go.

22 August 1944. I get a day off and get a little "sack time" in. I decided to go to Cerignola and trade off my cigarettes for good things to eat, almonds, olives, cheese, and Spumante wine. When I got home I went

to the Photo Lab and developed some of my pictures. Then back to my tent to write letters to home.

23 August 1944. Well today is supposed to be another "milk run" We are going to Ferrare, Italy to bomb some bridges on the Poe river in Northern Italy. We are trying to trap the Germans from escaping northward. It didn't sound too bad but when we get there the Germans must have moved all their big guns by rail to protect the target. It must have been more important than Intelligence thought. As we made our run to the IP the sky was black with "flak". It sure didn't look like a "milk run" to me, especially when I had to stay still on the 10 second bomb run, which was at only 22,000 feet. Too low! A blast caught us near the nose and blew Sgt. Cornell out of the nose turret. Fortunately it did not hurt him but scared the life out of him from the concussion. The next blast blew our bomb bay doors off and blew holes in the hydraulic tank and cut a lot hydraulic lines, as we dropped our bombs. Another burst got us as we rallied off the target. This burst knocked my foot off the rudder so hard I thought I was hit in the foot. I looked down and could not see any blood. I then got a call from the waist that we had a rudder cable sheared by piece of "flak" that had come through the fuselage. Fortunately the B-24 had dual rudder cables for such a situation.

I called back to the waist to see if everyone was OK and no one was hit back there. About this time I am covered with hydraulic fluid, which is red and looks like blood but does not smell like it. I am not hit. The hydraulic tank is quite close to cockpit and I got sprayed. I then smelled smoke and called it out to the crew just as Lt. Keegan informed me that we had a fire in the heater and; he had shut off the fuel to it. That was quick thinking. The heaters on this aircraft were South Wind heaters, which are fueled with gasoline! A piece of "flak" had come through the aircraft and cut the gas line to the heaters.

As we got out of the danger area we began to assess our damage. No one was injured, thank God. But our aircraft was out of hydraulic fluid, which made our hydraulic system inoperative. This meant that the landing gear would have to be lowered manually as well as the flaps. Also we would not have any brakes unless the accumulator was full of hydraulic fluid. We checked the pressure on the accumulator and Sgt. Merfeld, my engineer, said we had enough pressure to make one stop. Sgt. Merfeld would have to pump the gear down manually when we got home.

Looking back into the bomb bay I saw Sgt. Beauvis trying to tape up some of the leaking hydraulic lines that were spraying all over. He was on the narrow catwalk, which now was covered with slippery hydraulic fluid. He did not have a parachute on and was slipping around 20,000 feet above the ground!

Well we got back to the base and we pulled out of formation, after informing the lead ship of our predicament. We would land last so not to block the runway for any other aircraft that was landing, if we should crash.

I set up a pattern and it was decided now that I still had enough pressure in the accumulator to make one application of the brakes. Sgt. Merfeld got the gear down after 76 rotations of the crank and it was locked. I made a slower than normal approach setting up for a short field landing and hit the first 10 feet of the runway. Before we were on the final approach I told everybody available to get as far back in the fuselage as possible so we could keep the nose gear off as long as possible to make the aircraft slow down quicker and also drag the tailskid.

As I toughed down I cut the throttles to idle and we were doing about 90 mph and the runway was 5000 feet long, so there was no room for error. So with the weight in the back I could hold the nose up very easy and the old B-24 slowed right down and I did not have to use the brakes. In fact I had to use power to get off the runway and made a turn with power and no brakes. After turning off the runway I used the brakes to make one stop and shut down. A tug came out to get us and towed us to our parking place.

After parking we all got out and surveyed the damage. We looked at our ground crew chief and he couldn't believe we made it back. He had heard that of the 26 B-24s that were on the raid ten aircraft were seriously damaged with two landing at other bases. They could not make it home. I thanked the Lord again for sparring us.

24 August 1944. Well after that last mission they gave us two days off so they could repair the damage to "Organized Confusion" our B-24.

I met the Flight Surgeon, Dr. Schutenik, and told him I was through flying after that mission. He laughed and quoted the odds of me making it now with only two missions to go. I told him if he was so sure I would make it to fly the next two missions with me. He said that I was the brave one and not he. We laughed it off and had a beer together at our Officers Club. It was a converted cow barn.

I went down to see how my ground crew was doing on our aircraft. The crew chief gave me a cigar box full of "flak" pieces he had found in the aircraft. As we were checking the stuff out I found a piece of "flak" that believe it or not had numbers on it that were the same as the last four numbers of Lt. Keegans serial number! This was a time that his number came up but did not connect, luckily.

26 August 1944. After awakening me, my friendly Sgt. gave me my usual weather briefing said "This was next to my last mission". It was supposed to be another "milk run". I about hit him with my shoe.

It was a beautiful morning when we got down to briefing but when they took off the cover from the target map I saw it was to Bucharest, Rumania! We were to hit the German barracks at the Baneasa Airdrome. We have 30 B-24s loaded with 100 pound bombs. We were lucky this time there was no "flak" to speak of at the target but there was plenty of it coming home. The mission was successful and we were reported to have killed 10,000 German troops and destroyed numerous aircraft on the ground. Once again we arrived home safe and sound. One more mission to go! Only I was a bit reluctant on the way home when we got a lot of "flak" over Sofia. In fact we lost the Deputy C.O from the 743rd squadron and another aircraft that was not from our squadron. Lost two aircraft on a "milk run"!

Our call sign for our tower at Cerignola was "Carol". After landing we went to debriefing and afterwards I took my whiskey and headed for my bunk. I was bushed not only from the long mission, 7 hours and 10 minutes, but from the mental strain of hitting such a hot target on my next to last mission

27 August 1944. We got the day off so I went down to the photo lab and developed some more of my pictures to bring my album up to date. I also got a lot of pictures of the aircraft in our group from the GIs that ran the lab.

I was standing watching a ball game later, when we were "buzzed" by a fighter aircraft. Everybody looked up and said that was a funny looking P-

51. I said that was not a P-51 but a German Me-109! I started running for the airstrip as it made a pattern to land. As it landed it was met by the MPs in a Jeep with machine guns on it as the Me –109 taxied off the runway. The Me-109 had old Army Air Corps insignia painted on the wings, the white star in a field of blue, with a red center to the star. It was painted on top and bottom of both wings with a big American flag on both sides of the fuselage. They wanted to make sure we did not shoot them down before it got to Cerignola.

After shutting down the Me-109 the pilot got out and went to the aft section of the aircraft and opened a hatch near the tail and out came Col. Gunn the C.O. of the 454th Bomb Group! They shared our runway area, which was parallel to ours. Everyone was flabbergasted included the MPs.

It seems that Col. Gunn had been shot down over Ploesti, Rumania on the 17 August 1944 the same raid I was on. He was interned in a Rumanian POW camp. Somehow while there he contacted a Rumanian pilot who was fighting for the Germans. The Russians were about to invade Rumania and threatened the entire position of the Axis in the Balkans. This was about 27 August 1944.

The Rumanian pilot agreed to fly Col. Gunn back to Italy in his Me-109. Col. Gunn got into the fuselage through an access door in the rear of the fuselage and hung onto the bracing inside of the aircraft, while the Rumanian pilot flew him back to Italy

I heard later that Col. Gunn tried to fly the Me-109 and ground looped it on take off and damaged it. I also heard that after wrecking the aircraft they gave the Rumanian pilot a P-51 to fight against the Germans.

I later found out the true story behind the liberation of Col. Gunn by my friend Bob Goebel, a P-51 ace, who was in Italy the same time I was. Here is a short resume of the operation: In the middle of August 1944 the Red Army crossed the eastern border of Rumania and threatened the entire position of the Axis in the Balkans. On the 23rd, King Michael, who had never been particularly fond of the Nazi partners of Rumania, summoned marshal Antonescu, the head of the government to the Royal Palace. They met in the Casa Noua, a small building inside the Palace grounds. The King asked Antonescu to break with the Germans and negotiate surrender with the Soviet Union. Antonescu refused. Twenty three year old King

Michael promptly had him arrested. Officers who were loyal to the King stepped forward to carry out the order. Antonescu was furious and told the assembly, "You'll live to regret this. Tomorrow you will all be hung at the "Palace Square". Shortly thereafter, the King took Rumania out of the war, and the new government issued an ultimatum that the German forces were to leave within three days. The German Luftwaffe Commander, Lt. Gen. Gerstenberg, responded by bombing the Palace, the government offices and military targets in and around Bucharest. Amid this military and political confusion the guards at the POW camps abandoned their posts and the allied prisoners, no less confused, tried to figure out what to do with their new-won freedom.

The ranking officer among the prisoners at this time was Lt. Col. James A. Gunn. He had been shot down over Ploesti on the 17th of August 1944, and so had been in camp only a few days before the confusion erupted. Col Gunn was not shy about taking action; the problem was that he could not locate any Rumanian in authority with which he could discuss the situation. He visited the enlisted men's camp on the other side of the city and found essentially the same situation there. The reason was that the incessant German bombing had destroyed the government offices and all the communication facilities and the provisional government was temporarily located in a wood outside the city

Finally, he was able to locate the new HQ and to speak with the head of the War Department, Lt. Gen. Raeovita. He made one demand and one request. The demand was that the allied prisoners be removed from the dangers of the bombing and shelling in the city to somewhere safer. The request was that he be given an aircraft to fly to Italy and arrange for the repatriation of all allied POW's in Rumania. He also wisely promised to arrange for a bomb strike against Baneasa Airfield, the base from which the German strikes were being launched. The General promised to evacuate the Allied prisoners to another camp a few miles away and to pass the aircraft request to the Chief of the Air Force. The POW's were subsequently transported to the garrison near Bragadiru, 8 kilometers south southwest of Bucharest, mainly through the coordinating efforts of an interned Dutch Admiral Dorman, who spoke Rumanian fluently

At this point, Col. Gunn was taken in tow by a Mr. Rico Georgescu, who was the Secretary of State and Minister of National Economy and actually spent the night with him, finally retiring at 4 a.m. Early the next morning, Georgescu escorted Gunn to a meeting with the Secretary of the Rumanian Air Force. He informed Gunn, through an interpreter, arrangements had been made to fly him back to Italy in an ancient, twin-engine Savoia-Marchetti. Almost immediately, they departed for the Popesri Airdrome, where they found the aircraft, pilot and two armed guards who were to accompany the Colonel to Italy. The pilot's enthusiasm for the flight was under whelming and the guards seemed to be on edge and suspicious of everything. It came as no surprise to Gunn that 20 minutes into the flight the pilot turned back claiming engine trouble although the American officer thought that both were running quite smoothly.

As he stepped out of the aircraft he was met by a Rumanian captain, Constantine Cantacuzino, himself a Me-109 fighter pilot of considerable renown and a member of the Royal family. He spoke excellent English and proposed to fly Col. Gunn to Italy if he would agree to lie prone in the aft fuselage of the aircraft. Col. Gunn was quite willing to do this and as they discussed the flight in more detail, Mr. Georgescu appeared and informed Gunn that the interim President of the new government wished to see him. On being taken to him, the President, Dr. Maniu, made an impassioned plea to Gunn that upon arrival in Italy, he convey; the desire of the Rumanian government to be occupied by the British or the American forces. Dr. Maniu, as well as many other Rumanians were terrorized at prospect of the Russian occupation. Gunn promised to make the representations, although in his own mind he realized the impracticability of such a turn of events, and did in fact relay on this proposal at MAAF HQ with the expected result.

Cantacuzino and Gunn proceeded with the mission planning but were unable to find any suitable maps of Italy. Finally Gunn sketched out the details from memory on a piece of cardboard, which would enable the Rumanian pilot to find and land at Gunn's home field at San Giovani near Cerignola. Since Gunn would have no oxygen they settled on an en route altitude of 6500 meters (about 19,000 feet) Cantacuzino vetoed Gunn's suggestion to cross the Adriatic at wave level to stay under Allied radar, claiming the 109 engine was too unreliable. He preferred to stay at altitude until half way across the Adriatic Sea and then begin a high-speed let- down into Italian air space

One last bit of preparation was the painting of the America flag on both sides of the Me-109s fuselage. While painting was in progress, Cantacuzino drew Gunn aside and expressed his fears that the plan was much too widely known and that the possibility of being shot down by the German fighters which were still operating in the area, was very real. He suggested that a departure time on the following day be freely passed around but that they should actually get away as soon as the painting was completed. Gunn was provided with some warm clothing and the radio equipment removed, which would allow him space in the fuselage. On the pretext of trying out the arrangement, the 18"x18" panel was removed and he crawled in, lying face down on the space provided. As soon as he was in, Cantacuzino replaced the cover, jumped into the cockpit and off they went. The time was 1720 on the 27th of August.

The flight was uneventful, Col. Gunn found that by pushing on a spring-loaded small door covering a pilot's step near his head he could see downward but could only tell if they were over land or water. Once they reached the Italian coast, the pilot had no trouble following the crude map right to the San Giovanni air strip. As he and Gunn agreed, he lowered his gear and flaps and circled the field once, rocking his wings slowly before attempting a landing. It worked. The British anti-aircraft gunners held their fire and allowed the 109 to land, toughing down at 1930. As he taxied to a stop on the parking area, a crowd of curious onlookers rapidly gathered around the 109. Capt. Cantacuzino, obviously enjoying himself, stood up in the cockpit, asked for a screw- driver and to the throng that he had a surprise for them. When he removed the panel, Col Gunn crawled out, stiff, dizzy from hypoxia but otherwise in good condition.

After a quick round of salutations from his friends on the base and a quick bite too eat, he telephoned 15th A.F. Headquarters. M/G Twining was not available so he spoke to Charles Born, Director of Operations. He was told to bring Cantacuzino and get to Ban as soon as possible. It was a one- hour drive to Ban and the planning began that night. The initial phase of the rescue plan was called Operation Gunn. It was laid out on the 28th and begun on the 29th of August 1944. The first phase consisted of sending three P-51s back to the Popesti Airdrome to verify that it was in Rumanian hands and that air evacuation activities could indeed be conducted from there. Capt. Cantacuzino was to fly one of the returning fighters the other two were to be experienced American pilots who would escort him back and be prepared to take whatever action was necessary, in the event there was an attempt at treachery. The two pilots chosen were Lt. Col. William Daniel and Lt. Walter Goehausen both from the 31st fighter Group. They arrived at Ban on the morning of the 28th and, on being advised that they were to participate in a very high risk mission were given the opportunity to opt out. Both immediately agreed to go. Goehausen was given the honor of checking the Rumanian out in the P-51, which of course he had never flown before. Goehausen remembers him as a polished gentleman, and very sharp. When the Lieutenant gave him various airspeeds for gear down, approach, stall, etc., he converted them from miles per hour to kilometers per hour instantly in his head. Goehausen watched his first take off, air work and landing and was mightily impressed. He handled the P-51 on that first flight as if he had been accustomed to flying for a long, long time.

In the course of the many hours that Goehausen spent with the Rumanian ace, he learned something about his background of this former adversary. He remembers him as a darkly handsome man with certain flair. Before the war he had flown transport aircraft of the Rumanian National Airline and was an accomplished acrobatic pilot. By this time he had amassed a great deal of combat time and experience. He stated matter-of-factly that he had engaged in hundreds of air combats and had 64 air victories, including P-38s, B-24s, and B-17s. He seemed to enjoy discussing air tactics with Boehausen and recounted a very tough fight he had with a P-38, and only through luck, finally shot him down. To other interrogators at the 15th AF HQ he mentioned that he commanded the 9th fighter group equipped with the Me-109G and was located at Roman Airdrome near Iassi with fighter units of the Luftwaffe. When the Rumanian capitulation was announced, he kept a nervous eye on the German units occupying the airdrome with him and the next day flew his group to Popesti Airdrome near Bucharest, he lead his group in attacks against the German claiming 12 of the attackers for the group of which four were shot down by him personally. In four days time he had gone from attacking American aircraft to fighting against his former comrades. He was merely a soldier and a patriot he stated, who fought against his country's enemies.

The plan for Operation Gunn was for the two American pilots and Cantacuzino to take off at 0800 on the 29th for Bucharest, Lt. Col. Daniel would lead, the Rumanian would fly his wing and Lt. Goehausen would fly a position on the outside of him, forming a loose echelon

The assigned radio call signs were:

Captain Cantacuzino	call sign - FUNNEL
Lt. Col. Daniel	call sign - NORMAL
Lt. Goehausen	call sign - HOMEMADE

We three were to proceed directly to the Popesti Airdrome where the Rumanian would go in to land. Lt. Goehausen was to provide top cover while Col. Daniel went down and circled at low altitude within visual range of the airdrome, awaiting a signal from the ground. Immediately upon landing, Capt Cantacuzino was to assure that the airdrome was still firmly in the hands of Rumanian forces. Having satisfied himself that this was so, he was to communicate with the waiting P-51s via flares, which had been provided to him for this purpose. The choice of signals was follows:

Double yellow star means the airdrome is held by Rumanian forces and all clear for the B-17's to proceed to land.

Double red star means the situation is unsafe for landing of Allied aircraft.

Single green means stand by for 5 more minutes.

If no signal were received within 15 minutes after he landed, the airborne P-51's would assume that the situation was unsafe for the landing of Allied aircraft. As soon as the signal was received or when 15 minutes had elapsed, whichever occurred sooner, the P-51's were set course for Ban and establish radio contact with "BIG FENCE" on channel "A" as soon as possible. When contact was established with "BIG FENCE" they would use one of the following phrases to indicate the status of the Popesti Airdrome.

The phrase, I have zero six gallons of gas repeat, "zero six" would mean that the Popesti Airdrome was firmly in Rumanian hands and all was clear to dispatch the B-17's.

The phrase "ceiling and visibility zero zero, repeat zero zero" would mean that the situation was unsafe for the landing of Allied aircraft at Popesti and the B-17's were not to be dispatched.

After the participants were briefed on the details of the plan one of the senior staff Colonels took Guehausen aside and told him that if Cantacuzino tried anything funny on the way to Bucharest, he was to shoot him down without further ado. The Lt. confessed afterward that what had seemed like a straightforward order by a staff officer in the HQ at Ban might have proved to be a little harder to accomplish in practice.

All three aircraft were off on time at 8 o'clock and everything proceeded according to plan until they reached their cruising altitude over Yugoslavia. At this point Cantacuzino began sliding out away from Daniel until he was about 100 yards off his wing. Goehausen was puzzled by this odd behavior but quickly slid in behind the Rumanian's P-51 with his sight and gun switches on. Cantacuzino careful not to make any sudden moves that might be interpreted as hostile, fired a short burst from his machine guns and then eased back into his former position, where he continued for the rest of the flight. Since Goehausen never saw him again, he was not able to ask the Rumanian what he was trying to do. However, considering the conditions that existed in Rumania air space at the time, it is not difficult to figure out. He was reviewing the possibilities of encountering the Luftwaff fighters and knowing that the three of them would be in the fight of their lives, began to wonder if he had trusted the loaded guns in the P-51. He found out that he had. Whether this was an oversight by the American personnel or had been done deliberately is anybody's guess now. The rest of the mission went as planned. After landing Cantacuzino gave the "all clear" signal to the circling P-51's who headed back at maximum continuous power until they were in contact with BIG FENCE. They immediately relayed the appropriate coded message, which signaled the

The Me-109 that flew Col. Gunn out of Romania to Cerigola inside of the fuselage, after he was interned in the POW camp

start of the second phase of Operation Gunn.

Meanwhile, as part of the planning for the second phrase, the 5th Bomb Wing had been tasked with sending two B-17's with full combat crews and fuel to Ban earlier that morning to be fitted out to carry personnel and equipment in their bomb bays. Immediately after this installation was completed, the equipment was loaded. At 1000 the crews and passengers were told to stand by at the operations building ready to take off on 30 minutes notice. The passengers, with their equipment were a team of twelve O.S.S men with two radio communication sets and 250 gallons of 100 octane gas for Cantacuzino's P-51. The ranking officer of the party was Col. George Kruger, HQ, and MAAF, who had been previously in charge of a Balkan rescue mission operating with the Chetniks in Yugoslavia.

Soon after the transmission from Daniel and Goehausen was received at 15th AF HQ, the two B-17's were on their way, with escort of 32 P-51's provided by the 305th Fighter Wing. The bombers landed at Popesti at 1530 and were met by Mr. Georgescu. After disgorging their loads, the two aircraft took off at once for the return trip and the O.S.S.

party was taken into Bucharest and set up headquarters in the home of one Demeter Bragadiru at 5 Aleea Mondrogan. For some unexplained reason, the O.S.S. Radios were unable to establish contact with Ban. As a consequence, Capt Cantacuzino was sent to Italy again at 1715 on the 30th with a letter to General Twining assuring him that all was still in readiness for the implementation of the evacuation plan. Operation REUNION II scheduled for the following day and REUNION III for the 3rd of September.

Meanwhile in Bucharest, Col Kraiger undertook to round up all the prisoners and move them to Popesti for the flight out. There were about 800 at the camp near Bragadini, another 110 were at Pietro Sita and an unknown number had taken off on their own and were scattered about the city, a few of them partaking of the new-found Rumanian hospitality. The prisoners, at Pietro Sita were mainly survivors of the 1941 low-level raid which had been held at Tinisul de Jos near Brasov. Admiral Dorman had arranged to move them closer to Bucharest. These American Airmen had a close call en-route, for just as they were leaving the camp they ran into the German Army retreating from Bucharest toward Hungary. Admiral Dorman had arranged to arm the prisoners from a small arsenal at the camp and all were ready, at a signal to fight to prevent their being shot or transported into Germany. They pulled the trucks off the side of the road and prepared to fight for their lives, if necessary. The German convoy, however, rolled on without stopping. The Americans arrived at Pietro Sita at 2300 and were hidden in the homes of Rumanian residents. Arrangements had been worked out ahead of time by the Admiral for the prisoners to be taken, one or two at a time, to the different homes where they were well treated. They were essentially immobilized in Pietra Sita by the steady stream of German troops falling back through the area. Princess Caradya commandeered five trucks, hid the men under blankets and proceeded through the lines with the excuse that she was going to pickup civilians trapped in Bucharest. All 110 prisoners finally arrived at the camp and joined those that had been moved out of Bucharest.

The problem now was to move everyone from the camp to the airdrome early the next morning for the pick-up. Col. Kraiger was able to arrange for the Rumanians to provide 27 buses, which arrived at the camp at 0500 the next morning. By 0600 a large number of men had already been moved the 14 miles to Popesti Airdrome. He sent trucks out to find something to eat for the men while he organized them into groups of 20 placed around the perimeter of the field at 150 foot intervals, so that when the B-17's would arrive at 1000 they could taxi up, to each group of men, load up and take off again with a minimum of delay.

The execution of operation REUNION had been assigned to the 5th Bomb Wing because the B-17 bomb bay doors were strong enough to support the internal racks for transporting the prisoners. The 2nd and 97th Groups were to provide 38 B-17's outfitted with these racks. Two of the aircraft were equipped for litter cases. The plan was for the aircraft to proceed in three separate waves of 12 aircraft each. The first wave was to take off at 0800 with each subsequent wave following at one hour intervals. The fourth wave consisting of; two aircraft fitted with litters was to take off last at 1100. Two doctors were to go in the first wave in order to attend to and prepare the litter patients for transport by the fourth wave.

The Me-109 that Flew Col Gunn out of Romania

The 306th Fighter Wing was responsible for escorting the B-17's and providing adequate cover for them during landing and take off at Popesti Airdrome. The wing was additionally tasked to strafe parked aircraft at an airdrome near Reghin. 94 P-38's of the 1st, 14th and 82nd Fighter Groups and 158 P-51's of the 31st, 325th, and the 332nd were dispatched.

When each wave was about 30 miles from Bucharest, one flight of escorting fighters would leave the bombers and go directly to the Popesti Airdrome. These fighters would look for the same signals from the ground that had been used for Operation Gunn, i.e., a double yellow star was the O.K. signal, a double red was the unsafe signal. Upon receiving the signal, the fighters were to return to the bombers and communicate as follows. A series of small dives and zooms would mean that that it was O.K. to land, rocking the wings followed by a sharp breakaway would mean the bombers were to return to base. If the mission was on, the bombers were to circle to the left with landing gear down while the fighters provided airdrome cover. Landing, loading, and take off were to be accomplished as quickly as possible.

That morning Captain Cantacuzino returned with the fighters and bombers yet again to Popesti. Just before the arrival of the first wave of B-17's, a lone P-51 swept across the field at tree top level, did a perfect aileron roll, pitched out, dropping his gear and flaps and greased the fighter onto the grass field. It was Cantacuzino. Almost immediately thereafter the B-17's appeared and began circling to land. The mission proceeded as planned except for the one B-17, which blew a tire on landing. There was a certain amount of apprehension as the prisoners entered the bomb bays and realized that there were no parachutes for the trip back. Since the alternative was totally unacceptable, they seated themselves on the plywood racks and were soon on their way. The two doctors managed to treat 39 patients at the very poorly equipped and run hospital and to bring all of the patients, 10 litter cases and 29 sitting patients to the airfield in time for the two litter aircraft to take off at 1425. That day a total of 739 prisoners were evacuated.

REUNION II on the following day, the 1st of September, consisted of one formation of 16 B-17's. One suffered a burst wing tank but the aircraft that had blown a tire the previous day took its place. On this phase,

393 prisoners were flown out including 12 walking patients and hospital attendants. On the next day, Col. Kraiger, taking the final steps to wind up the Operation, paid a formal farewell call on Mr. Georgescu, Prime Minister Santanescu, and President Maniu. A few additional stragglers came in that day, some reluctantly leaving the good life they had found several days before when the guards disappeared.

REUNION III was flown by 3 B-17's and 1 C-47 on the 3rd. The C-47 was used to bring a replacement wing panel, strapped beneath the fuselage, and a crew of mechanics to repair the B-17 with the ruptured wing tank. The B-17's with the final 29 POW's and Col. Kraiger on board took off for Italy at 1530 essentially completing the operation. One POW, T/Sgt Peter Tierney, too ill to be moved, was left behind with 2 doctors to attend him. All told, the total operation succeeded in rescuing 1162 men of whom 1127 were Americans, 31 British, 2 were Dutch Naval Officers, 1 was a French Sergeant and 1 was of questionable origin.

Of the Americans, the breakdown by command was as follows: 15th Air Force, 445 Officers and 608 Enlisted men for a total of 1053, 8th and 9th Air Forces, 30 Officers and 44 Enlisted men, for a total of 74.

A committee of 4 Officers from Headquarters, Mediterranean Allied Air Forces was sent to Ban to report on the operation from the 27th of August to the 3rd of September 1944. One of the conclusions of the committee was the "The Fifteenth did a well-nigh perfect job". A simple statement certainly true as far as it went. Perhaps in wartime such an astonishing feat is taken as a matter of course. But how could a relatively low level Command, take upon itself the authority and responsibility for removing 1200 men form a hostile theater in the presence of the enemy and two other national forces of unknown unpredictable intent. Surely the opportunity for disaster lurked everywhere. Losing many aircraft and crews even without 20 prisoners in each was enough to make the most daring of Commanders blanch. But the 15th seized the moment and none were lost.

In five days time the 15th HQ, personnel with an opportunity by Captain Cantacuzino, validated his proposal, did the necessary planning, modified the aircraft, dispatched the forces and equipment and safely evacuated all of the personnel. That the whole incident is a little known footnote to history in the Air War in Europe during WWII testifies to the prodigious feats, which were accomplished routinely with hardly a backward glance. I wonder how many people even have ever heard of this.

I have finally found this history of the Me-109 that landed at our field when I had one more mission to go for my 50 missions. Thanks to my friend L/C Bob Goebel a P-51 ace in Italy during the time I was there and was my top cover on 8 missions with me.

Well it is the 28 August 1944. Today is the day, my last mission. I can hardly believe it. But I am sweating out the target. It is supposed to be a "milk run". When we got to briefing, it doesn't look too bad. We are supposed to bomb bridges in Northern Italy. I remember what happened the last time we tried to bomb bridges.

We put up 31 B-24's and our target is the railroad bridge at Avisio and Pecheria. Their destruction was to disrupt the German retreat but we did not do a very good job. It is hard to hit a bridge from 24,000 feet. When we got there we must have taken them by surprise. It seems we had light "flak" to nothing at all and got away unscathed. It seems the group in back of us got it and one of their B-24's was damaged severely but made it back safely.

We rallied off the target and were homeward bound at speed. When we got home and parked "Organized Confusion" for the last time I scratched my name on the windshield molding before I got out. When we got out Sgt. Merfeld and I got down on our knees and kissed the ground, we had made it! We had our picture taken on our knees holding up the Form one, our flying record for the day, saluting our last mission. We had flown 50 missions in 3 months and two weeks! I had lost 20 pounds.

As it turned out we flew more missions than the rest of the crew that came over together and they still had 4 missions to go. The crew decided they were not going to fly any more missions unless they flew with me. I told them that I would wait for them on the ground until they finished. They all finished up safe and sound except Lt. Don Keegan, my Bombardier, who on his first mission with a new crew took a piece of "flak" in the head that went through his steel helmet and they had to put 16 stitches in his head to patch him up.

Well after finishing my missions the CO asked me if I would like to be Tower Officer in the control tower. They would promote me to Captain and I would not have to fly anymore combat missions. Just fly locally to get my flying time in. I told them that I wanted to fly another tour in a P-38. When I enquired about flying the P-38 with the 1st Fighter Group, near Foggia, they informed me that I would have to go to Alexandria, Egypt to get my gunnery indoctrination, and then go back into combat. I told them I had just finished 50 missions in a B-24 and I wanted 30 days leave before going back into combat so I could go home and visit my wife and my family. I was in the throes of deciding what to do when I got a letter from home. With everyone wanting me to come home they thought that I had enough combat. So I decided to go home and not press my luck. I sure would have liked to be the shooter for a change rather than the "shootee". By the way I remained a 1st Lt. for 5 years. Of course if I took the job as Tower Officer I would have been stuck for the rest of my career and would not have had the wonderful flying jobs I had.

I now had time off since I had finished my missions so I "bummed" a ride to Naples in a B-17 and got to fly co-pilot. It was my first ride in a B-17, quite a "bird". It took only 30 minutes and I was seeing the sights around Naples. I stayed at the GI billets for the five days that I toured the area. I ate eggs and chips, my favorite dish in Italy. I went to Pompeii and to Sorrento and tried to get back to Capri but you need special orders to get there since it was strictly for R&R. I got a chance to go to a few special services shows, USO shows and went dancing at the Officers Club as usual. It was a little better than the one at Foggia. I finally decided it was time to report back to my base so I went to the local military airdrome, Cappuccino Airport and hitched a ride back to my base. This was on 2 Sept 1944.

6 Sept 1944. They needed a pilot to go Rome to pickup some personnel who were getting off R&R and bring them back home. So I volunteered and took Sgt. Merfeld and Sgt. Vincent, who had finished their missions, with me in the old B-24.

We landed at a small strip very close to Rome, which had a lot of assault gliders parked on the base. After I landed the tower directed me where to park on the turf surface. We parked and went into operations to call the troops that their transportation was here to pick them up. We got there early, so no one was ready to until 5pm, it was now noon. We got a ride into town and had lunch and saw a few sights. I rounded up the troops while we were there to make sure everyone was ready to go and we all went out together.

After we pre-flighted the B-24 and everyone was aboard I cranked the old bird up. As the engines were running the tower contacted me to use minimum power taxiing out since all those gliders were directly behind me. He did not want us to blow them over and damage them. As I gave the power to the B-24 I had to make a sharp turn to avoid a building adjacent to our parking area. As I started our turn to avoid the building all of a sudden our left gear went down to the hub of the wheel. We were stuck! It seems that we had bombed this strip and they filled the craters with dirt and did not compact it, so when I started my turn with all the weight of the B-24 it sunk out of sight. We all got out while the emergency crew brought over a Cle-Track. It looked like a tank and tried to pull us out but to no avail. So we all decided to go back to Rome and RON. I informed our operations at home what happened and the crew was trying to get us out by tomorrow. As we left they were in the process of jacking up the aircraft and putting steel planking under the wheel and would get more equipment to pull us out. The next morning after having a nice night visiting all the nightspots in Rome we went out to try and "unstuck" our aircraft.

They had gotten the PSP under the wheel and had dug a small ramp so the wheel could roll up out of the hole. Now the trouble was that the wing tip was almost touching the ground. They brought back the Cle-Track and again gave it a pull but the Cle-Track did not have enough power to get the job done. So they brought in another one! They hooked on and I thought they were going to tear the gear off the B-24. This did not work either. By this time my Sgt.Vincent was getting exasperated with the whole operation. He ran over to one of the operators and took his spot and on his first try pulled us out. It happened that the operators were new to this vehicle and did not know that it had an emergency low gear for just this purpose. Sgt. Vincent was an old hand with type of equipment. There was a big cheer when he pulled the old B-24 out

We all climbed aboard and I cranked her up again and taxied out and took off. We had quite a few people aboard, about 30 people. I knew we were loaded because my tail skid was touching the ground as we taxied out. We made it home safe and sound and everyone was glad they did not have to ride in a 6X6 GI truck back home.

7 Sept 1944. I made two round trips to Rome today taking personnel up and bringing people back. I got 3+30 hours of flying time already for the month of September. When I got through I had my orders to return home. I had to go to the replacement depot first in Naples to await further transportation orders to the States. I was to arrive no later than 10 September 1944. I think I got two days travel time.

I got my gear all packed and did not even know who was going to get my tent. Lt. Scott had been my roommate; he was a Navigator from Texas. I had fixed up the tent very nice. Board floors, chest of drawers, mattress on my cot, etc. I packed a lot of stuff in my foot locker that would go by surface vessel. I stuffed my B-4 bag with all my uniforms and my short coat. I had a large manila envelope with all my records and my 201 files, plus my G.I.45 Colt automatic under my leather jacket.

I said "Good Bye" to all the troops, which were few since our rate of attrition was 100% turn over in a year. In addition I said "Good Bye" to all my friends in the Photo Lab who did all the pictures for me. Just before I was about to leave I saw Lt. Lou Nixon, who got shot off my wing with Maj. Langford near Brenner Pass on our way home from one of our missions. They had evaded and escaped from Yugoslavia, and were air lifted to our base by a C-47 by the English. He was reported missing in action and he wanted me to tell his wife he was OK. She lived in Pacific Palisades, California. I assured him I would do this and left the area.

When I reached Naples replacement depot everybody was living in tents at a large racetrack north of Naples. It was quite a ways out of town as I recollected, since I walked it one night. We had the run of the place but were supposed to check in every day to see if our orders were up to go home. So I went off to town and lived it up. Saw all the USO shows, went to all the Red Cross dances, chased all the girls and had a ball.

It was hard to find a place to stay over night in Naples. The locals were not supposed to rent to any military personnel due to security. So if I couldn't find a place I would have to go back to the "repple depot", I did not like that. I think I only had to go back once. I met a little Scottish girl from Edinburgh; she worked at the Red Cross officers Club. She was very nice to me and put me up for a few 'nights. She was also a great dancer. (I was a rascal!) She wanted to marry me and have me take her back to the states.

18 September 1944. I finally got my orders to leave for the States. It was by air! I had heard through the grapevine that anyone who was awarded the Distinguished Flying Cross would fly home. I had the DFC, and the Air Medal with 3 oak leaf clusters, the ETO Ribbon with 6 battle stars and also the Presidential Unit Citation. It seems the rest of the troops took the boat.

We flew in an old "Gooney Bird", C-47, to Oran, Algeria and then to Casablanca, Morocco. When we got there they put us in a compound and we were not allowed to leave. It was nice quarters compared to what we were used to staying in. We could not get out to see the city or the sights I guess they were afraid we would get our throats cut if we went into town since the place was overrun with German agents and wild Arabs.

The place had a big courtyard inside with horseshoe pits. I have always been a horseshoe pitcher and played with an old fighter pilot, Serverio Martino from Framingham, N.Y. He flew P-47's.

I can't remember how long we stayed at this place but on the 23rd September I celebrated my 29th birthday there. We managed a little party after playing horseshoes all day. We went to the makeshift bar and had a little booze, which was in the compound.

25 September 1944. I finally arrived back in the good old USA by C-54, from Casablanca to the Azores, to Newfoundland, to La Guardia Airport New York City. On the way the pilot asked me if I wanted to fly the C-54. So I went up to the cockpit and flew the old "Bird" for an hour, so I got a little C-54 time.

We were billeted at Fort Totten, N.Y., and had the run of New York City. So off to New York City with another fighter pilot who flew P-38's, named Capt. Hod Meyers. We went our own way and I got a room in a hotel near Times Square. I went out on the town and met a girl. I took her to dinner at a nearby restaurant, which was having a dance contest. Well we won it and got our dinner free and tickets to the Latin Quarter.

The next night I went dancing to Woodie Herman at the Pennsylvania Hotel. Girls were plentiful for our boys in Uniform who were fighting the war. Especially the ones with those silver wings on their uniforms. Somehow I lost my hat in all the living it up, so the next day I went to Bonds, a clothing store at Times Square and bought a new one. To this day, every time I see a picture of Times Square I look for Bonds.

I finally had to report to number one Park Avenue to get my Transportation Request (TR) to get me to the Reception Center at Monterey, California. I was supposed to go by train and my reporting date was 2 October 1944. As I was standing in line I saw a Colonel go through a door to another room and I heard him request air transportation to California by American Airlines. So I walked in and asked the Sgt., at the desk for the same thing. I got it without a bit of hesitation. So off I went to American Airlines while all the rest of the troops were taking the train!

It was an old C-54 and it had trouble so we had to land at Washington, D.C. We had to RON here until they could fix the trouble. We were off the next day for Burbank, California. As I was getting my baggage I ran into an old friend, who I hadn't seen in years. It was Harry Mundy, who was a Navy Pilot Lt. Jg. Same equivalent rank as a 1st Lt. my rank. We went to San Mateo Jr. College together and belonged to the Junior Birdmen Of America, which I was commander of our squadron. We made many model airplanes together. We reminisced until my transportation arrived to take me to Hollywood. I made a visit to an old friend before leaving for Monterey.

4 October 1944. Left for Monterey in another commercial DC-3 to Sacramento with a stop at San Francisco. On landing at San Francisco I was told that I would have to get off. It seemed that I did not have a high enough priority after fighting in the war and surviving 50 combat missions some "feather merchant" had a higher priority! I could not believe my ears after flying all the way from Naples, Italy and now I could not make the last short leg of about 45 minutes to Sacramento. My Mom And Dad with my wife Florence were waiting for me at Sacramento. I was a little perturbed, to say the least, since there was no aircraft available until the next day. They were waiting for my call to tell them where to meet me.

I took a Taxi to 3rd and Townsend Street for the train station and when I got there they were filled up. I then took another Taxi to the Greyhound Bus station. Got a ticket and they took my B-4 Bag. I called home and told them that to meet me at the Bus station in Sacramento. They put my B-4 bag aboard the bus and I was standing to get on but being polite I let the ladies on first. When I went to get on they said that there was no more seats left for me that I would have to wait until tomorrow! By this time I was fuming and I was in a rage. They went off with my bag and I got another Cab and had him take me out to the on ramp to the Bay Bridge. By this time it was dark and I started to hitchhike, which was against all rules and regulations for a 1st. Lt. in Uniform to do.

I was only out on the road a few minutes before a young fellow picked me up. My luck was changing he was going to Sacramento and would drop me off at the Bus station. Well we beat the bus in by a half hour! Since there were no freeways in those days we were really going. He was a "hot rodder" and I was hanging on and praying that we would make it.

He let me out at the Bus station and I thanked him. I walked into the station and saw my wife and my folks looking out toward the Bus entrance. I sneaked up in back of them. They of course were elated to see me. After hugging and kissing my Mother said that I looked like a movie star in my tailored Palm Beach Uniform with a sharp looking battle jacket. I had all my ribbons on with my silver wings along with my 15th Air Force Patch. I have to admit I did look sharp, weighing only about 125 pounds by this time.

I related all my experiences upon getting home and thanked the Lord I made it. I guess I hadn't been home for more than a week when Florence told me she wanted a divorce! That is why she wanted me home. She said that she did not want to tell me while I was still flying combat. That was thoughtful of her. It seems she had met someone else. I guess I was too much for her. It was not too much of a blow to me. She did not want any children and I always wanted a family. After hearing this news I said goodbye and took my old Ford V8 1936 convertible and was off. I stayed with my folks for about two weeks

During this time we visited all the Hitchcock family, which was on my mother's side, who had not seen me in quite a while. I found out that my cousin Jack Sankuhle had been killed in the South Pacific at New Guinea, when the ammunition-ship they were unloading came under attack by the Japanese and exploded. My cousin Richard Gratton was a doctor aboard a Navy ship some where in the South Pacific. I think Jack was an ensign in the Navy.

While I was visiting my folks I went to visit McClellan Army Air Base, where I used to work and saw a few people that were not in the service, I used to work with. Also I visited the 1830 Pratt and Whitney overhaul shop. My Father was the Chief Inspector for these engines. He took me up and down each row to meet the mechanics that were working on them. Introducing me to each one and telling them that I was the reason he was so "hard nosed" on his inspections. I was flying a B-24, which used 4 of these engines on it. He was really proud of me and I loved my Dad. In fact one of the engines came to the 454th Group with my Dads stamp on the yellow tag! Flying combat our lives depended on our engines.

After staying with my folks I was off to San Francisco to see all my old buddies and friends. Now I was "foot loose and fancy free" I made it a point to have a ball. I looked up one of my friends that acted in my movie that I made when I was a member of the Sherman Clay Camera Club, Mr. and Mrs. Hohn. I had used their home as the place to shoot my movie. I found that Mr. Hohn had cancer of the stomach and was in very bad shape Dollie his wife was a very happy person and we always had a good time with her. I asked her if she would like to go dancing at the Fairmont Hotel. Her husband urged her to go since she had not gone anywhere since he became ill. We had a great time. She was an excellent dancer. She could not get over me since she always considered me as a youngster. She was only 3 years older than me.

Well after painting the town red, I had to get to the reassignment center at Santa Monica. So off I went in my fast Ford to Southern California. I got there early and had a ball in Hollywood. I had known a lot of people while I was a Cadet. I looked them up, mostly the opposite sex, and had a real great time. The war was still on so we had to wear our uniform at all times and it was a mark of a hero for the ones who survived the war and was home. The women were plentiful, especially to the pilots with those silver wings. I made all the night clubs in Hollywood and went to my old hangout at Olivera Street in Los Angeles. I went to the La Golandrina and the El Paseo Mexican restaurants and the rest of the clubs on the street. I used to go there when I was a Cadet. I would go back to this place for years to come and am still going there with my grandchildren.

26 Oct 1944. Finally it was time to get to Santa Monica and get my new assignment. I was assigned to Victorville AAB, California. That wasn't too bad; I would be close to Hollywood and could live it up on weekends.

3 Nov 1944. I arrived at Victorville AAB, California, and signed in. They gave me my quarters an old GI barracks with open bays a two-story job. There were only 10 of us in it so far. I was assigned as a B-24 pilot but I had no love for big airplanes and never flew a B-24 again. I got my flying time in an AT-11 and an AT-7 both trainers for bombardiers and Navigators. They were made by Beech. It seemed like we were just killing time until a new assignment came out. I wanted to go to the South Pacific and fly P-38's but my request was turned down. It seemed I had a letter in my 201 file that stated that I would be better off to go to instructing since I had such a rugged tour in Italy, and should not be assigned to further combat. So that stopped my tour as a fighter pilot.

All we had to do at Victorville was check the bulletin board daily for any assignment, or had a duty. I suggested to some of my new friends that we ride up to Big Bear for the weekend and live it up and chase the girls. It was so nice there and at lake Arrowhead that we got a couple of Lt. friends at the base to check the bulletin board everyday for us, and stayed up at Big Bear and Arrowhead.

One night we went dancing to Anson Weeks, a well-known band at that time, I thought the female vocalist sounded familiar. As I looked at her from a distance she looked familiar, also. As I danced I got close to the bandstand and sure enough it was a girl I used to compete with in the amateur programs around San Francisco, during the 1930s. We sang a lot of songs competing with each other on the same programs. It depended on the whims of the audience, who would win. Sometimes I won and other times she would win. She was now singing for Anson Weeks and married to the Bass player.

After she got through singing and the Band stopped for an intermission I walked up to the bandstand. The minute she saw me she recognized me, even in my uniform. I had not seen her since 1936. She had a terrific voice. Her name was Caroline Hauk and now it was 1944. I used to date her and ride her on my motorcycle. Her mother always said that she was 16 years old but she was 14 at the time. She introduced me to the band and wanted to know if I was still singing. Just for my own pleasure I told her...We jabbered about old times until she had to get back on the job. They would be there for only three days, so that ended that, I haven't seen her since.

We had quite a time at Big Bear and Arrowhead but it was now getting old. I wanted to get back to flying and get a good assignment. I went to the assignment Officer and asked if there were any schools open that I could qualify for. He found that I had the necessary qualifications to go the Armament School at Lowery Field, Denver, Colorado. I told him I would take it just to get out of here. I was also told that if I were among the top of the class it would be a step to making regular officer in the Army Air Corps. I got my orders on 16 Jan 1945. In the meantime I was back to Hollywood living it up. Then I had 3 days left I went up to see my folks and tell them about my new assignment.

While I was visiting, my folks introduced me to the girl next door. Her husband was in the Navy on a ship somewhere in the South Pacific and she was home alone. I did not think much about it at the time but it seemed she went for men in uniform. Her name was Irene Nielson. I did not know it at the time but she was a Mormon (Latter Day Saint) I of course did not know anything about the church then. Little did I realize that some day I would be a member and go through the temple in Los Angeles, Ca.

16 Jan 1945. I got my orders for Armament School but instead of Lowery Field it was to Buckley Field, about 10 miles east of Denver. I loaded up the old 1936 Ford Convertible Coupe with all my gear and went back home to see my folks again. They lived on Jasmine Street in Del Paso Heights just east of Sacramento near McClelland Field the Army Air Depot. I had 13 days delay en-route to get to Denver, so I had some time to spend with my folks before leaving for my new assignment.

While I was home my Dad tuned up the old Ford so it would run good on my trip to Denver. My Dad was an excellent mechanic. He had that fine touch and insight when it came to repairing automobiles. I would inherit his mechanical abilities and would teach Auto Mechanics at Manual Arts High School in Los Angeles after I retired from the Air Force. I would repair all my Daughters cars at one time or another through the years.

I went around seeing all the relatives and saying good bye again. I took Irene Nielson to San Francisco to see the sights. Went to see my Uncle

Sgt Merfield and Lt. Bill Disbrow. We just finished our 50 missions

Edwin Hitchcock and his wife Marie to show him my car, and to show him that it was still running after the last time I was there and blew a valve spring at 100 mph. My uncle Edwin was a speed merchant, and liked fast cars. After I got back from combat I had a fellow put a 49S Ford block in the 1936, which was a Mercury 1941 engine. I had it all "souped" up to go fast and it did. So when I visited him the first time he wanted to see how fast the car would go. Well we went out on the March Creek Road, near Concord, California, and proceed to roar down it at 100mph when I broke the valve spring. The next day I took it to J.W. McAllisters, where I used to work in San Francisco. I knew almost everybody there so Duke the shop foreman took the car upstairs to the shop and had it going before I knew it. This made me happy that they had fixed it so quickly as well as the price they charged me, which was nominal. They would do anything for me since I was in uniform.

After living it up for a week or so, I decided it was time for me to head for Denver. In the meantime a friend of the folks needed a ride to Denver, so I took him along. On the way he was telling me how fast he made it to Denver in his Century Buick. Well he should not have bragged about it because I showed him some real speed. We were cruising 100mph all the way through Nevada since in those days there was no speed limit. I think I made it at least two hours faster than he did. He was quite impressed with the old Ford.

We stopped for gas at a lonely gas station somewhere near Elko, Nevada, to refuel. As we were coming out of the station I noticed a girl hitchhiking. It was now getting dark and the temperature was about 32 degrees. Naturally I stopped for her and put her in the middle of us in the front seat. I immediately noticed that she was pregnant and at least 7 months along. She wasn't much over 21 years old if she was that. She told us that she was headed for Chicago. It seems her boyfriend had deserted her so home was the only place to go. She had no money and there was no welfare in those days. I told her I would gladly take her as far as Denver, which was as far east as I was going, even if it was a little crowed in the front seat of the Ford. I had a rumble seat but it was too cold for anybody to be riding there, besides it was full of my gear.

We made Salt Lake City in nothing flat and stayed over night there. I paid for her room and her meals, since I felt so sorry for her. We were up at the crack of dawn the next day and were off to Denver. I took US40 highway, which went out of Salt Lake City to Steamboat Springs, Rabbit Ears Pass, and Berthoud Pass. Little did I know that I would be climbing up to 11,000 feet to get over the Rockies through a blinding snowstorm. The reason I was going this way was because I had goofed off too long in Sacramento and this was the shortest way to Denver and my new assignment.

As we climbed the Rockies everything was great until I was climbing Berthoud Pass. I had no chains and the road was covered with about 3 inches of snow, which was icy. Also I did not have any anti-freeze in the radiator. I did have a winter cover for the front of the grill to keep the engine warm so our heater would work in this cold weather.

We must have been about ten miles from the summit when I hit a slick spot while making a climbing turn in the road. I immediately spun out as I made the turn. Luckily I spun to the inside of the turn and went into the bank backwards. I would not be here if it had gone the other way over the side. It was a long drop into oblivion.

We got out and let the girl drive as my friend and I pushed the car out of the bank. We went back down the hill to get a running start to make the grade. While we were trying to get the car out of the snow bank the radiator froze and it started to boil. I closed up the radiator cover and let the engine cool down and then started stuffing snow into the radiator. It finally thawed out and we were on our way again.

All this time from Steamboat Springs we had not seen one car coming or going our way. In fact traffic was very sparse since we had left Salt Lake City. In these days people did not use this road much in the wintertime especially when it was snowing and it was at night.

We finally made it over Berthoud Pass and were heading down hill toward Denver when my lights started to dim. I then noticed that my generator had stopped charging at low speed. I was being very cautious not to get too much speed on this slippery road and at the speed we were going the generator could not keep up with the load of the lights and the heater going. I put the Ford in second gear to get more RPM to keep the generator charging enough to give us brighter lights. We did not have very bright lights in cars in those days anyway. I was doing about 40mph going down this snow covered road and being very cautious in the turns. We finally made it into Denver that night and got a couple of rooms and "sacked out". I was bushed.

The next day I paid for the rooms and bid my hitchhiking girl friend farewell, after giving her five dollars and wishing her luck. I then dropped my friend off at his destination.

28 Jan 1945. Got to Buckley Field in time and signed in. I got my quarters; an old GI tarpaper barracks with a pot-bellied stove in the center of the bay. I knew I was not going to stay in it very long. Quarters for Officers in those days were something to be desired.

24 Jan 1945. We started school and to me it was going to be quite easy if you did a little studying and memorization. Some of us could not stand the tar paper barracks that we were in so we decided to move into Denver to the Shirley Savoy Hotel, which was in downtown and convenient to everything. We pooled our transportation so all of us did not have to drive every day and shared the gas. We could also study as a group on the way to Buckley Field, asking each other questions to cover the daily subjects.

We went to school from 0800 to 1600 hours daily except for Saturdays, Sundays, and Holidays. So we had quite a lot of free time, which we spent flying, seeing the sights, skiing, and chasing the girls. We would hit the Shirley Savoy Bar for a cool beer every day after school for a little R and R after a crushing day at school.

I was on per diem but it was not enough to quite cover my expenses, it never did, but we were having a ball. Denver was noted for being a servicemens town and we were proving it.

While I was at school I managed to go for a weekend to a Dude Ranch in the Rockies and rode horseback all over the ranch. We ate at a large community table for our meals, which were great. It reminded me of the time I used to ride horseback to see my girlfriend when we had our large ranch in Westley, California. We also went to Colorado Springs to see Pikes Peak and visit the Garden of the Gods. We were always doing something, which made the time fly by.

Getting our flying time in consisted of flying some old BT-13's. There were old basic trainers that I flew as a Cadet. I flew these for about three months and then we got some old AT-6's. I was eager to fly one since I did not get a chance to fly one when I was a Cadet. I always wanted to fly everything I could get my hands on. The AT-6 had a 600 hp engine on it and it performed much better than the BT-13. It also had a retractable gear, which made it a little faster. It was also a good acrobatic airplane so we could "rat race" all over the sky like good fighter pilots. They had a P-38 in the hanger that I wanted to fly but they never got the thing in commission while I was there. We did have one P-38 pilot in our class but he did not seem very interested in flying it.

While I was at Buckley Field my wife Florence got her final decree for our divorce so now I was really a free man and glad of it. I had been corresponding with Eileen Nielson in Sacramento. She lived next door to my folks in Del Paso Heights, California. After about three months she decided to come out to visit me. She took the train from Sacramento to Denver, where I met her.

At the time I was sharing a room with my friend Capt. Paul Warf from Oklahoma City who was going to school with us. We moved into a less expensive place to conserve our finances. So when Eileen got there she moved in with me in a new room in the same hotel. In the meantime Germany surrendered so the war in Europe was over. Now we had to get the Japanese to surrender and we would be through fighting.

So while I was at school Eileen got herself a job so she would not become bored. We took many trips skiing and to Este National Park. We made all the parties at the Officers Club. Little did I know at the time that she had been married in Mormon Temple (The Church of Jesus Christ of Latter-day Saints). In fact I did not know anything about the Mormons except that the early church members had a lot of wives. It seems I had been involved with a few other Mormon girls at one time or another and did not know it until later. One thing I do know they were the always best looking in the crowd. I did not know much about formal religion at the time except that God is love.

Eileen and I had a great time while we were together in Denver. I gave her her first airplane ride in a B-13. I gave her a tour of the Rocky Mountains, which were beautiful at the time, with snow on their peaks.

In the meantime, I was doing well in school in fact I was top man in the class. I was still getting my flying time in the BT-13 and the AT-6. Then one day I was taking off in an old AT-6 when the impeller in the supercharger broke just as I picked up the landing gear. The engine just about quit and was running on about 4 cylinders out of the 9 it had. It sounded to me that it was running too rich, so I began to lean the mixture out with the mixture control. As I did this it began to run a little better enough to maintain about 500 feet of altitude in the pattern, which I had. I limped around the pattern and called the tower that I had an emergency and they called back that I was on fire as black smoke started coming out of the cowling and enveloping the cockpit. By this time I was on the final approach and had my gear down to land.

I got the aircraft on the ground and the fire trucks were chasing me down the runway. The AT-6 started to slow down as I was trying to stop short for the fire trucks, they pulled up along side of me to hit it with the foam, just as I was getting out. I jumped out on the wing as the AT-6 was still rolling slowly and jumped off the wing just as the fire trucks hit the aircraft with the foam. The parachute hit me in back of my leg and threw me off balance so when I landed I twisted my knee and fell down. I did not think too much of it at the time so Eileen and I went to a dance at one of Denver's Parks. Well after dancing it up until late that night I woke up the next morning with a knee as big as a balloon and could hardly walk. Eileen drove me to the Base Hospital and they put me there for a week with water on the knee. They had to tap my knee to get the water out. After I got out of the hospital I had to be very careful when I walked. I got back on flying status immediately but could not go dancing for quite a while.

One day when I was crossing the street in Denver, I stepped off the curb wrong and fell down in the street, very embarrassing especially in uniform and the Cop was thinking I was drunk. I told him I just had a trick knee. Years later I would have a little arthritis in this knee, but it did not stop me from skiing or dancing.

Well the last three months of school went by in a hurry. In the meantime Eileen went home after getting a letter from whom I did not know or what it contained but off she went back to Sacramento. I found out later from my mother that it was from an old boy friend and she went back home to be with him.

After Eileen had her sojourn with her boyfriend she came back to me in Denver. It would be about two weeks before I graduated from Armament School. I graduated with a 4.0 grade average, which was tops in the class and one of the highest grade attained at the school since it was started. I was quite proud and the CO of the school, Major West, congratulated me and stated that if I tried to make regular Officer in the Army Air Force my stay and my grades at the school would help a lot. He also gave me a very fine recommendation.

Before leaving school one day I had this other Officer that drove a new Chrysler Convertible who was always talking down my 1936 Ford V8 Convertible. So when we got out of school one afternoon we all jumped in our cars and headed for Denver. As we left the gate at Buckley the Chrysler was ahead of me with a full load of Officers in the car. The road to Denver was a two lane in those days but the only traffic on it was base traffic. I pulled up and passed the Chrysler and pulled in and then he passed me with them all waving at me like I was never going to catch them. Well that did it, I quickly accelerated up in back of them and when we got to sixty mph I pulled along side of them and shifted into second gear and accelerated to 80mph and left them with their mouths hanging open. They never did catch us. I had Capt. Warf with me, which gave him a real thrill. The old Ford would really go. Always on the edge.

The next day this lst Lt. who owned the Chrysler wanted to know what I had in the Ford because no 1936 Ford could go by him like I did. I lifted up the hood on the old Ford and all you could see was an old flat head engine with a single carburetor. He could not see the inside of the engine, which contained a ¾ race camshaft, ported, polished, high compression heads, a 1941 Mercury 49A block with more cubic inches than a stock Ford block. I guess it gave the engine over 150 hp instead of the original 100hp. He never said a thing about my old Ford again.

10 June 1945. Eileen and I had a leisurely trip back to Del Paso Heights, California. I had gotten 10 days travel time plus 10 days leave after attending school.

On arriving home my folks, Eileen, and myself decided to take a few days vacation together and we went to Lake Tahoe, California. In all my travels this was one of the most beautiful places in the world. Did a little fishing, swimming, and just relaxing.

I wanted to marry Eileen but she did not want to divorce her husband who was overseas at the time. Deep down I think she did not want to divorce him since they were married in the Mormon Temple. So I let it got at that. My Mother did not think it was such a good idea since she saw how she carried on with her boyfriend when she came home from Denver after receiving a letter from him.

With my leave over I bade everyone farewell and headed back to Victorville Army Air Base, California, my home station. I reported in and got my old BOQ back. A lot of new troops were there from all over so I suggested they let me show them Hollywood and all the girls and bright lights. So after getting all settled down, off we went to Hollywood. Our first stop was the Melody Lane Cocktail lounge at Hollywood and Vine streets. We all ordered beer and looked the crowd over. The place was packed with servicemen and girls. I noticed a very good-looking girl come in and sit down and ordered a drink of some kind. She was the prettiest thing I had seen since going to Hollywood. I then noticed a Marine enlisted man starting to harass her. I could not hear the conversation but the girl got up and went by me to the restroom. The place was very crowded so she had to squeeze by me as I was standing at the Bar. When she came back I asked her, "If the Marines had the situation well in hand?" She said, "No". I then asked her if she would like to get out of this place and to go to the Beverly Hills Hotel. This place in Hollywood or Beverly Hills is where all the Movie Stars hung out. It was quite exclusive in those days but not too expensive for a single 1st Lt. on flight pay. She said that she was ready to get out of there so off we went leaving my friends with their mouths open and leaving them in the wilds of Hollywood for their first time there.

This gorgeous creature would eventually be the Mother of all my four wonderful children, Dorothy Fay Cox. She had just gotten off from dance rehearsal at Earl Carroll's Night Club on Sunset Blvd. and stopped in to call her mother at the Melody Lane Restaurant. All the phones were busy at that time so she came in and sat down to wait for one of the phones and have a little refreshment at the same time. This is when the Marine accosted her, but the Army Air Force came to the rescue.

We went to the Beverly Hills Hotel Lounge and then I drove her home all the way to Torrance, California. It was a long way in those days since there were no freeways. When we got there Fay introduced me to her Mother Gladys Cox and her Brother Bob. Her father was at work at Columbia Steel in Torrance. I made a date with her for the next weekend for a big party at the Base Officers Club at Victorville AAB.

When I got back to Victorville all the fellows had made it back safe and sound and were surprised to see me leave the bar in Hollywood so quickly with the prettiest girl in the place, with a touch of class

Well I picked up Fay in Torrance on Saturday and off we went to the Base at Victorville. It was about 100 miles from Torrance and being no freeways we had to take surface streets all the way. There were quite a few traffic signals along the way so we could not make very good time until we got out of the Los Angeles area. Then we began to cruise. I had the old Ford all cleaned up and shined so it was quite an eye catcher in those days. The Officers Club party was a huge success and the band was great. We danced until the wee hours of the morning. Fay was a fantastic dancer and we got along great. She wore a red formal that made her look like a Starlet from Hollywood. In fact she was the prettiest thing there. I had to chase the other officers away. I was very much impressed with her by the time we got back to Torrance. The only thing to mar a perfect weekend she got sick on the way home. She must have got something that did not agree with her at Buffet the night before. As I raced to get her to a gas station a motorcycle cop pulled in right behind me and asked me what the big hurry was. I must have been doing 60mph and told him Fay was sick as she jumped out of the car and headed for the restroom. He did not give me a ticket but told me to slow down. Being in uniform helped. We were going to have another date but when I got back to the base I had orders transferring me to Dalhart AAB, Texas, the following week. In the meantime I called Fay on the phone and gave her the bad news, just when we were getting to know each other.

21 July 1945. Off I went to Dalhart, Texas, to my new assignment. I loaded up the old Ford with all my gear in my B-4 bag and away I went. I took route 66 to Flagstaff, Albuquerque, and to Tucumcari. Here I turned off to Dalhart on a dirt road. I wondered what adventure this new assignment would bring. This would be my first assignment in Texas.

I found the base and went in and signed in. It was not very big but had all the necessities. I signed in for my quarters and unloaded my gear. I got cleaned up and preceded to town to see what it had to offer. As I was going out the gate I noticed a girl walking on the side of the road toward the gate to the base. I stopped and asked her if she wanted a ride she got in and was very grateful that I stopped for her. She had just terminated her job at the Base and was leaving the state for a new job. On the way to her house I asked her if she would like to go to dinner with me and show me the town. She agreed and I waited for her to get ready and we went off for dinner. We had a very nice evening together and she showed me all the very limited places to go. It was a very small town. I took her home and thanked her for a very nice evening and that was the last time I would see her. She was gone the next day.

I was assigned to the Bombsight section under a Capt. Buckley. There was not much to do since the war was now winding down in the South Pacific. Dalhart AAB had a lot of old B-29's to ferry to a sub base for storage. I hated big airplanes but this was the only thing they had at present to get my time in.

One day on the line I saw a Bell King Cobra P-63 fighter aircraft sitting on the ramp. I immediately asked who owned the aircraft and could I fly it? The Operations Officer told me to go ahead. So I read the Dash One (Operational Instructions) after which I got myself a parachute and got in and cranked up after giving myself a cockpit check. I taxied out and was running up the engine and checking the magnetos when I got a call form the tower to return to the line immediately. I then began to wonder whose airplane I had stolen. I taxied back to the line and was greeted by the maintenance Officer. The P-63 had a red-bordered tech order on this airplane to check the main spar for cracks before flying it again. They took it in the hanger and I found out later that it had cracks in the wing spar.

These are radial cracks around the wing bolts due to using a dull drill when they drilled the holes or just metal fatigue. I was going to handle it very gently anyway. It would have been my first flight in and operational WWII fighter, I was bound that I was going to fly a combat fighter.

In the meantime, I was corresponding with Fay and she had called me on VJ day to share my joy that the war was over. The 14th of August 1945.

I got a call from Fay that she was in Amarillo, Texas, so I dashed down to pick her up. She had to get a room in a Hotel before I got there. She had asked someone where to stay and she got very bad advice. When I got there I had her get here gear together and I moved her out and got a place in the best place in town. When we went to the Officers Club on the Base she created quite a stir. She was the prettiest thing ever to hit this part of the country. All the Bachelor Officers were drooling. One night I won $64 playing Bingo, so we celebrated my good luck.

Since there was not much to do on the Base since the war was now over and we had delivered all the B-29's to storage I could get off quite regularly. So Fay and I went to Eagles Nest in the Mountains of New Mexico for a weekend. It was a small summer resort in those days near Taos, NM. It was about 100 miles from Dalhart. After two weeks Fay had to go back to California, so off she went after I took her to catch the train at Amarillo, I knew I was going to miss her.

So with nothing much to do on the Base after Fay left, I decided to start a Base football team. I put a notice in the Daily bulletin and on the Bulletin board for all interested personnel to sign up in the Gym. There was lots of interest. So I got a B-17 to fly down to Lubbock, Texas, where they had a lot of surplus football gear, and loaded up and flew it all home.

16 Oct 1945. I was put on orders as the assistant Coach of the Dalhart AAB, football team. They made a Captain head coach even though it was my idea. We had a great time and it made a lot of the troops happy. I got to fly the team with a Major pilot in the B-17 to the football games. We did not play too many games but had a lot of fun. We played Nebraska State Teachers, at Kearny, NE., and Canyon City State Teachers College, Texas.

I no longer had something interesting to do than I got orders to transfer me to Colorado Springs, Colorado for recruiting duty. I was fortunate to have been asked if I would like the assignment. I jumped at the chance to get out of Dalhart. Where the only thing between you and the North Pole was a three-strand barbed wire fence and two strands were down on it. It was really out in the "Boondocks".

In the meantime, before I got my orders I built a water injection system for the old Ford. It was so high compression and the gas we were getting was so pour that it was "pinging" on fast acceleration. The water injection stopped this. In fact a Taxi cab started to race with me one day coming out of the Base at Dalhart. I whipped him so badly and so quickly he stopped me and asked what I had under that hood. The water helped very much. Always on the edge.

So I loaded up the old Ford again and was off to Colorado Springs. It was now 9 Nov. 1945 and I would sign in the 10 Nov. 1945 to my new assignment to the recruiting section. My Boss was Col. Irving (Twig) Branch, an ex AVG pilot He explained that now that the war was over everyone was getting out of the service and his job was to try and keep as many in the service as possible. They were depleting the greatest fighting force ever seen in history. Before the war ended they had a system of points you received for combat duty, overseas duty, medals, etc., added up to a certain number. If you had that total or more you could request a discharge, if you were not key personnel, you could be discharged. Now that the war was over one did not need the points. Just request a discharge and you were out.

My job was to give lectures at all the mid-west Bases in the Base Theater on the advantages of staying in the military and the benefits of the retirement system, also, schools available and Air Mission duty, etc. I did a lot of research before I tried to persuade anyone to stay in the military, especially in the Army Air Force.

I started ferrying around recruiting teams in a C-45. Later they got me a B-17 with it being painted with all the Air Force Insignia's on the sides of the aircraft and the name "The Volunteer" was painted on the nose.

The way I got checked out in the B-17. They needed someone to take a recruiting team to Deming, N.M. Col Branch called me into his office and asked me how much first pilot I had in a B-17. I answered, "None". Then he asked me how much four- engine time I had and I replied "That I had 575 hours at the time". He then told me he wanted me to take a team to

Deming, NM. in the B-17. I then asked who my co-pilot was. I found out that the co-pilot was a fighter pilot and had never been in a B-17. Well we got out to Peterson Field where the B-17 was parked, got the team aboard, climbed in ourselves, and proceed to ask the crew chief, "How do you start this thing?" That was the crowning blow just like a cartoon. He helped us get cranked up and we taxied out. Takeoff was no sweat, just like the B-24, and away we went to Deming. When we got there I forgot I was flying a tail-dragger and proceeded to land it like B-24 and bounced it, needless to say what goes up must come down and I made a great recovery.

The team got out and booed me for my landing; little did they know that was my first landing in a B-17. By now it was getting dark. My second landing would be a night landing. I knew the Crew Chief was in a state of "shock" by now. No problem when we got back to Colorado Springs, I paid attention to what I was doing on the landing and greased it in, with a big sigh from the Crew Chief. In those days a pilot was supposed to be able to fly anything if he had enough nerve and I would fly anything they would let me.

It was my job to ferry the teams around the Bases in the mid and southwest. I went to Pratt AAF, Kan., Hanford AAF, Neb., McCook, AAF, Neb., Deming AAF, NM Great Bend AAF., Kan., Albuquerque, AAF, NM. Sioux City, AAF., Iowa., Wendover AAF., Utah., La Hunta AAF., Colo., and Sioux Falls AAF, S,D.

Later they took the B-17 away and gave me the C-45 again. It seemed the B-17 was too expensive to operate for the results we were getting. So I had a 1st Lt. and a master Sergeant with me when I got up to give my talks. We all gave our opinion on staying in the Army Air Force and answered the questions anyone asked. I had the authority to call on the Base Commander at the Bases where we stopped and get authorization to speak to the troops in the Base Theater.

I remember one trip we had to make on the train due to weather. A GI got drunk and was causing a disturbance on the train. I was the only Officer aboard the train. This GI was trying to beat up the Conductor. They called me to break it up due to my rank, but the GI was really drunk. With the help of some of the troops we subdued him and handed him over to the MPs at the next stop. Never a dull moment, especially when you are the only

Officer aboard. This would happen again in Japan a few years later.

In the meantime, I was calling and corresponding with Fay. During the Thanksgiving Holidays I dashed out from Colorado Springs to California to see her. I left after work on a Wednesday and drove all night through the snow at Flagstaff and finally had to give up at Kingman, Arizona. I was beginning to fall asleep at the wheel. After getting about 4 hours sleep I was on the road again and arrived in time for Thanksgiving dinner. In those days there were no freeways or 4 lane highways they were all two lane and not too wide in places. I did not have any chains as usual but did have anti-freeze in the radiator, since it got cold in Colorado Springs.

I had Thursday evening, Friday, and I started home on Saturday night. I drove all the way back to Colorado Springs so I would be at work Monday morning. I had traveled over 2000 miles just to see Fay, in three days.

I called when I got back to Colorado Springs so Fay would know I had made it safe and sound. We then decided that we would get married. It would be cheaper than running back and forth from Colorado Springs and paying for all the telephone bills, and the wear and tear on the Ford and me.

I got leave for Christmas, 1945, and drove back to Torrance again to pickup Fay. I got 11 days leave for Christmas so I did not have to go quite as fast as I did for Thanksgiving. But I was moving right along. I was always on the ragged edge.

I picked up Fay and met all her relatives. Then I drove up to Del Paso Heights to my Folk's home for Fay to meet them. It was quite a moment since Eileen lived next door and she saw me drive up. After we were in the house for about 15 minutes Eileen came dashing in and made a scene even though her husband was home. She was jealous since she lost out. After we had visited all my relatives we headed for Colorado Springs. We always said that we were married on New Years Eve in Tijuana but decided against it. We were married on 20 September 1946.

As we were racing down the US99 Highway, I was passing a truck about 80mph when the left rear tire blew. It was no sweat I accelerated pass the truck and came to a stop on the shoulder of the road. Of course the tire was shot. I put on the spare and away we went. Fortunately Fay's Dad gave us an old tire for an extra spare. I had the extra spare in the rumble seat with all our gear. So we were racing through the Mojave Desert at night when the tire blew again on the right rear wheel. Well there was no stopping, since there was no way I could put the tire on the wheel since it was not mounted and was laying in the rumble seat. I just kept on going on the flat tire, slowing down to 45 mph. At the time we were about 45 miles from Blythe, California. Of course by the time we got to Blythe the tire was in shreds and smoking. It did not do the wheel any good either.

Everything during the War was rationed, gas, tires, food, etc. That was why I had no new tires. The tires I had were re-capped three times. It just happened that when we got to Blythe it was past midnight and the rationing was over. It was now 1946. So when I pulled into a gas station I could buy a new tire and not use the old one that Fay's Dad had given us. The only drawback about buying a new tire was the cost. I had no checking account only a savings account. I had only enough money to pay for gas and food for the trip and Fay did not have a penny. Buying the tire took almost all my money. What a fix to be in. We decided that we had enough money to get somewhere near Raton, NM. That was done by figuring the distance and getting 18 miles to the gallon of gas, if I slowed down

We got the new tire mounted and a full load of gas and away we went. We got as far as the Colorado Border where I traded the old tire for a full load of gas. We were in luck. We made Colorado Springs and checked into the Antlers Hotel. We did not have a dime between us. In those days you did not have to pay in advance for your room, especially in the best Hotel in town, fortunately for us. They don't do that today.

New Years was on a Friday so we got to Colorado Springs on Saturday evening so all the banks were closed the next day, Sunday. I went back to the Garage on Sunday morning and borrowed five dollars from the old fellow who was the attendant. He knew me since I would park the Ford there every time I would come down to the Antlers Bar. Also there was $50 waiting for me at the Western Union. A loan I had made to Lt. Segal but the Western Union was closed until Monday.

The $5.00 gave us money to eat on until I could get my money from Western Union on Monday morning. When I did we were "flush again". I think our room only cost 10 dollars a night. So we were off the next morning to find a rooming house. We found one then we had a place to stay until we found a little place to buy.

Within a couple of weeks Fay found a little place we could afford. It was a little house at 2304 East Boulder. It cost 4500 dollars with 500 dollars down with payments of $25 per month. It did not have a bath or shower so I had to have one put in. It was only one bedroom but it had a large living room and a small kitchen. It sure beats paying rent.

In the meantime, I applied for a regular commission in the Army Air Force, desiring to be a career Officer. I did not make it on the first try but made it on the second time around at the interviews at Biggs AAF, Texas.

I was taken off recruiting duty, since they had to cut down on the number of personnel in the office. I was assigned as Assistant Information and Education Office. My Boss was Major Jim Turner, a Louisiana Boy who also flew B-24's in Italy when I was there. We became good friends and had many parties at our little house for him and his girlfriend. He got "riffed" (reduction in force). We kept in touch and I finally met him again in 1948 in Japan. He was a Master Sergeant crewing a Generals B-17. He was stationed in the Philippines at Clark Field. That would be the last time I would see him and I lost track of him. We were stationed in town at Colorado Springs at 2nd Air Force Headquarters. It was quite convenient for Fay and me since our little house was on the same street as 2nd AF HQs, only a few blocks away. I could walk home if I had to. We lived on East Boulder.

Fay made our little house very livable and we were very comfortable. Before our friend, Jim Turner left we used to have a lot parties at the house and had a lot of fun together. We had a favorite steak house at Manitou Springs, where we would have dinner together quite a lot. We toured all the sights, the Garden of the Gods, Pikes Peak, Leadville, etc.

Fay wanted to do something so she got a job at Alexander Pictures, at the north end of town. They used to be an airplane company manufacturing the Alexander Eagle rock. Now they were making movie commercials and Fay got a job making commercials, which would be shown in many theaters throughout the United States. In fact some people we met later claimed they saw her in a theater in Fort Worth, Texas, Denver, and many other cities. She did Jewelry, house hold products, etc. She got $10 per hour when she worked, which was not bad pay for that day. This was before TV commercials came into vogue. She was a real star of the commercial circuit in 1946. Then she got pregnant with our first daughter, Sherry Ann and could not continue.

In the meantime, I noticed an ad in the local newspaper that anyone interested in Auto Racing please be at a certain address at 8pm on a Friday night. This was sometime in April 1946. Of course I was there and the fellow who was organizing the race was Jimmie Good, who I would meet years later at a sports car race at Wickenburg, Arizona. At the meeting there were about 10 or 15 people. We got the rules and regulations for cars and drivers. Which stated that the cars could be altered in any way, except the engines could not be altered from a flat head to an overhead valve head. It was inferred that they would be a type of "Hot Rod" roadster. There were no weight restrictions. They could not be a one man racing car but had to be a modified roadster. After the meeting I decided I would build a racer for the dirt track.

I went out and found an old rusty Model A Ford block with a hole in the side of it for $5.00. I had it all cleaned up and the hole welded up. I then proceeded to have it bored out to 4 inches for oversized pistons with a model C Ford crankshaft, which was counter balanced. I then put oversized valves in it with a Model 97 Stromberg, downdraft carburetor. I would later install a Wico magneto for my ignition system.

I took leave to go to the Indy "500" in Indiana. This was the annual 500 mile race at the Indianapolis Speedway, which takes place every Memorial Day. So off Fay and I went in the old 1936 Ford Convertible to Indianapolis. We did a lot of things on the trip besides seeing the first Indianapolis 500 since the end of WWII in 1945.

We went to Anderson, Indiana to buy a racing camshaft from Roof Manufacturing Company for my racer. We then went to the races at Indianapolis. Getting to races was a chore. The traffic was terrible. We started at daybreak and it took us 3 hours to go 3 miles. They did not have a good traffic control in those days and since it was the first race in years they had not figured out the traffic control for so many cars.

If I remember correctly, servicemen got a discount on their tickets. I had my 16mm Movie camera with me and I got to take some pictures of the races and also got into the pit area since I had my uniform on. Paul Robson won the race in an old car since the only new car was the Novi

Special. It was a very advanced car for the day with an internal supercharger on the engine. In fact it was so powerful that it twisted the shaft off the supercharger after qualifying fastest in the race. Now it was out of the race. This car would become a legend at the Speedway for many years but would never win even though it was the fastest car each year at the race.

I could hardly wait to get home to finish my racecar. I would call it the "The Disbrow Special". This would be my first "Disbrow Special". I would build another in later years. Only for blowing the cap off my last US Royal tire, which I had recapped twice and had lasted through the war, our trip home was uneventful.

After getting home I started on my racecar. I got and old Model "T" Ford chassis at the wrecking yard along with a Willys Overland front axle, which mated to the front end of the "T" frame. It made it nice and low, since I stepped the spring hanger in front (suicide front end). I also stepped the rear spring hanger, which made the bell housing of the engine about 4 inches from the ground. I put a bobbed tailed "T" Roadster body on it using the gravity fuel tank that was installed in the body. I painted the whole car a bright red with number 77 in the side. The people that did my welding on the car did it free if I would put their name on the side of the car. The name was "Cox Welding", so I got all my welding free.

I had ordered a 5.1 to 1 rear end gear for the model "A" rear end that I had installed. This would allow me to run in high gear while the rest of the racers had to run in second for the size of the track we were racing on. It was like a hazard course up and down with very short straight ways.

After I finished the car some of the participants came over to our house to see the car. It was a big surprise to them. It was strictly a California design, very low and light. They wanted to see it go so I got a push to start it and I spun the wheels in second gear, from a standing start. Of course they did not know what I had done to the engine to make it go, especially the new Roof racing camshaft.

Since I had gone to Indianapolis I was unable to finish my racecar for the first race but on the first time out I broke the track record. I won the heat race and was leading in the main event when the battery box broke pulling the battery cable off and killing the engine. I had not installed my Wico Magneto as yet. I was out of the race until next week.

I got a call from my Mother in July that my Dad was very ill and I got an emergency leave. I flew out to Del Paso Heights in a C-45 with another pilot. We landed at McClellan Field and he took the airplane back to Colorado Springs. After seeing my Dad the pilot would come back and pick me up.

It seems my Dear Dad had Cirrhosis of the liver and was in bad shape. He did not have a regular Doctor but an Osteopath. I was wondering why he did not get a regular Doctor and put him a regular hospital. I then took him home and told my Mother to get him a regular Doctor and I had to leave. I tried to comfort my Dad before I left and cheer him up. I got a call from my Mother on the 6 August 1946 that Dad had passed away.

I took the C-45 again with another pilot so he could bring it back when he dropped me off at McClellan Field. I would get everything in order after my Dads funeral so I could bring my Mom back to live with us. I packed up all my Fathers tools and gear. I loaded it in a trailer I had bought for $50. My Mother sold her house and said "Good Bye" to all her friends and off we went in my Dad's pride and joy, a 1932 Auburn Convertible Phaeton, pulling the luggage trailer full of tools and parts my Dad had collected over the years, which would be very useful to me

Everything went well until we got to Truckee, California, when the trailer hitch came loose. I had enough tools to fix it in no time. So off we went again. We stayed at Elko, Nevada the first night. The road of course was a two lane and made traveling a little slow by today's standards. Especially when I was pulling a very heavy trailer.

We were on the road to Salt lake City just past Wendover when I lost a wheel on the trailer. It was now getting dark. The road was two lanes and was raised up about six feet from the desert floor for drainage and had very narrow shoulders. There was no place to park without blocking traffic on the highway. So I pulled off down the side of the bank on the sand. I walked back down the highway and luckily found the wheel. It had pulled the wheel off right through the lug nuts, which were still on the hub. I could not believe it. Now there was no way to hold the wheel on the hub unless I found some big washers. After searching through numerous boxes in the trailer, of nut, bolts, and washers I finally found what I wanted. My Dear Dad had left me quite a collection.

I finally had to take the hub off because the lug bolts had come loose in the hub. I had to bolt the wheel directly to the hub through the brake drum. By this time it was dark and I was wondering if the old Auburn would be able to pull this load back up on the highway, since were six feet below the road on the sand I got in and cranked up and gave the Auburn all the gas it would take and just about got it back on the highway when the it started to spin the wheels and bogged down. I tried again but just could not quite make it. I put my Mother in, to drive and I got out and pushed. As I was pushing the car a car stopped and some people got out and helped me push the old Auburn and the trailer back on the road. I thanked them and away we went to Salt Lake City.

I was going to drive all night to make up for the lost time but my Mother made me stop and we got a Motel. We were off again the next day, after breakfast, taking US30 to Rocksprings and Laramie, Wyoming. We got to Golden, Colorado about midnight when I had a flat tire on the Auburn. What else could happen? Nothing was open so I had to change the tire myself. The Auburn had Kelsey-Hayes wire wheels with split rims. These were very dangerous to change. You had to take off a locking ring with a special tool to get the tire off then you had to make sure the ring was locked in its groove so it would not pop out and hit you when you filled the tire with air. I finally got it changed and luckily my Dad had a hand pump so I could fill the tire with air. I finally finished the job since my Dad had all the tools to do the job. Off we went again but had to stop since I had driven all night and I was bushed and needed a little rest.

After getting some rest we finally made it to Colorado Springs sometime that afternoon. It had been quite a ride and I was glad to get home and Fay was very relieved when we finally showed up. It had taken us about three days pulling that heavy trailer.

Before my Father died and I was still with recruiting I had been flying to different bases taking the recruiting teams there. I made one trip to Fort Worth, Texas and dropped a team off and had to fly back the same day to Colorado Springs, Peterson Field. I was by myself and it was my first night flight in a C-45. As I was filling out my flight plan an enlisted man asked me if he could hitch a ride with me to Colorado Springs. I was happy to have a Sgt. fly co-pilot with me who could help me navigate at night.

I had checked the weather and the winds were from the west at 25mph, which later turned out to be 50mph at 9,000 feet. The weather was clear but there was no moon out and it was pitch black. Well I took off and headed for Colorado Springs. I knew there was a light line, a navigation aid for night flying, running through Pueblo, Colorado, to Kansas City and I would cross it on the way. I also knew the Rockies loomed out of the plains quite sharply. I did not want to hit those mountains. I was trying to use my Radio Compass to pick up a radio range station but to no avail. I could not pick up any radio stations.

Well I thought I passed the first light line but could not see the lights of Colorado Springs or lights of a town anywhere I looked. I knew by the time I was flying that I must have passed the first light line. I knew there was one more light line that went from Cheyenne, Wyoming to Omaha, Nebraska and I better not pass this one as my fuel was getting really low by this time. I had nothing in one tank and ¼ tank of fuel in the other

Out of the corner of my eye I thought I saw a green flashing beacon off to my left and asked the Sgt. if he saw it. He verified that it was sure enough a green beacon. By this time I was running on fumes. All I could think of, was what, I was going to tell the Colonel why I bailed out of a perfectly good airplane that ran out of fuel in the black of night.

Well the Lord was looking after me again. As I approached the field I noticed that there were no runway lights but just perimeter lights. I quickly chose the diagonal to be the longest area to land on and put the C-45 down. As I touched down the red fuel warning lights came on, I was out of fuel! I coasted up to a little building that had the beacon and the windsock on it and stopped. I got out with my passenger and was it cold. I then noticed that there were patches of snow on the ground. I also noticed that the field was a large square sod strip, no definite landing area. I was glad I was wearing my Army Short coat. I found out later the temperature was around 30 degrees.

I walked up to the little building and knocked on the door. The top half of the door opened and there was a young lady standing there. I asked her where am I? She laughed and said, “Sidney, Nebraska”. I asked, “Where is that”? She said, “Come in and I will show you”. She opened the rest of the door and let us in. It was nice and warm inside as she pointed to Sidney on the map on the wall. I could not believe it. I had missed Colorado Springs by about ten miles but I could not see the lights of the city because there was a mountain in the way blocking my view so I went right on by. Now I was 100 miles from Colorado Springs. If I had had more altitude I would have seen it.

The young lady called town for some fuel. A truck finally arrived with two 50-gallon drums of fuel and a hand pump; before the fuel arrived the young lady supplied us with hot chocolate and cookies, which hit the spot.

After getting nice and warm I decided it was time to get out and pump the fuel in the C-45. This was done by hand, which kept me warm. As I was pumping I decided that the weatherman had given me the wrong winds aloft, which made us drift farther off course than I was supposed to. Also I was fudging to the east to keep away from the mountains. That was why I had missed Colorado Springs.

Having finished refueling, thanking everybody, and filling out the Army Air Corps form for obtaining the fuel from a civilian company, we were off, but not before the young lady told me that I was not the first one to come in there lost. Even a B-24 and many others were disorientated landed there. We made Peterson Field in about 45 minutes. When we got there no one had even missed us, this day in age they would be looking for us after we were over due 15 minutes. We were over due about 2 hours.

When I got home Fay asked, "Aren't you a little late?" I then told her what happened. I had taken a little detour to Sidney, Nebraska.

With the war over there was not too much to do but go to parties at the Officers Club. We had a lot of good bands come to play there. We even had Stan Kenton and we had a great time dancing to this good music. We also had a lot of parties at our little house on East Boulder. We made a lot of good friends while we were there.

Of course, when I got back in car racing again there was plenty of excitement. I raced from June until the snow began to fall and it got cold. I sure had a lot of fun and a lot of publicity. They called me "Bullet Bill" in the newspapers. I was always breaking the track record it seemed every time I raced. I was always racing against Herb Byers a local who drove a "hopped up" Model A Ford Roadster. We would race neck and neck every race. If I got the jump on him I would win if he did he would usually win.

It sure was exciting for the crowd. Herb would years later win Pikes Peak Hill climb.

In the meantime, I had my Mother living with us. She would not come out to watch me race. When my Dad raced she would not go out and watch him. Fay was 7 months pregnant but came to every race to watch me go. I always gave the crowd their moneys worth with my complete broad slides on some of the turns at wide open throttle. With two straight exhaust pipes coming out of the bottom of the car it sounded like an Indianapolis car.

Col. Branch came out to see the races and offered me a flight in a P-80 Jet when he got it, if I would let him drive my racer but the P-80 would not get there before I was transferred to Roswell AAB, New Mexico.

With racing over, due to the weather, Fay would have her first baby in the worst snowstorm in the long history of Colorado Springs. I had to dig away the 6 foot drift of snow piled up on our garage door before I could get the old Ford out to take Fay to the Glockner Hospital. It was the 2 November 1946 when she began to get labor pains. I got her in the car with her bag of stuff to take with her. I got in the car and wound up the engine and let the clutch out and away we went in reverse hitting the snow bank in the driveway and bounced through it into the street. I must have spun out a couple of times on the very icy streets. We made it to the hospital safe and sound finally. There were no military hospitals in the area so we had to go to the civilian one. It was the Glockner about 5 miles from our house. We got there at 7PM and I waited until 3am in the morning when the nurse came by and told me to go home that Fay was not going to have the baby just yet. She would call me when she was going to have it.

I reluctantly went home and I got a call at 8AM in the morning from Fay that I was a proud Father of a bouncing baby girl of 6lbs. I sure was a proud father that day. Of course I was passing out the cigars. Between us we decided to name her Sherry Ann Disbrow. I used to work for Sherry's Liquor Store in San Francisco many years ago, and Sherry sounded just right.

Well the good life at Colorado Springs, 2nd Air Force, had to end after we bought our nice little house. We had many visitors including Fay's Aunt and Uncle Savage. We no more had Sherry Ann when I got my orders to transfer to Roswell AAB, New Mexico. Sherry was born on the 3 November 1946; we got our orders to move on the 16 November she was only 12 days old. I traded the old Auburn for a 1937 Ford Convertible, which I still regret. My Mother drove the 1937 Ford, Fay drove the 1936 Ford Convertible, and I drove my racecar that I had to make street legal. We had one week to get to Roswell, AAB, N.M. so we did not have time enough to sell our little house, which would turn out to be a pain.

It was quite a sight all of us in trail with me at the rear wearing my crash helmet and goggles since the car had no windshield. I also had on a big sheepskin coat to keep me warm. I didn't have any of the niceties of a normal car it was strictly a racing car. No fenders either and winter was rapidly approaching.

On the way my Mother ran out of gas in the 1937 Ford. I had to hook on to her and tow her about 20 miles to a gas station, otherwise the trip was uneventful. The country was the stark wide-open spaces a great contrast to where we had come from.

When we drove into Roswell I created quite a scene with red racer bellowing as we came down the main street. I got out and had to leave the engine running since it had no starter. You had to push it to start it. I was asking where the Air Base was and the nearest Motel in town. When I got back to the car I had quite a crowd around it. Of course all the questions started especially how fast it would go. I could do an easy.100mph with the low gear ratio in the rear end and much more with a normal gear ratio. It had so much power that I had to re-enforce the model "T" frame with angle iron

We found a Motel and bedded down for the night and the next day I reported to Roswell AAB, for duty. In the meantime Fay was looking for a house to rent or buy. She found a converted "chicken house", which we rented temporarily. There was not too much room for me and Fay, my Mother and Sherry, but we managed.

It took about a month or so to find a house in a new housing development, in a new area of Roswell. It was so new that the streets were not paved. This would be 706 South Union Street. So we moved into our new house and I was eligible for a GI Loan. Which was nice even if it only had two bedrooms and one bath. That was the way they built them in those days.

I was assigned to be the Information and Education Officer for the base. I had a nice big room and office for administering the GED tests to the personnel who failed to get their High School diploma before enlisting in the service.

I got quite a few enlisted men their diplomas as well as their state bonuses for serving in WWII. I even got the Base Commander his state bonus. His name was Colonel William Blanchard, who would later become the Asst. Chief of the Air Force. Fay and I taught dancing at the Officers Club and taught Col. Blanchard how to dance. He would later die young in Washington, DC.

Roswell AAB was the home of the 509th Bomb Group who dropped the atom bomb on Hiroshima and Nagasaki with the B-29's. We were in the 8th Air Force Command, which had its Headquarters at Fort Worth, Texas. I got some good flying here by flying the mail shuttle from Roswell to Fort Worth in an AT-6. I also got to fly the C-47, B-25, and"ugh" the B-29. I almost got checked out in the P-51 by a reserve squadron that moved on the Base but they were having too many accidents with a bunch of new pilots of their own to check me out. Besby Holmes was the Operations Officer I think. He was on the raid of P-38's in the South Pacific that shot down Yamamoto. Busby is no longer with us but passed away in 2002.

We took leave and went out to California to show off the new baby. This would be sometime in June 1947. We all got in the 1936 Ford Convertible, Me, Fay, my Mother in the front seat and Sherry in the depression in back of the front seat where the top fit when it was down. It was a bit crowded but all the gear was in the rumble seat

Before we started back to Roswell my Mother bought us a used 1946 Buick Sedan so we could ride back in comfort. In the meantime, I had bought a four cylinder Chevrolet racing car. I got it for a very good price and would tow it back to Roswell with the 1936 Ford, for the race track a fellow and I were going to build in Roswell. He was the operator of the Base Gas Station, Pat Baldinell. We were going to get all the garages in town to build racing cars for the track.

After a nice visit with all of Fay's relatives and thanking her Mom and Dad for letting us stay at their little house on Torrance Blvd. California, we were off for home. I would be driving the 1936 Ford towing the Chevy racer and Fay would be driving the Buick with my Mother and Sherry.

We took route US66 through Needles, Ca. Globe, Williams, Flagstaff, Winslow, to Holbrook, Arizona. We turned off at Holbrook for Socorro, NM, a short cut to Roswell. It was winter and there was snow on the ground. I made the mistake of not checking the heater on the Buick before we bought it. Of course it was warm in Torrance and I did not think of it. It did not work and Fay and my Mother were freezing and I was nice and cozy in the Ford. My heater worked great since I installed it and had a winter front on the radiator, which kept the interior nice and warm.

We stopped and I traced the wiring and found the wire to the control had come loose. I fixed it and it got warmer immediately. This made everyone happy and warm.

As we climbed over the mountains to Socorro, NM, it was below freezing and I was leading. We came around a sharp turn in the mountains at about 9 pm. It was very dark. All of a sudden there were a lot of red flares in front of me. A car had skidded on the icy road and went over the bank. The Highway Patrol and a wrecker were there trying to get the car and the occupants out. I immediately pumped the brakes gently to keep from locking up the wheels but with the racer behind me pushing the extra weight made it hard to stop. I finally had all the wheels locked up and was still slowly sliding down the hill. The Officer was wondering why I was not stopping and I told him the wheels were locked up on the ice. I finally came to a stop and told the Officer that my wife was coming in back of me and to get some one up near the corner to flag her down ahead of time so she will be able to stop. Just about that time Fay came around the corner and immediately started to pump the brakes so as not to lock up the wheels and came to a stop before she hit me. The Officer congratulated her for being such a good driver. They let us go on in a few minutes so we could get down to a lower altitude where it was not freezing and no more ice on the road.

This wasn't the last of our troubles. The Buick froze up. The Don Lee Cadillac Co., where we bought the car, forgot to put anti-freeze in the radiator like I told them. After I got home I contacted them and told them what had happened. After I took the Buick to the base Hobby Shop and took the engine out Don Lee sent me a new short block free and I rebuilt the engine. It is nice to deal with a reputable company. The ice had cracked the block.

After Sherry was born, Fay said that she wanted to have the baby blessed. So on Sunday I went with her to The Church of Jesus Christ of Latter-day Saints (Mormon) building in Colorado Springs. There were not very many people there as I remember. While at Roswell the LDS Missionaries came over and I decided to take the missionary lessons. They came once a week for dinner and the lessons. I sure gave them the third degree. One was a returned Navy Lt., if I remember right. We had something in common, the military. Of course I wanted to know what happened to the golden plates that Joseph Smith had translated into the Book of Mormon. They had most of the answers but I was not thoroughly convinced, although the religion seemed to me the most sensible of the ones I had come in contact with. I did agree to go to Church with Fay once in a while when it did not interfere with my racing or flying. We met in the local Funeral Home. I guess there were not more than six people attending when I went. Of course it was hard to understand everything at once and the meeting was short since there were so few people. This was in about March 1947. I guess we only had a sacrament meeting, I can't remember.

We finally started our racetrack, which was 1/3-mile dirt track, which was hard packed. It was on the road to the Base. We did not have enough money to put in a grandstand at first but got a small one later on. I think we charged one dollar for adults and 50 cents for children and the military. We did not make any money only for expenses. The only profit I made if any was from the prize money I won.

Before we built "Roswell Speedway" Pat Baldinell had a track like the one in Colorado Springs. It was built in an old gravel pit, which was like a circular cross- country race. We had only one race there in which I raced the Chevy four "banger" I beat everybody with ease and almost lapped the field, in 5 laps. I was the only one that wore a crash helmet. It was a Clymer and was made out duralumin. Everybody was astounded on how fast the Chevy 4 was and how it sounded. Just like an Indianapolis car. It had hit 113mph at the dry lakes in California. It was like a one man racing car. You sat in the middle of the body, which was made from an old Dodge roadster body and narrowed. It also had a Franklin steering gear, which was very fast.

Our next race was at our new track, "Roswell Speedway". We advertised it in the local newspaper and over the local radio station. I can't remember the call letters but "Lefty Frizzel" got his start there at the same time. I also advertised it on the Base since Servicemen got in for half price. We gave 40% of the gate for prize money to the drivers.

The first race I had the Chevy and my "Disbrow Special", number 77, at the starting line for the qualification heats. I had an enlisted man drive my old 77 for me as I was driving the Chevy.

On qualifying the Chevy was flying, when after 3 laps I came in the pits with the engine missing it was only running on 3 cylinders. It hardly slowed down a bit with the miss. I took off the hood and found that I had broken a valve rocker arm and it had a big hole in the block! It seems that the valve adjustment on the rocker arm had come loose and had pushed the valve through the head of the piston and everything exploded sending the broken connecting rod through the side of the block. A good racer shot. To make matters worse the "Disbrow Special" had the main bearing go out. My debut at the new track was a bust.

I had to rebuild the "Disbrow Special", since there were no parts locally for the Old Chevy; I had to have a car to race. I rebuilt the Ford in the Base Hobby Shop. I added and aircraft oil pump to have full oil pressure feed and did away with the splash system it originally had. I also added twin Stromberg Model 97's carburetors to the intake manifold plus aluminum finned high compression head. It was ready to race again.

By the way, I was the instigator for the first Base Hobby Shop in the Army Air Force. In fact Gen. LeMay sent down two of his representatives to Roswell AAF, to look at our installation. This was the start of Hobby Shops throughout all the Military Installations everywhere. SAC was the first besides us to make them available to all military personnel.

Our track was having quite a bit of success with a lot of local cars as well as one car coming all the way from Monahan, Texas. We also had two new cars built in the Base Hobby Shop with Ford V8's in them.

Since we were having so much success and having a good crowd another old Speedway, a ½ mile track, decided to give us competition. This little town of Roswell could not support two tracks, so we finally folded up and went there to race and let them have all the responsibility for everything. It took that burden off of me and I tended to strictly racing.

Before we left our track we had a lot of V8 Ford racers show up and it made it hard for the old four "banger" Model A Ford to keep up. I had to go wide open the whole time, right through the corners. In one race I had passed a car just entering the turn and he ran into me flipping me into the air and landing upside down and the side of the car caught my head between it and the ground. Lucky I had my crash helmet on. I did have a lump on my head but without that helmet it would have been much worse. As usual I gave the crowd their money's worth for the day. In practice I would come down the straight-a -way and do a spin right in front of the grandstand and keep right on going.

One day the woman wanted to have a woman's race but would not race unless my wife Fay was in the race. So I put her in the old Model A Ford number 77. Well she got in old 77 but did not realize how quickly it turned and how easy it was to broad slide the corners. She had never driven it before. In the first turn it scared her, but she finished. I have movies of this race some place.

Another time at the old track I was racing old 77 and I was overtaking a car and I passed him going into the turn and he spun out. I thought nothing off it until leading the race my radiator hose came off and I had to drop out of the race across from the grandstand and the pits. I saw this fellow coming toward me and thought he was going to help me get the car back to the pits. I had just taken my crash helmet off as he got close to me. Before I could say anything a fist was in my face and he knocked me to the ground. I could not believe it what had happened. All the dust on my face went into my eyes. I got up and he was calling me names and threw two more punches at me but missed as I weaved away and I then let him have one right in the jaw, which knocked him down and he was very slow to get up. I did not have presence of mind to finish him off with a few good more punches. Instead I made the mistake of grabbing him around the neck. He slipped out of my grasp as I fell down. He then started to kick me in the head and jumped on my back, as I was face down hitting me with his fists until somebody pulled him off of me. As I got up he was nowhere in sight. I found out later that the Kenney Brothers put him up to do this to me. They thought I had run into their car in the corner, which made it spin out. I didn't touch their car and they were going to teach me a lesson. I had driven their car a couple of times but it was so out of balance that it spun at the least provocation. I refused to drive it anymore until they fixed it. The new driver was having much more trouble controlling it than I had. So this was their way at getting back at me. He was the one that spun out just as I passed him.

I found out later that the fellow who started the fight was the town bully. He drove a bread truck for some local bread company and after this fight he was scared to come on the Air Base. All my friends were waiting for him. Also I heard I had broken his jaw.

I could not believe that of all days the Base Commander, Col. Blanchard, was at the races that day and was watching all this from the grandstand. The next day was his staff meeting, which I had to attend. I walked in with a pair of dark glasses on to hide the big black eye I had. He made the remark during the staff meeting that I hadn't faired to well yesterday at the racetrack. When I first built the track he was pleased that there would be something for the enlisted men to do on weekends besides getting drunk and getting into trouble, since Roswell was in the middle of nowhere with not much entertainment.

In the meantime, all the racers moved to the ½ mile dirt track on the other side of town. I had a lot of servicemen building cars in the Hobby Shop. This was now under my control as part of my Information and Education Office. We managed to get a lot of surplus equipment from other bases that were closing up or did not need the material. We had both a metal shop and a wood shop with working lathes. We had a welding shop, a tool crib, boring bar to re-bore engines, brake drum lathe, drill presses, grinders, etc. It was a complete shop and as good as any commercial shop. I even re-built the engine in the old 1936 Ford V8 there. When I had finished the job I had polished all the aluminum plus the carburetor inside and out. I painted all the rest of the engine. I then put it on an engine stand. I put a sign on it stating that this is the way I wanted all the engines to look like when they left the shop.

I have always been a busy person so along with being I&E Officer, getting my flying time in, which by this time I had flown the PT-22, BT-

13, AT-17 UC-78, AT11, B-24 B-25 B-17, B-29, C-45, C-47 and the P-38, or racing my car or another owners car, Fay and I taught dancing at the Officers Club once a week at night.

While I was at Roswell I got promoted to Captain in the Army Air Forces Reserve. I was AUS (Army Of The US) and had applied for reserves, AAFR, when I did not make regular officer the first time. This was the 24 May 1947. It did not affect my present rank at the time. I applied again for regular officer and was called to Biggs Field, El Paso, Texas. This would be my second interview.

. I lucked out, during the interview I talked about flying the P-38, which was my favorite aircraft at the time and was also the favorite aircraft of one of the Colonels on the Board. So I must have made a good impression because I made regular officer on the next list on the 13 Nov 1947 with a date of rank for 1st Lt. of 23 Sept 1943.

Fay, Sherry and my Mother went with me to El Paso, Texas, where Biggs Field is located. We had a nice time since I took a little leave with the trip. We went to Juarez, Mexico, which is just across the Rio Grande from El Paso. We stayed in a Hotel in El Paso and would walk over the bridge to Juarez to have great Mexican food and went to a few nightclubs carting little Sherry Ann in her buggy with us.

Winter came and racing was over and we were still having the LDS Missionaries over every Tuesday for dinner and lessons. They were making me really study since I had many questions to ask, some, they did not have the answer at the time but would have it for me on our next meeting.

I got a lot of good flying time at Roswell and many good cross-country flights in everything from the AT-6 to the B-29. I remember one incident in particular. I was flying Co-pilot with Capt. Paul in a B-29. We had been to Maxwell Field, Alabama and were returning home to Roswell. Usually Roswell had the best flying weather in the world but this day a front had moved in. It made for low ceilings and rain. As we approached Roswell the weather was deteriorating and it was raining we had to let down on instruments for our approach to the base. Capt. Paul instructed me to make sure of his altitudes and let him know when we reached minimum of 400 feet. Make sure he did not go below this minimum, if we did not break out in the clear we could go to our alternate airport. I also was to inform him when I saw the runway on the letdown. Fortunately I saw the runway at about 500 feet and called it out, since he was flying instruments and was not looking out. We landed without further incident.

Roswell AAB was not bad, we had a lot of fun at the Officers Club but I wanted a flying job instead of being an I&E Officer. So when I got my orders to go to Japan, I was happy. I sold the house and loaded up our possessions and away we went in the Old Ford Convertible. I had been at Roswell from 31 Dec 1946 to 1 March 1948. During that time I had raced at Artesia, NM, Carlsbad, NM, and Hobbs, NM. I had won at all three places and had a great time. Fay's folks came out to see us as did her younger brother Bob. It was the Land Of Enchantment. I was ready for a change. Sherry was 16 months old at the time and a lovely little blond girl we loved very much.

I sold both of my racers and the Buick my mother had bought us since she went back to Oakland, California, some months before with some friends. We still had the Ford V8 Convertible. I decided we did not need two cars, so the Buick went so we did not have the expense of driving two cars to California.

We took thirty days delay en-route and drove to California. We took route US70 & US 80 on the way out. It took us through El Paso, Texas, to Los Angeles. We would see Fay's folk's first then drive up to the Bay area and see all my relatives and friends, including my friend Bob Lively and his family. We had a good visit with my Mother before leaving for the Far East. She was staying with my Aunt Marie Hitchcock in Concord, California.

Before leaving the Los Angeles area we had to have a new car to take to Japan. I went looking for a new Cadillac Convertible to bring to Japan. I went to Hollywood one day in the old Ford to find one. This was the most likely place to find a good one, since a lot of people in this area drove Cadillac's.

I hit a lot of places including the Cadillac dealer on Vine Street but to no avail. Cars were still scare since the ending of the war. It had been a long time since any new cars were being produced. I was about to give up when I went into a used car lot on Vine Street and was just nosing around. A salesman came out and asked me it he could help me. I said that I was looking for as new Cadillac Convertible. I guess he did not think I was serious, since I had on an old pair of Levi jeans and my old A2 leather flying jacket which had my old insignia and my rank on it. It seems after a bit of talking, I told him what I wanted it for and that I was still in the Service and wanted to take the Cadillac to my new station in Japan. I also told him I was a combat pilot in WWII. He said that his boss was a reservist and wanted me to meet him. After meeting his boss and relating my story he said that he had just the car I needed. It came in two days ago in a caravan from New York and they were detailing it right now before putting it on the lot. He asked me if I would like to see it of course my answer was positive. So away we went to see this "Caddie".

We pulled up to a garage a few blocks away and we walked in. It seems they had just finished the Cadillac and it looked like a million dollars. It was beautiful. It was gunmetal gray with a wine colored convertible top. It had a gray leather interior with every accessory on it that Cadillac made at that time. It also had wide white sidewall tires on it. Of course I had to drive it and it drove like a dream after the old Ford. I was afraid to ask him the price but after the demo ride I asked. He said that since I was a serviceman and going overseas he would let me have it for $3100 since there would be no trade in. He did not want my old Ford.

Since we were passing through Los Angeles to Japan I had no checking account and only a dollar in my pocket. We did have a savings account but I had left the bankbook with Fay. I told the boss I wanted the car and would bring my wife and would pay cash for it if he would take one-dollar deposit. He took it and I told him I would be back tomorrow with the money and left. I jumped in the Old Ford and dashed from Hollywood to Torrance in record time since there were no freeways. I told Fay what had happened and then went to the bank to get our money for the Cadillac.

The next day we got all dressed up and headed for Hollywood and our new Cadillac Convertible. It was a big contrast from the day before. I now had on new slacks, white shirt, with tie, new sports jacket with brightly shined shoes and my dark glasses. Fay looked ravishing in one of her neat outfits.

When we arrived he had the Cadillac in the back of the lot with a "Sold" sign on it. When the Boss saw us he came out. After introducing Fay to him he looked at me and said that I had gone Hollywood already with all my new gear and dark glasses. So we bought our first Cadillac, which would not be our last. We are still driving them after 56 years.

We left the old 36 Ford with Gladys and Mordecai (Mont) Cox, Fay's folks to sell while we headed for San Francisco and the Bay area. We had to go to Fort Mason to get the information for Fay since she could not travel with me but would have to wait about 5 months before she and Sherry could join me in Japan. I had to get information on shipping the Cadillac to Japan, also. When we drove into Fort Mason all the Lts. were "bug eyed" over the Cadillac Convertible. Everyone either wanted to buy it or trade me their car for it. It would be the only new Cadillac Convertible in all of Japan at the time.

I was off on the USS Blachford, what a ship, a real scow. It took us 11 days to get to Yokohama, Japan. I found out on orders that I was supposed to go to Okinawa but when I got to Yokohama they were changed to JAMA, Tachikawa, Japan, arriving on 9 May 1948.

It was quite a long ride, 7000 miles across the Pacific on this old tub. I spent most of my time playing gin rummy with a newfound friend, Lt. Alex Sentes, who, incidentally went to the 49th fighter group at Misawa, Japan. I was always dreaming up something to break the monotony and make the Troops laugh. Like wearing our tailored made uniforms with our battle jackets and scarves around our neck or at times wearing our A2 leather jackets with our leather flying helmets to chow. It was fun and made the time pass faster and better.

It was a magnificent sight coming into Tokyo Bay. It was a clear day and you could see Mount Fuji looming up to over 12,000 feet right out of the Pacific Ocean to that height. It still had snow on the top of it. It would make a good checkpoint.

After landing at Yokohama at the 2nd medium port, we were loaded in GI trucks and taken to a replacement depot. Here I found that my orders had been changed from Okinawa to JAMA, Japan. It would be the Japan Material Area. It would be at Tachikawa, about 20 miles NW of Tokyo. This made me happy but I would be assigned to be the Asst. Troop Information and Education Officer, this would be the same job I had at Roswell. The area at the Base would be called the 13th Air Depot, which changed to the 4th Air Repair Squadron, APO 704. I wasn't too happy to be in I&E again as an assistant. Since they were only authorized one I&E Officer, they found me another job.

They finally assigned me as Asst. Chief of Manufacturing and Repair of the Depot on the 13 August 1948. In the meantime I was getting my check out in the AT-6, which I had already flown a bit stateside so it was a formality. This was at Base Flight, which also had two P-51's, a C-46, a C-47, a B-17, a B-25, and 4 AT-6s. It was just like I liked, I could finally fly the P-51 Mustang!

After being assigned to Maintenance s Asst. Officer to Manufacturing and Repair Section it seemed that they needed a Flight Test Officer for the Flight Test Section. I guess they had seen my Form 5, my flight record, and had noticed all the different aircraft I had flown to date. They included the PT-22, BT-13, AT-17, UC-78, B-24D, J, H, AT-11 AT-7, AT-6, P-38, C-47, C-45, C-47, B-17E, G, B-25, and the B-29. I also had over 1000 hours of flying time. So I got the dream assignment for someone that loves flying all types of aircraft. Since I did not have any formal training like going to the flight test school at Edwards AAB they made me acting Chief of Flight Test Section. JAMA was the main Depot for the Far East, so all aircraft arriving for any organization had to go through the Flight Test Section before being released to the organizations. Almost all the aircraft I would have a chance to fly.

This part of my flying career was one of the best, I flew everything I had enough nerve to get into and that was anything. So on the 21 Oct 1948 I became the Acting Chief Of Flight Test Section. I had been flying for the Flight Test Section before I got the job from Lt. Mix.

In the meantime, I had been passed over for regular Captain but made it on the next go around. I don't know how they promote people and never will. I made 2nd Lt, Army of the US, AUS, on the 5 Dec 1943, made 1st Lt, 2 July 1944, made Captain in the USAAFR (reserve) 29 May 1947, made my regular Army Commission as 1st Lt, 13 Nov 1947, which made me resign my reserve commission as Captain. I then got passed over for Captain in the Regular Air Force. I finally made Regular Captain, 25 Oct 1948. I passed over again for regular Major after having a date of rank of 1 July 1948! I made regular major 28 April 1952 with a date of rank of 6 Dec 1951. Backing up my date of rank each time was a little unfair since I was competing with people who always had more time in grade than I did.

. Being a new Captain was a "shot in the arm" for me after being a 1st Lt for almost 5 years. I now was still acting Chief Of Fight Test with Lt. Sam L'herisson and Lt. Wegman as my helpers.

Before I went to Flight Test I made sure that I got a chance to check out in the P-51. I went to base flight for my check out. It would be shooting 3 landings from the back seat of an AT-6. This was supposed to give you the perspective of the long nose on the "Mustang" and how blind it was on the ground. It had a 7 foot nose on it. After shooting the 3 landings I read the operating instructions in the dash one. I then asked some experienced P-51 drivers what I should know about the aircraft. One of the most important things to remember was to roll in at least 3 degrees of right rudder trim for take off or you may not make it. The aircraft had so much torque at full throttle that it will veer off the left side of the runway if you don't have enough rudder trim for the torque. I would roll in 5 degrees of right rudder trim to be on the safe side. Also to watch that last quarter of throttle when pushed to wide open, which consists of 61 inches of manifold pressure and 3000 RPM. The power comes in like a lion. That is where the torque grabs you and you must have a strong right leg. Also, on a go -a-round make sure that you roll out the cruising trim as you push up the power; the torque will roll you into the ground if you slam the throttle wide open. I saw this happen at Roswell while I was there trying to get checked out in the P-51. The P-51 hit the ground and the pilot luckily came out through the bottom of the aircraft as it broke up doing cartwheels down the runway. He was still strapped to the seat and tried to get up and run. He thought his back was broken, since he could not get up and it was just the seat was still strapped to him.

With all the good info from all the pilots that flew the P-51, I was ready to go. One other thing, you were not to intentionally power on stall this airplane. I got strapped in, cranked up, and taxied out to the run up area, checked the "mags" and gave it a coolant check then made sure I had the 5 degrees of right rudder trim in. I taxied onto the runway lined up, and eased the throttle to the "beast". I pushed the throttle continuously keeping myself straight down the runway and waited for that last bit of throttle, they were right. The power came on in a big rush. I locked my right leg on the rudder to keep it straight and at about 100 mph I came off the ground and picked up the gear and the flaps and away I went, what a thrill. I was finally flying the P-51

I climbed to 10,000 feet to give me room for a little air work and become familiar with the "Beast. After doing stalls and rolls I was ready to shoot my first landing. I came into the pattern pulled back the power and pushed up the rpm for maximum thrust, dropped the gear, checked for the green lights, called the tower, I had three in the green, dropped the flaps and came around the base leg and slowed down on the final to 120mph, I flared out and three pointed it in as everybody was watching. It had a "built in landing" I greased it in. You just hold the stick all the way back "in your gut" to lock the tail wheel at the crucial moment so when it touches down you cane keep it straight down the runway. The wide gear makes it simple to land. It is hard to see out of the P-51 in a three -point attitude. If you were a "long legged midget" it would be better. In order for me to see out I had to have the seat up but to get full rudder I had to have the seat down. I made sure I always could get full rudder so I would have to look out both sides of the windshield to keep her straight down the runway. I could not see straight ahead. On taxiing you would have to "zigzag" back and forth to make sure you were seeing everything.

I taxied in and received all the congratulations on my first ride in the "Mustang" from then on this was the aircraft to fly fast in. It was a 400mph aircraft at altitude, the fastest fighter in WWII. From then on I always 3 pointed the aircraft as I always did with any tail dragger, including the AT-6. I have noticed now-a-days that most of the new pilot's wheel land it, no guts.

My first hop at flight test was co-pilot in an A-10A (PBY), on 19 Oct 1948. What a bird, 90 knots it would do everything, take off, cruise, and land. I wanted to land it in Tokyo Bay but the crew chief advised me very quickly that the hull had a leak in it and was on a red cross for any water landings. It was restricted for landing on the runway only. So after "buzzing" around for about an hour, with the throttles on the ceiling Navy style, we came in and shot a few landings, me making two of them, which were considered my check out.

21 Oct. 1948. I flew a test in an L-5E liaison aircraft built by Cessna, a

puddle jumper but fun to fly. During the month of August I flew 12 flights in 5 different aircraft. These included a T-6, A10-A, L-5E, C-45F, and a C-47. I was getting in some good flying, which I surely enjoyed.

Nov. 1948. I flew 19 different flights that included the B-17G, C-47-A, Q-14, C-47D, and the AT-6.

In the meantime, Fay and Sherry arrived with the Cadillac Convertible on the MATS ship. It landed at Yokohama at the 2nd medium port. It was a great day since I had not seen them for 5 months I left in April 1948 and they got there in September 1948 just in time for my Birthday, what a nice present.

There was no housing for them on the base so they were billeted at the Gora Hotel in Hakone National park. It was about 50 miles from Tachikawa. I got leave to meet them in Yokohama and get the Cadillac off the ship. It seems the Cad did not come on the same ship so a staff car drove us from Yokohama to the Gora Hotel at Hakone. When we got there it was quite impressive. It was a nice modern Japanese Hotel that the occupation had taken over for the Officers dependent housing. We got a very large room on the third floor. It was very nice and lots of glass all around. I think there must have been at least 50 dependents living there so everyone had a great time.

With my leave up I had to get back to work at Tachikawa, there I found they had changed the name of the base from JAMA to FEAMCOM, Far East Material Command. In the meantime we got the Cadillac Convertible and were the object of much attention where ever we went. It was the only Cadillac Convertible in Japan at the time. General MacArthur had an old 1941 Limo but that was the only other one I ever saw in Japan.

Sherry created quite a sensation with the Japanese with her blond hair. Every one of the Japanese wanted to touch it. She was two years old at the time and as cute as a "bug's ear". Fay used to dress her in very cute clothes, which made her stand out that much more.

Since there was no base housing yet I commuted every Friday after work to the Gorah Hotel and started back every Sunday evening late. I stayed in the BOQ during the week. All the husbands with wives at the Gorah Hotel did the same thing, until they got base quarters. In the meantime the wives were living it up going on sightseeing tours and seeing all the local sights. This being in a National Park there was lots of places to go and see. Then when the husbands got there on the weekend it was party time. They always had a live band on the weekends for dancing. We had a great time. If it had been closer we would have never left.

We finally got temporary quarters at Yokota Air Base after leaving the Gora Hotel and living in the FEAMCOM BOQ for a short time. By Christmas 1948, we would be in our nice two- bedroom apartment at Fuchu Air Station. I was about 3 miles from my work at FEAMCOM. This made it very convenient. It was good to get settled permanently in our new quarters.

Once we got settled the LDS Missionaries found us and we would have them to dinner whenever they were in our area. We would have cottage meetings at our house for other LDS members that were in the military. We would attend Church when we could make it on a Sunday to Tokyo. I was not a member yet but Fay was a strong influence on me. I knew she would like me to become a member and be active in the church.

The church needed money for the building fund in Tokyo so Fay made arrangements to hold the first American style fashion show at Hibia Hall in Tokyo. As models she used volunteers from the Officers wives club at FEAMCOM. She made arrangements for all the latest fashions in the United States to be shipped over through a local importer. She really worked hard on this show so it would be a success. She even had a musical combo to play during the show, which she got from the NCO Club.

The night of the show there was a gigantic rain and wind storm. We could not believe it. The admission was only a dollar (360 yen) in 1948. Since the Japanese economy was not too good we made it reasonable enough that most could afford to come. When Fay and I got to Hibia Hall that evening we were surprised to see Japanese everywhere waiting for the box office to open and it was raining "cats and dogs". There were umbrellas everywhere. Indeed the Lord was looking after us.

We hurried in and everything was all set up. On stage there was a big book of Vogue Magazine in the center with all kinds of flowers for decorations around it. The models would come out of the book and I would take their hand and lead them to center stage. It was quite impressive and certainly "Wowed" the Japanese as we found out later when the show was on.

When the box office opened, the Japanese would flow in like a big wave. Before the performance started the place was full with standing room only and there were a lot of people standing. When the performance started there was lots of "Oohs" and "Aahs" as the different designs came on the stage. Fay modeled one outfit in red and with an Ostrich Feathered hat and it brought down the house with applause. As the models came out the Combo played "A Pretty Girl Is Like A Melody".

During the intermissions Fay and I danced so the models would have time to change into their next outfit. The first dance we did during the first intermission was the Rumba. On the second intermission we danced the Tango. The applause was tremendous I guess they had never seen a live Tango before. Our Combo was terrific as our accompanists.

Well even with the foul weather for the fashion show it was a huge success. We made 3000 dollars clear for the LDS Church and the Japanese were very pleased. The show was covered by all the local newspapers and a lot of pictures were taken. The Church got a lot of publicity. We were very happy it turned out so well in such inclement weather. It was due to the Lord answering our prayers. Today there is a Temple in Tokyo for all the deserving saints to attend.

In the meantime, I was really enjoying my job at Flight Test. Being at an Air Depot all the aircraft arriving for delivery to the organizations in the area had to come through the Depot. So most of them would need a flight test and my section would do the testing. The Depot also pulled all the inspections on all the Generals aircraft in the area. I got to fly the test after the General MacArthurs C-47 "Batan" came out of inspection. I had to fly with his personal pilot.

During the month of December 1948 I made 18 flights, which included the Q-14. This was a little drone aircraft. It was radio controlled from a mother ship over the target so the Anti-Aircraft crews could see if it could be shot down, what a waste. It was built by Culver who built the Culver Cadet It was made out of wood and had a 150hp Franklin engine in it. This engine gave the little aircraft with a 20 foot wingspan a speed of 150 mph at 5000 feet. It was so fast that it used to get away from the mother ship at times if the pilot let it get too far ahead of him so they switched from a C-45 to a B-17.

I also flew for the month of December, the T-6, C-47A, C-47B, L-4J, B-17G, F-51D, plus my first Helicopter the H-6. I did not think much of the Helicopter. My check pilot was a Lt., I can't remember his name but he would be the first Helicopter pilot to fly a Helicopter across the Atlantic. He was married to the daughter of the Commanding General of FEAMCOM, General Doyle, my boss.

On my first ride and check out the main rotor box failed and we made an auto-rotation landing. I was lucky to have a very good instructor with me. It was quite a thrill; we had already made 4 landings before it happened.

Christmas came and we had a big party at the Officers Club on Christmas Eve but I had duty on Christmas day. We had the L'Herisson's over for dinner. I took movies of this. Fay had a house girl and a house boy to help her with the housework and mind Sherry.

I forgot to mention, that while we were at the Gora Hotel I played Santa Claus for all the dependent children who were there. I was dressed up in my Santa suit and walked in with the HO, HO, HO's, and Fay was holding Sherry. When Sherry saw me she asked her mother why Daddy was playing Santa Claus. Fay had to keep her quite so the rest of the little children would not find out. Sherry was only two years old at the time, but sure knew who her father was.

30 Dec. 1948. I got a real thrill when the P-51 I was pulling a flight test on blew the nose seal on take off. It dumped 5 gallons of oil all over the windshield and I could not see so I opened the canopy and pulled down my goggles and looked out the side like a navy pilot, they always open the canopy on landing. I was immediately covered with oil. I called the tower that I had an emergency and was making an immediately landing. By this time I was quite a greasy mess in the cockpit. I got in OK and taxied up to my parking spot with oil all over the P-51. They had to condemn my parachute but I got a new tailored made one in return. I also had to trade in my flying suit. I had to take a shower and change all my clothes that I was wearing at the time.

The crew chief that worked on the aircraft said that he guaranteed the plane for its first test hop and he would come back off his leave to fix it if anything went wrong. I have a picture of him installing the new nose seal on the old "bird" on his leave.

The New Year was upon us and there would be a big party at the Officer Club. It was a brand new one. It was a great improvement over the old one, which had been an old Japanese office building. Since I was not a member of the Church at the time I liked a cold beer as well as whiskey and 7up. I sure was not living the "Word of Wisdom"; I did not know what it was at that time. Before this when I first came to FEAMCOM I tried Manhattans but got drunk on them one night and got sick after that I could not stand them. I did switch to Martinis later but later in life I would mend my ways. We did have a great time at the new Club on New Years Eve.

The New Year started with a bang. My first flight test was a P-51. I was climbing out after take off to test the automatic cut in for the supercharger. The supercharger would shift from low blower to high blower at about 16,000 feet. This would make your manifold pressure go from 30 inches to about 42 inches, which gets your attention very quickly if you are not expecting it. It came in at the right place and I now was climbing up to see how it performed at 27,000 feet and above. I just passed 27,000 feet when I reached up for my throat mike, which seemed to be chocking me. The only trouble with that I was not wearing a throat mike I was wearing an oxygen mask with the mike in the mask. I then realized I was starving for oxygen. I looked down and the red light was on for my oxygen supply. I immediately rolled into a dive to get down where I could breathe again.

Later in the month testing another P-51 I noticed after take off I smelled smoke. I always wore a crash helmet and an oxygen mask while testing fighters. One of the feared emergencies for a test pilot is an in-flight fire. Fortunately as I smelled the smoke I could smell insulation burning it was an electrical fire. I shut off all the electrical power after calling the tower of the emergency. I opened the canopy to let the smoke out of the cockpit and went to 100% oxygen pulling my goggles down so I could look out the side of the aircraft to see where I was going. I then looked around and it seemed the smoke was coming from back of the canopy. After making a successful landing I taxied up to my parking spot and shut down. The crew chief jumped up on the wing and saw smoke coming out of the dynamotor that sits back of the pilot in the rear of the canopy, which was the culprit, another day in the world of a test pilot.

When the weekend came around we usually got away from the base and went to Tokyo, where Fay liked to look for all the bargains. We would hit all the BX's and PX's we could find as well as all the little stands on the Ginza. The Ginza was one of the main shopping areas in Tokyo. It is amazing how much the Japanese product has improved since 1948, during the occupation.

We managed to buy two beautiful 9X12 Chinese rugs, while we were there. They were all made out of wool and were one inch thick. They weighed 140 pounds a piece. One was champagne and one was blue. They only cost 300 dollars each! I kept them a long time and should have sold them when we came home. Being made of pure wool they would mildew if they got damp or wet. I had them for about 30 years before I neglected them. We also acquired many oriental artifacts. Noritake flat wear, sterling silver service for twelve, sterling silver tea and coffee service with the sterling tray. I even went to Okinawa and got a screen, which they were famous for. I brought it back to Japan in a C-47.

We traveled to see the largest cast out of bronze Buddha in the world at Kamakura, Japan. I have pictures and movies of Sherry at this historical place. She is running around the area in her little red dress. We also watched the first outboard motorboat races to be held in Japan in Kamakura bay. One of the Officers who was in charge of Manufacturing and Repair at FEACOM had built himself an outboard racer out of mahogany that was the crating material for a wing that came to our area from the Philippines. He had engine trouble and did not finish.

Fay had become pregnant just before leaving the Gora Hotel and she had to go to Johnson AB to have her delivery, since that was the closest GI Hospital available. Her doctor was and old Austrian and very experienced. He had been the personal physician for Madame Chang Kai Chek before the war. While at Fuchu we had two servants, a house girl, named Onasan, and a house boy named Kopei. They could take care of the house when Fay was not there.

As usual babies always come at the most inappropriate times. Fay started to have labor pains at midnight in a raging storm. In fact it was a typhoon. So we jumped in the Cadillac and raced for Johnson AB, which was about 20 miles away over dirt roads. We were going as fact as I dared. Everything was ready when I got there but after waiting 4 hours she still did not have the baby. Her Doctor told me to go home, since I could not help her and I was not allowed in the delivery room. Dear little Sherry was with me, since our help did not live-in; I had to take her with me. She was sound asleep on the couch waiting for me. So we drove back home in the storm again.

In the morning I got a call from Fay that I was a proud Father of a lovely little girl. I immediately jumped in the Cadillac and was off again for Johnson AB to see my dear wife Fay and my beautiful new baby girl. During all this time the typhoon was raging through the area and I could hardly see to drive and the wind was blowing a gale so we named our new daughter, Gale.

Gale was a Japanese citizen until she turned 21 years of age and also a citizen of the US. At 21 she had her choice but until then she had dual citizenship. I had to go to the US Consulate to get her official birth certificate. She was born at Johnson AB, Irumagawa, Tokyo Prefecture, Honshu, Japan 21 September 1949.

Gale was a beautiful baby even the nurses remarked how pretty she was. She was a 10- month baby, practically full grown before she decided to enter this world, (Ha). There were quite a few ten month babies. It had something to do with the water?

After a week in the hospital I went and picked up Fay and our new baby girl Gale. I had been visiting Fay and the baby every day until my leave was up. I had to go back to work after I got them home.

I forgot to mention how I met Lt. Don Disbrow who was stationed on the Tachikawa side of the Base. I was on the FEAMCOM side with a common runway in between us. He was attached to MATS, Military Air Transport Service. We called them the "trash carriers". Well I was flying a test hop in a P-51 and I had just landed and was taxing up to my parking place when I saw this Lt. standing along side of it. I shut down and opened the canopy as he jumped up on the wing and asked me if my name was Disbrow? I assured him that it was and asked him "Don't tell me there is another one". He then asked me, "Where did you get a crazy name like that?' He had gotten my movie film by mistake in his Squadron mail and he decided to deliver it in person to see who this other Disbrow was and make sure I got my film. Ever since that day we have been friends. He was a swinging bachelor at the time. For laughs we would go to the Officers Club on the Tachikawa side and he would pass Fay off as his new wife. Of course they did not know me, and Fay would show her ID, which would read Fay Disbrow. It only worked once but was fun at the time, since some of the troops knew who I was.

Since we now had permanent quarters we were having the LDS missionaries over for dinner and lessons about once a week. We were also having cottage meetings from time to time for the LDS military in our home. I still was not a member of the Church as yet. But I was attending Sunday school with Fay and the children, intermittently. We had Gale blessed by the missionaries so she had a good start like Sherry Ann. I thanked the Lord for my wonderful family and all of us were in good health at the time.

One day as I had just completed a test hop I got a phone call from Fay that Sherry was lost with another little boy in our same housing area. He was "Herky" Bjorum, Lt. Bjorum's little boy. We had come over to Japan on the same boat together and were friends. I immediately found out that the MP's were now looking for them. I was off for home in a flash to help. By the time I got there they had found the two of them wandering around in all the mud in the rice paddies adjoining the area. Fay took Sherry in and scrubbed her down. Fortunately she had all her shots for just such an occasion. Never a dull moment.

At Flight Test we would get in projects of aircraft. Sometimes it would be P-51s, or C-47s, or F-82s, etc. We had just finished a P-51 and L-5 project and now had gotten a bunch of C-47s. Fortunately I had been flying base flights C-47 so I was current in the airplane. Of course there was also smattering of other aircraft to fly which was sometimes one of a kind like the C-45, B-17E, T-6, B-29, H6, etc.

Since I had all the C-47s in flight Test I was made instructor pilot. Lt. Don Disbrow was slated to go to the states to pick up a C-47 but was not current at the time. I was the only place with C-47s in the area and I was an instructor pilot. I took him up in the old "Gooney Bird" and got him checked out.

Lt Bill Disbrow in his Hot Rod Racer with his father-in-law, Monty Cox, in back. Roswell NM 22 June 1947

During the year of 1949 I got a lot of diversified flying time in. Toward the end of the year we had a project of F-82Gs the "Twin Mustang". This was an all weather fighter with a large radar pod between the fuselages. It was quite powerful having two V-1710 Allison engines on it with counter rotating propellers. The engines developed 1500 hp a piece. On take off you would get 3200rpm with 67 inches of manifold pressure. It flew on one engine so easy that you hardly noticed the engine was out. I could come across the field and feather an engine and pull up and do a roll. The Tech Rep for Allison said that the engines could pull 100 inches of manifold pressure with water injection for war emergency!

I guess I had about 50 of these "birds" going through Flight Test. Its armament consisted of six 50cal. machine guns in the wing between the fuselages shooting straight ahead so there was no deflection shooting. I delivered the last one personally to the 68th Fighter Interceptor Squadron at Itazuke, Japan, on the 8 May 1950. Ten years later almost to the day I was assigned to JAMA, I was assigned to the 68th FIS at Itazuke, Japan, in May 1958. I was assigned as Deputy Commander and Maintenance Officer.

During 1949, I got my instrument check from Lt. George L. McGinnis in an old C-46, which I had never flown before. George said no sweat it is just like the Old C-47. I met him again after we both retired in Sacramento, California, and he was still flying and instructing. I just had him give me my Bi-annual flight check at Lake Tahoe airport in his Cessna 206. He lives in Roseville. This would be on May 1985.

While I was at Flight Test at FEACOM, George used to help me out if we had too many aircraft to test fly. Lt. Sam L'Herisson was one of my test pilots so between us we flew everything that came along. George was also the Base Operations Officer and I have his name on a lot of copies of my Form 5, flying record.

I just got a call from George's wife that he had just passed away. I could not believe it but he looked real yellow when he came up to give me my check ride. He had cancer of the liver another old pilot to "bite the dust". He died in June 1985.

Racing at Artesia, NM. My tire flys off as a racer trying to pass, hits me

It was uncanny that his funeral was held at The Church of Jesus Christ of Latter-day Saints Chapel in Roseville, California, when he was not a member of the Church. I found out later that his wife's daughter was a member and was a good influence on him so they had the services at the LDS chapel.

I forgot to mention that Lt. Hudson was the project officer for the F-82s. He would call his organization when an F-82 was ready for pick up. Later Lt. Hudson would be credited with his RO Lt. Frazier for shooting down the first aircraft in the Korean War a North Korean "Yak: He was a member of the 68th FIS at Itazuke Japan, which I became a member 10 years later.

During December 1949 we were flying mostly F-82s, plus a few At-6s and C-47s. I got my first test hop in a B-29. I only got in 12 flights for December due to foul weather, etc. Of course New Years was coming up and we would be having our big party again at the Officers Club. It seems General Doyle, the CO of FEAMCOM, wanted to put on a skit for the party. "Lo and Behold" he wanted Fay to be in it with him and to help him with the script. Knowing her background as a former Earl Carroll Dancer in Hollywood and she was always putting on Fashion shows plus entertainment at the Officers Wives Club, she was selected by the General.

She called me one day and she was in a state of shock. She said that General Doyle was coming over to see her about the show for New Years Eve. I told her to act natural and offer him some coffee. As it was she thought he was real nice and they had a nice visit. The night of the big party the skit was a huge success. It was a parody of the "Face on the bar room floor".

I think it was some time in November or December that a Capt. Kelly came from Headquarters, Fuchu, and JAMA, by way of Headquarters Wright-Patterson, Ohio, and Flight Test center and took my job. This was in 1949 and I was quite put out after all the work I put in but he out ranked me and was promised the job before he left the states. Also I was not trained as a flight test pilot but got my training the hard way by on the job training. I had saved "Uncle Sam" a lot of money by not bailing out when I had an in flight emergency, I did have the job first but someone higher up put him in the job.

I was still a test pilot although he brought a friend of his along as his assistant Lt. Peeples, who was a big "blow hard". I was assigned to OIC of the Tool Supply, which was soon phased out and they sent me back to the flight test section as assistant OIC of the flight test section under Capt. Kelly. We didn't see eye to eye for a while but we became good friends after he found out that I was a returned Combat Pilot with 50 missions and more diversified time than he did plus I could fly as good, or better than he could. He also had never been in combat. We now had Capt. James Kelly, Lt. Sam L'herisson, Lt. Wegman, and me who took Lt. Peebles place. I still was doing most of the flight-testing.

January 1950 was a slow flying month, since I still had the tool supply to contend with. I only got 6 flights in which included the T-6, C-45, F-82, and I finally got checked out in the F-80 since I still had the tool supply I had to fight to get checked out in the Jet. They checked out everyone but me. They went to Yokota AB, which had a 10,000-foot runway. I had talked to Dave Davidson, the Allison Tech Rep and got the scoop on how to start the F-80A. It was a beast to start. After the briefing from Dave I went out on the line and started the F-80A. It had a very different starting procedure than any of the later models. It was a manual start using the I-16 pump switch, which if you didn't use the right procedure you would shoot flame out the tail pipe about 50 feet in length which naturally would send the crew chief into a state of shock trying to shout at you to shut the I-16 switch off.

Well I was finally given the green light to make my first Jet flight. It would be at FEAMCOM on 16 January 1950. Everyone else had to go to Yokota AB where they had 10,000 feet of runway to make their first flight. I would be flying it off a 5000-foot runway with ten-foot fences at each end. I always thought I made my first flight in 1948 but was mistaken when I looked at my Form 5.

The F-80 did not accelerate very fast. I had taxied on the runway to the very end so there was no runway behind me, which is useless. I then ran the "bird" up to 100% holding the brakes until it stabilized I then released the brakes. As I said it did not get going very fast, not like a P-51. As I was charging down the runway I noticed that the end of the runway was coming up I looked down at my airspeed indicator and it was finally passing through 100 mph. I needed 120 mph to lift the nose wheel off the ground to get airborne. Just as I passed the 4000-foot marker I had 120 mph I pulled the stick back gently and rotated off. I picked up the gear and flaps, and then things began to happen. I looked down and I was doing 300 mph going right over Johnson AB, which was about 10 miles off the end of our runway. I immediately started a sharp climb to get out of every ones way in the traffic pattern. I zoomed up to 20,000 feet where I could relax a little and look around, all this time I was running at 100%. I pulled the power back to cruise, at 96% and did a little air work to see how this "beast" handled. I did rolls, chandelles, stalls, etc. After feeling things out I was ready to come in for a landing. In those days you made a tactical approach, which was a 360-degree overhead approach. You would approach the field going straight down the runway at pattern altitude, as you passed the end of the runway you would drop your speed brakes and break into a 360 degree turn and pull about 3 Gs to slow you down to drop your gear and then as you came around on the approach you would drop your flaps and land. Well I made my approach at about 170 mph and pulled the throttle to idle and put the dive brakes down but I was still going like mad, I had no propeller to slow me down. I came around and dropped my gear and flaps then it began to slow down and landed about 100 mph and put it right on the numbers. This baby was still going fast but when I toughed the brakes it started to slow down really nice. This flight was one of the thrills of a lifetime. Of course flying the P-51 the first time was thrill but not like this without a propeller. From then on this was the only way to fly. You could get up to 35,000 feet and be flying almost 500 mph and that gets you across the ground in a hurry. It made all propeller driven aircraft obsolete as of now, I was hooked. I did not get much flying time this month but the flight in the F-80 jet made up for it. I only flew the C-45, F-82, and 2 F-80Cs.

I forgot to mention, Christmas for the children for 1949. It had gotten around that I played Santa Claus for the children at The Gora Hotel in 1948 while we were waiting for base housing. I was volunteered to play Santa Claus for 1000 children at Tachikawa side of our base. I would do it on one condition, that I could fly one of the L-5Es I had in flight test and land it on the football field and greet the children there. Everything was going fine until someone higher up thought it would be too dangerous for the children who might get too excited and run into the propeller. I finally had to ride on top of a fire truck with my large bag of "goodies". Well with the siren blaring and me on top of the fire truck we were off until they almost threw me off the truck in a three G turn but we eventually made it to the base Gym where all the children were waiting.

It was really something me playing Santa to all those little ones, Ho! Ho! Ho! and them pulling at my beard to see if it was real. Also setting them on my knee and asking them what they wanted for Christmas. It was good that my two girls, Sherry and Gale were not there they would have given me away. To top things off I was O.D. for Christmas Day. We had celebrated on Christmas Eve.

February 1950. Was little busier than January, I had 17 test hops in C-47s, P-80Cs, T-6Ds, T-7s, and F-82s.

I forgot to mention my trip to the Philippines, Clark Field, on the 14 Dec 1949. My crew consisted of Lt Charles Wilkinson as my co-pilot, M/Sgt Grubb as my Crew Chief, Capt. Marsh Hovey as my Navigator, and S/Sgt Asiala as my radio operator. I took colored movies of this flight. Everything went well to Naha AB, Okinawa, where we refueled. We then took off for the Philippines and were to skirt the island of Mindanao to the east but the Navigator took us straight down the center of the island. It was a very dark night with no moon and it was winter. We went right over "Huk Hill" on our approach to Clark Field. The "Huks were the outlaws in the area and would come into Manila and shoot up the town and disappear back to "Huk Hill" to their mountain retreat. "Huk Hill" was about 50 miles as the crow flies from Manila. The "Federalis" would chase them up and down the hill but never catching them.

As we approached this "Huk Hill" on our let down to the pattern we saw a lot of fireworks shooting from the top of the hill. Since it was close to Christmas we thought they were having an early celebration.

We landed and taxied in to our parking place. The Airdrome Officer was waiting for us. When we got out he asked if we had any holes in us since went directly over "Huk Hill" and they were shooting at us! It was a restricted area for aircraft since they would come under fire. It was not in

Our 1947 Cadillac convertible we took to Japan on our first three year tour. FEAMCOM 1948 Tacikawa, Japan

the NOTAMS (notices to airmen) so we were not informed of the danger but lucked out since we had no holes in us they missed us.

The aircraft we flew down was going to overhaul so we would have to wait for transportation to pick us up to fly us home. We got a ride into Manila in another C-47 and went to the Avenue Hotel for our billets. This was right down town in the middle of Manila. As we entered the Hotel it had a big sign stating that there were no guns allowed in the dining room. It seems since the "Huks" were on the rampage everyone in town was armed.

After we all got settled in we went out to see the sights. We went to the Manila Hotel which was the Headquarters for General MacArthur when he was stationed in Manila. We even took in some dancing. The dance hall was one of the biggest in the world. It seemed as big as a football field. They had a night curfew so we had to be careful. We did a lot of shopping for beautiful crocheted Army and Navy tablecloths.

We rode on the many "Jeepnies" which were used as taxis; these were made from old GI Army "jeep" left over from WWII. There were hundreds of them running around Manila. They were painted and decorated in wild colors to the individuals taste and imagination. It was quite a thrill riding in one of them. They were all would be race drivers and would race each other down the street. After seeing all the sights and doing all the shopping we were ready to go back home and go to work again. During my 21 years in the USAF I would visit Manila quite a few times

I had been flying quite a bit and could not get any leave at the present time so I saw and ad in the daily bulletin for ski racers for the team. When General Doyle saw it I heard he approved it because I needed a rest. I could not ski a "nickels worth" at the time but the manager of our ski lodge was Capt. Loran Trubschenck. He was an excellent skier and I thought I could get a few lessons from him. I got to take the whole family with me, including our maid. We had a great time and took movies of the trip. They gave me a little loving cup, which said on it "The most fantastic skier", when we left the Lodge. I still could not ski. Later on we would go to another Ski Lodge called Odawara. the Lodge was operated by Special Services. I took more movies of this place and after many years I transferred them to VCR tapes. We rode the train to both places and were picked up in a snow cat to ride up the mountain to the Lodges. The weather was beautiful at both places, which made it very nice for skiing. I could still not ski very well but beat everybody at the pool table after skiing. It was real reasonable to stay at these Lodges, since they were under Special Services.

We still spent our weekends mostly going to Tokyo shopping and browsing around in all kinds of shops looking for bargains. Fay got a full length Mink coat and we got a tea service set with the tray, all sterling silver plus service for twelve flat ware, ivory statues, etc. We bought lamps, rugs, vases, silk screens, miniature ivory statues, etc. I was broke buying all the bargains. It was a shopper's paradise during the occupation. I was not collecting stamps at the time or I could have had a fantastic collection real cheap but now I have to pay much more for them.

We were living at Fuchu AB, in a nice 2 bedroom apartment upstairs in the complex. We had a house girl, Ono and a houseboy, Kopei. I decided to make a movie with my old 16mm Bell and Howell movie camera, with them in it. We had a lot of fun and had a running gun chase with two jeeps. I borrowed one of the MP jeeps and got the rest of the cast from some of my more adventurous friends. I shot on weekends. The plot was the Russians were going to try to blow up the bomb dump. The title of the picture was "Menace". We had lots of shots of spies, etc. We had the preview at the Officers Club. Everyone seemed to like it. I also took movies of the beautiful area of Japan as well as their colorful festivals. I took movies every where we went

April 1950. This was a slow month since I still had the tool section as well as doing flight- testing when they needed me. I was still qualified to fly anything they had in flight test, but they always got first choice.

1 May 1950. This was May Day, the Communist Birthday. Everyone was restricted to the Base on this day, except for an emergency. Before the restriction the "Red", Japanese, would seek out US military personnel and civilians and "hassle" them quite a bit. One time they turned over their cars and set them on fire. To avoid all this they put the Military on the restriction.

We had celebrated Easter and Fay and the children dressed up but I was restricted to my uniform, which I wore always, especially off base.

Flying in May was a little better than April and I took a cross country ride in an AT-6 to Komaki and back just to get out of the local pattern for a change. We also got the last Q-14 ready to fly and delivered it. I hated to see these little drones go. It was so much fun to fly and they were fast for their size.

June 1950. It had been rumored that the North Koreans were building up their Army to invade South Korea. Of course it was shrugged off as a rumor, so we went about our business of getting the aircraft in flight test flown. I was thinking of going home to the states, since our tour would be over in October 1950. We were what people were calling "short timers". I got 27 hours of flying time in this month with 17 landings. I got a cross country to Ashiya in an old "Gooney Bird", the C-47D.

As things would have it Fay and I were at a party at the Officers Club at Fuchu with General Doyle and the rest of the compliment of Officers, when there was a "drum roll" by the orchestra. The General then went to the microphone and made an announcement. He read a bulletin that the North Koreans had just invaded South Korea. This was Sunday evening the 25 June 1950. We could hardly believe it, another war!

The next day was flying as usual. I was assigned back to the flight test permanently by this time. We were waiting to see what the US would do. What would President Truman do and what the rest of the world would do. Of course General MacArthur was appointed Supreme Commander as we started to send troops into Korea, on the 25 June 1950. By this time we were trying to organize all our fighter squadrons and groups. The 49th fighter group at Misawa, the 36th fighter group at Johnson AB, near us, and the 8th fighter group at Itazuke with the 68th Fighter Interceptor squadron, along with all the support groups. The United Nations asked the US to aid South Korea, so we began to organize.

29 June 1950. General Doyle called me at flight test and asked if I still had the old C-47 in flight test. I told him I did and it was on a red cross (maintenance designation to ground the aircraft for a one -time flight to the Philippines for overhaul at Clark Field). He then told me to take it off the Red Cross and taxi it over to the Tachikawa side of the base when I got it ready to go and find out where they wanted me to go. It was ready by quitting time and I went over to Tachikawa with the C-47 and got my briefing. I found that I was to go to Taegu, Korea, with a load of 5000 pounds of Howitzer shells for the Army. I was to leave at 0600 hours the next day, 30 June 1950. I would land at Itazuke AB, Japan, and refuel. The weather was terrible with driving rain with very low ceilings.

I said "goodbye" to Fay and the children, Sherry and Gale and persuaded them that this flight was just routine but deep down I couldn't believe I was going to fight another war after flying 50 missions in WWII. At least in WWII I had 10 50 Cal. Machine guns protecting me on the old B-24 now I was going to war with only my 45 Cal Automatic pistol in my zipper pocket of my flying suit. Of course Fay did not know really what was happening but that was good so she would not worry too much.

30 June 1950. I finally got into the old C-47 and noticed the load sitting right in the middle of the aircraft fuselage. It didn't take up much room but was very heavy and explosive. I took off with my co-pilot, Lt George, and my crew chief Sgt. Aziala. We climbed up through the "soup" to our cruising altitude and headed for the homer on the volcanic island of Oshima. When we hit Oshima we made a right turn to Itazuke. It

was raining real hard and there was quite a bit of turbulence. I had made sure that our load was tied down securely. I did not want those boxes of howitzer shells shifting, which would be a disaster.

We had to make an instrument approach to Itazuke and had to hold until another aircraft landed ahead of us. After landing we were met by a group of Officers who said that they were off loading our howitzer shells and loading communication equipment aboard. We would go to Suwon, Korea, where is Suwon? It would be south of Seoul and a double track railroad goes from Pusan, Korea to Seoul and passes right by Suwon, you can't miss it it is a single concrete strip running north and south.. Don't land unless you get a green light from a light gun, no matter what anybody says on the radio. After you land, unload and pick up the wounded, if any and all the civilian personnel trying to get back to Japan.

We took off for Suwon. Our first checkpoint after crossing the strait between Japan and Korea was Pusan. There I found the double track railroad going north out of Pusan. I dropped down to about 1000 feet or less right over the railroad tacks. I would pull up every time we came to a tunnel, then drop down again right over the tracks. I did not want the enemy to pick us up visually or on radar

I was listening to the fighter channel when I heard a conversation. "Hey! There goes a North Korean train down there" "Lets go down and get him" "You go down and get him I'm low on fuel and I'm staying up here". There was a long pause before the next transmission. Then I heard a very obscene phrase and "I missed him". There was another long pause and then "I got him". "Hey, I got a flame out!" "I'm putting it down, see you".

While all this was going on I was on the "deck" following the double track railroad. I had to pull up to get over a hill in front of me. When I pulled up to get over the hill I got to the top I could see Suwon and a cloud of dust coming off the runway. As I made my pattern someone said, "Look out for little friend", as I got the green light to land. Then I saw the P-80 on its belly along side of the runway. As I touched down I made sure I avoided him and as I went by the pilot waved. I was doing about 80 mph at the time. As I came to the end of the runway there was a Korean GI waving me into a parking place.

One of the P-51Ds I had in flight test for the South Africans, FEAMCOM 1950

On getting out I was met by a US major in a jeep and he said that we better go down and get the pilot of the P-80 who had just "bellied in". I leaped in the jeep with the major and off we went down the strip. When we got there it was a friend of mine, Lt. Ollie Olson from the 49th fighter group. He had already blown up the IFF and had the ammo from his machine guns over his shoulder. He remarked what good service he got for his pick up. He had just radioed in for someone to pick him up. I told him he was lucky I came in here. Let's get out of here we could see small arms fire in the distance. There was an F-82 in the ditch with an L-5 and a C-54 burning at end of the runway.

I asked him what happened and he said that he went down for the train and missed it the first pass and on the second pass it blew up in his face, knocking out his electrical system and his engine so he put it in the first strip he saw, which was Suwon. He radioed his wingman to have some one pick him up and said that it was sure quick service. I told him he was lucky that I landed at Suwon just as he crash-landed. I did not hear his

I am flying the Q-14 target aircraft over the Kanto Plain, Japan 1950

transmission to pick him up. Lt. Olsen hopped into the jeep and by the time we got back to the old C-47 they had unloaded it and there were about 15 people ready to go back to Japan.

When we got back to Itazuke AB, Japan, we found out that the North Koreans had bombed and strafed Suwon and the foot soldiers took it. We got out of there just in time I had been given film from the Public Affairs Officer to get pictures of all this, which I did.

1 July 1950. We got orders to land at Taejon, Korea, which was a grass strip, and pickup all the wounded and sick and anybody else that was trying to get back to Japan. I had Lt. Pecan as my flight nurse. When we came in for a landing I had to land over a hill. The runway was grass and did not look too long so I made a short field landing. It had been raining so I had to watch my braking but made it OK and turned right around on the wet field.

When I taxied back and parked there was an ambulance waiting for me. As it turned out it had only one person in it. They loaded him aboard on a stretcher plus 7 other people who were stranded due to the war. While I was giving the C-47 a preflight before starting up, I saw a lone unidentified aircraft, single engine, headed for our strip at a right angle. The Koreans shouted, "Enemy Aircraft" with everybody taking cover anywhere they could get it, even under the GI trucks that were parked in the parking area. I looked up and shouted that it was an AT-6 one of ours, which made everyone happy. With that I got in the aircraft and cranked up and got out of there as quickly as possible.

2 July 1950. We got the day off for a little rest and to find out where our next mission would be, since the North Koreans were rapidly moving south toward Taejon and our troops needed supplies.

3 July 1950. We were loaded with General Timberlake's Jeep and driver to take to K-1 south of Pusan on the southern tip of Korea. We took off without incident and proceeded to K-1, which turned out to be an old Japanese WWII fighter landing strip. It had no parking area so all the aircraft landing there had to land over the parked aircraft at the end of the approach end of the runway. You landed and when you got to the end of the runway you would turn around and taxi back to the other end and park next to the last aircraft that landed.

As we approached the runway I noted we were landing to the South over

Flying thr AT-6 Flight Test, FEAMCOM, Japan 1950

about 5 other aircraft parked at the North end of the strip. I made a pattern and landed. As we were taxing back to park at about three quarters of the way back there was a loud thump and the old C-47 stopped with a lunge. I could not believe what happened. It seems the old Jap runway collapsed under the load we were carrying and the left main gear sunk a tire width through the runway. Well there was instant pandemonium among all the personnel responsible for the logistics and unloading of the serving aircraft.

They quickly brought over a forklift to unload the jeep and the other supply equipment we had aboard to make the plane lighter, then proceeded to fathom a way to get the old "bird" unstuck. After many suggestions it was decided to get all the Korean workers in the area of the strip to get under the left wing and all lift at once on a signal with a GI 6X6 truck hooked to the tail wheel with a chain pulling the aircraft backwards. After much effort and a lot of "ooshing" it came out to everyone's relief and shouts of accomplishment. Now the aircraft that were holding in the pattern could land, after we cranked up and took off for another load.

On our next flight I found that they had filled the hole with gravel and marked it with a red flag. It seemed that the Japanese used more sand than cement in these old strips and this one was made on a delta, which made it a little weak for our heavy load on the old C-47.

We made a total of three trips this day and on the last trip it was dusk. We set up our pattern and landed. As we slowed down and started to make our 180-degree turn to taxi back down the runway the left tire blew! There we were blocking the runway again so no one could land.

It seems the strain on the tire as the aircraft was pulled out of the hole had weakened the tire and it blew with the heavy load we were carrying. I must have made a smooth landing or it would have blown on touch down. Luckily they had a lot of C-47 tires on hand so they could change it in a hurry since they had all those aircraft holding waiting to land.

While we were getting unloaded on our subsequent trips I took pictures of all the proceedings, which included a picture of a Korean pilot servicing his L-5, a small spotter aircraft it had four "Bazookas" on it. Two on each wing strut. He had two North Korean tanks to his credit he would fly down a road where the tanks were reported and he had an electrical switch in the cockpit to fire the rockets. He would wait until he was real close and then he would blast them before they knew what happened. They would not shoot at him because he would call in the fighters.

Well after getting our tire fixed and our load unloaded we headed back to Itazuke, Japan. When we got there and landed General Doyle's Aide was waiting for us. He gave us the good news. There was a new crew to take over our "bird" and we were to return immediately with him to FEAMCOM in the Generals plush B-17. They had 150 P-51s arriving on the Boxer Aircraft Carrier for the war in Korea and they all had to go through flight test and I was needed immediately. It felt good to get back home after living in a flight suit for almost a week with my .45 automatic in my flight suit zipper pocket. I was at least going to get a shot this time myself if we were attacked.

5 July 1950. It was back to the old grind. For the rest of the month I would be flying 12 P-51s, 6 F-80Cs, 4 C-47s, and 2 T-33s. I had a little excitement; upon feathering the prop on one of the engines on the C-47 on a test hop one of the props would not un-feather so I came in on one engine, no sweat

Since Fay's birthday was on the 4 July, we had a belated celebration for her and for me getting back from Korea. We now had a very nice Officers Club, where we could go to dinner. We had a lot of Japanese places to go for dinner consisted of Sukiyaki or Tempura, both were very good. The Tempura would be served right from the cook, which was deep-fried. We liked going to the native restaurants in the area of Tokyo. When we went to Tokyo we would make a full day of shopping and dining. If we went on a Sunday we would try to make the Church meeting in Tokyo. Both Fay and I had tailor made clothes. I had some beautiful Harris Tweed sport coats made for $15 apiece I supplied the material. Fay had a lot of nice dresses made from a place in Tokyo. The Japanese lady who ran the place was married to a Japanese fellow who was one of the Japanese Olympic swimmers in the 1936 Olympic games in Los Angeles. He also survived the Hiroshima atomic bombing and was to be examined periodically for his injuries and radiation he was subjected to.

August 1950. The Air Force had changed the symbols on us for different flight categories. It was now S-24 from X-3 for a fight test. Experimental flight test was X-1. Administrative flights were A-2 and so forth. Confusing to start with but we became accustomed to it shortly.

I don't know if I mentioned that the Air Force had changed our wonderful US Army Air Force uniform from our "pinks and greens" to blue. It was quite a let down. In the old days everybody knew who we were, an Officer in the USAAF. The new blue uniform you couldn't tell us from a Greyhound bus driver. It also wasn't tailored like the old uniform. They wanted it to look like a civilian suit. I always hated it except for the dress uniform which had a lot of class. They eventually changed that, too. Their summer uniform was not bad they were called silver tans. I can still get into my dress uniform and my silver tans.

I was flying so much and getting hot and cold going to altitude that I got a back spasm. As I finished this flight in an F-80C I parked and reached up to lift myself up to get out of the aircraft, it hit me. I had to have the crew chief and his assistant lift me out of the cockpit and the pain was excruciating. They took me up to the flight surgeon at the hospital where the "Doc" gave me an examination. He then sent me home for a week of rest and relaxation, R&R. I lay around the pool and soaked up the sun on my back, which helped a lot. It seemed that the vent for the air conditioning in the F-80 and the T-33 blew right on your back. With it being 120 degrees on the ramp when you strapped in the jet and you would turn on the air conditioning on to cool off when airborne. On take off it would throw snow in the cockpit. You would cool off real nice including your back. When you got to 35,000 feet the outside temperature would be a minus 40 degrees outside. Even at 40 below you were nice and comfortable in the cockpit. I was never cold in the cockpit on a test hop. The pumping of the adrenalin kept one warm. Of course that cold air on your back eventually took its toll and all test pilots who flew jets would experience a back problem at one time or another.

The rest around the pool and at home did the trick. I was never completely cured although the Air Force gave me a back evaluation when I retired years later. I later found out from a Chiropractor, if I took Dolomite the spasms would go away. I did this and have had no more trouble. If I don't take it the spasm will return with the right circumstances.

While I was relaxing at the club pool I had Fay and the children with me and we had a real nice time together. I was teaching Sherry and Gale how to swim. I took movies of this along with Fay teaching them how to swim. Our family was due to rotate to the states in April 1950 but we were frozen due to the Korean War. We had to put in an additional year in our tour of duty. This made it a three- year tour from a two- year tour. We did have nice quarters, which made the extra time bearable. Sherry and Gale were not school age as yet so we did not have to worry about that and Fay had help in the house, which made it nice. We had to pay 20 dollars per month for two servants.

September 1950. This was a busy flying month as well as Gale's birthday, one year old on the 21 September, and I was 35 on the 23 September 1950. Also in this month I delivered the last F-82G personally to the 68th Fighter Interceptor Squadron at Itazuke, Japan. It was on the 8 September 1950. Nine years later I would return to Japan for another tour of duty and would be assigned to the 68th FIS, as the Deputy Commander and Maintenance Officer. We would be flying the F-86D and the F-102.

This month entailed flight-testing the aluminum and steel rocket fins for the 5.2 rockets carried on the wing rocket pods on the F-80Cs. These fins were made under contract with the Japanese. I also would test the nose and tail fuses for the napalm tanks, which were carried on the same wing pods on the F-80Cs.

Capt. Kelly, I, and Lt. Wegman would make the first tests at Miho gunnery range. The first test was for the Napalm fuses. We would use nose fuses on one tank and the tail fuse on the other. We would drop the tanks one at a time. Our target was an old bridge on the range. The consensus of opinions was to get down low and "scrape" the tanks off for accuracy.

We flew up to the range in diamond formation and upon arriving we broke off in a trail. I was second to drop my tank. We dropped one tank at a time whereas in combat you would drop both tanks at once to keep the aircraft trimmed, since each tank weighed at least 600 pounds a piece. It was quite a thrill dropping one tank at a time. That 600 pounds hanging on one wing made your trim way out of whack. You had to have pressure on the stick to catch it so you could roll in the trim rapidly with your thumb. It was quite a thrill dropping the napalm, especially at the very low altitude, 50 feet at 400mph. I swear I could feel the heat from the tremendous explosion.

After the mission the General called up and wanted his Aide to fly one of the missions. Naturally he did and it finally turned out he was presented with the Distinguished Flying Cross and so was Capt. Kelly. I could not believe it. Of course neither of the two had ever been in combat so this was a way to get the DFC, what a laugh. I got nothing since I already had the DFC awarded for outstanding airmanship in combat after flying 50 missions in WWII in a B-24.and I did most of the napalm and rocket testing. I guess that is the way the ball bounces.

The rocket test would be air to ground. I was to start my run from 4000 feet and go into a 45 degree dive at no more than 300 mph indicated and fire the rocket at no less than 1500 feet of altitude and pull our before I hit the ground.

On the first run I got all set up at 4000 feet and started my 45 degree dive and got a little anxious and fired too soon and missed the target. The steel fins worked OK. On the second run I was determined to hit the target this time. I got to 4000 feet and put the old F-80C in the 45 degree dive at 250 mph and at 1500 feet I fired, thinking I had a dead hit, since I had the target right in the cross hairs in my gun sight. The rocket went about 500 feet in front of me as I started my pull out the rocket made a 180 degree loop and headed right for me. In the split second I almost shot myself down but I whipped the F-80C in a tight descending turn and it missed me just going over the right wing. It seems that I had steel fins on the first rocket and aluminum on the second one, which tore off upon firing this mission was being viewed from the ground by range personnel and they were wondering what was happening as I was making those evasive maneuvers on the second pass. By the time I landed at Miho strip the rocket was standing in front of the operations shack with no fins on it. It showed that aluminum fines were unsuitable and that the steel was the only way to go, so all the rest of the fins were made of steel.

I also had to test carrying two 500pound bombs on the wing tips of the F-80C. One bomb on each wing tip attached to the shackles that usually hold the tip tanks. The test would be conducted at our sub base at Kisarazu. This was across Tokyo Bay about 30 miles east of Tachikawa. The test consisted of climbing to 5000 feet and go into a dive with a pull up at least 4 "Gs" to see if I could pull the bombs off the shackles. I conducted the test over Tokyo Bay so if one did come off it would be in a safe area. After making four runs I decided that I could not pull the bombs off, so the shackles would be safe in combat.

We found out later when we got the large Beech fuel tanks, that carried 360 gallons of fuel, the shackles were still strong enough to carry the weight of 2160 pounds on the wing tip. Of course the strength of the shackle was limited to how many "G" forces you put on the shackles when the tanks were full. When I finished my test and was coming in for a landing at Kisarazu AB, and I heard the tower tell an aircraft taxing out to hold its position because he had an F-80 in the pattern. The aircraft taxing out was a Navy F9F, their first operational Jet. It had the same engine as the F-80C.

During lunch before my test at Kisarazu I got talking to a Navy CPO with wings. His name I found was CPO Smith and he had written a few books on flying reciprocating engine aircraft. I also found out that he had never flown a jet aircraft. He had a Navy F9F in the hanger and he wanted to fly it. He had no one to give him a cockpit check and information on the flying a jet aircraft. I gladly volunteered to give him a briefing on flying a jet type fighter and gave him a good cockpit check. I also gave him a walk around pre-flight of the aircraft. One thing I stressed was the slow acceleration of the jet aircraft on these particular models. I told him to make sure he had 120 mph on the airspeed indicator before trying to lift the nose wheel off the ground for take off. He should keep the elevators in neutral as he proceeded down the runway keeping good rudder control and at 120 mph apply a little back pressure on the stick to bring the nose up and the jet would lift off in a flash and would climbing at 250 mph at between 6000 to 10,000 feet per minute! Also before take off line up on the runway, hold the brakes, run the engine to 100% RPM wide open to the stop to see if the engine RPM is reading 100%. If not don't go!

After the briefing I offered to fly the aircraft for him before he attempted to fly it to make sure it was operating properly. He insisted that he could handle it, although most of his flying time was not in fighters but in cargo aircraft. In fact I don't think he had any fighter time at all much less jet fighter time.

Listening to the tower I told them that I would go around and let the F9F take off. As I watched he ran up the engine and must have gotten

100% because he released the brakes. As I watched in disbelief the jet ran the full length of the runway, 6000 feet, and never got off the ground and went off the end of the runway in a very nose high attitude and hit the sea wall just off the end of the runway. This sea wall was the dock for unloading aircraft at Kisarazu. The Jet disintegrated as it hit the sea wall. I was horrified as I set up my pattern to land. The landing was quite tricky, since everyone was running across it to see what happened along with all the crash equipment dashing toward the accident. Then a helicopter got airborne and was hovering over the crash sight by the time I taxied in and parked. The helicopter took the pilot in a mad dash to the hospital at Yokasuka Naval Hospital but he died en-route.

On inquiring of the witnesses on the ground, it appeared he had a nose high attitude all the way down the runway instead as I instructed him not to get the nose off the ground until he had 120 mph. The jet was in a stalled attitude the whole length of the runway and would not fly in that attitude no matter how much power you had. He went off the end of the runway in this attitude. I also asked if they jet sounded like it was at full power. Sometimes if you don't have the friction lock tight the throttle will creep back on take off, if you take your hand off the throttle. Your hand should never leave the throttle on take off only for picking up the gear and flaps after take off. I asked if the flaps were down, everyone agreed that they were. If the flaps are not down on take off it will lengthen the take off run on a short runway where you will not get off the ground in time before you are out of runway. I surmised that he simply stalled the aircraft all the way down the runway and it would not fly in this position.

I flew my F-80C back to my home base, FEAMCOM, to make my report on my bomb test and related what happened at Kisarazu. I was very surprised that the Navy never called me as a witness to the accident investigation. In fact it was hushed up I never saw or heard of the incident ever happening. I always wondered if CPO Smith was even authorized to fly that F9F. The next time I went to Kisarasu I went to the salvage yard and the F9F was gone. It seems that every time I landed at Kisarasu something seem to happened

I was flying a C-47 from FEAMCOM one day and had a Major Grubb aboard bumming a ride. We were in the pattern at Kisarasu, when all of a sudden I noticed we were loosing power on one engine. Of course I pushed both throttles up to full power and fed rudder and aileron to overcome the yawing of the dead engine. Major Grubb rushed up and said, "What's wrong?" when he saw the aileron up more than usual, especially when we are flying straight and level. I said that we just lost an engine. He asked, "Which one?" I said that I did not know, as I saw him looking at the feathering buttons on the top of the cockpit. Too many pilots have feathered the wrong engine and were coasting instead of having a good engine with power. We were in the pattern at the time so there was not too much "sweat"

I was turning base leg for my landing, turning into the dead engine, which you should not do unless you know your aircraft. We landed without further incident and I learned that I could fly the C-47 with full power on one engine and turn into the dead engine.

We later ran the engine up upon landing and it appeared to be OK. I surmised that the weather conditions were such this day that we had picked up carburetor ice from the quick letdown over Tokyo Bay, from 5000 feet to 1000 feet to the pattern and the temperature and humidity was just right to form ice in the induction system. When we landed the temperature was warm and melted the ice. Of course I gave the engines a good power check before taking off for home and made sure that the carburetor heat was working.

Another trip in a P-51 "Mustang" was a real thrill. I was taking the P-51 to Kisarazu to have it painted after finishing all the overhaul work on it. I had given it a flight test first and everything appeared OK. I took off with out incident with minimum fuel for the short trip to "Kisser". When I let down for the traffic pattern I made a 360 overhead approach, breaking to the left and pulled the throttle back and pushed the prop pitch up to high RPM, I leveled off and reached for the gear handle to drop the gear. The gear handle on a P-51 is near the floor near your left foot. For me to reach it I had to lean way over and could not see where I was going for an instant. As I tried to push the handle to the down position it would not budge, it was stuck solid. I called the tower and told them I was having a little gear problem but would try all my tricks I knew to get it down. I had already tried the emergency gear extension handle and it would not budge either. I had heard of pilots putting their foot on the gear handle trying to get it to move and then broke it off since it is made of pot metal, then you are in real trouble.

In the meantime I am "chugging around" the pattern trying to get the levers to move with no luck. The tower called me and wanted to know what my intentions were. I told them that if I couldn't get the gear down I was going to belly it in on the runway. This created panic in the tower since Kisarazu only had one active runway and no taxiways. You would land, stop, turn around and taxi down the runway you just landed on back to the ramp to park your aircraft. If I bellied the P-51 in, it would close the only runway they had and no one could land until they could get the P-51 off the runway.

Capt Bill Disbrow flying the F-82 Twin Mustang over the Emperor's Palace in Tokyo, Japan 1949

As I was thinking of all the things I might do the tower called again and wanted me to go back to FEAMCOM and belly the aircraft there. By this time I was on minimum fuel and I was not flying over Tokyo Bay with

Capt Bill Disbrow in the F-80C, our first operational jet FEAMCOM Flight Test, Jan 1950

a chance of going down in the "drink". I told the tower I would try to get the gear down one more time and had an idea that might work. After trimming up the old "bird" to fly hands off at about 140 mph I grabbed the gear handle with my left hand and the emergency extension handle with my right hand. I made a very positive movement at the same time with all the strength I could muster. Low and behold the gear popped down and I got the green lights that the gear was down and locked. Thanking the good Lord I landed without further incident. The Lord had gotten me out of a tight spot again.

By this time while I was trying to get the gear down a big crowd was out on the ramp to watch the P-51 belly in. When the gear finally came down there was a big roar from the crowd as they waved their caps. After I landed I taxied up to the hanger and shut down. I described the sequence of events I went through to finally get the gear down. After many congratulations they rolled the P-51 in to the hanger to give it a retraction test. The tower was very much relieved since I did not have to belly the P-51 in. They were

The F-84E at Flight Test FEAMCOM Japan 1950

watching me the whole time with their binoculars with a big sigh of relief when the gear came down.

The maintenance crew put the P-51 up on jacks so they could give it a retraction test to find the trouble. When everything was all set they retracted the gear which came up just like the book said but when they tried to lower it the crew chief could not budge the gear handle to the down position. He was a burley man and was quite chagrined that he could not move the gear handle. I hollered not to put his foot on the handle since it was quite easily broken off with the excessive pressure. He then tried my trick but to no avail, the handle would not budge. The gear system in the P-51 operates on 3000 pounds of hydraulic pressure so it is hard to overcome.

The crew chief after trying everything could not get the gear to come down. They finally had to take the inspection plates off to release the gear up locks, manually. The gear finally popped down. After a little adjustment to the up-locks the gear worked as smooth as glass. It seems that as I was trying to get the gear down in the air the wing had enough give at 140 mph to release the bind on the up-locks for me to overcome the bind.

For the month of December 1950 I had flown 34 test hops in 9 different aircraft from the T-6 to the F-80C. I delivered the last F-82G, Twin Mustang, to the 68th FIS at Itazuke AB, on the island of Kyushu, Japan. This was in 1950 and little did I dream that I would become the DCO of the 68th FIS 10 years later almost to the day that I came to FEAMCOM.

On my days off we would tour around the outlying districts of the Tokyo area. We always attracted a lot of attention wherever we went in the Cadillac Convertible it being the only one in Japan at the time. Also Sherry Ann our first daughter had beautiful blond hair, which was very rare to see in Japan. All the Japanese people wanted to touch it and feel it.

It was Gale's and my birthdays in September. Gale was one year old. Fay baked her a little cake with one candle on it. I was 35 on the 23 September. Gale was walking by this time. She was a good baby no trouble at all as long as you kept her fed and changed her diaper on time.

October 1950. We had a project of L-5s plus the usual P-51s, F-80s and T-33s. The L-5s were used as spotter aircraft. The pilot would try

Playing Santa Claus for the children at Tachikawa A.B. Japan, 1949

to spot enemy gun emplacements so he could call the fighters in to strafe them. We gave the South Koreans some of these aircraft for spotting. The Cessna.Aircraft Co manufactured the L-5 and they turned out to be a very good utility airplane. They were also used for flying ambulances.

We also had a lot of P-51s to fly to get ready for Korea. I personally flew 8 flights in the P-51 this month. In fact we were so busy trying to fly all the test hops off that we had to bring in some qualified Base Flight pilots to help. One of these pilots was Captain John Bull Sterling an old WWII fighter pilot.

As I was landing this day in a P-51, John was taxing out for take off in a P-51. I taxied up and shut off and went into my office to see what was next. I talked to my crew chief and line chief, Sgt Grubb, on the write-ups on the aircraft I had just flown and to get it ready for delivery.

I was assigning aircraft to my other pilots when over our radio in our operations office, which we used to monitor each test hop, in case they had any trouble, came the voice of John. He was having gear trouble in the P-51 he had just taken off in. I got on the radio and asked him what the trouble was. It seems he put the gear down to come in for a landing and he had a red light on the left gear, indicating it was not down and locked. I told him to make a low pass over the runway and I would check it visually. I ran outside of the office, along with every one else that was around; with my binoculars .to check the gear as John made his low pass. As he came by I noticed that the left gear was out about a foot and hanging there. The right gear was down and so was the tail wheel, fully extended.

I went back into my office and got on the radio and told John what I saw. Then I told him to retract the gear to see if it would retract and lock. As I listened he picked up the gear and my line chief, Sgt Grubb, checked the gear out to see if it came up and locked. The right gear and the tail wheel came up but the left gear remained in the same position. I then told John to pull the emergency gear release handle to see if that would drop the gear manually. He tried this with negative results. The left gear stayed in the same original position while the right gear and tail wheel came down. I told him to pick up the gear again and if the right gear and the tail wheel came up to not fool with it any longer, since the sequence valve is out of sequence he would not be able to control the gear at all.

I flew this H-5 helicopter at Flight Test FEAMCOM, Japan 1949

The emergency procedures are in black and white in the operating instructions, the "Dash One". I tried them all and told John if the gear would come up again, the right main gear and the tail wheel, belly it in on the runway. I would have the crash crew out waiting for him. Just then a strange voice came over the radio. It was the Flying Safety Officer, L/C Timothy O'Keefe. He told me to have John shake the aircraft to see of that would make the gear come down, since it would work once in a while. I radioed John and told him to shake the gear to see if the gear would come down after putting the gear handle in the down position again letting the gear go to the down position. This was against my better judgment but I was out ranked by a L/C and he was giving a Captain the orders. A P-51 is easy to belly in and the repairs are not too extensive if it is done right.

Well John really shook the old P-51. In fact he broke the actuator on the good gear and now it was dangling loose and the other gear was still in the partial up position. I had a feeling this would happen. Now what! I told John he could still belly it in but John wanted to bail out and L/C

O'Keefe gave him the OK! I was fit to be tied. We were losing a beautiful aircraft that was needed just because I was out-ranked by a L/C, who never flew a P-51. He later became the Assistant Chief Staff of the Air force but did not last very long and died of a heart attack. I think we were the same age. I ran into Tim many times after leaving FEAMCOM. We went to all weather instrument school together at Moody AFB, Georgia in 1953. Well John was going to bail out and wanted to know the best way to get out. I told him the consensus of opinions was to roll on your back and fall out. The bail out area was to be Miho Gunnery range away from all the populated areas. Miho was about 50 miles from Tachikawa. I was to fly up with the Fight Surgeon in the L-5 so I could mark where he landed after he bailed out so the rescue crew could pick him up as soon as possible.

I got the Fight Surgeon loaded in the L-5 and took off in the same direction John was heading but at 150 mph slower. As we got airborne I called John on the radio and asked him his position and altitude so I could find him. Also what was the best area to bail out? With all the chatter on the radio we began to pick up a lot of airborne spectators. I then called Tokyo Center to notify all aircraft in the vicinity to depart immediately to protect anyone from being hit by a stray P-51 after the bail out. As we approached the bail out area I heard and exclamation come over the radio, "Dammit", I dropped the clock". It seems John was trying to get the clock out of the instrument panel while he was waiting for us to arrive in the area. He was removing the clock for a souvenir. As the clock came loose he dropped it and now was trying to retrieve it in between his feet. I could see him now and called him to re-brief him on the bail out. Roll on your back with forward trim in and fall out. As I cleared the area for the bail out, John made a 360-degree turn and rolled on his back. I was about 1000 feet below him and my altimeter was reading 4000 feet. I watched him roll on his back but was surprised that John was not coming out of the P-51, he was still in the cockpit and I mentioned it to the Fight Surgeon who was in the back seat of the L-5. Then all of a sudden John came whizzing out of the cockpit and went right by us with no parachute deployed! As I raced after him in the L-5 I was shouting to myself "pull the ripcord". Then all of a sudden the chute blossomed out to the relief of the Flight Surgeon and me. As I got closer to John I noticed that the chute was swinging back and forth and he was going to hit going backwards. He hit going backwards in a rice paddy. As I banked around to get a better look he laid motionless. After what seemed an age he began to move. He sat up and waved to us. By this time I was no more than 50 feet above him in a steep bank watching him. After he waved I took off for Miho, after wobbling my wings to acknowledge his wave. As I gained some altitude to see Miho, where the rescue vehicles were, I noticed a jeep already on its way in our direction. I flew over the jeep and made a turn in the direction where John landed, so the jeep could take a fix on me. I would circle over John until they arrived and picked him up. I was back at Miho Operations waiting to get John's story, which did not take very long.

As we waited at Operations for John the Flight Surgeon got out his supplies from his bag just in case, when John drove up in the jeep. As I started to ask all the questions why he bailed out, etc., John gave me his story as the Flight Surgeon checked him over. Why he bailed out? He always wanted to be a member of the "Caterpillar Club". Why he didn't come out of the P-51 immediately when he was on his back? He made such a coordinated roll that he stuck up in the cockpit. He then pushed the stick forward and he flew right out. Why he did not open his chute immediately? He said that he wanted to see what a delayed jump felt like.

As the Flight Surgeon had John take off his leather flight jacket out fell the clock, the florescent lights and the Form one (the flying record of the aircraft). Since there wasn't anything to do while he was waiting for me to get to the bail out area in the L-5 he decided to take apart everything he could and stuff it in his jacket so he would not lose it when he bailed out. After the Flight Surgeon checked him out he was no worse off from his bail out so we flew home, less one good P-51. The P-51 went into a rice paddy missing a farmer's house by about 100 yards and burying itself up to the tail of the aircraft, so ended my day of the 27 October 1950.

I forgot to mention that John B. Sterling had knocked off the tail on the Generals B-17 one day. I gave him an orientation ride in an F-82G and after we parked he tried to step off the wing on to the tire like a P-51 but the F-82G is much higher than a P-51. Well he missed the tire and bumped his head on the stationary propeller and split his head open requiring 16 stitches. He was also riding in a T-33 and failed to lock the canopy, which sucked his arm out and broke his shoulder. It seemed that John was an accident going to happen every time he left the ground. I did not request his services anymore since his wife called and did not want him to fly at flight test any more.

31 Oct 1950. I took a routine supply run in an old "Gooney Bird", the C-47, to K-14 Korea. We all took our turn flying supplies to Korea, since FEAMCOM, was the supply Depot for Korea. By the time I would get home I had landed at K-14, Iwakuni, and Tachikawa and would log 11+30 hours of flying time. On the way over to Korea we were flying at 11,000 feet altitude over the Sea of Japan when the right engine quit. At this time we were on solid instruments in thick clouds. I was monitoring the carburetor heat gauge and had full carburetor heat on to prevent ice from forming in the induction system. The ice was so thick on the wings that I was using the de-icing boots to break the ice off the wings, when all of a sudden the right engine quit it was quite a shock. Trying to fly instruments on one engine and trying to reach the carburetor de-icing fluid switch, which was mounted on the overhead panel was no easy matter. I hollered at my engineer to turn on the de-icing switch for the carburetor as quickly as he could. When he did the engine started right up again. There was a big sigh of relief in the cockpit. We had no more solved this emergency when the propellers started throwing ice off the blades and the ice was hitting the side of the C-47 like gunshots. It had been quite an exciting day until we broke out in the clear over Korea at 11,000 feet where the air was warmer and melted the all the ice off of us as we let down for our landing.

Part of this mission was combat time since we were in the combat zone part of the time. I think that by the time I left Korea for and returned to the US I had logged at least 14 missions. I was supposed to get an air medal for every ten missions but I had 5 Air Medals already from WWII so I did not push it like I should have since they were giving them to everyone else.

On the way in to Kimpo we saw a lot of our big tanks going to the fighting front. I took movies of these just before we landed at Kimpo AB, Korea. After we landed there was a squadron of P-80s landing after a mission. Then another squadron took off on a mission and after they were

Lt "Ollie" Olson in front of his F-80 after a belly landing in front of me. A train he straiffed blew up in his face and he put it in Suwon just before I landed in the C-47. Suwan, Korea, 1 July 1950

airborne a squadron of P-51s took off for a mission. I recorded all this on my 16mm Bolex movie camera. It was quite impressive.

After we got our C-47 off loaded and refueled we took off for Iwakuni AB, Japan to refuel on our way back to home base at FEAMCOM. I logged 8 hours of actual instrument flying on this trip. We were in weather the whole flight. I had to make instrument approaches at all our stops except Kimpo AB, Korea.

1 Nov 1950. Today I will be making and endurance test with the new long range Beech tip tanks. These new tip tanks were to increase the range of our new jet fighter the F-80C. These new tanks carried 365 gallons each on the wing tip of the F-80C. This meant that I was carrying over 1290 pounds on each wing tip! I would be carrying 1083 gallons of fuel, more fuel than a C-47. What I did not know was they did not have any baffling inside of the tanks to keep the fuel from sloshing back and forth as you changed attitude. Also the F80C would be 616 pounds over

Loading everone about my C-47 who were trying to get out of Suwon, Korea, including Lt. :Ollie" Olson. 1 July 1950

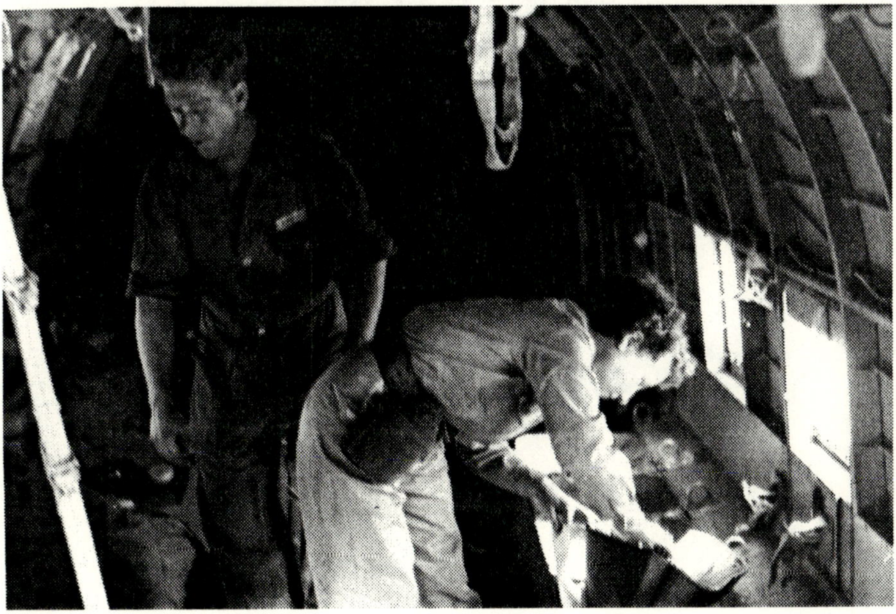

Lt. Pecan, my flight nurse administers to the wounded aboard my C-47 at Taegu, Korea 2 July 1950

One of the casualties we picked up at Taegu Korea being loaded into the ambulance at Itazure A.B. Japan

My C-47 stuck in a hole in the runway , K-1 Korea 3 July 1950

its normal gross weight. I was to take off from Tachikawa and fly to the Misawa Radio Station reverse course and fly home again monitoring my fuel use all the time and record the amount of fuel I used on the round trip. I was to climb to 30,000 feet level off and reduce my rpm from climb speed, 100%, to 96% for cruise. I was to climb out at a steady 250 mph indicated if possible. While I was taxiing out I noticed that the wings on the F-80C were flexing much more than normal with that extra fuel on each wing tip. Our runway at Tachikawa was only 5000 Feet long in those days so I got as close to the end of the runway as possible, in fact I had the tail pipe hanging over the access road that went from FEAMCOM to the Tachikawa side. I stopped all traffic until I was on my take off roll. I held the brakes and ran the engine up to 100% and checked everything to be "in the green" and released the brakes. With the extra weight the "old bird" did not accelerate as fast as it should but I was patient and let her run until I had 120 mph. I looked up and I noticed the fence at the end of the runway was getting mighty close and I had only 100 mph I still

A Korean pilot working on his L-5. Note the Bazookas on his wing struts. 3 July 1950

let her run and glanced down at my airspeed indicator and noticed I had 120 mph. I eased the stick back and skimmed over the ten-foot fence by a couple of feet it seemed as I cleaned up the aircraft. As I started my climb out everything seem to be OK. I was keeping my climb speed at 250 mph like I should and everything was in the "green". I leveled off at 30,000 feet and pulled the power back to 96% for cruise power. Then I noticed that the aircraft was hard to keep level. It had a tendency to want to porpoise. Even after I trimmed it hands off it would not stay there for any length of time. The fuel was sloshing around without any baffles in the tanks. It took a real fine touch to keep the oscillations to a minimum. It was very aggravating and tiring. Then I noticed that one wing was getting heavier than the other. The tanks were not feeding together. I kept trimming it up until I ran out of trim the sniffle valve was stuck on one of the full tanks allowing the tanks to feed one at a time, which was bad. If the full tank did not feed at all I would have over 2180 pounds hanging on the wing tip and the aircraft would be impossible to control. I had to make up my mind when I was going jettison the tank since I was over a populated area.

The troops waiting at Itazuke A.B. Japan to get airlifted to the front in Korea, 3 July 1950

Getting un-stuck

I finally had both hands on the stick trying to keep the aircraft level with full aileron trim in, which was just about to become unbearable. I then decided to rock the wings more than they were rocking to see if I could get the tank to feed. After much rocking and praying to the Lord the tank began to feed, the aircraft then became gradually more controllable.

I reached Misawa in about 1 hour and 30 minutes and made a 180-degree turn over the Homer and started for home. The F-80C was still trying to porpoise since I still had plenty of fuel left in the tips, which was still sloshing back and forth. Fortunately the weather was clear and the air was smooth so that kept the porpoise to a minimum. Upon approaching my jet let down for Tachikawa I still had fuel in my tip tanks. That meant I would be landing with at least a full internal load of fuel. The runway was only being 5000 feet long, which did not mean much to me in those days except I would have to hit the very end of the runway to utilize all of it. I touched down right on the "numbers" and used my brakes sparingly so I would not scuff a tire. As the F-80C began to slow down I braked a little harder and turned off the runway like I always do with minimum fuel instead of a full internal load. I recommended they install baffles in all future tanks to alleviate the porpoise caused by the sloshing of the fuel. Also make sure the "sniffle valves" worked properly. On this test I had flown approximately 1200 miles on about 700 gallons of fuel and was airborne 3 hours and 5 minutes. I still had at least 450 galloons left, which would be good for at least two more hours or more of flying time, depending on your altitude. You could go a long way with 5 hours or more of fuel at over 400 mph. For the month of October 1950 I put in 38 flights in 11 different aircraft including the Generals B-17.

At the end of December 1950, a boatload of F-86As came in on the aircraft carrier "Boxer". On the way across the Pacific there were high seas. The aircraft were tied down on the flight deck and got a lot of sea spray. Even though they were cocooned for this spray some of them developed electrolysis on the wheels and the trailing edges of the ailerons. These aircraft had to be repaired before being delivered to the 4th Fighter Group in Korea. They flew some of the repairable aircraft to us at the Depot to be repaired and flight- tested when we were through with the repairs. Major Jabara and Lt. Gibson were the project officers for these aircraft both of these pilots became "Aces" in the Korean War. Major Jabara was already a WWII "Ace".

We got one F-86A ready for a test hop. I had never seen an F-86A only in pictures. So I asked Major Jabara how to start the "beast". He said that I could not fly their aircraft. I reminded him that the aircraft was mine when I signed for it when it came in for repairs. It would be his when I gave it a test hop and signed it off for delivery to his outfit. With that Lt. Gibson spoke up and said he would show me how to start the "monster". I got my flying gear on and proceeded to the aircraft and climbed in. Lt. "Hoot" Gibson showed me how to start the aircraft plus answered all my questions on how it flew, what to look for, etc., etc. I had a good 5-minute on the ground briefing and check out. I cranked up, which was easier than on the old F-80A. I taxied out, lined up, ran the engine up to 100% and released the brakes and was gone. I said to myself this baby really gets with it. I was off the ground in a flash and was climbing like a sick angel to 30,000 feet. Upon reaching 30,000 feet I began to put the aircraft through its paces. Stalls, slow flight, etc. noting everything on my kneepad; I then did a few rolls and started down to the field. Everything checked out OK. I asked the tower for permission to make a high speed pass over the field. I was cleared and I came across the field at .95 mach. The controls were a little stiff at this air speed; little did I know that the aircraft was restricted for this airspeed below 5000 feet. This was the fastest aircraft I had flown to date and what a great airplane to fly. It only had aileron boost like an F-80 that is why the controls got a little stiff at speed. This flight made my day for the month since it was on the 31 December 1950. I had gotten a lot of good flying time for the month. It also ended a good year of flying.

As a family we celebrated all the holidays with the children. The 4th of July was also Fay's birthday. Labor Day was a good day for sightseeing. We traveled quite a bit around the area. Halloween was a trick or treat night with my help. Thanksgiving was always great to give thanks to the Lord for all our blessings, especially for our wonderful family. Now Christmas had passed. I think I had OD on Christmas. I did go home briefly for dinner and to see the children and their presents they received on Christmas Eve. Sherry was 3 years old and Gale was 1. We also went to some of the Japanese celebrations. They put on very elaborate shows. Now it would be New Years Eve and we would have a big party at the Officers Club. We would start the new year of 1951.

Jan 1951. I don't remember but my flight log showed that I flew test hops on New Years Day. We had such a backlog of aircraft to test hop and get ready for delivery to the outfit fighting in Korea, was the main reason. I now was back as the Chief of Flight Test instead being the Assistant OIC. I flew every day until the 7 January 1951, flying 10 F-80s and 2 L-5s. Then I got 2 weeks leave since I got orders to transfer me to Korea as CO of the 101st Field Maintenance Unit at Pusan, Korea. I could not believe I was being transferred to the war zone with only 6 months to go on my three-year tour. I even went to see General Doyle but his Deputy saw me instead. He advised me it would be good for my career. So with his advice I decided to go. He also told me that I was the only one actually qualified at FEAMCOM for the job with my flying and maintenance background. I came home and broke the news to Fay I was going to Pusan, Korea for good until my 3 year tour was up. She still had the option of going home with the children but she was determined to stay until we all could go home together, since she was pregnant with Patty.

I finished up the month getting everything ready for my transfer to Pusan, Korea, which actually took place on the 5 May 1951. I was awarded my Senior Pilots Wings on the 12 February 1951 along with my green instrument card. During this era, green instrument cards gave you the ability to land and take off in zero-zero weather zero visibility and zero ceiling. Actually it was a ticket to kill yourself if you were not an excellent instrument pilot. I finished up flying a lot of F-80s, C-47s, B-17s, L-5s, L-16s, AT-7, and a C-45, flying 34 flights for the month of February.

I also had a supply flight to Korea and on the way home I stopped at Pusan to check out my new job as to location and mission. I found it was on the south west side of the runway. Everybody lived in old WWII pyramidal tents. The organization was completely mobile. It was the 101st FMU. It was a retriever outfit that retrieved all the aircraft that were shot down on our side or were wrecked by accident or other means. This meant going right up to the front lines at times looking for downed aircraft. The organization was attached to the FEAMCOM but was on the same field as the 35th fighter Group, which was our supply source at times. I can't remember the CO's name but he was a very tall person and I wondered how he managed to get in and fly the P-51, which was their primary aircraft. We were a tenant outfit to the 35th Fighter group. After surveying the place I called home to let Fay what I had found. I then got back in the old "Gooney Bird" and headed for home.

I got all my gear together for my transfer to Pusan (K9) Korea, said "goodbye" to Fay and the children, also to our house girl and houseboy. Fay drove me to my hanger at flight test where I had an L-17 (Navion) to deliver to General Timberlake in Korea it would be his flying staff car. I was fortunate to be able to fly myself to my new assignment. It was to be delivered to K-37, which was near Taegu. This was also near FEAMCOM headquarters in Korea.

5 March. I threw my B-4 bag in the back seat of the L-17. Said "good bye" to all my troops at flight-test and took off for Itami, Japan to refuel. After refueling my next stop would be Iwakuni AB to refuel, this was an "Aussie" base. Next stop would be Itazuke AB, Fukuoka, Japan. Little did I know at the time that I would be stationed at this base in the future. I landed at Itazuke and refueled and stayed over night. The next day I headed across the Sea of Japan for Korea. I landed at Pusan, where I met my Adjutant, Lt. Norsworthy and the rest of my crew. I then arranged for Lt. Norsworthy to pick me up at K-37 after I delivered the L-17 to the General. I went to FEAMCOM HQS. And signed in and got my new instructions from the CO. By this time my ride was waiting for me to take me back to my new home. When I went to HQS I met my new CO, I can't remember his name, and also an old friend, Major Austin Miller, who we visited at Komaki, Japan. He was stationed there with his family. We had been stationed together at Roswell, AB, NM, in 1947. I jumped in the back seat of the T-6 and Lt. Norsworthy flew me back to my new outfit, the 101st Field Maintenance Unit. I was now Commanding Officer of the 101st FMU. My administration personnel were Lt. Norsworthy as Adjutant, a Master Sgt. as my First Sergeant, and a corporal as my clerk. I had thirty Enlisted Men who were my mechanics, etc. We had our own mess hall, latrines, and later our own showers.

Our mission was to pick up all downed aircraft on our side of the front line. We would send a crew out to repair the aircraft at the site if it was repairable. I then would fly it home to be made ready for combat again. If it could not be repaired at the sight it would be dismantled, and trucked to our unit. If it was beyond repairing and had no good used parts we would blow it up or give it to the local Koreans. It would be immediately cut up and melted down and made into pots and pans and souvenirs that would promptly be bought by our GIs.

10 Mar 1951. I found out that I had 4 different aircraft at my disposal. An L-5, T-6, C-45, and a P-51, the P-51 was a wreck that was written off but repaired later to be my own personal aircraft. All these aircraft were used depending on what the mission was that day and how far away the wreck was.

Three days after getting acquainted with my organization I got my first call from HQS. There was a P-51 down on an old MASH strip next to the Haun River, a place called Chang Wawn-Ni. I got the coordinates on the map, jumped in the L-5 with Lt. Norsworthy in the back seat, and was on our way to locate the P-51 and to survey the damage. After flying for 2 hours and 30 minutes I finally spotted the P-51 on a gravel strip. I made a low pass to check the surface of the strip and the wind direction. As I made a pass over the P-51 I noticed that it had nosed up and the prop was bent around the nose section. I set up a pattern and landed. I then taxied up alongside the old "Bird" and parked. We got out to take a survey of the damage. Most of all we were sure it needed a new propeller. W saw many bullet holes in the aircraft with signs of a coolant leak. That meant a new radiator. When I looked closer the radiator was perforated. A barrel of coolant would be needed. The pilot who was flying this aircraft must have gotten it very hot so we would need spark plugs plus a couple of magnetos. That seemed to be enough to get the P-51 back to Pusan, which was about 250 miles away. I arranged for one of my maintenance crew to drive up in a GI 6X6 truck to help make the necessary repairs to allow me to fly it back to our organization where we could put it back in shape for combat. I noticed that the aircraft had only 50 hours on it since it was completely overhauled. We rounded up a Korean soldier and posted him at the site and got in the L-5 and headed for home at Pusan.

It took a while to order all the parts for the P-51. They had to be flown up to the downed aircraft in a C-47. The prop is so big on a P-51, eleven and a half feet in diameter that it would not fit inside of the C-47 but has to have a special fixture to mount it on the belly of the C-47 to get it up to us.

We finally got word that the C-47 would be on its way so I got in the C-45 with Lt. Norsworthy, my crew chief and his assistant with all their tools. We then took off for Chang Wong-Ni.

17 March 1951. We got there ahead of the C-47 so the four of us removed the bent prop from the P-51. With the prop removed we started to remove the cowling as the crew chief and his assistant started to remove the radiator, which is a real mean job. By this time, the old "Gooney Bird" arrived with the prop attached to its belly, which was fairly easy to remove. The four of us carried the prop over to the P-51, which was quite heavy over 200 pounds. The rest of the gear was inside of the C-47 including the 50-gallon drum of ethylene glycol for our coolant.

We immediately installed the prop on the P-51, since there was no place to put it except on the rocks, which was unacceptable. We lifted it up to the prop shaft and it slid right on the prop shaft. The crew chief got out his big wrench and we tightened it up with as much torque we could get. After getting all our parts off the C-47 the old "Goon" took off with the parting salutation "Good Luck", after seeing what kind of condition the P-51 was in. As they departed, the rest of the crew arrived from home in the truck and the work progressed rapidly.

Lt. Norsworthy and I flew back home since the P-51 would not be ready that day. The next day we flew back up in the C-45 and the P-51 was ready to start up. It had been sitting for over a week and I didn't know how good the battery was. After the radiator was installed I had to fill the system with coolant. The C-47 had brought us the 50-gallon of ethylene glycol, which had to be mixed with water for the cooling system. I had an empty number 10 can to pour the coolant in the aircraft after it was mixed. I would have to pour it into the header tank on the nose of the P-51. I had two waterproof cardboard boxes one for water, which I got from the river that was adjacent to the strip and one for mixing the water with the ethylene glycol. I enlisted a Korean boy to run over to the river and fill the box with water and bring it back and I would have him mix the ethylene glycol and water in the other box, 3parts of water to one part of glycol, this was done with another number ten can. After he had mixed the two together he would hand me the full number ten can up to me and I would pour it in the header tank. The P-51 took 21 gallons of coolant. He made many trips and I got "saddle sores" straddling the nose of the P-51 by the time it was full. Also the prop spinner would not fit the new prop. They are tailored to fit each prop on installation.

We had been here now for three days trying to get this "bird" in the air. The temperature was about 34 degrees and the wind blowing off the North Pole. It was miserable. We had flown up and got here at 0800 hours and it was now 1600 hours, I was ready to go. Everything was ready now for the moment of truth. I got in with all my gear; turned on the necessary switches, after a careful cockpit check, hit the starter switch and the primer at the same time. The old Merlin started to turn over and all of a sudden it started with a big roar of the engine. It started right up much to the surprise of everyone including me. After letting the P-51 warm up I gradually ran the engine up to RPM and started to check the magnetos. Right "mag" 125rpm drop not too bad. Left "mag" WOW! 500 rpm drop not well at all. I shut down after running the engine up and down to try to correct the trouble but to no avail. You can only run a P-51 up to 30 inches of manifold pressure holding the brakes any more power will make it nose over so it has to be tied down at the tail wheel to get a full power check. We had no way of doing this. I got out and told the crew chief to change the magnetos. This is usually the trouble with a P-51 if it sits too long and is not flown or at least once a day.

The crew chief and his crew started to change the two magnetos, which did not take too long. I got back in and tried it again. Left "mag" 125rpm drop, right mag 500 rpm drop, no change! Now there was only one thing left to do, change the spark plugs. I left this for last since it was easier to change the "mags" than 24 spark plugs.

The crew chief got up and took off the cowling to get to the spark plugs. He tried the first spark plug and was really tugging on the wrench when it broke! That did it. I told everyone that I would fly it home on the good magneto if it got 3000 rpm and 61 inches of manifold pressure on take off. This was take-off power for the P-51. Of course everyone was quite tired and disgusted by now. They had done everything to get the "bird" in the air and it was not cooperating one bit.

20 March 1951. I was going to get this P-51 home or else. I got in again and cranked up and was ready to fly this old "bird" home. I taxied to the end of this rocky strip and turned around and faced into the wind. I noticed an old bridge directly in my take off path. I had to get airborne with enough altitude to clear the bridge hoping the engine did not quit before I got there. I held the brakes and ran the engine up to 30 inches of manifold pressure with flaps down and slammed the throttle wide open. As I glanced at the instruments I noticed that I had normal take off power. It was a little tricky with all that power coming on all at once but I managed to have enough right rudder trim in to help me hold it straight down the strip and bumping over all the rocks. I jumped into the air, picked up my gear, "milked up" my flaps, waggled my wings at Lt. Norsworthy and my crew, I was on my way. Lt. Norsworthy would fly my crew chief back in the C-45 and the rest of the crew would drive the old GI truck back.

I had just passed Taegu AB, when the engine started to act up. This was about 100 miles from Pusan. I immediately ran the power up to maximum cruise and gained 2000 feet of altitude to 12,000 feet. The engine was missing and banging but ran smoother with the higher power setting. I then put the P-51 in a highs speed letdown to Pusan. Everything was in the "green" on the instrument panel and the engine was running smoothly.

As I approached our runway I was really moving and not having a radio I started to wobble my wings donating that I did not have a radio. I was right on the deck and was making a tactical approach, which is a pull up, going straight down the runway with a 360 degree overhead turn to the runway. Just as I was getting to the peak of my turn I pulled the throttle back to run up the prop pitch for landing mode when the engine let out a loud explosion with fire and smoke covering the cockpit and quit right there.

I was almost on my back by this time and was trying to look over my shoulder to find the runway and was very busy trying to restart the "beast" and not stall out in this precarious position, the next 20 seconds I was very busy. I bent the old P-51 around in a half roll and found the runway as the big four bladed propeller started to stop and slow me down like a rock. I kept my air speed and as I approached the runway there was a big fence on the end of the runway and I skimmed over it with minimum airspeed and thumped the old "bird" on the runway. I thanked the Lord for helping me make it onto the runway without hitting the fence. During all this time I had to put my gear and flaps down before I landed.

As I was rolling down the runway with the engine stopped and the prop still, I noticed a GI truck running down the taxiway beside the runway keeping up with me. I coasted into my parking area and stopped, rolling the canopy back. The truck driver stopped and hollered at me, "Is that was a 35th fighter group aircraft", "I replied that it was not. He said, "Thank goodness" and turned around and left. By this time it was dusk and none of my crew even knew that I had landed. I walked into my tent office and they couldn't believe it was me they did not expect me until the next day. Not being right on the runway they did not here me since the engine was not running at the time I parked the P-51. They heard the explosion but did not go out to investigate. Most of the base ran out to see what happened, after hearing the P-51 coming in at high speed and then the explosion. They figured the aircraft blew up.

21 May 1951. The next day the line chief tried to start the "beast" and found that the engine was frozen solid. I really "lucked out", since I talked to the pilot who nosed the aircraft up at Chang Hown-Ni after he made a forced landing there. He told me he flew it at least 15 minutes with the coolant on the peg (125 degrees Centigrade or better). The old Merlin engine in the P-51 is only good for 8 minutes at that temperature. I know the Lord was watching over me to be able to fly over 200 miles on that engine and one magneto.

The next day I was off to Taegu, K2, to pickup a pilot from HQS to give him some field experience. We had another aircraft down at Suwon, K38, to evaluate. On landing we found an F-80C down and shot all full of holes. Fortunately it was on a good field that had the 4th fighter group as tenants where I could bum some parts.

It seemed that we had a crew chief there already who was taking the old engine out of the F-80C and had a new one to put back in. He was just finishing up and needed a new aft section to put on the aircraft since the original was almost blown in two, which ruined the original engine at the same time. I went over to the bone yard and found a good tail section.

While the crew chief was getting the aft section on with my help, I had sent the other pilot home in the aircraft we flew up in, an L-5. As I gave the aircraft a preflight I noticed that the tires were practically brand new and thought to myself the pilot that dead-sticked the F-80C in was a good pilot not to wipe out the tires on landing at Suwon. I got in after everything was tightened up and proceed to start up and between both of us we set the idle and 100% on the stops. I was ready to go as I started to taxi out I noticed that there were two big thumps. The pilot wasn't as sharp as I thought he was. The tires were worn to the tubes. I could not see this since it was on the bottom of the tires when I was looking at them. I taxied back and shut down and told the crew chief what was wrong.

While the crew chief was in the process of taking off the wheels I went over to the 4th fighter group Maintenance Shop to bum a couple of tires. After much discussion I convinced the OIC that the tires off the F-86A were the same size as the F-80C and they would fit on. The only difference was that the F-86A tires had more plies than the F-80C. All I had to do is bring over the old wheels and tires and they would mount them for me. He gave me a jeep and a driver to go get them.

By the time we got back to the F-80C the crew chief had the wheels off the aircraft ready to put the new tires on. I took them back to the 4th FG and they were changed in no time at all and the crew chief had them installed and I was off for home to see who owned the aircraft.

It was confusing to the tower when I called in for my landing instructions, since the F-80C had two different numbers on it, one on the tail and one on the fuselage. It only took 40 minutes to get home, since I was loafing along. After getting home I had my Adjutant call around to find out who owned the aircraft. After two days we found that it was owned by Itazuke AB, Japan, so on the 24 march 1951 I got in and flew it to Itazuke, where no one would claim it. They thought it might belong to Tusuki AB, on the other side of the island of Kyushu. So again I climbed in the F-80C and took off for Tusuki AB. Just as I was in the landing pattern for Tusuki AB, the cockpit began to fill up with smoke. I made a really short pattern and landed after declaring I had smoke in the cockpit.

After landing I was met by the Airdrome Officer and another Officer from the outfit inquiring as to whom the F-80C belonged to. His opening statement as I got out of the cockpit was, "Don't tell me you brought that old dog back?" It seems they thought that the aircraft was "class 26", not repairable, and did not think that they would ever get it back. They did give us thanks for being able to repair it. I had the OIC sign for the aircraft and then I had to bum a ride back to Pusan in an AT-6. Oh for the life of a retriever pilot.

General Doyle was the CO of FEAMCOM as well as my CO. He was known to make unannounced inspections. This day he did it to me at 0600 hours in the morning. The first thing I knew about it was when my first Sergeant opening the door of my tent and exclaiming, "The Generals here!" I jumped out of bed and got my pants on and the General stood in my doorway and started on me, "Why wasn't the organization up and working?" I'm trying to salute and get the rest of my uniform on. He walked out and waited until I got dressed and started in on me again. Your organization should be utilizing all the daylight hours in a time of war, etc. When he finally finished I told him we were totally dependent on the 35th Fighter Group for our supplies, etc. and they do not go to work before 0800 hours. It would be unproductive if we were out at 0600 and nobody else was working at that time. He left and I thought I had, had it. He came back later and apologized, since he found out that the base did not go to work before 0800 hours. That was a load off my mind although I wondered if this affected me not getting promoted to Major the first time around on the regular promotion list.

There were other wrecks to inspect along the Haun River near Seoul, Korea. It seems there were two aircraft down on a sand bar on our side of the river. The fighting line was the Haun River we were on the south side and the North Koreans were on the north side.

I took the C-45 for this trip because I had to take an Officer from HQS with me as co-pilot and observer. As we approached the Haun River I noticed a lot of foxholes on the ridge of the hills as we were passing over. I then noticed that they were our GIs and they were waving at me. As we came to a bend in the river I noticed the two aircraft on their bellies on the sand bar, east of Seoul. I then let down real low to about 100 feet and noticed that one aircraft was an AT-6 a spotter aircraft and the other one

Flying in a supply mission for the troops at Kimpo Airport, Korea from Japan in a C-47 Nov 1950

was a P-51. As I circled to come back for a second look I noticed a tank coming out of a group of trees and dashing up to the P-51, the hatch on the tank came open and a GI jumped out and ran over to the P-51 and opened the gun bay doors and grabbed all the ammunition and went back to the tank and gave it to the other GI. He then went back and proceeded to unscrew all eight of the gun barrels and bringing them back to the tank. When he was finished he waved and was gone. The P-51 uses the same 50-caliber machine gun as the tank. In a fight the tank burns up lots of barrels, and they were getting spares just in case.

In the meantime while I was circling watching what was going on I did not notice that the north side of the Haun River was lighting up like a "Christmas tree". The North Koreans were shooting at us. I immediately pushed up full power and got out of there by staying on the deck and using evasive action. Fortunately we were not hit.

When I got back home I called HQS and told them that the two aircraft were in no mans land, between both front lines. They would have to wait until the battle line shifted in our favor before we could get to the aircraft. Our boys did benefit from the P-51 by getting the ammo and the gun barrels for their tank.

7 April 1951. We no more got home when we got a call that there was another P-51 down at a place called Chung-Ju. This was a MATS strip that was used to bring in men and supplies for the war effort. This P-51 had to have an engine change since it also nosed up on landing and bent the prop around the nose just like the other one I had flown out of Chung Wang-Ni. This was out in the field again and we had no facilities for making engine changes on a P-51 at that time.

I sent up a crew in a 6X6 GI truck with a bomb service crane on it to lift out the Merlin Engine. After a day or so I flew back up to see how they were doing. I found out the crane on the truck could not lift the engine high enough to get it out of the aircraft. With the usual "Yankee" ingenuity I found that they had dug two holes in front of the landing gear and rolled the P-51into the holes, which lowered, the aircraft down low enough to get the bomb crane to lift the engine out. Then they could put the new engine in and pull it out of the hole to its normal position so they could put the new prop on, which would finish their work. I did not have a chance to fly this P-51 back to our home base since I received my orders to return to the ZI, zone of the interior, stateside before my crew finished the P-51.

In the meantime I had my own personal P-51. We made one good P-51 out of two wrecks and all the spare parts we had from other salvaged P-51s. It was named "Red Raider". I had the local parachute shop make me a red flying suit out of a red nylon parachute. I wore my metallic pink helmet with yellow wings painted on the front and in the circle had "BILL" painted. I kept the flying suit until I retired and traded it for a welding outfit to another pilot. I found out that nylon melted on you in a fire, which was not good. My old helmet finally cracked and I got a new model with the new visor on it instead of having to wear goggles. I had no armament on the P-51 so everything I picked up would go in the gun bays. My P-51 was faster than most GI P-51s, since I was not carrying any armament, only a steel plate under my seat and at my back. This made it very light, relatively speaking. Somebody had "ratted" on me because one day I got a call from General Doyle who heard I had a P-51 that wasn't on paper. He said that he wanted to see that P-51 back in Japan when I rotated to the states. I said, "Yes Sir".

I had heard that anybody that had there tour extended by the Korean War over their normal tour and had dependents in Japan would be rotated to stateside at their request. I had been on my tour of duty for 3 years, which was one year over my normal tour of duty. This made me eligible to rotate to the states. I had already submitted my request to HQS and on the 16 April 1951, I loaded my gear in my P-51, "Red Raider". I was wearing my red nylon flying suit and my metallic pink helmet, as I said a "good bye" to all my troops, and blasted off for Tachikawa, Japan, and home.

The weather at the time was terrible so I had to file an instrument flight plan. All this P-51 had for instrument flying was the basic artificial horizon, needle and ball, for a radio it had only a 4-channel push button VHF. For navigation I had an old Bendix *to and from and left and right needle* for doing aural null type of identification of the station. As you would approach the station on course the sound of the identifier would gradually get weaker and weaker until there was no sound at all as you passed over the station you were homing in on. The P-51 was not known as a good instrument aircraft. The secret of flying good instruments was to keep the aircraft trimmed up constantly to fly hands off.

I took off and climbed through the overcast and rain to 10,000, telling myself all the time be gentle with the controls. I leveled off and trimmed up. I had my flight planned out and got the winds aloft at my flight level. I was to fly dead reckoning using winds, air speed, time, and distance. I made my first leg right on schedule listening to my station on Honshu, Japan. There was a break in the overcast so I could see the ground momentarily so I could place my position visually and was over the station, right on course. I turned to my new heading and switched to the next homer. I started my time for my new heading and leg. I then tuned in Komaki Radio my homer for this leg. When my time was up for this leg I called for a steer to O-Shima island homer my next leg. They gave me a call and corrected my heading by about a degree, I was right on course. I was above the overcast so I had no way to check my position visually. I then flew to O-shima homer and broke out of the overcast in the clear. This homer at O-Shima is on an island in the entrance to Tokyo Bay. I called Tokyo Control and closed my instrument flight plan and flew into the area VFR for Tachikawa.

I was making a high-speed letdown and was looking for our home at Fuchu AB which was an upstairs apartment. I buzzed the place at about 350 mph to let Fay know that I was home and to get over to the Flight Test hanger to pick me up. She heard me as well as the rest of the people in the complex she told me this after I landed and called her.

You can't imagine the look on my crew chiefs face as I got out of the P-51 with that red flying suit on and that pink metallic helmet. His remark was, "Now I've seen everything". Especially with the name "Red Raider" painted on the side of the P-51 which was dirty and had oil streaks on it.

After getting two weeks leave to get everything packed and celebrating our transfer to stateside we left for Yokohama, Japan on 10 April 1951. We would leave by ship, the President Cleveland. We had to sell our Cadillac to an American personnel since we did not want to take it home. We had a staff car take us to the Port. Fay was 4 months pregnant with Patty by this time. I thought a nice slow cruise home would be better than riding MATS aircraft home and be there in a couple of days. The cruise on the liner took 11 days.

We went by Okinawa to pick up freight and passengers. On the way to Okinawa we ran into a typhoon, which gave us a real wild ride. Everybody was seasick but me. When we landed at Okinawa there were boats washed up on shore as well as a Navy PBM flying boat with all kinds of debris. After we left Okinawa we headed for Hawaii.

Of course this boat ride got boring for something to do, especially on a GI chartered ship. We were the first Officers with dependents to come home since the freeze and the extension of our tours. They were not ready for all these people with children and how to entertain them. To break the monotony I decided to make a movie aboard ship called "Murder At Sea". I used many of the dependents and friends aboard and had a lot of fun. We even used the ships radio operator to add a little realism to the picture.

They had movies aboard for the children and it just so happened I had my own production of the "Bronco Kid". It was a western and the children got a big bang out it even though it was a silent production with titles.

11 May 1951. We finally arrived home to salute of all the fireboats in the San Francisco Bay. They greeted us as we passed under the Golden

The first F-86A to ccome to combat in Korea. It was later called the MIG Killer. I am giving it a flight test. My first flight in this aircraft

101st Field Maintenance Unit Orderly Room, Pusan, Korea

Gate Bridge. Home sure looked good after being gone for 3 years. It was Gale's first look at the United States, since she was born at Johnson AB, Irumagawa, Japan. We docked at Fort Mason and they marched all the troops onto the dock for roll call. I saw my Mother waving at me behind a low fence that had been erected to keep the visiting crowd back. Here we were in formation and they were egging me on to break ranks and run over to her. Well I did and I gave my mother a big hug and a kiss just as the news photographer took our picture. This picture wound up on the front page of the Call Bulletin newspaper a big paper at that time for the Bay area. It had a caption of "War Hero's Return" a write up of my exploits and my mother's address. For over a week people were calling her who she hadn't heard from in years. She had remarried after my Fathers death and of course she had a new name from Disbrow to Horn.

We finally got released with our orders to go home and I couldn't believe that I was assigned to Recruiting duty for the Los Angeles Area. We all went to my mother and her new Husband Henry's home to celebrate. Henry drove us to their new home in Berkeley. As we drove up to the house there was a big sign

A P-51D Mustang on it's belly at Kimpo Airport, Korea, March 1951

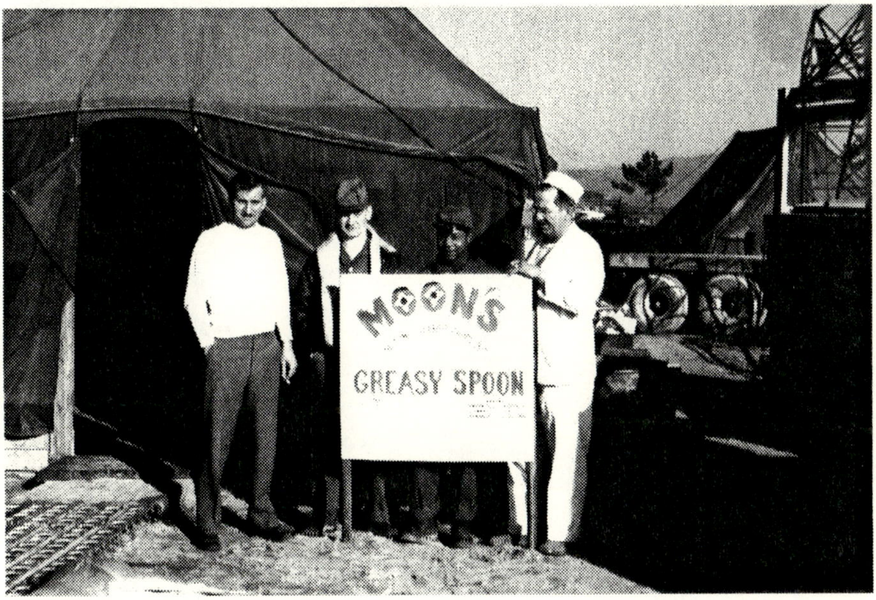

My messhall crew at 101st FMU, Pusan, Korea April 1951

over

the

My work area for the 101st FMU at Pusan, Korea April 1951

Capt Bill Disbrow and his crew going on a "Reccie" mission.
Pusan, Korea February 1951

entrance saying "Welcome Home Bill and His Three Girls". I took a picture of this and I still have it.

We stayed about a week or so while I was searching the wanted ads for a new Cadillac Convertible. I finally saw an ad that offered a 1949 Cadillac Convertible, low mileage, yellow for $3200. We went to see it and of course it was beautiful. Just like a new car. I had the first overhead valve engine in it which was a big improvement over the old flat head our 1947 had. The engine was named after the designer; it was a "Kettering" engine. It had only 21,000 miles on it just broken in. We drove it and it was just like a new car. We immediately bought it and had our second Cadillac Convertible. The first time out I almost got into trouble trying to make a left hand turn and turned into the wrong lane after driving on the wrong side of the road for three years. The Japanese drive on the left hand side of the road like the English. We visited all the points of interest in the Bay Area, including the Zoo, San Francisco, Fisherman's Wharf, and all the old spots I knew in the old days.

Well after packing and saying goodbye to Henry and my Mother,

I don't know where all the spectators came from but they were watching us work on the P-51D Chung Chu, Korea April 1951

Here I am sitting on the nose of the P-51D filling the header tank with coolant with a #10 can. the system holds 21 gallons! April 1951

we were on our way to Los Angeles in our new Cadillac and to my new assignment and to visit Fay's folks. Gladys and Mordecai Cox were Fays Mother and Father. When we left for Japan in 1948, they lived on Torrance Blvd., in Torrance, California. They now had moved to 4816 - 9th Avenue in Los Angeles while we were in Japan. This house was an older home but was bigger and had much more room. So we stayed with Fays folks until we could find a place of our own. In the meantime I had reported to my new assignment at the old Mode-O-Day building on Washington Street in Los Angeles. This was Headquarters for the Army and U.S. Air force recruiting. My new assignment was OIC of the Los Angeles Recruiting District. This took in Santa Monica, Culver City, Florence Avenue, Central Avenue and East Los Angeles, with my office at Sunset and Vine Streets in Hollywood! What a deal, which included my own staff car to drive around to check all my stations at least once a week.

I found out immediately, being a WWII and a recent Korean returnee that I was in demand to give lectures at all the different civic clubs in the area, the Lions, Rotary, AFA, etc. They called it the "cream chicken circuit", which was usually severed for lunch. I also gave talks at the local High Schools, depicting the advantages of going into the USAF as a career. I always wore my uniform with all my ribbons and my Command Pilot wings to make a good impression for the people. Fortunately I had taken many colored pictures of my operations in Korea as well as movies, which provided an interesting program for the people that attended the different civic clubs. I was asked more than once to return.

Recruiting at Sunset and Vine in Hollywood was quite an interesting place. I would get many so called entertainers and movie extras that wanted to enlist if they could get into special services, so they could further their careers. Of course I could not guarantee anything in those days but would submit their request with their qualifications.

At lunchtime I would wander into any one of the local eateries along

This P-51D nosed up at a MASH strip. We had to put a new prop, mags and radiator. I flew it out on one magneto to Pusan 250 miles away. It quit in the pattern while landing.
This is my crew Chung Wa Ni, Korea, April 1951

A bombed out bridge near Seoul, Korea. March 1951

Vine Street and would find a Hollywood actor. William Conrad, the young chinaman that played in Charley Chan, as number one son, Jimmie Durante, Jerry Lewis, Red Skelton, Warner Olin, who played Charley Chan, Mickey Rooney and many other bit p[layers. It all was very interesting.

I used to check my stations at least once a week. Culver City station was my favorite. My Sgt. in charge had movie connections at the movie studios there. So I would get to visit the studios to see what new pictures they were shooting at the time. One day we got on the set of the "Korean Story" with Robert Mitchum. They had a mock-up of an old C-47 fuselage that was called the "Voice". The real one was built at FEAMCOM in Japan when I was Chief of Flight Test and I was the one to make the flight test on the aircraft. It was full of amplifiers and a small generator to run the power for the huge speakers that they had aboard. The speakers were attached to the belly of the C-47. It would get the North Koreans attention immediately, trying to get them to surrender. On the movie version it had only a small radio amplifier and a small generator for power. After they got through shooting the sequence my Sgt. introduced me to the Director and told him

Seoul, Korea after a bombing of the city in March 1951

that we built the original "Voice" in Japan. I told him that there was much more equipment aboard than they had. He remarked that nobody would know the difference. That is how the movie business is run.

I also saw them making "Northwest Passage" with Spencer Tracy and Buddy Baer. While I was standing watching them getting ready to shoot the scene, I noticed everybody was snickering. I was wondering what was going on. As I turned around I was looking at a big belt buckle. I looked up and it was Buddy Baer, the ex-prize fighter, who was huge. He was at least 6 feet 6 inches tall and weighed 275 pounds. He was playing a mountain man.

Fay was pregnant with Patty at this time and as usual I was at work when the event took place. Fay and her mother were visiting with her Grandmother Day in Torrance when Fay began to have labor pains that were very close together. Since Fay had driven the Cadillac down to Torrance and her mother could not drive them so they called Fay's uncle Henry Day to drive her to the Torrance Hospital. By the time I was notified in Hollywood Fay had had a baby girl, number three. I dashed down to Torrance from Hollywood to see my new offspring. This was on 4 September 1951. There were no freeways to Torrance in those days so it took quite a while to get there on the surface streets. I would take Western Avenue all the way to Torrance Blvd., make a right turn and I was there.

Patty was our third girl and a new little spirit from the Lord, for us to take care of and rear to adulthood. We had her blessed at the Arlington Ward of The Church of Jesus Christ of Latter-day Saints, which was only a two blocks from the house. It was very convenient to be so close we could walk to Church. I do not know who gave her blessing but it will be in the records.

The missionaries from the Church (LDS) were coming over to the house regularly and were giving me a continuation of the lessons. So I finally decided I might as well join the Church. Besides I owed it to the Lord for protecting me through all the years of flying and surviving through WWII and Korea. The two missionaries took me out to the Orange County Stake to the baptismal fount and I was baptized by Elder Veloy Eugene Griffin, on the 6 September 1952.

During this time I was getting my flying time at Long Beach Airport. I was flying the old familiar C-45, T-7, and the B-25. I took my instrument check in the B-25 and renewed my green instrument card. During this time a green instrument was a valuable asset to your flying career if it was used right.

One morning I had to report at HQS in the Mode-O'Day building. When I got there I had orders to attend Recruiting Management School at Fort Benjamin Harris at Indianapolis, Indiana, for 30 days. The family could not go with me since it was TDY. I was lucky to get an airplane a C-45 from Long Beach to fly myself to my new TDY assignment. I had a co-pilot with me so he could fly the aircraft back to Long Beach.

It was a good school patterned after the Dale Carnegie Institute. It was to give one confidence in speaking as well as speaking to people that were interested in joining the USAF or the Army. In a class of 45, I graduated 11 in my class.

When we graduated and the class was over we could seek any means of transportation we wanted. I thought it would be nice to ride a train, the Union Pacific Flyer from Chicago to Los Angeles. I had never ridden a train in the United States except when I was a little boy in 1920 going from San Francisco to Fort Bragg, California and back to see my Grandmother in Oakland, California.

I thought this would be a real treat. Some of the "troops" were from Chicago so I got a free ride with them in their car. They dropped me off at the Union Station in Chicago to hop the Union Pacific Flyer, 36 hours from Chicago to Los Angeles was the time they advertised and I was off. After this ride, which was rough, boring and slow, I haven't ridden one since. I was sure ready to get off when we reached Los Angeles.

I gave many talks at different associations and civic clubs. I received many nice letters of appreciation and was asked to return again many times. I also talked at the High schools in the area. I would show the movie on the F-86 fighter pilots. One Principal at one of the high schools remarked, after I gave a talk to the student body that was the quietest the students had ever been at an assembly. He said that I had them spell bound describing my war experiences and my test flying. He was very grateful and would encourage the students to think about as military career. There were at least 1500 students at this assembly. I also got a nice letter from the Los Angeles chapter of the Air Force Association. The letter came from the

The city of Pusan, Korea April 1951

president of the Chapter. I returned to give them another performance, which they also enjoyed.

During this time my old Air Force friend Don Disbrow came down from Vacaville, California, to see us. He had his girlfriend with him and we all went out on the town to Hollywood. We ran into Liz Taylor, John Wayne, and a few other characters. We had our picture taken at "Don the Beach Comers" and had a real blast. I still have the picture, which is rare since Don is now deceased.

Fay and I used to go to Hollywood once in a while to Ciros and the Mocambo to nightclub and dance. Ciros was the best nightclub in Hollywood at the time. All the movie stars used to hang out there. This particular night we went to Ciros and Desi Arnez was there with his orchestra. As he started his Latin American music we got up and started dancing to their great beat. I saw Desi watching us dance. We were staying up to his beat in a Rumba and I noticed everybody watching us. When we finished he clapped for us as well as all the rest of the people in the club.

Landing at Chung Chu to check on being repaired by my crew, Chung Chu, Korea April 1951

He played all his good Latin music for us and we stayed until the place closed. We had a great time and Desi enjoyed playing for us.

We were still looking for a house so we decided to by a lot instead. I met a fellow in the real estate business in Hollywood and he had some lots for sale that we could buy. He had this view lot just above Sunset Blvd. with a fantastic view of the city and ocean. We bought the lot for $3500 and found a contractor that was building a standard type of home to fit any lot for a very reasonable price but before we could sign the contract he went broke. Then I decided to design my own house. I made a model of it built out of balsa wood. I had to find someone to build it for me. By this time I had been on recruiting for a year or more and I was getting a little uneasy since I had a rare specialty MOS, of Flight Test Maintenance Officer.

One day I was out at Long Beach Airport to get my flying time in and I parked alongside a fabulous looking sports car. It was parked in front of the weather office. I immediately went in to find out who owned the car. I found out that it was the weather Officers car. He had the body built at the

Another P-51D being repaired in the field, Taegu, Korea 1951

My crew working on the P-51D changing the engine and prop.
Chung Chu, Korea April 1951

the Korean retired farmers watching the crew work on the P-51D
Chung Chu, Korea, April 1951

Glasspar Boat Company in Costa Mesa and he helped design it with Bill Trip. It cost $600. I just had to have one. It looked like a Jaguar XK-120 from the side and an Austin Healy from the rear and had its own front end styling. I came home and described the car to Fay and told her I was going to build a Sports Car with this body on it.

The next weekend I went down to Costa Mesa to see where the bodies were built. The bodies were molded in a form out of fiberglass. They would put in a layer of fiberglass cloth then a layer of fiberglass matt and so on until the body was about an eight of an inch thick. After talking to the owner I ordered my body. He mentioned that they would be at the Los Angeles Fair at the Pomona Fair Grounds and would demonstrate how strong the body was. We all went to the fair and saw the demonstration of a man with a fire axe trying to cut a hole in the "turtle deck". He could hardly knock the paint off the body, since it had such resiliency.

I got a call one day that my body was ready for pickup. Now the problem was how to get it home. I borrowed my Father-in-laws pickup truck and off we went to Costa Mesa to get my body. They help us load it at Glasspar and we were lucky when we got home we had the Mormon Missionaries there to help us unload it. By the way, the body only weighed 200 pounds. It was light but awkward to handle but we got it off without doing any damage to it. We set it on two sawhorses before I could fit it to the chassis, which I had already started to build.

I bought an old 1932 Ford frame from the local wrecking yard and hauled it home. I then began to degrease it and clean it up. I then took out the cross members of the frame so I had two bare frame rails. I then proceeded to put in a 1940 Ford rear cross member to take the late style spring for the Columbia rear axle I had acquired. The Columbia axle was a two speed, which I had traded a Crosley full race engine I brought back from Japan. I got a dropped front axle for it from the Bell Auto Parts in Bell, California. The engine was a Ford flat head, which was bored oversize to 3 3/8 inches and the crankshaft, was stroked form 3 7/8 inches to 4 1/8 inches. This would give the engine good low speed torque and along with a compression ratio of 11 to one, a Clay Smith 284 2B camshaft, Lincoln ignition, Wiend Aluminum heads, ported, polished, relieved, balanced, and 3 model 97 Stromberg carburetors with a electric fuel pump. With this set up it should really go since the engine would be developing about 250 HP on Ethyl gas.

I no more got the body fitted to the chassis when I got transfer orders to Tyndall AFB, Florida. I took a delay en-route to finish my "Disbrow Special". I took the car up to the Peterson Publishing Company in Hollywood, when I finished it, so they could take pictures of it. This was the home of "Hot Rod Magazine" and "Motor Trend Magazine" at the time. I parked the car out in front of the building, which was on Hollywood Blvd. to talk to the people inside when a policeman came running in and asked who owned the car parked out in front. I said that I did and he said would I please move it. People are stopping on Hollywood Blvd. to look at it and it is causing traffic to jam up on the street I went out and drove the car around in back of the building to their parking lot. It had Chrome knockoff wire wheels made by Rudge. They had been on an Indianapolis racecar at one time and I had them chromed and re-spoked. The car was painted Lincoln yellow chrome, which was outstanding. Behind the wire wheels were polished aluminum disc brakes, which were built by Kinmont. The dash had a full set of Stewart-Warner instruments, with a 150 mph speedometer and an 8000rpm tachometer. The dash was made out of black Formica. The seats were upholstered in red and white tuck and roll Nagahyde. The rug was red to match the upholstery. It was a very striking automobile.

I was very pleased with the cars performance. It would go 135 mph at 5500 rpm and 0 to 100 mph in 16 seconds. It would cruise at 90 mph at 3000 rpm in high ratio of 2.54 to one and in low ratio it would top out at 135 mph with a 3.78 gear ratio. This was with 6.50 X 16 inch tires on the rear and 6.00 X 16 on the front.

Our first trip in the car was to San Bernardino to see our friends the Kelly's. They were stationed with us in Japan at FEAMCOM. It was an extreme pleasure to drive such a powerful and docile car. It only weighed 2100 pounds and the engine developing 250 HP on gasoline. This gave it a very good power to weight ratio as good as some of the most powerful sports cars of the day. It cruised effortless at 65 mph and the acceleration was outstanding. You pushed on the throttle in high gear and it would jump right out, passing a car ahead was effortless. It was a car that people would stop immediately and stare at it. It even startled people when I would pass them with its beauty and its sound. It had two glass-packed mufflers one for each bank of four cylinders on the V8 Ford. The tail pipes came out of the rear fenders with chrome tips. The car had no bumpers to spoil the clean lines. After a few "test hops" I made a tow bar for the "Disbrow Special". After we got all packed we said goodbye to all the relatives I hooked the "Disbrow Special" to our 1949 Cadillac and off we went to Florida. I forgot to mention that I had special nameplates made for each front fender that read "Disbrow Special", which would baffle all the people that read it.

Of course everywhere we stopped we would have a crowd of people around the car and asking what kind of a car it was. Some would say they thought it was a "Jagger". I would say that it was a "Disbrow Special" and they would say that they had never heard of it. I would reply that no wonder it was one of a kind in the World and I built it.

When I arrived at Tyndall AFB, Florida, I noticed I had picked up a lot of pits from gravel hitting the front fenders. I immediately took it to the nearest body shop and had it repaired and it looked as good as new. I should have taped it all up to avoid this.

When I reported to Tyndall AFB I was assigned to the F-86D training squadron. I was to learn to fly our first super sonic all weather interceptor aircraft, which was the first aircraft to fly by wire. This would be the first aircraft that I had to go to school to learn to fly.

In the meantime, Fay was setting up house keeping in our new beach house. It was a two-bedroom concrete-block house with concrete floors. It had only one bathroom, which was the norm for these homes. The floors were covered with asphalt tile all through the house. It made it easy to sweep the sand out, which was plentiful. We were only a block from a pure white sand beach, which was finer than salt. The beach was beautiful and Fay and the children spent a lot of time at the beach.

We were only in the house for a month or so when I got orders to attend the All Weather Jet Instrument School at Moody AFB, Valdosta, Georgia. We had just made a deal on a brand new home in Panama City. In fact it wasn't finished yet. When we were about to move in I noticed that it did not have a garage but only a carport, this is how they build homes in this part of the country. In California it was practically unheard of to not have a garage. I told the contractor to build me a 24X24 inside dimensions garage in back of the carport. It would have windows all across two sides of the walls. It would be made out of concrete blocks. In this very humid area a car would deteriorate very rapidly if left out in the elements. Having two cars it would serve as a garage as well as my workshop.

I was off to Moody AFB to learn to fly a jet aircraft in any kind of weather conditions. The jet I would be flying would be the Lockheed T-33, which I was quite familiar. I had about 100 hours of jet time in the F-80, F-84, T-33, and the F86A but not much actual instrument time. All my time was in flight test.

When I had my first ride and found our how they made an instrument let down I was startled. You home in on the high cone, the radio fix, at 20,000 feet and start your letdown to the procedure turn inbound, which would be about 11,000 feet, then hit the low cone at 1500 feet usually 3 miles from the end of the runway. I would ride in the back seat of the T-33 and would make a take off under the hood in the back seat. The safety pilot was in the front seat. He would taxi me out to take off position and line me up on the runway and give the controls to me. I would set my gyro to the heading of the runway, run the engine up to 100% release the brakes and hold my runway heading. When I got 120 mph I would apply a little back pressure on the stick and take off holding a two bar width on my gyro horizon for my climb out. All this time I would be holding my runway heading so I would not run off the side of the runway. I would climb out at a steady 250 mph after picking up the gear and the flaps. Your initial climb out would be 5000 feet per minute. I would climb to 20,000 feet and level off. I would then call Valdosta Radio letting them know my intentions. I would then do a radio range orientation using "A" and "N" signal to determine my position to the station. This was not too hard but things happen much quicker when you are flying a jet aircraft instead of a prop job, especially when you have to do everything yourself, such as reading your let down chart, remembering all the headings and altitudes, and flying instruments at the same time.

Letting down from 20,000 feet they wanted your air speed to be 150 mph. I just could not get myself to go this slow on a let down. Every time I would start to make my let down I would be at 200 mph or better. I told the instructor I thought that 150 mph was too slow, especially in weather when you needed good control of your aircraft I almost washed out of the program on this particular point. I finally had a check ride with another pilot and did it their way and passed the course. Not long after I had graduated they came out with a change in the let down airspeed to 250 mph with the speed brakes out just the way I suggested. I was real easy to do it this way and you had good control and you came down quicker.

While I was at Moody AFB, I met Col. Timothy O'Keefe who was going through the school with me. Col O'Keefe was the flying safety officer at FEAMCOM when I was there in the late 1940s. He was the one that caused me to lose my beautiful P-51 when the pilot could not get the gear all the way down and I wanted him to belly it in but Col. O'Keefe insisted on the pilot shaking the P-51 and we finally lost the aircraft.

Well Tim and I hung around together since I had the "Disbrow Special" with me and he didn't have any wheels. One night we thought we would take a trip to one of Valdosta's local roadhouses that had a bar and dancing.

It was out of town about 10 miles on a very straight road. I told Tim to fasten his seat belt and away we went. We were cruising at about 70 mph in overdrive when I kicked it down into conventional drive and pushed on the throttle. Tim asked about how fast we were going? I didn't say anything and since I had no dash lights you could not see the instruments. He took out his Zippo lighter and lit up the speedometer which was reading 125 mph at the time. He let out a yell to slow the thing down, which I did. I thought he would blow a fuse. It was the fastest he had ever ridden in an automobile and wasn't too pleased although the car was built to go that fast safely and was very stable at that speed. In fact you did not realize you were going that fast. He had a lot of respect for my sports car after that. We spent six weeks together and finally graduated and went back to our home bases. Tim went back to England AFB, Louisiana and I went back to Tyndall AFB, Florida.

During my stay at Moody AFB, I used to commute back and forth to Panama City on the weekends to be with my family. The first week I went home I was cruising along through Tallahassee, Florida, and as I got to the outskirts of town I dropped the car into overdrive. I did not see the Florida Highway Patrol car hiding behind a big billboard sign. I immediately started to accelerate and was up to my 70 mph in no time and the car was still picking up speed fast while the rpm was dropping dramatically. AT 70 mph I was only turning 2000 rpm. I now was picking up more speed there was no one on the highway from Tallahassee to Panama City and it was about 6:30 in the evening. It was very cold and I did not have a heater or a top on the car but I was wearing a big sheepskin coat over my uniform to keep warm. About 17 miles out of Tallahassee I thought I saw a red light behind me as I checked my rear view mirror. The road was very straight but went up and down like a roller coaster in spots and you could not see behind you very far unless you both came up on top of one of the knolls together. I kept looking back and finally saw the red light about a mile behind me. At this time I was cruising at 90 mph at 3000 rpm. I thought "goodbye cop" as I dropped the car into conventional drive and accelerated up to 135 mph and left the cop like he was standing still. After running at this speed for about 2 minutes or so I thought to myself this was the only road through the bayous to Panama City. There was no place to go and

I was driving a very distinguished looking car. The only one like it in the world! I was trapped so I slowed down and let him catch me.

He finally caught with me and stopped me. He got out and said that I was going too fast "Reckless Driving by excessive speed". He was going 90 mph and could not catch me. I thought to myself he was the one that was driving recklessly going that fast in that old Ford he was driving! He then asked if I was trying to out run him. I was going to say it would have been easy but I did not. He had been chasing me for 15 miles. He would not give me a ticket because I had California plates on the car so I had to follow him back to Tallahassee to the justice of the peace.

When we got back to the Judge in Tallahassee it was a typical southern Justice of the Peace type. Court was in session immediately. The Highway Patrol told his story to which I pleaded "Guilty" to get out of there as quickly as possible. The Judge said that will be $35.00. I asked if he would take a check. We had funds in the bank at Panama City but I wasn't sure of the name of the Bank since Fay opened the account there. I did not even have a check book with me but I was in uniform and they let me use a counter check. Not knowing exactly what the name of the our bank was I filled in a name of a bank I remembered seeing when we came into town, not knowing if it was right our not.

In the meantime two women were brought in for speeding that did not have any money. The Judge asked them if they have any thing of value, any watches, etc., I could not believe what I was hearing, it was truly southern justice.

After paying my fine I walked out to my sports car and the Officer who had stopped me was looking the car all over. He saw me and asked, "How fast will it go?" I said, "135 mph", as I got in and cranked up. I backed out of the police area and with a rap of the pipes I left for home once more. It was about a week later that I got a call from the Provost Marshal at the base to call the Judge. I did and he told me that the check had "bounced" which I knew it would. I said that I would send him another good one. He then wanted me to pay for the long distance call. I told him he was lucky to get a check and hung up. From then on after I would pass through Tallahassee and get to the big sign on the outskirts of town I would see the same cop hiding in back of the sign. I would drop the car in to conventional gear and rap the pipes and take off. He never chased me again.

April 1953. I was going to the F-86D All Weather Interceptor School. This would be the first school I would have to go, to learn how to fly an airplane. This was the first "fly by wire" electronic aircraft in the history of the Air Force, so you had to know all the systems and how they operated in case of an emergency. This was also the first super sonic aircraft for normal operations. You had to climb to above 40,000 feet and roll it on your back and dive straight down with full after burner going wide open. If you did it right you would go supersonic. It was a real ride! It would jump all over before it would penetrate the sound barrier. Once it was through it was real smooth but by this time it was time to pull out and it would jump all over again as it became sub-sonic again. It was a real wild ride the first time you tried this.

The first time I tried to go super sonic it did not go through, I was too low. I started at 35,000 feet, so I climbed back up to 40,000 feet and with full power and after burner I "split essed" going straight down and after a wild ride it went through. It was the transition from .99 Mach to 1.0 Mach that gave you the trouble. After I broke the sound barrier North American gave me a pin that said "Mach Buster" on it. It was quite an exclusive club in that year, 1953. Now in 2003 all the fighters are supersonic and do it going straight up. My, how things have changed.

It seems I was "Doubled Crossed" after I got 12 hours in the "Dog" F-86D and finished the program; I was transferred to the Maintenance and Supply Squadron Group at Tyndall as permanent party! I was supposed to go to an operational All Weather Fighter Squadron. They had looked at my Form 5, my flying record and found out I had all my time in flight test and decided to keep me there. I was assigned to be the CO of the Maintenance Squadron as well as the test pilot for the base. My squadron consisted of about 300 men. In those days you paid your men in cash once per month. The money would have to be picked up at the finance office at 0600 hours. I would be with my Adjutant and 1st Sgt. We then would count the money there and then take it to the squadron and count it again and put each mans pay in an envelope with his name on it. This would be done by me, my Adjutant, my 1st Sgt Perry, and my Company Clerk. After everything was ready we would go down to the maintenance hanger

Major Bill Disbrow in the "Disbrow Special" in front of the Mode-O-Day Building in Los Angeles 1951

and pay the troops.

Being CO of a Maintenance Squadron was not my idea of a good job. I would rather have been a CO of an operational flying outfit. I hated staying behind a desk in my office, which was not even on the flight line. So I was flying as much as I could by flying target for the school squadron, F-86D, and the GCI station. I also flew all the test hops I could on all the aircraft that came out of the shops. When I was not flying I was disciplining the troops. For "Failure to Repair", Drunk on Duty, AWOL, Suspicion of Robbery, Etc. In fact I flew up to Fort Benning, Georgia, to pick up one of my AWOL airman who was in the stockade there. I flew up in a C-45 with an MP. He was sure surprised to see his Squadron CO with the MP to fly him home personally.

One day our Chief of Maintenance gave us a barracks inspection and noted that the place needed painting. I got my 1st Sgt to round up some paint and bodies to paint the place. We then painted all the barracks in pastel shades. It was beautiful but the troops complained that it looked more like a WACS barracks. The Chief of maintenance was impressed so I did not mind if it looked like a WACS barracks.

At the time Col. Fred Gray was CO of Tyndall but later was transferred to Randolph AFB, Texas. He and I used to talk flying at the Officers Club Bar. He was a very "fly safe" type of person. He had heard that I was shutting the T-33 off in the air and making air starts, which we were discussing this day. He told me I could test the system on the ground and did not have to test it in the air. He mentioned that it was not a test flight procedure to do this. I argued that an in flight check of the system was the only sure way to know if the system worked in the air. His reply was that if you bust your "butt" it would be as pilot error if the engine does not start and you have to crash land. We left it at that since I knew of no one that did this test in the air. This not only tested the system under actual conditions but also checked yourself to see if you could do this. When I shut the Jet off I was always in the flame out pattern so if it did not start I always had the field made. I always call the tower to make sure there would be no traffic in my way.

Learning this procedure was to payoff very soon. I was giving an instrument check to a Lt. one day. After climbing out to 24,000 feet assigned altitude we were on actual instruments, solid clouds. You could only see the wing tips. The Lt. was doing his range orientation, still under the hood when he had a flame out! It gets real quiet when the engine stops. When it happened the Lt. asked me, "What I was doing? I said, "Nothing", with that he was so excited that he pushed the microphone button to talk to me and shouted, "Flame out"! He did not have to push the microphone button to talk to me it was a "hot mike". Of course when he hit the "mike" button to talk to me it went over the air to the tower and to anyone else that was on the same frequency. After he shouted he said to me, "You got it". Well I immediately hit the alcohol switch for deicing the fuel system as I watched the RPM wind down, I pulled the throttle back to idle and hit the "air start", and making sure the ignition switch was on. I caught the RPM at 8% and the engine started right up. I only lost 500 feet during the procedure as I was still flying actual instruments. That gave me nothing but confidence. There was nothing to it.

The Lt. wanted me to fly it back to the base and make the instrument approach with a GCA (ground controlled approach). He did not want anything to do with the aircraft after the flame out. I found out later that he had bailed out about a month before when he had trouble. I imagined that if the aircraft did not start doing the air start he would have been leaving which would have left me with no canopy.

In the meantime the tower was frantically trying to find out who had had the flame out. I called the tower and reported we were the one who had the flame out and we were running on the emergency system and requested an immediate approach to Tyndall. Everything went like clockwork and we landed without further incident. We had a 1500 foot ceiling at the time and GCA brought us right in on the money.

It got around how fast I had made the air start and it gave me confidence, especially when we were on actual instrument conditions. I don't think 1% of the pilots on the base ever had and actual air start in the air or even practiced one. It sure paid off for me and I would demonstrate it many times to all types of pilots.

There was a time I had a 2nd Lt. in the back seat of the T-33 on an emergency leave into LAX. On the let down into LAX I was going to demonstrate the air start procedure to him but a little voice said to me not to do it. After I came back three days later to fly back to Tyndall the aircraft would not start on the normal system or on the emergency system. I might have been in trouble since they found that the ignition coil was no good. That little voice had warned me and I had listened to it. The Lord had protected me again as well as many times in my flying career.

Christmas was coming on and we would celebrate it in our new house. Fay's folks Gladys and Mont came out to visit us and towed my 1932 V8 pickup out to me. I had to leave it in Los Angeles since I could only tow one car at the time and that was the "Disbrow Special". Mont towed the pickup with his GMC pickup truck. We had a nice visit. I think they stayed a month.

The sports car was still attracting lots of attention wherever I drove it. I wanted to enter it in the Sebring 24 hour road race at Sebring, Florida. I found that it did not qualify since it was a one off design. It had to be a production model of at least 50 copies. So they invited me to be an inspector in the pits or a pit-stewart. I was assigned in the Cuban pits.

They were driving a Jaguar D model. I was to watch that no extra parts were obtained outside of the pits except what they had on hand. Also only two of the pit crew was allowed over the fence of the pits to service the car. It had to be fueled by hand with big five-gallon cans with bit spouts. A fire extinguisher had to be available at all times. The race was a 24-hour endurance job. They raced all night with their headlights on. It was quite a sight seeing them come down the straight-a-way at over 150 mph with their lights on and passing other cars. The race had a lot of the world champions in it, like Juan Fangio, Sterling Moss and Briggs Cunningham driving his own car. Fangio as driving a Ferrari and Sterling Moss was driving an Aston martin.

May 1954. We went to Indianapolis, Indiana on leave to enter the "Disbrow Special" in the Auto Show there. We would also take in the race. On the way we visited the Kentucky caves with the children. We towed the sports car behind the Cadillac as usual. I covered the front end so it would not get pitted again. When we got to Indianapolis we checked into our Hotel and asked where the Auto Show was being held. The next morning we towed the car out to the Auditorium where they were setting up for the show. I unhooked the car and cranked it up and drove into my reserved spot, much to the surprise of everyone. Most of the cars were pushed in. I had stands to put around the car to keep the crowd from getting too close. I then spent the next two hours polishing it to a bright shine, including the chrome wheels, engine, etc. It looked like it had just come off the showroom floor. I had signs made that gave the name of the car plus the specifications including horsepower and top speed, which was 135 mph. Many publicity pictures were taken with no one in the car. Everyone with a camera was taking a picture of the car.

The night of the opening of the show we had a baby sitter for the children. This let us free to answer all the questions pertaining to the car. The car looked beautiful and factory built. The first Chevrolet Corvette was just across from us. It was not half as good looking as the "Disbrow Special" and we were drawing a bigger crowd.

The people attending the show were supposed to vote for the best looking sports car in the show. One night a familiar figure stopped by to chat, it was Mel Torme, the "Velvet Fog" singer. It seems he was playing at one of the theaters in town and he had a XK 120 Jaguar with chrome wheels on it. There would be votes for every category in the show, classic, antique, Hot Rod, etc.

If I remember right the show lasted at least for three days. On the last night of the show when the votes were counted I had won hands down. I won a nice trophy and $250 prize. We also got very good seats for the Indy "500" race, thanks to the show. We sat right in back of Maury Rose, a winner of the race in 1947 and 1948. He drove a Blue Crown Special racecar. This was one of the nicest vacations for the whole family even if it entailed a little business with pleasure. We really enjoyed ourselves.

After seeing the huge crowd that attended the Indianapolis Auto Show I got the "bug" to have my own custom auto show at Birmingham, Alabama. Upon researching the area and the people I found that there had never been any kind of an auto show in the area. There were over a million people to draw from.

I talked to my friend L/C Bill Morris and his wife Annette to see if they wanted half of the action. If Birmingham had a million people in it 1% of the people would be 10,000. If we charged $1.00 each for admission, that would be 10,000 dollars. I thought 1% was on the short side. We could sell the stage to a sponsor and cut expenses down for the rental of the Auditorium.

After finalized our plan for the show and our budget, we started. We found that the Birmingham Auditorium would be $100 per day including the decorations, which was great Fay an Annette went to Birmingham from Tyndall to get ads for our program and sell the stage. Fay sold the stage to the local Ford dealer in town. Also he just happened to have the Indy Ford Pace car as an added attraction. It was the one we saw at Indy. I now began to round up the ten best custom cars in the US, also, the best Hot Rods, Antiques, and Sports Cars. I guaranteed a $50 appearance fee for each entrant plus $100 for each class winner and a $500 for best of the show. The entrants began coming in immediately and we found that we would have plenty of excellent cars. We also got "Miss Cotton" to be Hostess of the show and award the prizes. We were even on the TV Talk Show in Birmingham with pictures of some of the cars. With all the effort and cooperation from everyone we thought we had a winner.

On opening night they were standing in line before the doors opened. We even had big searchlights, lighting up the sky. Our admission was only $1.00 for Adults and 50 cents for children and servicemen. Then it hit us, no blacks allowed! I was stunned being from California, I had no idea this would happen I knew nothing of segregation. We would have to have a special showing for the blacks, which we did not plan on and could not afford. This was the law in the South and they had a policeman there to see that it was enforced. I knew that if the blacks could have been able to come at the same time as the whites we would have made it.

We ran for four days and took in a total of $4000 or more, which was about $6000 short of our expenses. It was a hard lesson. The Tax people were there when we closed demanding their money on the spot from our ticket sales. We had to put off some of the prize money until we could raise enough to pay them off when we got home. I guess we offered too much to the competitors but, live and learn. Also Birmingham was not an automobile oriented town as yet. Both Bill and I took leave to promote the show so now we were back at the old grind again.

While flying into Birmingham at the beginning of our promotion I ran across my old ex-brother-in-law, Bud Abad. He was a Major and a pilot in the USAF. He had been shot down over Germany in a B-17 during WWII. I was the one to talk him in to going to be a flying cadet before I could go. I hadn't seen him in years. I found his name on the National Guard roster at the airport where I had landed. He was the adviser for the "Guard" there. I had a great reunion with his family.

After coming off my leave I was assigned to OIC of Quality Control for the base. This included Flight Test. I was back in my old element of Flight Testing, which I enjoyed more than any other job except being the Commander of a fighter squadron. I had four pilots in my Flight Test section, Capt. Kennedy I. (Sam) Bass, Capt. Jerry Hattendorf, Capt. Ed Powell, and Lt. Jack Harris. At times we would have other pilots assigned to the flight test section. One was Bill Janssen who later when he retired moved near me in Garnerville, Nevada, (1988). He was still flying at the time and so was I.

Flight test had its tense moments, hours and hours of boredom with seconds of stark terror. We had a lot of fun along with the job. We were the elite pilots of the base. We would fly over 300 test hops per month. At times we would all take off in different aircraft, a C-45, a T-33, an F-86D and a B-25. After we would finish our test hops we would all join up together. I would be leading in the C-45 with the T-33 on one wing and the F-86D on the other with the B-25 in the slot. I would call the tower for a flyby and I would make a low pass over the field with this wild formation. This broke the monotony for the troops. Not only were all the troops watching on the ground but anyone in the air was too.

We all had call signs in flight test. The call sign for flight test was "sidewalk". My number was "sidewalk one", Sam Bass was two, Jerry Hattendorf was three, Ed Powell was four, and Jack Harris was five, so everyone could be identified when calling the tower for take off or landing instructions. It seemed I was the "enemy" whenever I took off and the other pilots were in the air. I would climb to 41,000 feet whether I was in a T-33 or an F-86D for my test hop. If I was in a T-33 and the rest were in F-86Ds I would be ready for a "dog fight". They could out dive me when I was in a T-33 because I would get into compressibility if I went over .85 Mach, the percentage of the speed of sound. With the F-86D, "the Dog", you could go super sonic. I was no match for them at that altitude but down at 20,000 feet I could hold my own.

On this particular day I was letting down and was just passing 35,000 feet when Sam went screaming right across my nose. I started after him but was in compressibility immediately. Compressibility happens when part of the aircraft becomes super sonic before the rest of the aircraft does. On a T-33 it will get into this effect at over .85 Mach. The higher you go the easier it is to get into compressibility. The aircraft starts to shudder and shake and will destroy itself if you don't slow down, so you put out the speed brakes to slow down. As Sam went by my nose I started after him and the T-Bird started to get the shakes. I immediately extended my speed brakes to slow me down while still letting down to an altitude where I could fight, which was 20,000 feet. I could hold my own in the "rat race" and not get into compressibility only in a screaming dive. After getting to 20,000 feet I expected to be "bounced" again. Sure enough Sam was on me and I started all my evasive action even went into a screaming dive and pulled 6 "Gs" on the pull up and he was still on my tail. I was going straight up and then I pushed the stick forward as hard as I could. I pulled one and one half negative "Gs" just before stalling out and went over the top of the vertical climb. This gave me a partial flame out and all the red lights in the cockpit came on. It gave me a partial "red out" when all the blood rushed to my head. Quite a thrill! I did lose Sam. I disappeared under his nose. I lost him and when we got on the ground he wondered what I had done to disappear so quickly. I said that it was a trade secret. We left it at that.

The next time he was ready for me. With Jack Harris on his wing in another F-86D he had an observer to watch me this time as Jack broke off. So when the "rat race" started Jack saw what I was doing. I couldn't pull that trick anymore since all he had to do was a roll on his back and he had me again. This not only tested the aircraft you were flying but tested the pilot's proficiency in flying. The F-86D was our first line fighter at the time.

We did get into a little trouble when our workload got too heavy and I had to borrow two pilots from the base flight section to help us out. It seems that after the pilots had finished their flight test in two T-33s they joined up and started to "rat race". Not being to experience in this sort of action, they had a mid-air collision. One bailed out, he could have saved the aircraft if he did not panic. The other pilot landed safely. They had brushed together bending a wing tip on one and knocking part of the rudder off the other one. He stated in the investigation that the T-33 seemed to be flying all right when his wingman checked it but he was reluctant to try to land it after the wingman checked the damage to his tail surface. I was to appear before the Accident Board, since I was responsible for all the aircraft in Flight Test and the pilots that flew them. I was asked if this kind of flying was tolerated in Flight Test. I said that the aircraft we were testing were fighter aircraft or fighter-trainers. To effectively test the aircraft for what they were designed for I did not see that "rat racing" hurt the aircraft but determined if the aircraft was a fit fighter to do the job that it was designed for. It was the responsibility of the pilot to fly safe and within his ability. The two pilots were awarded "pilot error" for the accident. I was exonerated and test flying with "rat racing" was still in!

I think of all the years of being in Flight Test, and test flying aircraft myself; we had no serious accidents with our regular pilots. There was one

P-51 bail out in Japan and a collapsed nose gear on an F-86D. Capt Ed Powell was the pilot at Tyndall AFB, Florida. Both of these accidents were attributed to material failure and maintenance error. We never had a pilot error accident, but we sure had our thrills at times.

One day I took off in a C-45 on a test hop, this is a twin Beech aircraft, and it was at Tyndall, AFB. After going through the test it was time to test the feathering device for the propellers. I feather the left engine first and flew along for a few minutes to see how the aircraft flew on one engine. It was OK so I un-feathered the prop back to normal. I then feathered the right engine and flew along on one engine again. I then tried to un-feather the prop and it would not un-feather. My co-pilot said, "Now what do we do"? I said, "Watch this". We had 5000 feet of altitude at the time and I put the C-45 in a steep dive and started the prop wind milling. At the same time I hit the started button and the engine started and the prop un-feathered. An old trick and it works most of the time if you have enough altitude.

Another day I had a T-33 test hop after an engine change. I gave the "bird" a good preflight before take off. I got in cranked up and taxied to the active runway. I took the runway and holding the brakes ran the engine up to full power to see if I got 100% RPM for take off. When it did and everything was in the "green" I released the brakes and was on my way. At 120 mph, I applied the backpressure to the stick and was airborne. I picked up the gear and flaps. What was that, as I felt the aircraft slightly shudder at about 150 mph, checking the oil pressure and everything else with a quick scan of the instrument panel, everything seemed normal. I made a maximum 180 degree climb turning back over the field so if anything was going to happen I had the field made. As I was climbing east towards Mexico Beach, I was closely monitoring the instruments when all of a sudden my helmet hit both sides of the canopy and the aircraft started to shake violently. I immediately pulled the throttle to idle and made a steep 180 degree turn back toward the base, which was 15 miles away. I noted quickly that I was at only 5000 feet high. I then dropped the gear and now was gliding. I called the tower and told them that I had an emergency. I had an engine failure and would try to make the runway. To get all the emergency equipment out, in case I went into the trees short of the runway. I could see the base with its two 10,000 foot runways. It looked quite a ways away but I was sure I could make it if I did everything right. I still had the throttle in idle to make sure I had hydraulic pressure and the aircraft was still vibrating since it was idling at 6000 rpm. When the engine blew it was turning at 11,000 rpm! I looked at the instrument panel and had hydraulic pressure but no oil pressure. I passed the low cone of PAM the radio fix at 700 feet and then I knew that I had the field made as my airspeed at the time was 200 mph I put down the speed brakes to kill off some of my speed then put it right on the runway and shut the engine off. Just as I passed the low cone I heard a pilot waiting for take off clearance, say to the tower, "I would like to make a running take off ahead of the emergency". I immediately called and said, "If you get out on that runway I'll land right on top of you". That ended that!

After making a normal landing I had enough speed to coast all the way down the runway and off onto the taxiway as the fire trucks followed in back of me. As I came to a stop and opened the canopy everybody was motioning to get out of the aircraft, "Get Out!" "Get Out!!" I looked back and it was smoking up a storm. I could be on fire any second. I could hardly get my oxygen mask disconnected so I could get free from the aircraft and get my helmet off. I got out of the cockpit and jumped down from the cockpit to the ground. Gave all my gear to the Flying Safety Officer in his jeep and went back to the T-bird and jumped back on the wing. I then opened the plenum chamber doors to let all the smoke out of the engine compartment, just before the firemen were going to hit it with the foam.

It seemed the rear main bearing in the engine failed and allowed all the hot oil from the engine to flow into the hot tailpipe, which caused all the smoke. The oil had such a high "flash point" it was not going to catch on fire, although it looked like it was. I am glad that I did not let the firemen hit the engine and the aircraft with the foam. It ruins all the parts as well as the engine if it is not washed off immediately.

There was another test hop waiting for me when I got back to my operations. So I again took off right away. When I got back they had the engine out of the T-33 and I went over to take a look at it. I found that the buckets on the turbine wheel, which are normally 6 inches long, were now only 2 inches long. The turbine wheel had jumped out of the engine when the bearing broke and started cutting into the aspirator section. It had cut through part of the section of the tail pipe, my thrill for the day!

Karen Lynn was born on the 27 August 1954, at the Tyndall AFB, Hospital. As usual I was not there when she was born but out at the Base beach with Sherry, Gale and Patty. School was out and I was the sitter for the day. In those days the fathers were not allowed in the delivery room. My 1st Sgt Perry came to the beach to give me the good news that I was a proud father of another baby girl and mother and child were doing fine. I dashed to the hospital to see Fay and my new daughter Karen. She was beautiful as usual. Now I did not have a chance with five females in the house but they were all lovely.

On fast Sunday we had Karen blessed at the LDS Church. Now I was sorry I could not bless her myself. I realized now how important it was. I was sorry I wasn't worthy enough to do this and had not taken the Church too seriously. I was falling away to the peer pressures of the military "good life" of parties and more parties. Tyndall AFB was a good duty with plenty of flying time but it was not doing a thing for my religion and obeying the Lord's commandments, especially living the "word of wisdom" it seemed that I was always flying off on weekends.

My Mother, Audrey Horn, lived in Berkeley, California and our overhaul facility was, American Engineering at Oakland Airport. I would take our T-33s out there that way I could see my Mother and my Step-father Henry depending when the repaired aircraft would be ready to exchange for the one I just brought out. I did this about once every two months. Being stationed so far away it was nice to be able to fly out so quickly, four and one half hours from Tyndall! This would take four or five days driving day and night in the car since Tyndall was 3000 miles from California.

After we drove the old 49 Cad over 100,000 miles I traded it for a 1952 Cad Convertible. We drove that one for over 50,000 miles and traded it off for a 1954 Coupe Deville. This would be the first hard top we would own, after driving nothing but convertibles for years. We drove throughout Florida while being stationed there.

Before Karen was born we took a trip to Mexico to see my Aunt Mary Villaran in Guadalajara. This would be in 1953. We drove the 1949 Cad from Tyndall to Laredo, Texas. We drove from there to Monterey where we stayed overnight. From there we drove to San Luis Potosi where we stayed overnight. We then drove to Guadalajara where I found my Aunt Mary, who was my Fathers half sister. Her husband was Trino Villaran. They lived in a nice three-story home in a nice residential area of Guadalajara. We stayed about a week and saw quite a few places of interest. We took in the market places and bought a beautiful Sombrero. We also went to Tacapaque a famous town nearby. It was noted for its furniture, pottery, ironwork, etc. They would ship their products all over the world. We visited Lake Chapala and the artist colony at the town of Ajijic on the shores of the lake. It had a large American settlement of nice homes and a nice golf course. We were thinking it would be a nice place to retire. Everybody had maids that were very reasonable. After leaving Guadalajara we drove over the mountains to Mexico City. It is about 450 miles over this route. The shorter route would be through Queretaro but the road was not finished as yet.

Upon arriving at Mexico City we found that the San Francisco Hotel offered the best rates for the whole family and was right down town. We went to the Bullfights since all the great Matadors come to Mexico in the wintertime from Spain. We lucked out; they were filming the movie "The Brave Bulls" with Anthony Quinn. The film crew was getting actual shots of the real matadors who were doubling for Anthony Quinn in the picture. They were real good they would kill the bull with one thrust of the sword. The crowd was going wild. They were throwing Mink coats, jewelry, etc into the ring. We later saw the movie and it was a classic. We also went to Xochimilco the floating gardens near Mexico City. The Mexicans actually call it the "swamp". It is the remains of the ancient lake that Mexico City is built on today. It was a very nice trip by boat all through the many channels covering the area. After staying a week in Mexico City we headed for home. We went through Pachuca, Victoria, and McAllen, Texas, back to Tyndall AFB.

Back at Tyndall the old routine started again. Flying test hops and going on cross country flights. I was disappointed when I wasn't selected for promotion to Lt/Col. It was kind of a slap in the face since I considered myself as one of the best pilots in the Air Force. It seemed that flying did not count; it was never mentioned in my Officers Evaluation. They wanted administrators or a "desk jockey". I hated the thought of staying behind that desk and flying only four hours a month to keep my proficiency up. I was the one they always called on to fly one of the Colonels or pick up someone special. This seemed not to count. Of course I had not finished my four years of college which was now required for the new pilots coming into the USAF.

I was transferred from the CO of the Maintenance Squadron to OIC of the Quality Control Department. This made me happy since I was also in charge of the Flight Test section. My office was right on the flight line. I now had it made when it came to flying. When I was CO of the 3625th Maintenance Squadron, I was on the other side of the base across the highway from the fight line, which was about a mile away.

With my background in Flight Test it seems they wanted me to get proficient in the F-86D so I could do the flight tests on them. The "Dog" as it was called, did not have a very good flying reputation at this time. If you were not careful on the start it would get an overheated and you would have to change the engine. When you flew the "Dog" there was two kinds of pilots, ones that had no hot starts and the ones that had one already. It would give false fire warning lights in the air. This was quite disconcerting, since if it was a real fire you had just 8 seconds to bail out before it blew up! I knew the procedure if the forward fire warning light came on. This was the bad one and it was red. I would quickly check my fuel flow meter and see if it was normal and the tailpipe temperature was normal. If they were normal it was a false reading if not it was a fire! Get out! . .

One student pilot flying at 20,000 feet one day had the forward fire warning light come on. I don't think he even retarded the throttle to see if the light would go out or check any of his instruments. He immediately bailed out after calling the tower at Tyndall he had an emergency and was leaving the aircraft. Well the aircraft was so trimmed up that it flew 150 miles after the pilot bailed out. It had been a false fire warning light. The aircraft eventually ran out of fuel and landed itself in a big field in Alabama. It would have been easy to repair only there was a big tree in the middle of the field, which the aircraft hit sliding along on its belly. The damage was extensive since it cart wheeled and tore the wing off. I was president of the Accident Board at the time and would investigate the accident personally.

In 1954 we drove out to see my Mother and Henry in Berkeley, California. She bought us a house trailer since she did not have enough room for all of us. After visiting for a few days we pulled the trailer to Los Angeles it see Fay's folks. When we got there they wanted to go with us to Mexico to see the Mexican Road Races. These races were sports cars and sedans. The Lincoln had been winning it from the first. In the sports car class the gull winged Mercedes-Benz Coupe won it. It started at Tuxtla Gutierrez near the Guatemalan border to Juarez. It was a 1,000 miles long with stops along the way.

We drove down the west coast of Mexico, which was on the start of a new road that Mexico was building at the time. It was called the Pan-Americana. It was mostly dirt when we got well into the interior. We crossed rivers on railroad bridges and one time on a bridge made out of rowboats! Everybody got out and let me go by myself pulling the 24-foot house trailer with our 1949 Cadillac. As I was crossing on the boats the timbers that were on the top of the boats began to crack with the weight of the "Cad" and the trailer. The Mexicans kept flagging me on and calling our "Mas" "Mas". I made it across just in time. One of the timbers broke as the trailer wheel passed over it but I gave the old "Cad" 'the gun and made it to solid ground.

We drove through Hemasillio, then to Guaymas, Mazatlan, Tepic, Guadalajara to Mexico City. We showed all the sights to Gladys and Mont, Fay's folks who had never been there. When we got to Mexico City we found a trailer park to stay in. After getting settled Mont and I went to see the cars that were going to be in the race. They had a parking area where they were getting prepared for the race. When we got there I thought I recognized one of the people on the Lincoln team. I went up to the car and sure enough it was one of the people from Bell Auto Parts in Bell, California. I used to go in there on my recruiting tour when I was in Los Angeles. Roy Richter was the owner at the time. He did not like me trying to recruit his young men from behind his counter. I bought a lot of racing equipment from him. When the Lincoln crew saw me they greeted me warmly. I went up the mountain before the start of the race to watch them come by and to take movies of them. The dates on my colored slides are 12 December 1954.

We would go back to Mexico almost every year. We would to see my Aunt Mary and her husband Trino Villaran. They would move a couple of times in between visits but always in a nice home and neighborhood. One time when we were visiting them my Uncle Trino got a little drunk on Tequila and he told me that my name was not Disbrow but Gomez! My Aunt Mary heard him and came out on the porch where we were and grabbed him by the ear and took him in the house and chewed him out in Spanish.

My Father gave me the story that he was born in Nogales, Arizona. The Catholic Church in Nogales had burned down that had all his records. His Father was the paymaster for the silver mines in Nogales, Mexico, and he was killed in a hold up. He was an Englishman and his name was Disbrow. My Dad had no birth certificate for the US. When he applied for a Civil Service job at McClelland Field in Sacramento, California, he had to get one of his friends that he had known for 30 years to vouch for him that he was an American citizen. I think Richard Olson was his friend who had worked for my Dad for years as an Auto Mechanic.

What my Uncle Trino had told me was intriguing. I never got any results from trying to trace my Dads genealogy through Arizona and I can see why, he was not even born in the United States. Aunt Mary was his half sister whose maiden name was Puga and she was born in Los Angeles, California. Later when I would retire from the USAF I would go see my Uncle Ignacio Leyva who had a store in Colima, Mexico, to see if I could get more information on my Father. He gave me the wrong information on where his mother was born he was my fathers half brother. He said that his mother was born in Acaponeta. I would finally get the right information from my Aunt Mary on one of my future visits.

One day just as we were ready to leave work we got a call from the Base Commander that Senator Bob Sikes from Florida wanted a fly by at Blountstown if we could get some aircraft up. I went to the flight test section and asked the "troops" who would like to give Bob Sikes a fly by? They were all ready to go and I would be leading. We would be flying four F-86Ds in formation. We were supposed to make one pass from south to north in front of the viewing stand and one form west to east. We were not to get lower than 500 feet altitude. We all joined up in a diamond formation. I think Capt. Sam Bass was on one wing, Capt. Jerry Hattendorf was on the other wing and Lt. Jack Harris was in the slot. We made a nice run at 1000 feet from south to north on the first pass and I signaled to get in a left hand echelon as I made my turn to the west to come to the reviewing stand from the rear. I dropped the formation down to 500 feet and ordered the flight into trail position as we turned to the easterly heading for our last pass. At about a mile from the viewing stand I called for afterburner now! We went over the viewing stand at about 600 mph with full after burner on. Just as we passed I called for a vertical climb with multiple rolls. I bet we almost blew the viewing stand away. Bob Sikes never called us again for a fly by.

I had become tired of Tyndall and put in for Air Mission duty. I had not made L/C and I needed a change. I had been CO of the training squadron for about three months when I got orders for a one-year tour on an Air Mission duty with the Japanese teaching them how to fly and maintain the F-86D the only trouble with the assignment it was a one year unaccompanied tour, which meant that the family could not go with me. That brought up the hackles on my neck. We agreed that I would bring the family over at our expense and live off the Japanese economy. Since we had spent three years there we knew how to live on the Japanese economy. We had been at Tyndall AFB for five and a half years.

Before I could go overseas again I had to go after an F-86D at McConnell AFB at Wichita, Kansas. At the time I was the most qualified F-86D pilot on the base to go get it. It had been there for about 3 months and they could not get the airplane to operate properly. I got one of my pilots to fly me up to McConnell AFB in a T-33. His name was Major Flotorp. After we landed we went over to the old "bird" to take a look at it. They had serviced it since they knew I was coming but when I climbed into the cockpit it was a mess. They had left the canopy open for some length of time. It had been full of dust and then it had rained on it. I got the ground crew to clean it up for me. Then after a good preflight I got in and cranked it up. After my start I noticed that the red light was on for the generating system. I checked all the circuit breakers and the switches but it did not make any difference. After I shut down I asked the civilian (who was the crew chief) why they hadn't fixed it. He remarked that they had no parts for this type of aircraft. The F-86D

In the "Disbrow Special" at Tyndall AFB, FL. after winning the Indianapolis Auto Show "Best Sports Car"

had the J-47 jet engine in it. There was a B-47 Bomb Group across the way on the other side of the field. They used the same engine and to go over there and get me a generator. Whoever landed this aircraft here in the first place left it on the civilian side instead of on the military side of the airport. He came back later with an electrician and they found out that it was the voltage regulator and they had one at the Bomb Group. They finally got the voltage regulator changed and I cranked up to give it a test hop to see if everything was in good working order. Major Flotorp was waiting for me to see if the aircraft was safe to fly before he returned to Tyndall. This aircraft was to be going to Fresno North American for project "Follow on". Here they would overhaul the aircraft and remodel it completely and lengthen the wings and call it the F86L.

I took off for my test hop and after putting through my test series it seemed to perform OK. I landed and put all my gear in the rocket pod, waved "good bye" to Major Flotorp as I taxied out for take off. I ran up to 100% on a rolling take off and as I got airborne I picked up the gear and heard a loud thump, the pod had come down as the gear came up. All the forms flew out I learned later, but my uniform, which was in a plastic bag, wrapped around the pod pylon. I did not dare retract the pod manually because it would cut my new uniform in half. So I left the pod down. I called the tower and they verified that a lot of paper flew out of the pod but there as something still stuck in there. That was my uniform!

I left the pod down and climbed to altitude. With all that drag I only got to 25,000 feet and it was slow going at that. I was going to Lowry AFB, Denver, Colorado. I had to watch my fuel so I would make it and it was getting dark.

It was a very dark night with no moon. As I approached Denver I could see Lowry Beacon and I was homing in on the homer. I landed and taxied up to the directed parking space and shut down. I hollered to the Airman, who parked me, if there was a bag in the pod? He said that there was and it was the first time he ever saw an F-86D land with its pod down. I told him what had happened and got my uniform out of the pod and got transportation to the BOQ, got changed and went to dinner at the Officers Club.

The next day I made sure that I placed my uniform bag in the back of the pilot's seat just in case. I had called the operations at McConnell AFB and was told that they had retrieved some of the forms. I told them to send them to North American Fresno, California. I took off from Lowry AFB and my next stop for fuel was Hill AFB, Utah. I refueled and was off for Fresno, California. As I was climbing out I noticed that my course took me right over Yosemite National Park. I had always had a secret passion to buzz the valley. As I spotted Half Dome I started my dive in after burner from 35,000 feet I aimed right where Mirror Lake should be and I was really going. As I went over Mirror Lake I was just about 500 feet in a steep vertical bank to make the turn into the valley, as I did I could see the shock waves coming off the wings. I was then over Camp Curry and rolled out of the bank. I was right on the Mach 0.99. As I passed over the trees at the end of the valley I did three rolls and disappeared over the trees into the San Joaquin Valley and landed at Fresno. I told them what had happened to the forms and was on my way back to Tyndall on a Commercial Airliner. This was sometime in March 1958.

I was on my way to Japan a couple of weeks later so nobody ever knew what had made that terrific boom in the valley until after I retired and the aircraft I was flying had been changed to an F86L with a new serial number and designation. It couldn't be traced.

After I retired I took the family to Yosemite for our vacation and we were taking the nature walk with the Ranger at the top of Glacier Point. As we were walking along a couple of Navy jets passed over us about 1000 feet high. I mentioned that they were still on oxygen. He stated that they don't get very low any more. Something came through the valley about three years ago and made a tremendous boom they thought it was an earthquake. It had echoed so loud through the valley. They surmised it had to be an airplane since one of the Rangers thought he saw circles of smoke going out of the valley over the trees. That was me rolling. I told him that it was me that did the buzz job. He wanted to know what kind of aircraft I was flying. I told him that it was the F-86D the fastest operational aircraft at the time it would go supersonic in a dive. I was almost supersonic when I went through the valley that is why no one saw me. I was gone by the time they heard me. I always told my pilots if you ever do a "buzz job" do a good one once and never go back or say anything about it. If you get caught it is a $100 fine per month for 12 months and you go to the bottom of the promotion list!

Tyndall was now getting rid of their F-86Ds it was sometime in December 1957. Tyndall was now under Air Defense Command. They would be getting the F-102 all weather supersonic fighters, which I would get a chance to fly before leaving Tyndall. I was designated to deliver the first F-86Ds to Moody AFB, Valdosta, Georgia. I took three of my pilots and we delivered the first four F-86Ds to Moody. We took off for Moody AFB, Georgia in a nice diamond formation. As I called the tower for landing instructions I told my flight to echelon to the right and I wanted all four aircraft on the runway at the same time when we landed. The runway at Moody was wide enough for two F-86Ds to land side by side and the next two aircraft would land in back of us. I said that I would take the right side to leave enough room for the rest of the aircraft on the runway. It seemed that the whole base was out to greet us. We all landed just as I planned but Capt. Hattendorf who was last on the runway pulled his drag-chute. He was afraid he was going to over run us. It still looked real good all the cameramen were there, taking our pictures, which would be in the Base newspapers as well as the local newspapers

Before I would leave Tyndall AFB, I would fly the last F-86D out of the base to the "Follow on" project to Fresno, California. This aircraft was a "Hanger Queen" and had been in the hanger for about three months before they decided to get rid of it. It had a bad maintenance record and nobody wanted to fly it. In fact I was the only one current to fly it on the whole base so I volunteered to fly it to "Follow On" at Fresno, California.

I gave it a good pre-flight and was off to Fresno. I was going to refuel at Big Springs, Texas but as I was flying along I noticed that one of the drops tanks were not feeding, which would restrict my flying time quite a bit. I decided to land at Reese AFB, Texas. At that time they were flying B-47s at Reese and it was a SAC base, which is usually slow service since they always have the B-47 flying on alert. I called the tower to see if they could start me. It took a special APU to start me. It had to have about twice the amperage as a regular one. They told me they could start me so I landed. What they did not tell me that they were having a big mission and could not refuel me right away. I told the refueler that only one drop tank was feeding but give me a full load.

After waiting about 3 hours I was fit to be tied. It was now dark when they told me the aircraft was ready to go. As I gave the pre-flight to the "Bird" I noticed that they had not filled the empty drop tank. The fueler thought since one was not feeding he would not put fuel in the empty one. I was about to explode. All the tankers were gone to the B-47s and I would have to wait again to get any fuel. I told him to forget it and jumped in and taxied out for take off. I ran the "Dog" up and hit the afterburner and skimmed over right over Wherry housing. I was irate! I knew better to land at a SAC base. Now I had to land again at El Paso International instead of Biggs AFB, Texas (Which was another SAC base). I got refueled just the way I wanted and had to land again at Phoenix Sky Harbor at the Nation Guard Side to refuel again.

I forgot to mention that when I left El Paso I climbed to 35,000 feet and set the aircraft on autopilot and tuned in Safford, Arizona, commercial radio station, which usually had nice music on it. It was a beautiful dark night but the stars were bright and sparkly. As I settled back at altitude I looked ahead and saw a bright light coming directly at me and very fast. I just had time to punch off the auto and make a break to the left as this object went by me and then climbed straight up with orange and different colors emanating from it, the object went right up until it was out of sight I almost spun in trying to watch it. It was the first real UFO I had ever seen and I watched for them all the time. In fact I always carried my camera with me in case I ever saw one. The objects rate of closure was so fast I did not have much time to observe it real good. The distance from me could have been about one quarter mile or better as it went by. I landed after this encounter at Phoenix and told the Sgt.Crisbell, the duty NCO, about it. He stated that the Guard pilots see them all the time. I was not about to make an official report of it and being interrogated like I was some sort of a nut.

I finally got the old "Dog" to the project at Fresno after landing another time to refuel since that drop tank was not feeding. It took a lot of trim to keep the wing up with all the fuel on one side. That would be my last flight for Tyndall AFB, Florida.

One thing about the military they pack all your belongings and move all your furniture and put everything in a big moving van. All you have to do is make sure you mark all the boxes so you will know where everything is when you go to unpack. We loaded up the old Cadillac and headed for California.

I had orders to attend survival school again, which I did not think was right. I had enough days delay en-route to take care of this before I would have to ship out to Japan for a second tour of duty there.

We would stop at Fay's folks in Los Angeles and then we would all go up to Berkeley to my Mother and Henry's house. We all stayed about three days and it was time for me to head for Reno, Nevada, and Stead AFB, where the survival school was located. When I got there I asked them at registration if I had been to the school before did I have to go again? They said that I did not, I was lucky. When I heard the good news I immediately called Fay and had her fly up to Reno so we could have a last good vacation together before I would have to go overseas alone. We had a lot of fun and met a lot of nice people. After about a week of living it up in Reno we started for home in the Cadillac. We drove up to Truckee, California and then to Lake Tahoe. I think we spent a night at South Shore and saw one of the shows. The next day we drove down HWY 395 to Los Angeles and home.

I don't remember how I got to Travis AFB, California I guess the whole family came up with me so they could drive the "Cad" to Los Angeles. When I got to Travis AFB I was told that the aircraft to Japan was leaving from San Francisco International and the last bus was leaving right now I said my quick good byes and hopped on the bus and left.

We were flying a Super DC-7 I think, a prop job. We would land at Hawaii for our first refueling stop and then into Midway Island then the Haneda International Airport, Japan. It was almost 10 years to the day since I was stationed at FEA MCOM in April1948 now it was April 1958.

I was to report to Headquarters at Johnson AB where my daughter Gale was born. After reporting in and getting settled in the BOQ I went back the next morning to get my assignment. I found out that I would be going to Komaki AB. I would be teaching the Japanese pilots how to fly the F-86D. I would be attached to a small USAF unit that was stationed there. I thought I was going to be the CO but I was told I was the DCO and there was a L/C who was presently the CO. In the meantime I told the project officer who was giving me my assignment that my family was coming over at my expense. I was told that they would try and get my orders changed to regular duty at one of our organizations so I could bring the family over at government expense. I would report to the Komaki unit until they got my orders changed and found a replacement for me.

I went down to Komaki AB and met the CO of our unit and a tour of our little detachment and the Japanese organization and all their aircraft. I wasn't there very long when I got orders to return to Johnson AB. They had found a replacement for me but were still trying to find a unit that could use my skills. After a few days of seeing all the old spots I was assigned to the 68th Fighter Interceptor Squadron at Itazuke AB, in southern Japan on the island of Kyushu. It was considered the Florida of Japan.

Lt. Kowal flew up to Johnson AB to pick me up in a T-33. I put my gear in the nose of the aircraft and we were off to Itakzuke. I was very familiar with Itazuke since I had been there quite a few times on our last tour. I had also delivered the last F-82G to the 68th in 1949 now I was going to be the DCO of the outfit almost ten years to the day since I had left Japan on our first tour.

L/C Harford P. Jenks was the CO of the squadron. We had 25 F-86Ds.

We also had three flights in the squadron, Red, Green, and Blue flight. The behind the line pilots were in Black flight. I was one of these since it was for all pilots that had administrative jobs. I would still be getting to test hop the aircraft. I was also the oldest one in the squadron and had more diversified time that anybody on the base. When the Form 5 clerk saw my flying - record it was not long before everyone knew it.

All new pilots coming into a new squadron had to get checked out in the T-33 before they could fly it solo. Lt. Kronebusch would be my check pilot. I had to fill out all the questions on the written test for the operation of the T-33 before we could get airborne. I got that over with and we went out to the aircraft and I got in the front seat and Lt. Kronebusch got in the back seat. We took off and went through all the normal flying procedures to see if I could fly the aircraft safely. One had to demonstrate a flame out landing with the throttle in the idle position simulating a flamed out engine. As I was approaching the "high key" to start my flame out pattern I asked Lt. Kronebusch if he ever had a real flame out in a T-33 and made a real air start? He said that he never had a real flame out or never made a real air start. With that I shut the engine off. I looked in the mirror for the wild-eyed reaction I always got when demonstrating this. I said, "Quiet isn't it!" I then said that an air start is real easy if you don't panic. Make sure that your ignition switch is on and gang load your fuel switches, hit the air start switch and watch the rpm come up immediately as you bring the throttle up to idle. As I made the air start I left the throttle in idle and told Lt. Kronebusch that I would not cheat and move the throttle to put any power on and came right around the pattern and land. I asked him if he would like to try it but he declined. I would do this with Capt. Al Nelson who was the Operations Officer and made a believer out of him, too.

My primary duty with the 68th FIS at Itazuke was Maintenance Officer with additional duties as DCO and test pilot. The first thing I found was the pilots were not using the autopilot in the aircraft. I was told that the autopilots never worked so I telephoned the Lear Tech Rep and got him over to find out why the autopilots did not work. I had him "peak" up all the autopilots and showed my technicians how to do it and to keep them that way. It was a 65 pound item in the aircraft that was not being used.

I would later demonstrate how to use the autopilot during actual rocket

The "Saber Cotillion" entertainment at the Officer's Club, Tyndall AFB, FL. Chorus line from the Officer's Wives Club. Fay Disbrow, 3rd from the left. 1 Dec 1956

firing, which it was designed for. I had a flight of three of us being vectored to the target. A B-57 was towing a big "rag" target. On the first pass the GCI station did not get us lined up in time so we had to make a second pass. On the second pass I got all lined up and picked up the target about 12 miles out. We were making a ninety-degree beam attack on the target. As I picked up the target on the radar I ran the "pipper" up on the blip of the target and locked on. At this time I was flying on autopilot. The autopilot was flying me right on a collision course for a hit. I reached over and selected 24 rockets. I was not going to miss the target after having to go around on the first pass. I gently monitored my heading to keep the dot in the center of the target circle. It was dead center as I looked up to make sure I was locked on the target as I fired my rockets. What a blast! I could hardly see from the smoke of the rockets but it looked like a hit to me as I radioed the target aircraft. There was a very acrid smell in the cockpit form the cordite explosion of the rockets.

The target aircraft called back that I had knocked the target completely off the cable of the tow ship. My wingmen were not too happy about that they did not even get a shot. The tow plane had to go back to the base and get a new target installed.

I proved my point that if you use the autopilot it is much easier and smoother to fly the target dot especially when you lock on. I told the other pilots how easy it was to do and to use it more often for good hits. I also told them it was easier to look up to make sure you are locked on the right target with the aircraft on autopilot because there is no deviation in your course when you look up.

I found out that I was the first behind the line pilot to knock the target off the tow ship I also found out the CO of our Squadron was a " hump pilot" in China during WWII flying C-46s, etc. he got out after the war and was recalled during Korea and then stayed in. This was his first assignment to fighters.

The "Saber Cotillion" - Fay Disbrow 2nd from left 1 Dec 1956

I was assigned to "Field Grade" quarters on the base. It was nice to get the best for a change. It wasn't like stateside but it was good for foreign duty. I had two rooms and a maid who cleaned every day and made up my bed and generally kept the place nice and tidy. I had Fay on the list to get to Itazuke and it took about five months to get her over with the children. In the meantime I was flying quite a bit and getting the gist of the job which started out as Maintenance Officer plus Flight Test Officer and the Deputy Commander of the squadron. It was great to be in an operational combat ready Squadron with lots of young pilots and a lot of "Esprit De Corps". I didn't realize it then but I delivered the last F-82G from FEAMCOM personally to the 68th in 1949, now almost ten years to the day I was back in Japan on my second tour of duty.

While waiting for the family to get over I was made payroll officer for a radar station at the tip of the island of Kyushu, Japan. During this time in the military everyone was paid in cash. So I carried a Colt .45 and had two MPs with me. I had to ride the train to Nagasaki and after waiting in Nagasaki for three days they sent a jeep to pick us up and drive the rest of the way to this radar station that sat on a mountain at the tip of the island of Kyushu. It was a weapons carrier and not a jeep that picked us up at the end of the railroad line, which actually went far past Nagasaki.

We were greeted like royalty since we had all their money for them. We stayed over night after paying all the "troops" and the next day they took us down the mountain to a boat dock where we took the scenic boat ride back to Nagasaki. On the way back we passed "Battleship Island". From a distance it looked just like a battleship and was bombed many times by our Air Forces. As we passed by I found out that it had a big coal mine underneath the bay.

When we got back to Nagasaki we had a chance to see "Ground Zero". There was a big statue in a park where the atom bomb was dropped. The statue was a large figure of a man with his finger pointing upward to the sky to donate where the atom bomb came from. They also had a large museum with the history of the bombing with all photographs of Nagasaki before and after the bomb blast. It was interesting to note that our government warned the Japanese to evacuate the city as we were going to bomb it. We even dropped leaflets of warning which they had some of these on display of the catastrophe that was coming but they did not heed our warning. There were 78,000 killed and 75,000 wounded in the fraction of a second when the bomb was dropped! The people saw a lone B-29 in the sky but it did not mean a thing to them since one B-29 did not scare anybody. They had been bombed before and could withstand the damage. It was a total surprise to them even after we had dropped the bomb on Hiroshima.

I got word that Fay and the girls would be flying over on Pan Am. I took leave to meet them at Haneda Airport in Tokyo. I flew up and had everything arranged it was great to be a Major since rank has its privileges. I got a staff car to pick them up at the airport and we stayed in the military hotel in Tokyo. We did a lot of sight seeing and went to the old places we used to go when we were here on our first tour in 1948. Of course Gale was born at Johnson AB and Sherry was here before now we had Patty and Karen.

After seeing everything we wanted and my leave was about up we got on JAL and headed for Itazuke. We had a nice Japanese house waiting for us with a live in maid. It had 4 bedrooms to take care of everybody. It was near the base in a place called Kaskabaru. We wore no shoes in the house since it was a Japanese house and shoes were not allowed in the house. Your shoes were left at the door and you put on slippers to enter the house. It kept the floors nice and clean and shiny. Our live in maid was Yoko Yamamoto. She was a jewel about 35 years old and was much bigger than the normal Japanese woman. She looked after the children like a "Mother Hen". She also taught them a bit of Japanese and was learning English at the same time. She went everywhere with us like one of the members of our family.

It didn't take long for the Church of Jesus Christ of Latter Day Saints group to catch up with us after our records arrived from the States I was interviewed by the group leader, Capt. Heber Butler. I had not received any position in the church since I left the Arlington Ward in Los Angeles. This would be after I was baptized, 6 September 1952. I was never ordained a Deacon, so was immediately ordained by Brother Richard D. Morton who was and Elder in the Church. He was also a pilot in the 8th Fighter Wing. We began to attend church regularly and I was advanced into the priesthood by being ordained a Teacher by Brother Morton following that I was ordained a Priest by Brother Loras Burk Tangren, 10 Jan 1960. I finally was ordained an Elder on the 18 September 1960.

We were a small group so we had to meet in the community center on the base. We had a very active group and we would raise money by putting on carnivals at the center. Fay and I were given the job of the head of the MIA (mutual improvement association). She was in charge of the girls and I was in charge of the boys. We would have dances and parties, potluck dinners, swimming parties at the base pool and all kinds of activities to keep us all close together. We had many pilot officers as well as enlisted men in our group. I even think we had a few civilian workers in our group. I had my greatest advancement in the Church while I was stationed at Itazuke AB. It was all due to Brother (Capt) Heber Butler and his Counselors who were all pilots to push me and "Goad" me into being a good LDS member. It was a surprise to the members of my squadron the 68th FIS that I was now a good member of the Church and was living the "Word of Wisdom" and going to Church every Sunday when I was not flying on official orders.

We finally moved out of our house at Kaskabura for a much larger house off base. It was near the Japanese Army Camp and had been a Japanese Officers club. It was about a mile from the base at Kaskabaru, which was the Headquarters and the air base was at Itazuke, it was actually two bases one for Headquarters and one for Flying. Our house was about in the middle of the two bases. It was typical Japanese house with Katami mats on part of the floors and the hallways were polished mahogany. I think it had at least 3 or more bathrooms. It also had a maid's room, sewing room, dining room, family room, a master bedroom suite, and two bedrooms for the children. We brought most of our personal belongings with us including our TV. It was quite a laugh to watch "Gun Smoke" and a lot of other American programs with Japanese dubbed in for the voices. We got fairly good reception off the antenna since there was no cable in those days, 1958. The children would watch all the cartoons of Bugs Bunny, and all the rest with the Japanese dubbed in. It was quite a treat for Yokosan, since there were only a few TV sets in the area. She would teach the children Japanese so they could understand some of the words. The children all picked up Japanese quite quickly and Karen who was not in school as yet learned faster than anyone since she was with Yokosan quite a bit and Yokosan would speak to her in Japanese all the time.

Karen was finally enrolled for a half a day session in Kindergarten on the base. Everyday she would walk down our road to catch the school bus that stopped at the bottom of our road. We lived on the top of a small hill overlooking the valley where the both military complexes were based. We had an acre of ground with fruit trees and a big garden with many flowers and bushes. As you came up the hill on our road you came to two large cement posts with cement Japanese lanterns on the top. It was very picturesque. It had a large parking area but no garage. We hired a full time gardener, a full time seamstress, and a part time houseboy to polish the floors and wash the cars and had Yoko for our live in maid. This all cost only $40 per month! We were really living.

Fay enrolled the girls in a Japanese dance class. They all looked so pretty in their Kimonos. They all did very well especially Sherry. She got so good that they made her a teacher to teach other students. She also put on a recital at one of the largest theaters in Fukuoka with another girl from her dance class, who was a good friend of hers. They did the typical Japanese Geisha dances in their beautiful Kimonos. The Japanese audience gave them a great reception with much applause. Sherry was 13 years old at the time and had golden blond hair, which drove the Japanese wild.

We went to a Japanese resort Hotel on one of my leaves. It was very nice and had a golf course, hot baths, etc. We took everyone with us including our maid Yokosan. It was beautiful and was located in the hills with a very nice view of the area. It also was reasonable priced in those days. We had a suite of rooms to take care of everybody. The rooms were typical Japanese with the Katani mat floors.

At the time we were there they were having a Japanese Convention at the Hotel. As I was passing a large room used for an auditorium I heard all this music and applause down the hall. Being curios I went down to the door and looked in to see what all the noise was coming from. It was full of Japanese men all in Kimonos and on the stage were three Geishas dancing to the Samison, a three-string guitar like instrument. One Japanese man saw me and motioned me in to take a seat and watch the show. When the first act was over I said to the Japanese man that I had a "Josan" a girl that could do the same dances. With that he insisted that she come and dance for them. There were about 300 Japanese men in the place. I went back to our room and told Fay and Sherry what had happened and that the Japanese wanted Sherry (Shess) to dance for them. Lucky we brought all the children's Kimonos with us. We got "Shess" into her Kimono and Fay fixed her hair up into a bun like the Geishas. The Geisha wears a wig but "Shess" had enough hair to put it up high on her head to look similar to the wig of the Geisha. The big difference was it was a beautiful golden blonde. I brought her over to the hall since no women were allowed in the hall. She did her dance with the other Geishas while one played the Samison. Well "Shess" did as well or better than the Geishas and brought the house down with applause. She had to do all her dances that she knew before they would let her off the stage. I can't remember what they gave her in appreciation for her great recital. I was so proud of her and she looked so pretty and had such poise. That was the highlight of our trip. I can't remember the name of the resort but it was well know in Kyushu. We would go on many more trips with Yoko and the children while we were stationed at Itazuke. We always made it a point to stay in Japanese Hotels so we could learn their customs. This made it a very enjoyable tour of duty. When the girls arrived in Japan in 1958, Sherry was 12, Gale was 9, and Patty was 7 and Karen was 4.

Japan had always been known for its earthquakes and typhoons. Fay and the children had been in Japan for about 6 months when there was a big typhoon. It seems I was on a special assignment to Taiwan aboard a C-119. While I was in Taiwan the typhoon hit Itazuke. The winds were so strong that it blew the tiles off the roofs of some of the dependent housing. Fortunately our house stood up OK but the house next door lost many of its tiles. The Lt. who lived there, I can't remember his name, was a member of our squadron. When you are in the military everyone is like a big family and help one another. So things were not too bad.

While on my trip to Taipei, Taiwan I stayed in the Imperial Hotel with the rest of the crew from the C-119. We had a beautiful bungalow along side of the big swimming pool this Hotel was owned by Madame Chiang Kai Chek .the wife of General Chiang Kai Chek. It sat up on a hill overlooking the city as well as the airport where we landed. While we were waiting to have dinner one evening an entourage of men walked through the lounge I looked up and saw an older distinguished Chinese gentleman coming across the room. He was dressed in the older Chinese robe with the typical Chinese beanie on his head. The rest of the people with him were in western dark suits. I recognized him immediately. It was General Chiang Kai Chek and I said it to the group that it was the Generalissimo they said I was crazy but I knew it was him from all the pictures I had seen of him. After they all passed through the lounge a Chinese gentleman came back and said that we were supposed to have stood up for the President of China. I apologized for everyone stating "We were not sure who he was". We did not see him again he went to a private room with his bodyguards and left by a different exit. I was told that he never retraced his footsteps. It was a precautionary practice against being assassinated. The Red Chinese wanted him dead since it was his goal to reunite China and his everlasting fight against Communism.

Upon touring the city with one of my fellow officers I noticed a four-wheeled rubber tire wagon coming down the main street. It was loaded with large blocks of granite and we could not believe our eyes. A lone Chinaman, "coolie", was pulling it all by himself and he was just a little fellow. He was very muscular and had a harness on his body and one on his head to pull the load. It was unimaginable I just could not believe it. As we stood on the curb watching this poor "coolie" inch his way down the street with this outlandish heavy load we noticed he was coming to a slight rise in the road that went over a railroad track. Just as he was making a great effort to get up a little more speed to make it over the rise a truck got in his way and he had to stop. When the truck finally got out of his way he tried to start this heavy load. I saw that he was struggling and just could not start up this load on this little rise to get over the railroad track. No one was paying a bit of attention to the poor man as he kept struggling. I ran out with my friend and helped push the load over the railroad tracks for him. After we got him over the railroad track and got him going again he could not stop thanking us. My heart went out for him what a way to make a living. He was the poorest of the poor of the Chinese people. I thanked the Lord that I was blessed to be born an American with a wonderful family and occupation. I took pictures of this event since it would be hard to believe by explanation.

We finished our business and got the C-119 loaded. We had purchased a lot of bananas for a Luau party that we were having back at Itazuke and they were loaded aboard with the rest of the stuff. We all got in and cranked up and taxied out for take off. When the magnetos were checked there was too much drop on one engine so we had to taxi back to the line to get it fixed. By this time it was 95degrees in the shade and about 110degrees inside of the aircraft. After about three hours we were to start up and go again. It was real smelly in the aircraft by this time with the entire bananas aroma permeating throughout the airplane. We arrived back at Itazuke to find that the typhoon had roughed up the place quite a bit. I was wondering how the family had faired and if our house had blown away. I called immediately after landing and found that everyone was OK as well as the house.

Our church group at Itazuke was interested in raising money for our group. We would put on carnivals, which proved very successful. We would have dart games, ring toss, etc. Each one had its own booth. We would have the carnivals at the community center on the base. We had quite a few people to draw from since there were 5000 people stationed there. We would put on bake sales and anything else we could think of that would bring people in. We had a very aggressive group.

We had a big retreat for all the Priesthood Holders in Japan at the Mt. Fuji Hotel (a beautiful old Japanese Hotel). It was located at the foot of the mountain. We had many meetings and I was confirmed an Elder there. We had all our Elders from our group there. So we all decided to climb Mt. Fuji, which is 12,104 feet high. We started at the 7000-foot level after a ride in a GI truck to the trail that led up the mountain. As you climb the trail it is covered with lava and has many switch backs and it is so steep you can see the top of the mountain. We all bought walking sticks, which was branded at every rest stop. This hiking stick was about 5 feet long and one and one half inches in diameter. It had enough room for all the brands as you made your way up the mountain. I also had a Japanese flag on mine with bells. As we were climbing up the mountain there were small Japanese men carrying cases of soft drinks on their backs and were practically running up the trail right past us and made no stops until they got to their special rest area or to the top of the mountain. They did this every day and it showed they were in great shape. We finally made it to the top and up the stairs to the house at the top. I lay on the floor and called for oxygen as a joke. It had taken us six hours to get to the top and it was covered with clouds when we got there. After a short rest we started back down the mountain. This time we did not follow the trail but went straight down the side of the mountain. It was covered with loose lava pebbles. We actually ran down the mountain taking about ten footsteps per step. We fell down many times but were having a ball we made it to the bottom in about an hour.

We had a great time during the retreat. At the final meeting of about 1000 people, whom did they call to give the closing prayer but me, which was the first time for me! The Lord gave me the strength and the words to get through it without much trouble. Having the priesthood is the greatest blessing one can receive being able to act in the name or the Lord.

On arriving back at the base at Itazuke it was back to the old routine and flying. Every so often Itazuke would have flights to Hong Kong and I could take leave and fly down to do some fantastic shopping. This time I was able to take Fay with me and we had a fantastic time. I had been there a couple of times before so I knew most of the good places to go. We bought all kinds of stuff including a USAF Dress Uniform for $25, which I still have. Also a suit for $19, which I had measured in the morning, a fitting at noon and wore it to dinner that same night! We had dinner at the Golden Phoenix restaurant. This place was in Kowloon and had a black peppered sirloin steak for two for seven dollars, which included dancing to a large orchestra. Fay bought a Chinese "Chesong" dress tailored made in red satin and gold lame for seven dollars! She bought many other goodies and had a blast.

A movie company was making a film while we were there and we saw William Holden on a street in Hong Kong and said "Hello". We rode the rickshaw and went to the top of the Tram with its beautiful view of Hong Kong and Kowloon. We met our friends at Repulse Bay, Lt. Ray Bryant and his wife Bonnie, and had lunch at the floating restaurant at Aberdeen. I was taking movies of most of this trip with my new Bolex Rex 16mm movie camera. This is a famous restaurant that has been featured in many movies that were made in Hong Kong. We had a wonderful time and would return to Hong Kong many times even after retiring Fay and I would return for the great shopping bargains and atmosphere. We would also visit the Philippines, Okinawa, and Japan again.

Between flying and putting on the entertainment at the Officers club I would take leave and we would visit many of the fine resorts on Southern Kyushu, as well as the many fine spas. One of our trips took us to a lovely Hotel at Beppo on Kyushu. It was noted for the beautiful gardens and hot springs. It was believed that these hot springs would cure most anything and were very popular.

We drove in and had the valets unpack our car. As we entered the lobby, which was very large, I noticed a large pool in the center of the area. It was like a big dish. It was about 8 feet in diameter and about a foot deep in the middle. In the middle of the big dish was one solitary fish about a foot and a half long and nothing else. As I walked around the pool I noticed that the fish did not take his eyes off me pivoting in the center of the pool as I made a 360degree turn around the pool. I was fascinated with this fish but went over to register at the Hotel desk to get our rooms. I had no more finished registering and as I turned around I noticed a Japanese gentleman walking back and forth like he was teasing the fish when all of a sudden the fish came right out of the pool after him landing on the marble floor and flapping around with its teeth snapping! With that the manager dashed out with a big towel and threw the fish back into the pool with the exclamation "Dami" "Dami" fish, which meant "crazy" "crazy" fish. I think it was a cousin of the Piranha. I found out later that it was indeed the cousin of the Brazilian Piranha. It was also a lot meaner and had bigger teeth. It was amazing for how big he was that he could get enough speed in such a short distance to fly right out of the pool into the lobby. I immediately told the children not to go close to that fish. Don't put your fingers anywhere close to that water or they would be missing a finger. I could not believe that they would have such a vicious creature in the middle of their lobby since Japanese children are always putting their fingers in ponds to attract gold fish. We spent a nice three-day weekend and had a lot of hot baths.

My Mother Audrey Horn and her Husband Henry were coming to visit us. They were on a tour of the Far East on the President Lines. They would stop at Hawaii then to Hong Kong, and then back to Tokyo, where we would meet them. After finalizing the dates they would be in Tokyo I took leave to meet them there with all our girls.

We took the "Kamikaze Flyer" the train from Fukuoka. The children had a ball on the train. If I remember right it was an overnight trip so we slept in bunks. We went to a hotel in Tokyo and met my folks and toured around Tokyo. I took them to all the old spots we had known on our last tour in Japan. We had a great time until it was time for them to go. It was nice to see my Mom and Henry after not seeing them for a year and they enjoyed the girls since they were a year older now.

Before Fay came to Japan, I enquired what type of automobile would be best to ship over. After asking around I found that a Cadillac Fleetwood or Limo would bring the greatest price. I wrote to Fay and told her what to get. It seemed that the Limos were scarce and if you could get one it would cost us $7000 cash to take it out of the country. We had to settle for the Fleetwood with all the appointments and it must be black! When the car finally arrived it landed at Ashiya, which was close to Itazuke and when we went to pick it up it was a beauty. Black with white leather interior and black seats with every accessory Cadillac offered.

When we got back to Itazuke I was immediately contacted by Japanese "scouts" from large Japanese firms in the surrounding area. The word got around real quick that there was a beautiful Fleetwood Cadillac in the area that would be for sale after it was in Japan for one year. That was the stipulation for selling foreign cars imported to Japan from the States.

We had a carport to keep it in and a houseboy to keep it cleaned and polished. We had 5000 miles on the odometer when it arrived in Japan we drove it very little just to keep the battery charged up and the engine in tune. When we finally sold it we were millionaires for a day in Japanese Yen. We sold the car for $8000. We sold it to the president of the steel mill in Ashiya. He sent his chauffeur over to drive the car and then came over himself and friends to get a demonstration, which closed the deal immediately.

I had a chance to buy a 1957 MGA sports Car from a Tech Rep who had to return to the States for $1500. It was only a year old so I bought it. I also bought a Hino Renault from the Japanese. Americans did not buy Japanese cars. I caused a little confusion at the base registration office. I should have cornered the market on Renaults. Later, there would be

21 Renaults on the base. It was built in Japan under license from French Company. It was a right hand drive and was very economical to operate. Of course GI gas was only 12 cents a gallon on the base while the Japanese had to pay 50 cents a gallon. Compare that to the price of gas today in the States! The car was a four- speed stick shift and I got a big kick racing the Japanese taxis, which were Datsuns. The beauty of the little car it could go down all the back streets without any clearance problem that I would have had in an American car.

Having been going to Hong Kong so many times and doing good shopping, I finally ended up with one of the best 16mm cameras in the world, a Bolex Rex 16. I had all the lenses for it plus a 35mm to 150mm Zoom lens and an electric motor drive. It had a built in fader and I had a title attachment also. It was the closest to a professional as one could get so I made a lot of movies of our travels and the children. I also had all the movies I had made prior to entering the service with me. I used to show them to our friends who would get a big charge out of them.

One day at the 68th FIS the subject came up if I could make a movie of the squadron like the one that had been going around the Air Force for a few years called "The F-86s Are Here". It was made by members of a fighter squadron in Germany and was a great comedy. So I decided to make a movie of our new aircraft the F-102, which had replaced our F-86s. I began casting the lead for the production. I selected my Electronics Officer Captain William "Bill" Morse. He was a natural born comedian. I decided to make it a comedy of the first checkout ride in the F-102. In fact the name of the production was "CHECK OUT'. It was shot in color and I "dubbed" in the sound track of narration and music with the help of one my good friends and pilot in the 8th FBW, Captain Ray Bryant. The opening scenes would be two F-102s in formation at 35,000 feet putting out beautiful vapor trails with the opening title superimposed on it. The opening music would be "61 Trombones" by Meredith Wilson. This would set the mood for the picture. It was quite a successful production with everyone in the squadron participating in it. It has been traveling around the Air Force for years. I don't know how many copies were made but I guess quite a few. Now that we have the VCR tapes I know many more will be copied on tape. In fact I made a copy of it on tape to preserve it.

I still have the original 16mm picture and the sound track that were used to make the original copy for Bill Morse. I still have an original copy and show it the 68th reunions.

As we were fazing out the F-86D I would deliver two to JASDAF (Japanese Self Defense Force). The young pilots like to fly my wing when I would get orders to deliver some of the F-86Ds. Lt. Jerry Newburger was one of the pilots that I took on one delivery to Komaki. As we approached Komaki I called Newburger and said that we would make an upside down let down and to hang in there. I rolled over at 20,000 feet and let down upside down he liked that as he stayed right on my wing. We rolled right side up at 2000 feet and came in for a landing at Komaki and gave the F86Ds to the Japanese.

The next time I had three F-86Ds to take to a storage area at Kisurazu near Tokyo. This was an old sub base for FEAMCOM on my first tour to Japan so I knew it quite well. I was leading the flight to Yokota AB, which was near my old base of FEAMCOM at Tachikawa. I was leading a flight of three with Lt. Ron Stull on one wing and Lt. Jerry Newberger on the other wing. After being airborne for about 30 minutes I noticed my gyro Horizon was tumbling and I had just checked the weather at Yokota AB and it was overcast there. That meant we had to make an instrument approach and I did not have any flight instruments. I called Lt. Stull to take the lead after I was sure all his instruments were working properly and I flew his left wing. We had adverse winds and were not going as fast as we usually do and were getting low on fuel. I noticed my fuel gauge was getting really low and told Lt. Stull to make a three ship GCA and landing since we were low on fuel. As we turned to the high cone I thought we were turning right when we were supposed to be turning left. I called to Lt. Stull and notified of the direction of the turn was left of which he replied, "I am turning left, Sir", boy did I have vertigo. We landed in a three-ship formation, which was easy on the big wide 10,000 foot runway at Yokota AB. It must have startled the GCA to have a three-ship formation all land at once.

We RON (Remained over night) and the next morning it was a beautiful clear day. We took off and I was going to give them a low level tour of the Chiba Peninsula on the way to Kisarasu AB. We did not get over 500 feet all the way down the coast of Chiba. Went over a lot of fishing boats and they had a real tour of the area at low altitude. When we arrived at Kisarasu we had to land one at a time since there were not any taxiways and when you landed you had to turn around and taxi back on the runway.

After delivering the aircraft to this storage area we were picked up and flown home the next day. That was the last of our F-86Ds, which would all go to the Japanese for training. About this time the promotion panel was meeting in the Pentagon for the selection of the new Lt. Colonels. I had been passed over the first time at Tyndall AFB, Florida. I was now sweating it out again. The only thing in my favor was if they passed me over again they had to retire me. Well when the list came out in September 1960 I was not on it. It was published in the Air Force times. It was very disappointing since people I knew who were on it were not as good a pilot as I was. This did not seem to count how many aircraft I saved the Air Force by not bailing out in an emergency but bringing the aircraft back safely to determine what had caused the emergency. Also that I had completed a WWII combat tour of 50 missions in a B-24 and had been awarded the DFC and the Air Medal with 5 Oak Leaf clusters plus a combat tour in Korea as commander of the 101st FMU at Pusan. With no breaks in my career from the day I enlisted as a Flying Cadet. After analyzing my career I found the first thing I failed to do was finish my College degree. I should have attended the University of Maryland College courses that were available on the Base. Like many of the Officers they had not attended college and got their degrees this way. I had an AA degree from San Mateo Jr. College, California, but it seemed the Air Force wanted all their Field Grade Officers to have a full college degree. I wasn't lazy I just wanted to spend more time with my family since I was always flying quite a bit. The second reason I was passed over was that I was one of the oldest Majors in the Air Force. I had been over 28 years old when I graduated from cadets. When I arrived in Italy for my combat tour I was older than the squadron commander. So not having a College Degree and being so old for a Major, 45, I was passed over for the second time. It was a little disturbing, since I had lots of commendation letters I had submitted to the promotion board. These letters were for outstanding performance and gratitude for the different projects I served on or was the project officer. This did not mean a thing I guess I liked to fly too much and hated to be at a desk job. One instance to getting a nice letter of commendation from a Base Commander happened at Itazuke. It was Armed Forces Day when Col. Jenks our squadron CO was away in Tokyo. The Base Commander, Col Riva called and asked if we could participate in the show. I now being in command of the squadron said that we would be happy to participate in the show. I got the "troops" together for volunteers who wanted to get into the act. I decided to take the most experienced pilots for this show. We managed to put up 12 F-86Ds with a lone ship for solo acrobatics, flown by Lt Dick Derr, which since has deceased. We all took off with me leading and formed up in formation in a three four ship diamond of twelve aircraft. We made our first pass at 1000 feet over the big crowd at the base. On our second pass I had the formation go to a four three-ship formation in trail of four elements. We formed up a distance away from the base so we could get all joined up in position and no one could see us from the base. We then came over Fukuoka in a long turn to line up for the runway from west to east. There was a large smokestack, which I was using for as a checkpoint so to get lined up in the turn. As we turned I was losing altitude rapidly and picking up speed to make a good pass. As I rolled out of my turn my wingman had it tucked in very well and we were lined with the runway. I looked at my air speed and we were indicating 350 mph and my altimeter was reading 100 feet and we were stepped down! The last aircraft was blowing dust off the runway and the noise was so excruciating that Sgt. Ewing, who was riding a horse dressed in the lightning lancer outfit, was bucked off. The letter of commendation from Col. Riva the base Commander after our performance was very pleasing, stating that he had never witnessed such a precision flyby being so fast and low with so many aircraft.

When Col. Jenks returned from Tokyo a few days later he congratulated me upon my leadership with a letter stating such. So Col. Jenks rotated to the ZI and a new commander took over the 68th, a Col. Marvin Miller, when all this time I thought I would be the new CO. I should have been if I had gotten promoted to L/C but it wasn't to be. I was transferred to the 8th Fighter Bomber Wing as Wing Flying Safety Officer waiting my retirement orders I was fortunate that during this time I could still fly with the 68th as well as base flight.

After finishing my movie production of "Check Out" everybody wanted to see it. It was quite a hit and even Gen. Milton saw it, which was the boss of the 68th FIS. After he saw the picture he asked me if I could do a production of delivering the weapon (the atom bomb) using the F-100. I said that I would be delighted to do it. I would use one of the 8th FBW aircraft. I would alert Col. Daniels, the CO of the 8th FBW, of my project.

This movie was to brief "Rosie" O'Donnell CINC of PACAF in Hawaii. I had to be very thorough and do a good job. I got my film from the base photo lab but they did not have any way to process it. I would have to send it to Yokota AB to have it processed. That would take to long so since there was a deadline for Gen. Milton to get the film and get to Hawaii with it. So to save time I would shoot a roll of film and then take it to Fukuoka to a Japanese photo lab and wait for it to be processed in their automatic machine, which would only take minutes, even though the film was classified

My pilots with the Commander of Moody AFB

Top Secret! Of course the film was never out of my sight at anytime and the Japanese processor did not know what he was processing anyway.

My pilot of the F-100 was one of the members of our church, Lt. Morton. The pilot of the plane carrying the weapon was Col. "Skeets" Gallager of the 8th FBW. I started by going out on the line with my camera, which startled the Air Police since it was a restricted area but I had a base pass good for any place on the base, Top Secret or not. The movie showed personnel loading the weapon on the F-100, then Col Gallager getting into the cockpit of the F-100 cranking up, taxing out and blasting off in afterburner, while I was on his wing position and in the back seat of the F100C with my camera shooting the whole sequence.

We were joined up with Col. Gallager and flew over to the bombing range where Col. Gallager would make a "Labs" maneuver. This consisted of a 3 "G" pull up into an Immelman turn, which is a roll at the top of a loop, going in the opposite of the entry of the loop. Half way up the loop, predetermined by the auto pilot release equipment, the bomb is released. It then flies out to the target in the original direction of the aircraft. In the meantime the aircraft is headed back to the original point of departure. The bomb describes a high arc to the target, which gives the aircraft a time to escape before the bomb hits.

Well on the 3 "G" pull up I was trying to film the action the pull on the camera almost broke my nose trying to follow Col. Gallager. So we went back to the base to see how I was going to avoid this and still get the action I needed. The next day after briefing Col. Gallagher to do the LABS maneuver again with another practice bomb, we drove out to the bombing range in a jeep. I had a radio so I could contact the Col. when I was ready to shoot the LABS from the ground. I was using a telephoto lens on a good steady tripod so I would get a steady shot. I had him make two runs one without the bomb and one with it so I could edit the entire episode showing the path of the bomb after it left the aircraft.

After Col. Gallagher did his last run and I got the bomb in the air I got in a helicopter with the practice bomb and flew over the target. I had the crew chief drop the bomb out of the helicopter right in the middle of the target circle as we hovered over it with me hanging our of the door getting the shot. Lucky I was tied in since I was hanging out so far to get a good

The Disbrow family 1958, Panama city, FL
Major Bill L, Disbrow   Fay Disbrow   Sherry Disbrow
Gale Disbrow   Karren Disbrow   Pat Disbrow

shot. We were about 50 feet high so we could not miss.

Of course, Col. Daniels wanted to see the results. Since he was the commander of the 8th FBW he thought it was his duty to see that I was doing a good job. Actually it was none of his affair since I was making the picture for Gen. Milton. So I would go in and bring the shots each time I would have them processed so he could see them. I had just about finished the film and then he wanted me to animate the LABS maneuver. I had to stay up half the night at the photo lab using a model of an F-100 and a black background. I would move the model about 2 inches for each frame of film I took. When it was shown it would be an animated picture of the LABS maneuver.

Well I finally finished the film just in time and was smart enough to make a master print from the original. Col. Daniels wanted to see the finished product and I informed him that the film was due to go on the courier to Gen. Milton today. He would be flying to PACAF tomorrow to brief Gen. O'Donnell in Hawaii with the film. So I had to leave it with him with the assurance that it would be on the courier. I had the duty that day so I was depending on him to get it there on time since I was going to take it myself to the courier before I had to go on duty.

I later heard through the grapevine that when Col. Daniels went to show the film he hadn't threaded the projector right and tore up the film. He then called the film Lab at Yokota AB and told them that he needed a copy immediately. They had made a copy but it was to dark but the General had no other choice but to deliver it anyway. I never heard another word on the movie. I often wondered whether Gen. Milton knew the whole story or if I got the blame. I will never know until I see the General again at one of our 68th FIS reunions. I was a fool not to have made a copy for myself but it was a Top Secret film at the time.

Before I got my orders to ship home we had ordered a new VW Westphalia camper. It was one of the very first of these models on the market, which we were to pick up at Nagoya as it was shipped from the factory in Germany. Fay and I flew up to Nagoya on Nippon Air Lines and then drove the VW to Yokohama to be loaded on the boat for the ZI. We left the children with Yoko our live in maid, while we were gone.

On our way up to Yokohama we were side swiped by a Japanese truck that was trying to pass us at night on a hill when another vehicle met him and he had to cut us off to avoid a head on collision. I chased him and caught him in a tavern and the company would pay to have our vehicle fixed. Our new car got its indoctrination real fast.

Fay and I got a chance to sleep in the camper and try it out on the way up to Yokohama. It was real nice for what it was made for but it was underpowered with only 40 hp. Later on they made the engine more powerful, which helped out a lot. We got the VW on the boat and spent a few days in Tokyo before flying back to Itazuke on Nippon Air Lines. I now had to make arrangements to get the MGA home. I found a Sgt. to take it home for me. You could take only one car home with you at government expense. I picked up the MGA at Oakland, California, where he lived.

We would fly home on an old "Connie" a Constellation made by Lockheed. On the flight into Hawaii we hit some good turbulence as they were serving lunch. Everything went all over the children and Fay. The stewardess cleaned up everything quickly as we were approaching Hickham Field, Hawaii. We then flew into Travis AFB but were diverted to LAX since Travis was fog bound and we could not land. We could not get off the aircraft since this was not a port of entry for overseas personnel. We then were flown back to Travis after the fog lifted. We went back down to Los Angeles to Fay's folks to arrange what I was going to do and where we were going to live. I had to be back at Travis AFB by the end of January 1961 for my retirement so we stayed with Glad and Mont, Fay's folks, at 48th street and 9th Avenue until we could find a place of our own.

THE RETIREMENT YEARS

After picking up my MGA I drove over to Travis AFB to see my old friend Major Don Disbrow. I had looked up Don's name in the telephone book at Travis AFB I called him when the secretary answered the phone and I said that this is Major Disbrow and I would like to speak to Major Disbrow, of course this caused confusion right off the bat. I talked to Don and went to see him in his office and he introduced me to all the personnel and explained our relationship. We were the only Major Disbrows in the Air force at the time. Don had gotten married since I had seen him last in 1952 and now it was January 1961. We had a great reunion and went to his house to meet his wife Eleanor (Bee) Disbrow. She had been Don's Flight Nurse flying out of the Philippines at Clark Field. We had a nice dinner and talked over old times.

When I retired at Travis AFB they asked me if I wanted the troops to pass in revue. I told them I would not put them to all that trouble so I left for Los Angeles. I had retired on the 31 January 1961.

So now I was retired and a civilian but being a regular officer they could call me back to active duty any time they needed me. We were deciding where to live when Fay suggested the San Fernando Valley. So we started at Thousand Oaks then Encino, Van Nuys, Canoga Park. After about 6 months of looking we went to a Real Estate office in Woodland Hills. It seemed they had a foreclosure but it had only two bedrooms it was a large house on an acre lot. It also had a circular driveway to a two-car garage. So we went out to see it and it was ideal except for only two bedrooms. The children's bedroom was big enough to get the two bunk beds in as well as their dressers. I think the room was at least 12 feet by 14 feet. I figured we could get by until I could enlarge the home to two more bedrooms and another bathroom, which would give us 4 bedrooms and 2 and one half bathrooms.

In all the years in the USAF I did not accumulate much money. My total pay as a Major on flying status was only $1007 per month in 1961. My retirement pay was $255 per month! In the USAF we lived well but it was hard to save very much money with four children. We got the home for $24,000, which I considered a bargain. The yard was huge with 17 fruit trees, plus 5 walnut trees, a horse corral with a three stall barn with a tack room and a dog run.

We saved $4000 but now my pay was 51% of my Air Force base pay of $1007, which was not much. I was lucky that I qualified for unemployment insurance, since the Air Force severed me and I did not retired on my own. This gave me another $250 per month. Not too much but it helped out until I found a job. We bought the house and I decided to draw up the plans on how to enlarge it for the whole family. I cashed in all our resources including my flying insurance. I had paid it for 10 years while I was on active duty in addition to my GI insurance. I did not need it anymore since I was not test flying any more aircraft. I think we paid $10,000 down on the house. I also borrowed $3000 from Mother and gave her my lots in Big Bear for collateral.

I drew up the plans for the enlargement of the house and I had them approved by the Los Angeles building department. I was surprised how easy it was to get a permit. Now that I had my permit I was ready to start on the foundation and figure our how I was going to match the roofs from the new construction to the old. I did not want it to look like an add-on.

I started to layout the foundation with string and stakes just like I had seen the contractors do. I had never built a house before or an addition. So I went over to the housing project near me and watched what they were doing and asked a lot of questions. I got a lot of good information. I also had the Los Angeles building code and examples for construction and strength of different size lumber and the size necessary for the span distances. I have always been able to build about anything I set my mind to, so this was gong to be a new project and experience. After laying our foundation to be attached to the side of the house, which would house the two extra bedrooms and bathroom, I started digging. This was no easy job like I thought it would be. It was hardpan and I had to use a pick ax instead of a shovel to start with. The foundation had to be 24inches square at the bottom and six inches wide from there to the top. It was an inverted "T". It took me quite a while with the help of Fay. It was 16 feet on two sides and 45 feet long.

In the meantime I found out that they were wrecking an old U.S. Hospital in Van Nuys. They were selling used 2X4X10foot lumber for 25 cents each with lengths up to 16 feet for the same price! This was all seasoned grade lumber. There would be no shrinkage. You had to load it yourself and haul it away. I also bought 1X12X16 foot lumber, etc. for 25 cents each. What a bargain. By the way the lumber was full of nails. They did not take them out they just ripped the lumber from the walls, etc. Monty would spend hours taking out the nails and straightening them out for use on the project. I had bought an old Ford ¾ ton pickup truck with a 4-speed transmission in it. It was a vintage 1941 and would serve us very well by carrying many loads of lumber at a great price for our new addition. I had my Father-in-law Monty Cox to help me, which was great. Two people can do the three times the work of one person.

I knew we wanted a swimming pool, since we had such a large back yard. I learned we had one of the best swimming pool plasterers in the business in our Church. He also knew all the best people in the business for each job that had to be done to complete the pool. Backhoe digger to dig the hole and shape it, the steel worker to lay the steel in, gunite people, etc. These people would "moonlight" from their job and work for me on Saturdays. I would pay them in cash as soon as the job was finished. I was contracting my own pool. I saved a lot of money this way and got a beautiful 41 foot by 20 foot pool half price.

Actually I had two projects going at once. The people on Saturday building the pool and during the week I was building the addition to the house. Fay's Mother and Father came out help me pour the cement for the foundation. I had boxed it all in with cross braces at the top to keep the boards from spreading when the concrete was poured. I also put in the foundation bolts in all the right places. I ordered the concrete and a big mixer showed up. I explained how I wanted to pour it into the forms. Well it came out too fast and I was trying to guide it into the forms and keep them from overflowing and shouting at the driver to stop the flow. After starting and stopping and lots of maneuvering we got it all in and leveled.

On Saturday the bulldozer showed up to dig the hole for the pool. I had staked it out, but each time I did, the pool seemed to get bigger and bigger. Of course it had to fit around our big patio just right so I made it fit. It would be 8 feet deep with a regulation diving board. The pool came within 6 feet of the house where we had a sliding glass door to our bedroom. We could open our door and jump into the pool.

The most expensive part of the house project was the plastering of the inside and out. All the wood except the shingles was used. The plywood for the over flooring was new ½ inch and was laid on top of the sub flooring for a nice smooth floor. It was better built than the original house. I even insulated the walls and the ceiling. The hard part was in matching the roofs. I had to tear up the original roof over the children's bedroom lengthen the rafters to peak in the right place to match the center of the addition. The front of the house was a straight 4X12 gable roof, so it was easily extended along the same roofline over the front of the new addition. I finally finished the roofs and had no leaks.

I then had to shingle all the new roof addition. When I bought the shingles they gave me a guide that showed me step by step how to install them. I also asked the man from whom I bought the shingles how to do the job. He suggested I buy a shingle axe but I used a snap line to get my shingles exactly straight.

This would be in the summer of 1962 the house finally got finished. One of the church members did my plastering inside and outside. It was like a donation since he only charged me $700. He only did real expensive homes in Hidden Hills and Woodland Hills so I new he was doing me a big favor since we were on a very low budget to build the addition.

Well with the addition finished the girls would have much more room, especially Sherry and Gale who would share the new large bedroom and with Patty and Karen sharing the old room. It was now so big that they could put their bunk beds down and use them as singles.

I installed a forced air heater in the new addition while the old part of the house had a floor furnace. This was a big improvement. Also the new addition had a large bathroom between the two bedrooms. I installed a large square sunken bathtub with a shower plus a large tiled counter with double sinks. It was a nice bathroom.

The pool was finished with a Tiki Hut and lights all around the pool area that could be operated from inside our bedroom. The pool was beautiful and large. I also had to put a chain link safety fence around the pool.

Well with all the construction the "cash flow" was going the wrong way so I had to look for a job and go back to work. I still did not know what I wanted to do. One of the members of our Church, Floyd Weston, gave me a tip on a job with Retail Credit Company as an investigator. I went to the office in Van Nuys and had an interview with the manager. He hired me on the spot. I was supposed to be able to type 60 words a minute but managed to get along real good after a week of practice. This would be in December 1963 when I went to work for Retail Credit. My job was to investigate new insurance policy holders to make sure the policy was on the right person, not bad debt artists. It was mostly for big companies. It was a very interesting job. I would get so many cases each morning in a particular area of the San Fernando Valley I would them map out my route and take off in my MGA to do my work. I would have about 15 cases a day (ten to start). I would get a flat rate for each simple case and more for complicated cases. After I was there for a while I got into the routine and it was easy for me to do. I had one particular case that no one in the office was successful in completing. It got so that they would give me the hard cases since I was older than anybody in the office. I presented an air of authority and could induce people to talk and answer questions that were pertinent to the case.

I got this case where a woman was making excess charges to her Mobil Oil company credit card, $1500, and making no payments. This had been going on for a year. They tried to pick up her credit card but every time they went to her door another person would answer the door and say that she was not at home and they did not know when she would return. I "cased" the place and it was a very nice neighborhood. I went to the neighbors to verify that she still lived at the address I had. I then noticed a For Sale Sign in front of the house with the name of the real estate office on it that were handling the sale of the house. I went to the real estate office and told them that I was interested in looking at the house and asked for her name and telephone number. Also would she be home if I went up to see it in person. They immediately called the woman and she said that she was home and I could come right up and see it. I dashed back to the house and rang the bell. When she answered the door I asked her name, which was the right name, I asked her for her Mobil Credit card. I was from the Retail Credit Company showing her my credentials. She was trapped and gave me the card. She then asked me how I got her telephone number. I told her it was a trade secret. I got $20 for this case.

I was making about $400 per month and with my $225 per month retirement pay it was just enough to live on if we were frugal. I had a Cal Vet loan on the house at 3%, which made our payment low.

My friend, Major Jay Ossiander, bought a house about six blocks from us in Woodland Hills. He had been my Maintenance Officer in the 68th FIS at Itazuke, Japan. He left Itazuke before I did and retired. He then went to "Boot Strap" to get his Degree at the University of Omaha. "Boot Strap" was for former US Military people to get their degree after leaving the service. After getting his degree at Omaha to become a teacher he came to California. He went to USC to complete his teaching requirements. When I met him again he was student teaching at Manual Arts High School in Los Angeles. We were discussing my job one day at our house and he asked me why I did not go into teaching? He told me you only have to teach six hours a day, get all holidays off, and get three months vacation every year so you can be with your family. Also the pays is good and they need teachers badly in the Los Angeles School District. He was quite convincing! After giving it much thought I decided to go and see if I could teach first year Algebra. I was a little reluctant about handling all those kids.

THE SCHOOL TEACHING YEARS

So I took time off from present job and went down to the Los Angeles School District Office and applied. They asked me what I could teach. I said that I wanted to teach first year Algebra. I was then asked if I had a masters Degree in Mathematics. I replied that I did not. They then told me that I would have to go back to UCLA and get a Masters Degree in Mathematics. I told them to forget it. I then asked if they had an opening in Vocational Education. They asked me again what I could teach. I then told them that I could teach Aeronautics and Auto Mechanics. When I said that I could teach Auto Mechanics the lady said that they needed an Auto Mechanics teacher right away. She then sent me to see Mr. Addlesack in Vocational Education.

This would be in January 1964. After being interviewed on my qualifications and my military and civilian background I was given a date to meet the Board. When I met the board they seemed very impressed with my background both in the military and civilian life. I was hired immediately. I had heard that they liked former military men for teachers. They were used to discipline and would keep it in their classes.

Two weeks later I was standing in from of my first class. I was supposed to have gotten and assignment in the San Fernando Valley but there were no openings at the time. My friend Jay was student teaching at Manual Arts High School in Downtown Los Angeles. They needed a teacher right away so since my friend Jay was teaching there I would go there. I would at least have someone there that I knew.

What a revolting development 90% percent of the school were black! What had I done, Jay did not tell me that the school was mostly black. I decided to make the best of it until I could transfer. I wasn't prejudice but I thought I would get a better start in a white school.

The first three years were not too bad. In fact I enjoyed it seeing the students learn and retain what I taught them. Ten percent were real smart and paid attention and ten percent were troublemakers and did not last long in my class. The other 80% went which ever way the wind was blowing.

I was surprised at the pay I started at $750.00 per month. When I was interviewed and they added up all my automotive experience and my military experience I was given nine years of experience on the pay scale. Then every year of teaching would move you up on the scale. Then with each year I attended UCLA I would get another raise on the pay scale determined by how many units I successfully completed. This was great in three months I was making more money teaching than a Major on flying status with 21 years of service in the USAF! This would be in March 1964.

I forgot to mention that I had to take a proficiency test at UCLA before I would qualify to teach Auto Mechanics. It was after I had another interview and I would have a week to prepare for the test. I told them that I would take the tests right now, which surprise the interviewer. I took the test cold and made 85% on my score missing some questions on theory, which I should have known. They were surprised that I had made such a high-grade taking the test cold when passing was 70%.

I taught basic Auto Mechanics, which was no problem at all, since I had a loving father that taught me all about auto mechanics. I had worked in his garage when I was a boy. My Dad was an excellent teacher and I got hands on experience. My Father learned his trade as an apprentice and that is how I was treated learning the trade. He always told me that I did not have to be an auto mechanic but a trade can never be taken away from you. It did come in handy I have been working on cars my whole life it seemed so teaching it was a breeze.

When I went to high school I never took auto shop. I was afraid I might get into an argument with the teacher about proper procedures of repairs. I figured it would be a waste of time when I could be taking a class that I really needed. I had that much confidence in my knowledge of the automobile at that time.

Since I did not have a B.A. College Degree I had to go back to College and get it. I graduated from San Mateo Jr. College in San Mateo, California, in 1935 with an AA Degree in Mechanical Engineering. Now in 1964 almost 30 years later I am going back to school!

The first two summer vacations after I started teaching I had to go to UCLA to learn how to teach. This gave me advance College credits for my degree. After finishing my tour at UCLA I had to agree to get my B.A. in Vocation Education, which meant getting at least 6 units per semester in advance college subjects. This would eventually give me a lifetime teaching credential. I forgot to mention that vocational education is the only subject you may teach without a college degree to start. For each three units of advanced college work or subjects you successfully passed you would earn salary units. This was a good way to advance on the pay scale. I would be at the top of the pay scale in six years.

In the meantime we were attending Church and I was installed as 2nd counselor of the Sunday School Program. Fay was in the Young Women's MIA. We were very fortunate to have a large home with a pool and a large patio. This allowed us to have the Priesthood gatherings at our home with Lords blessings. We were the first Saints to occupy the new building. I was also given the appointment as Scoutmaster to the Guide Scouts. This was a challenging assignment since they were all young boys. I managed to keep them busy with their assignments and I made everything interesting to them. With the help of a few prayers and the help of the Lord I was successful.

All the girls were going to school; Sherry Ann was going to Taft High School. Gale was going to Woodland Hills middle school; Patty and Karen were going to grammar school.

I forgot to mention that before I went teaching school my friend, Floyd Weston and I were going into the importing business. This would be in February 1962. We became fast friends by attending church each Sunday. He was also a pilot and we had lots in common. Floyd thought that kites, babies' diapers, men's suits, and coffins would be a good deal if we could get them at a good price. So Floyd and I decided it would be a good idea for me to fly to Hong Kong and look up all my old contacts when I was in the USAF. Floyd gave me $400 so off I went to Travis AFB, California to hop a plane space available to Hong Kong.

On the 23 February 1962 I got a ride from Travis AFB to Hickham Field, Hawaii and then to Clark Field in the Philippines. I could not get a ride into Hong Kong, since they only had special services rides once in a while and they had no regular schedule. I hopped Cathey Pacific Air Line from Manila after bumming a ride on a USAF C-47 to Manila International Airport. I had to pay my own way to Hong Kong from Manila.

When I got to Kai Tek Airport in Kowloon I proceeded to look for a "Hotel Person" for the Golden Gate Hotel where I stayed when I was on active duty in the USAF. There are always a lot of these people at the airport "hawking" their hotels. I found the one from the Golden Gate Hotel and off I went. The hotel was in Kowloon. When I checked in the clerk and the bellboy recognized me from all the trips I made into Hong Kong before I retired. I had a great time talking about the old days and how the area was growing. After I was shown my room and got all my stuff arranged I went out for dinner to meet my friend Macway. Macway was the owner of the tailor shop who made my entire tailor-made suits, shirts, and my USAF dress uniforms. They could fit you in the morning before nine o'clock then a second fitting at noon and you could wear the suit to dinner at 6pm! They were fast and accurate. You seldom had to go back for any alterations. They kept records of your sizes on hand so you could order anything you wanted by mail. If you gained a little weight they had a special form so you could measure yourself for your new clothes. I even had monogrammed white shirts tailor made in 1961 for three dollars a piece. A Dacron brown suit made for $16, Italian silk wool tailored made for $35, which would have cost at least $150 in the states. So if I could have them made for $35 a piece to Los Angeles we could sell them for at least $70, which would be doubling your money after paying duty on them.

I got swatches for all the available cloths for the suits and the forms for getting the correct measurements. I was assured if I sent the order by Air Mail I would have the finished suit in a week or ten days. The only catch was that I had to pick up the suit in person at the Customs at LAX and pay the duty on the package. After getting the suit question settled I went looking for a factory that makes diapers with the Velcro attachments. This would eliminate pins. After getting several leads I came to the conclusion that we would have to import them by the thousands in order to even compete with the plain diapers in the US. It would have been a first if I could have gotten them at a reasonable price since they had to be made of good absorbent cotton it was very expensive for the cotton cloth. Too bad I did not think of paper! We would have made it big since this was to come out much later in the US. We would have been the first with paper diapers! So the diaper deal fell through. I even had a sample with me that was cut to conform to the infants shape so it would fit well. With Velcro on it, it was a quick change job.

I then went looking for cheap kites. No one was in the market to make a few sample kites. Everything had to be made in lots of thousands and we were not prepared to handle this much merchandise at once. What I should have done was to contact stores at home before I left to have an outlet ahead of time for all the merchandise. At this time the money situation was a little tight and I did not have enough to buy a lot of anything.

I then went looking for coffins. I found them and got a free-guided tour of the largest mortuary in Hong Kong. It was quite an experience. They did everything in this 3-story building at the east end of Hong Kong. From manufacturing coffins to cremation and preparing the funeral. They had all grades of coffins from the very elaborate to just a plain hollowed out log with a top on it. I got all the prices and stated that I would contact them if we made a deal when I got home. After being there about a week I figured I had enough information. I called the aircraft military operations to see if there were any military flights going back to the Philippines or Japan. I could catch a flight to the U.S. if there was space available. Happily they had a C-124 going out the next morning to Clark AFB and they had room for me.

The next day I got on the C-124 and was on my way to Clark AFB in the Philippines. I had all the information and the samples I had accumulated with me. I stayed at the Clark AFB BOQ at $2.00 a day; which being a field grade officer gave me really nice quarters at a real deal. Being retired I had the same privileges as active duty personnel had. I visited the Officers Club and met a lot of old aquaintenances or friends of people I knew. I had great steak dinners at the "Rathskellar" restaurant in the basement of the "O" club. I used to stop there every time I went to Clark Field when I was on active duty. They had the best steak dinners in the Far East.

On 6 March 1962 I finally got a ride on a C-54 to Midway Island. We RONed there for a day or two and I got to see the "Gooney Birds" or Albatross trying to land after being airborne for days. We had hysterics watching them "wipe out" on their landing as they tried to touch down. They would knock themselves out as they would wrap up in a ball after going head over heals. They did not realize that they had to come in running. After being over the ocean for weeks at a time and gliding all the time they did not make very many landings and were not "current" on their procedures of getting back on the ground again. Another great laugh was watching them try to take off. They would run along flapping their wings trying to get enough airspeed to take off. Some would not make it and would have to make another try at it. This bird was not at home at all on the ground. After leaving Midway we made another stop at Hawaii at Hickam Field to refuel and RON. We then left for Travis AFB, California. After landing there I found out there was nothing going to the Los Angeles area I then had to take a commercial flight to LAX.

After getting home Floyd Weston came over to the house in Woodland Hills and I gave him a good briefing on what was available. We decided I should go back to Hong Kong. Fay would go with me this time. I had my Mother and her husband Henry come down from Los Gatos, California, to mind the children. Fay and I proceeded to "hitch" a ride to Hong Kong. This would be 1 July 1962 by the date in our passports. Fay and I went to Travis AFB to catch our space "A" flight. We thought we were going to have to wait along time but an old Air Force buddy, Bill Lawton, got us on a flight that just had a cancellation and we lucked out. We flew into Hawaii to Hickam AFB and stayed on the airplane. We then flew into Guam and got "bumped off". Someone with a higher priority and got our seats. We had to stay there a couple of days waiting for a new flight in the meantime I had a tooth looked after at the Navy Dental Clinic that was bothering me. I later had to have it pulled at Clark AFB when we got there. Fay talked nice to the space available clerk and got us a seat on a Boeing 707 into Clark AFB in the Philippines. By the way in those days a retiree could wear his uniform when going space "A". This gave you a little better prestige that you wouldn't have if you were in civilian clothes. This ride was on a US charter flight. Being in uniform they let me go up to the pilot's cockpit and watch what was going on. Of course they were on "George" the autopilot.

When we arrived at Clark AFB we got a ride to Manila but had to pay our way again to Hong Kong. We booked on Cathay Pacific for 64 dollars a piece in a Lockheed Electra. We got into Kowloon's Kai Tek Airport and I looked for the representative for the Golden Gate Hotel. I found him and he took us to the Hotel. We had a nice room since we had been there so many times before they took good care of us.

While we were there we made a few deals for suits to be delivered when we would send the measurements back to them. We got all the form's to fill

Flying formatioin in the F-86D over Kyushu Japan with the 68th FIS May 1960. I am leading and took the picture

out to do this. We had a nice time touring all the old spots that we had been to before we had left the Service. We did a little shopping for ourselves and then prepared to start home. When we were ready to leave we got a ride to Okinawa on a C-54 and it was at night. On the way we lost an engine about 100 miles from Okinawa where we were landing. I said to Fay don't look now but we just lost an engine. I said that no sweat we have three more and we landed at Kadena without further incident. After a couple of days of waiting we finally got a ride to Tachikawa AB, Japan, back to our old base where I was stationed from 1948 to 1951. We waited a few days and got a ride into Hickham AFB, Hawaii. This was on the 20 July 1962. We got bumped off and had to wait a couple of more days before we got a ride into Travis AFB, California. We stayed in the guest quarters while we were waiting and used the club facilities, it was very nice.

We finally got back to Woodland Hills and let my Mother and Henry relax a few days after having to mind the children while we were gone.

I forgot to mention that Jay Ossiander move near us in 1963. He was my Maintenance Officer when we were attached to the 68th FIS at Itazuke, Japan. It was nice to have an old friend close to me and we were able to have them over to our house to out door barbecues and visits. We even bought a beach house together in Ensenada, Baja, Mexico. The house was right on the beach south of Ensenada just north of Estero Beach. It was only $4000 for this two-bedroom concrete blockhouse. It had only two bedrooms and only one bathroom but had a nice living room and dining area. It had sliding glass doors facing the beach, which gave you a great view of the sunsets. It also had a big fireplace. It had a big patio outside our big sliding glass doors. We paid $30 per month for the land lease. After we bought the place we proceeded to fix it up. It was quite a nice summer home. We left the two wives down there for a week to paint, etc. Fortunately we would take turns going down since it was not big enough for two families at once. Jay and Suzanne had 3 children two boys and a girl and we had four girls. It worked our real well until we moved from Woodland Hills to Huntington Beach to our new home. When we first came to Woodland Hills it was nice and clear weather but after three years the smog was creeping up the San Fernando Valley and was just over the hill from our place when we left and we were at the far west end of the valley. It was with mixed emotions that I left Woodland hills.

Now back to my job as a teacher at manual Arts High School. Teaching Auto Mechanics was a breeze for me, since I knew my subject quite well. I had impressed the interview board when I showed them pictures of the sports car I built when I came back from Korea. It included all the publicity write-ups and magazine items plus all the rest of the cars that I had built over a period of years.

For the first three years I enjoyed it very much but it seemed that they liked to dump all the bums into auto shop. I found out the easiest way to control these people were to keep them busy, which I did. I had a regular schedule that everyone adhered to. I had lots of "mock ups" in the class. This included brakes, transmissions, rear ends, steering gears, etc., all of which could be taken apart and put back together again for hands on experience. Included in my shop was a lift with a complete Chevrolet chassis on it.

When a new class came in I would give them the routine. Work Monday, Tuesday, and Wednesday, review on Thursday and a test every Friday. The test would be graded after the time was up and everyone knew his or her mark for the day. I would pass the papers out to be corrected by other students so they would not be correcting their own paper. They liked knowing their grade immediately. They were told that the written test would count for one third of their grade. Their work projects would count one third and their notebook would count for one third. Their notebook consisted of pass outs that I supplied on all the parts of the engine and parts of the automobile. This would include the transmission, rear end, engine, brakes, etc. Each pass out had instructions on it to color code each different part. This notebook was very informative if it was done right. In fact I told the students to guard their notebook with their life or it would be stolen if they did not. Then the ones who lost their notebook would get new pass outs and had to do them at home to catch up. I usually supplied the colored pencils for them to work with. Of course each student had time in the classroom to work on his book since I did not have enough projects and facilities to keep them all busy at once. I had enough projects but not enough tools and supplies to keep everyone doing the same thing so my system worked quite well.

Another way I kept everyone busy and gave everyone an interest in the class was that I would take a smart student and have him teach the slower student. I would then quiz the slower student if he was ready for his oral and practical test. I would give the "instructor" a grade on how well his "student" did as well as the student. This worked very well, since everyone wanted to be an "instructor" it made them try harder. This system was practically fool proof and inspired the students. Everyone learned in spite of themselves. My pass outs were so great that a student who graduated and went to Trade Tech had his notebook stolen while there. He came back to me for more pass outs so he could have all the information he needed again. When I retired from Manual the new Auto Shop teachers wanted the master sheets for all my pass outs. It made me feel real good!

The first year of teaching at Manual I had to go to UCLA Summer

School to learn how to teach, etc. I had to attend two summers of this. The greatest thing I learned there was how to make these pass outs I used in my class.

I had mixed emotions about moving from Woodland Hills after putting all the work in the place but we were going to need a bigger home since the children were getting older and needed their own room. We only owed $13,000 on the home with a house payment of only $80 per month with a 3% Cal Vet Loan! The house was now worth $58,000 after paying only $24,000 for it. I guess I put about $10,000 in it in improvements that was a good investment. We wanted to refinance the mortgage to get money out of the place and have a low down payment for any new owner that bought the place since the Cal Vet loan was not transferable. That was a mistake! We got $20,000 but had to make the big payments until we sold the house. We thought we had it sold immediately and used our $20,000 to buy two rental properties that was another mistake! They were in Van Nuys and we were moving to Huntington Beach 60 miles away by freeway. Any other investment would have been better. We finally bought a nice home in Huntington Beach after supposing that we had our Woodland Hills home sold. It turned out that the people backed out of the deal at the very last minute and left us with two homes and two rentals. We finally had to come down on our price in order to sell it; in a hurry. We finally sold it for $52,000 taking a loss of $6000 plus all anxiety in the delay in closing the deal on the house.

The Real Estate dealer we had to rent, our rentals, had rented one of them without a thorough background check of the people. Fay and I had worked so hard to clean up and paint the interior of the houses. One renter was a single mother with 6 children and on welfare. Not only that but she was a "Bar fly" and left the children home alone. Her oldest was about 14 years old, I think, and the youngest was 3 years old. They moved in and I did not pay any rent at all for three months. We went to the Welfare Department to have them hold the rent from her welfare check but they could not do that and they were not responsible for her to pay her rent. She could do anything she wanted with the welfare check. We could not even evict her! The way we finally got her out was I took the front door off the house while she was gone. I hated to do this! I should have called

The Disbrow family having Sukiyaki at a Japanese restaurant
Our second tour in Japan 1959

authorities for child neglect but I did not know if they had such a law at that time. They finally left and of course the house was a shambles. We had to clean the place again and repair all the damage to the interior so we could try to sell it.

The other house was not much better. The people moved in and stayed only three months and moved our leaving us to pay the mortgages on both houses with no income coming from them. They moved out without any notice. We now had put the properties up for sale through a real estate dealer to see if he could sell them since we now lived in Huntington Beach on Avalon lane near Springdale and Warner Avenues. This made it very inconvenient to have the houses so far away in Van Nuys.

We had advertised the houses and finally found a fellow who lived in Van Nuys who had a boat to trade for our equity. The boat was a 65 foot overall ocean going yawl. It was 48 feet on deck and had 1400 square feet of sail. We had to pay extra money in the deal but it was better than those two houses and the boat was at Wilmington that was much closer to us. With

The 68th Fighter Interceptor Squadron
Itazuke AB, Japan 9 Mar 1959

the payment on the boat slip in Wilmington it came out to about the same amount of money as before but we had a boat much close that the whole family could enjoy. I wanted an airplane but had to settle for a boat.

The fellow we traded the boat for, checked me out on the operation of how to get in and out of the slip. This was real touchy since the boat was so big and the slips were so close together and the channel was so narrow. The boat was so big that it did not respond immediately. You had to anticipate every movement everything happened in slow motion. It weighed 25 ton!

Our first trip was to be to Catalina Island for a three day Holiday, which I think, was Labor Day. The family doubted my ability to find Catalina in the haze. I told them it a 14-year-old boy can sail his 26-foot sailboat around the world I can certainly hit Catalina Island. It was very easy navigating a boat since it was the same as navigating in an aircraft, which was dead reckoning.

When we got outside of the Wilmington Harbor I had all my girls put up the sails, which was 1400 square feet of sails! They got all but the main sail up, which had one inch hawsers attached to the sail and the mast was

40 feet tall. It was gaffed rigged so you not only had to lift the sail but the gaff rig boom. The mast was 12 inches in diameter at its base. I let Fay man the helm while I helped the girls get the main sail up and we were away. The only thing I was told about sailing a sailboat was not to jibe it. Don't turn down wind unless you shorten the sails. I was surprised how fast the boat would go in a moderate wind. It would go over 10 knots in a ten-knot wind. When we were about a half-mile from Catalina I helped the girls take down the main sail. My all girl crew consisted of Sherry, Gale, Patty, and Karen and their Mother Fay. They were taking down the rest of the sails as I started our Gray marine engine so we could motor into the harbor at Catalina with good control. The Harbor Master came out to greet us at the entrance to the harbor and directed us to our place of mooring. It was quite a thrill sailing this big monster down the row of parked boats. As we motored to our mooring spot I told the girls to catch hold of the bamboo pole that had our mooring hook on it to tie up. On our first pass they missed the pole as I threw the engine in reverse to stop the boat but it was not stopping. The fellow next to us yelled, "Go around", so we went around and tried it again. As I turned to go down between all the rows of boats again it was a little nerve wracking with this huge boat knowing how hard it was to stop. On the second pass Sherry caught the bamboo pole and we were moored in no time at all. There was a big sigh of relief. We had a wonderful time. The boat slept 10 people, had a galley, bathroom, ship to shore radio, a fathometer, and a radio compass. It had a 12 and one-half foot beam and had six feet of headroom and was very comfortable. It had a 36-inch tiller wheel; 100 gallons of water tank; 100 gallon fuel tank and we could motor for 10 hours at 7 knots on the engine.

We stayed at Catalina for three days. The girls had fun diving off the boat. We had a 16-foot dingy with a 10 HP outboard motor on it. This way we could get back and forth from shore. Instead, the girls were swimming back and forth from shore. We had a few small dingys coming by to see the girls. We were also invited aboard other peoples large boats parked next to us. It was fun since our boat was almost the largest boat in the harbor. It was also the oldest it was built in Rhode Island in 1915 by Hershoff, a well-known boat builder of that time. The name of the boat was the "Seminole"; it was a beautiful Yawl, especially under full sail. We made many trips to Catalina and also to Ensenada, Baja, Mexico. We had a beach house at Mona Lisa Beach, which was south of Ensenada about 10 miles near Estero Beach. We sailed down to our beach house with my friend Bob Elton who was a member of the Church. He was a good sailor and loved to sail our big boat. He had a 21-foot sailboat. We dropped him off at Ensenada harbor and then we proceeded to sail down to our beach house.

It was like sailing to the South Seas. We anchored off the shore of the beach house and got in our dingy and shot the breakers up to the beach right in front of the house. It was a blast and we stayed a week. It was something to see upon looking out our large glass sliding doors and see this large sailboat laying at anchor right off our beach and our dingy laying up on the beach.

We got a surprise when we started for home. I got the dingy in the water and pushed it our over the breakers with the family in it. I then got in and cranked up the engine and away we went. We drove right up to the boat and unloaded everyone and then I had to go back for all our gear. I got all the gear loaded and got in but the engine would not start right up and the breakers caught me sideways and over I went. I managed to right the dingy but the engine by now was soaked and would not start. I had to row out, which was a little longer than the motor would have taken. We finally got off and headed for home. Our adventures were not over yet. We didn't have much wind starting for home so I had to start our engine. I was not planning to motor all the way to San Diego where we could refuel. We didn't quite make it and ran out of gas about 10 miles from San Diego and it was night by now. I called the Coast Guard and they brought out some fuel for us and I had to pay a dollar a gallon! Gas in those days was thirty cents a gallon in 1964 but we were glad to get it.

After we got gas the charts and the lights that supposedly showed the direction to San Diego harbor confused me. It was about midnight by this time and it was dark as pitch. Luckily I slowed down and we were just creeping along trying to find the channel to San Diego and I did not realize that it was now low tide. All of a sudden we hit a reef that projected during the low tide. I immediately threw the engine in reverse and gave it full throttle and we backed off the reef. I went forward to survey any damage if any but there were no leaks. My Daughter Gale in the meantime was calling the Coast Guard again telling them what had happened. By this time the Coast Guard was back again and I was told to follow them into the harbor.

The next day there were some boys swimming around the docks and I asked them if they could dive under the boat and check for the damage I might have from hitting that reef. They were like a bunch of Otters. They immediately dove under the boat and when they surfaced I got the sad news. The blow had bent the lead keel sideways and it was loose. This meant a lot of drag for the rest of the trip home. We stayed a couple of days and finally started for home. We had to motor most of the way since there was very little wind at all. Upon arriving at home we were all bushed it had been quite a trip. There was never a dull moment in our family.

We would sail this boat many times to Catalina to both popular areas after having it repaired to the tune of $1500. Bob Elton would get charters to sail people over to Catalina for the day including the Boy Scouts. We would have them bring a nice lunch along for themselves and they could eat right on the boat. The people we chartered enjoyed it very much. One day Bob Elton signed us up for a race during the Newport Beach annual regatta from Newport to Dana Point and back. When we go there it seemed there were hundreds of boats milling around in the harbor waiting for the race to start. We were about the biggest boat in the race. Bob was at the helm and was trying to get a good position to make a good start but there were too many little boats in his way and we were nine minutes late on the start we were 19th at the start of the race in our class but ended up in 6th place. We passed a lot of boats since Bob had rigged up a spinnaker sail for us, which gave us a little more speed. After the race was over we headed back home to Wilmington. By this time the wind started to pick up and most of the boats headed for the shoreline. We took the direct route to Wilmington and we were quite a ways from shore when it started to get rough. We must have been a couple of miles from the shoreline at the time when we were about half way home and it really got rough and the wind was really blowing. The old "Seminole" started to dive under the large swells, which must have been twenty feet high. The waves were coming clean over the deck. By this time we had our "foul weather" gear on. We had another person from the Church to help as a crewmember. I was at the helm when I noticed that every time the boat would plunge into a large swell the anchor was coming off the deck and bouncing back down again, it wasn't lashed down! I gave the helm to Bob and I proceeded out along the deck to the anchor. This was a very precarious walk hanging on to the stainless steel railing, which was around the perimeter of the deck. It was a good thing that it was there or I wouldn't have made it. I had a life vest over my oilskins and slowly moved out to the anchor. I was swamped many times on the way out and hanging on for dear life. As I was tying the anchor down to the deck we hit a big swell that submerged the bow completely and I was suddenly under the ocean. As we came up it plunged again as I was tying the anchor down. It wasn't completely tight and my hand was underneath the anchor and I didn't even feel it my hands were so cold by this time. I finally got the anchor lashed down after seemingly taking in about a gallon of seawater. I finally got back to the cockpit and I was about drowned. By this time the wind was howling a gale. It was lucky we were in a sail boat which is much more stable in a storm than a power boat. Just as we started to head in toward shore there was a large gust of wind that blew out our mainsail at the bottom near the boom. My "Buddy" Bob Elton and my master sailor climbed up on the boom and shortened the sail. Without the mainsail we would have been in real trouble, since it stabilized the boat. It was so rough I was holding my breath while he worked. It was a dangerous job with the wind blowing so hard. After he got the sail shortened we sailed along without further incident. We finally sailed into Wilmington and docked the old boat after a harrowing time.

About a month later Bob wanted to sail in the "Transpac Race" I couldn't believe it. This was a race from the West Coast to Hawaii! The sails on the old "Seminole" were so old that we would never make it. When I took the main sail to be fixed the owner of the place wanted to know the name of the boat that the sail was on. When I told him that it was the "Seminole" he could not believe it. He had made the sails for this boat 15 years ago! It had lasted all that time. A new sail was unaffordable at that time so I had him patch up the old sail.

Bob and I ran more charters around the area and to Catalina. Bob was a "hustler" and would get the charters for us. We would split the profit. It was too costly to maintain this boat because it was so large. I finally traded it for a Stinson aircraft thanks to a fellow who wanted to restore the boat and had the airplane to trade. That was a great day when we got rid of the "Seminole" although we had a lot of fun and experiences while we had the old sailboat. They say that there is two great times when you own a boat when you buy it and when you sell it.

I made the trade for the Stinson somewhere around the end of February 1968. I then traded the Stinson for a Cessna 195 on the 6 March 1968. The Cessna 195 had a 275HP Jacobs engine on it. It was a good buy I traded the Stinson and $2000 for the Cessna 195. The day I was supposed to close the deal at Fox Field, Lancaster, California, we were going to go to Mexico in our new aircraft. We had loaded all our gear in the Stinson with Fay, Patty, and Karen and flew up to Fox Field. I had already consummated the deal so all I had to do was to preflight the 195 which I had never flown before. The fellow I was buying it from would only give me a ride. He would not let me land the airplane. He was not even going to ride with me as I checked myself out on my first landing. I told everybody to get aboard but Fay balked stating that I had to shoot at least one landing before anybody was getting in with me. I asked if anybody wanted to go with me as I shot a few landings. Karen said that she would go with her Dad. As we took off the fellow who sold me the aircraft told Fay, "Watch him bounce it" with that I made three perfect landings "greasing each one in three point". The fellow was startled since this was my first time I had ever flown this type of aircraft. It was notorious for creating bad landings. Fay then told him of my background and my experiences as a pilot, which amazed him. My luck wasn't to hold out. After getting everyone aboard with all our gear we headed for Mexicali, Mexico, upon reaching the airport and calling in for landing instructions we found there was quite a bit of traffic trying to land. I got in line and was trying to land as quickly as possible and I got to anxious on the landing. I did not let it stall in the three-point attitude and I bounced it. I immediately "pegged it" on the runway. That was the first and last time I bounced it again to any degree, I had learned my lesson.

We got to Guaymas, Mexico and it was a gravel runway. In those days there were not many paved runways around the West Coast of Mexico. We got a Cab to take us to the beach. We stayed 3 or 4 days I think and had a very nice time. We ate tacos on the beach that were cooked on an old piece of tin. They were delicious. The children went swimming and hunted for seashells. We watched the beautiful sunsets, as the weather was excellent we hated to leave. We flew back to Mexicali to alert Customs at Calexico we were coming so they would be there when we landed. You have to alert Customs so you don't have to wait or have to pay for overtime it you get there after hours.

When we stopped at Calexico we got a courtesy car from the airport, which was a Volkswagen Van. We all jumped in and drove back across the border to do a little shopping and to have lunch. After having lunch and got all our shopping done we drove back to Calexico Airport and hopped in the C-195 and headed for home. We kept the C-195 at Meadowlark airport in Huntington Beach. It was very convenient I could walk home if I had to since it was only about a mile from our house.

We belonged to the Huntington Beach Ward of the LDS Church when we first came to our new home on Avalon Lane, Huntington Beach. The Ward was located in the Community Center in downtown Huntington Beach. The Priesthood met in a metal building some distance away near an old oil derrick. Our facilities were indeed primitive after coming from a new Ward Building in Woodland Hills. As the Ward grew a new building was to be constructed for the members. In those days everyone helped in anyway they could to build the Ward Buildings and to reap the blessings for helping to share the load. This is where I met Bob Elton an Elder in the Church. He seemed to be a "go getter" and we would become very good friends. I would eventually teach him how to fly. He was a sheet metal man by trade and he was an excellent welder on any type of welding. Bob was also an avid sailor that is how we got together when I got the big boat. He taught me the fine points of sailing the "Seminole" which I mentioned before.

We both worked on the new Ward house, I was putting in the insulation in the roof with a staple gun and Bob was making all the gutters and downspouts for the roof. We finally finished the beautiful Ward house in the late 1960s.

Bob Elton and I were home teachers together, which made it nice. He was a good young friend and a returned missionary from Mexico. He helped me learn the Gospel and did any welding I had to have done. I told him I would teach him how to fly if he paid for the rental of the aircraft, which was a C-150. Since he always wanted to learn to fly this made him very happy and let him fly it once we were airborne.

I also became acquainted with another member of the Church Dr. Merlin Smith. He was a new pilot and owned a Comanche 260. It seemed that Dr. Smith heard that I was a pilot instructor and wanted me to get him his private pilots license with my instruction (I had gone to Long Beach Airport and got my CFI Instructors rating when I moved to Huntington Beach). When I was in the Air Force there was no place for me to get this rating. Everywhere I was stationed there was no FAA installation to give me my check ride so I used my G.I. Bill and got it at Long Beach Airport when I retired.

It seems that Doc Smith could not get an instructor to ride with him. Another member of the Church, Harry Jordan an ex USAF pilot, was Docs insurance broker who insured Doc's airplane. He took me aside one day and told me the history behind Doc Smiths flying. He had bought the Comanche 260 and then had to learn to fly. The Doc was flying with an instructor one day shooting landings at Orange County Airport when on a go around making touch and go landings he inadvertently picked up the gear instead of the flaps before he had flying speed and bellied the aircraft in. Harry told me to watch him if I was going to fly with him, I did "like a Hawk". After flying with him night and day he finally got his private pilots license. When I rode with him after he got his license he made a low turn to final approach from the base leg. I told him that was a good way to kill himself if he continued to do this. Doc Smith had his thrills. I was checking him out on his cross-country check from Orange County to Las Vegas then to Salt Lake City and back. We climbed to the altitude, which was 9000 feet and he proceeded to level off and trim up the aircraft and then to lean out the mixture to the engine. This was good operating procedure. As we were approaching McCarran Airport at Las Vegas he started his let down to the airport. As we were letting down I was watching him very closely. At about 7000 feet the engine quit! The Doc was in a sheer panic! He went around the cockpit switching the "mag" switches, changing fuel tanks, etc. He looked at me and said, "What am I going to do?" I was sitting there not paying a bit of attention to him all this time. Acting like nothing was happening. It is very quiet when the engine stops, which can cause a panic if you, don't know what to do. I looked over to him and said, "Push in the mixture control to full rich like you are supposed to do on a let down for landing. It is a checklist procedure". When he pushed in the mixture control the engine started right up. With that Doc said that I had just saved his life! He had no idea what was wrong. He never made that mistake again.

Doc finally sold his Comanche and got a Cessna 320, which was a twin-engine aircraft. It was a four place aircraft with all the latest electronics of the day installed on the instrument panel. It was also turbo-charged. Before he sold the Comanche 260 he wanted me to teach his nephew to fly, which I did and his nephew was a much better pilot than his uncle.

I had flown the Doc and Bob Elton up to Laytonville, California in my Cessna 195. The Doc was interested in buying some property in this area. After looking at the property we got into the C-195 and took off. It was a little short field that was private. He was surprised how easy I got off the ground and how fast the C-195 was.

Doc finally bought a place near Shannon Ranch a little dirt strip in Mendocino County. One day he asked me if I would like to fly up to see his new spread. Bob Elton went so he could make an estimate on fixing up the old homestead. When we were making our approach to Shannon Ranch strip the Doc asked me if he was a little short and I said to give just a little power to bring us up to the runway. With that he blasted the throttles and of course we were too fast. When he touched down he had to jump on the brakes and we slid to a stop on this short sod runway.

We looked the place over and Bob made his estimates. We then went back to the airstrip and took off for a little airport south of Shannon Ranch to refuel. We had to wait for fuel and by the time we were ready for take off it was getting dark. It would be dark as we approached the San Francisco area. We had been flying along in the black of night but the visibility was fantastic. You could see all the lights of all the towns along the way down the Salinas Valley. The Doc had all his new radio equipment going with his DME (distance measuring equipment). I asked him if he knew where we were. He had an IFR chart on his lap, which showed only the radio stations on it. No map of the area. He told me we were 60 miles from Priest Radio. It was real dark now and the towns were very prominent with all their lights on. Also all the airports had their beacons on, which you could see for miles. I asked the Doc if he knew what town was off to our right, which was Salinas, California. He didn't know, all he was doing was following the DME and the VOR. I asked him what if he lost all his electrical power. He said that he would call "Mayday"! He forgot that the radio equipment does not work if you lose your electrical system. That was a good lesson in pilotage. Use a sectional chart and know where you are at all times whether you are using all the navigation equipment in the world. It can fail and you want to know your position at all times. The Doc got so bad in his flying I heard that nobody would fly with him anymore not even his wife. I then heard that he moved to Ukiah, California, sold his airplane and took up playing golf.

One day as we were going to Church I noticed a sports car sitting among some trees in Woodland Hills. It was up on a hill next to a little duplex. I would go by this car every Sunday as we were going to Church. After viewing this car for about a year and watching it deteriorating I decided to stop and find out who owned it. I thought the car was an Austin Healy from a distance but when I got close to it I was surprised to see that it was a rare "Siata" an Italian racing sports car. I found out that a young man owned it and he worked during the day and went school at night. He did have a day off when I could contact him. The time to catch him was on Thursday evening. I finally contacted him and we made a deal to inspect the "Siata". It had a bad transmission and had a bad engine. We made a deal, I would trade him my MGA that was running good straight across for the "Siata". It seems some one stole the bucket seats out of the "Siata". I took the seats out of the MGA since he was responsible for the seats in the Siata. It took me about six months to get the Siata running. It sure was a pleasure to drive. I took the Siata to the paint shop and had it painted "Ferrari Red". It was beautiful and it sure attracted a lot of attention. Fay and I drove it to Hollywood to see the first showing of the racing movie "Grand Prix" featuring James Gardner. The car attracted quite a bit of attention while there. It was one of only 10 originals in the world.

The Society Italian Automobile Racing Touring Association, "Siata" in Italy, built it. The engine was a 2-liter V8, which was built by Fiat (120cu. in.). The engine was all aluminum wet sleeve block. It also was a 70-degree V8! Who ever heard of a 70-degree V8? The crankshaft had 8 throws on it! One for each connecting rod instead of 2 rods on each throw like a 90 degree V8 built in the US. To me it was a really weird engine; I had never seen one like it before. It also had a single distributor with two sets of points in it with a dual rotor with two individual coils, which were Magnetties. It ran like two independent 4 cylinder engines since it had a 180 degree crankshaft. I had never seen anything like it in my life and I was going to completely overhaul the engine without any service manual for the engine! I finally found a few people that knew something about the car and the engine. Alan Johnson was one who was a collector of engines, cars and etc. He was a gold mine of information. This was in 1964. I even bought a spare engine from him. Alan had this same engine in 1990! He had moved from Gardena, California to Fort Worth, Texas, where I visited him with one of my 68th FIS friends, Jim McDonald who lives in Fort Worth. One of my other contacts for the Siata information and parts was Salvatore Dinitallis in Van Nuys, California. He was a Ferrari expert and specialized in Italian cars. He was on the Ferrari Team as a mechanic at that time. I got some parts and a lot of information from him. He gave me an address of a company in Italy that built parts for the engine and car at one time. I wrote to them and received a letter back that they no longer made any parts for the engine and had no more parts in stock. I finally got a copy of a partial parts catalog and service manual, which helped out a lot. After I got the engine together I set everything with a dial indicator with a degree wheel on the crankshaft so everything would be right on the nose.

I drove the car back and forth to school. I was teaching at Manual Arts High School at the time. The car was in the school paper as the car of the month. I had used mostly used parts to rebuild the engine since new ones were not available. One day I burned a piston and had to find a used one to put in its place. I found one from one of my sources of parts. It was a chore to put it in since you had to remove the engine to get the pan off. Once you got the engine out it was much better to work on. I got it running again and continued to drive it to school. The car looked like a small Ford "Cobra" that was built by Carol Shelby so every time I came along side a Chevrolet "Corvette" he would want to race. I could beat him in first and second gear but when he hit third he had too much torque for me but I would always catch him in traffic. One day coming home from school on the Harbor Freeway an Aston Martin passed me and I caught up and passed him as he got stuck in traffic. We continued to blast down the Freeway and I was ahead of him as we went under the San Diego Freeway we must have been doing at least 70mph. As we came out of the underpass all the traffic was stopped. I immediately braked hard and stopped with no trouble so did the Aston Martin. We both had tremendous stopping power. My car only weighted 1500 pounds and had 12-inch brake drums and the Aston Martin had very large brakes, too. Well we had picked up a lot of racers and they could not stop and were up on the grass and all over. The fellow finally came along side of me and asked me, "What kind of a car is that?" "I replied a Siata". With that he was amazed he had never seen one before but had heard of them. He then said that it really goes. I said for a 2 liter it is a "Killer".

Vacation time was coming on and we were going on a vacation with the children. We had a little dog named Toro who was a "tiger". He liked to bite strangers if they invaded his territory. We left him with a boyfriend of Patty's in Seal Beach. After our vacation we came home and Patty wanted to get Toro. She wanted to drive the Siata so I let her take it against my better judgment. After getting the dog she was on her way home turning a corner when the dog saw a cat! He was death on cats! He jumped onto Patty's lap in the middle of the turn and pushed the throttle wide open. Being in second gear the Siata leaped across the street and hit a parked pickup truck. The Siata was mostly made out of aluminum, which included the body, transmission, rear end, suspension, brakes, wheels, etc. The frame was the only steel part in the car that is why it was so light. The blow of hitting the truck knocked the left front suspension right off the frame and wrinkled the left front fender my beautiful sports car was no longer beautiful. When Patty called me she was almost hysterical and crying when she told me that she had an accident with the car I asked her if she was all right. She said that she had the seat belt on which was and aircraft surplus 4 inches wide, which held her tight in the seat I immediately went over to see what had happened. After checking Patty out and calming her down the policeman who was there said that I was more interested in my car than my daughter. I then told him she was all right and the car was one of ten original left in the world. I had it towed back to Patty's boyfriend's house, which was close by since the towing charge was a lot less than towing it home and it would be less apt to more damage.

I would go over and work on the Siata on weekends and would finally straighten the frame where the suspension was attached and got everything lined up and bolted back together again. I drove it home and proceeded to drive it to school a few times looking for an artist to fix the fender. Being aluminum it took and artist in metal bending to straighten it out since the whole body was welded together in one big piece. I never did get the fender straightened out. I could not find a body man that could work aluminum. I drove it back and forth to school with the dented fender. Then one day it would not start and I can't believe what I did. I left the car sit for 9 years and never tried to find the trouble! I had so many other things going on that I had no time for it.

I would accumulate a few more cars including a British Ford, a 1957 Chevrolet Nomad Station Wagon, a 1965 Ford Station Wagon, and a mini Morris Station Wagon. All these cars were good buys if you could repair them. I could repair them since I had a big shop at Manual Arts High School where I taught Auto Mechanics. I had all the tools needed as well as my own, which made the jobs much easier. The school had a new Sioux Valve facing machine and a new hard seat grinder to do all the valve jobs; this was very handy since I had sold my valve refacer. Fixing and selling cars helped out in the financial department. It also kept me sharp so I could teach better and answer all the questions the teachers asked me about their cars at school.

All the girls were going to school at this time. Sherry was going to Orange Coast College in Costa Mesa, California. Gale was going to Marina High School in Huntington Beach along with Patty. Karen was going to Oceanview. Gale graduated from Marina High School in 1967, which left Patty alone until Karen showed up. They all had the same art teacher so when Karen showed up the art teacher could not believe he had another Disbrow in his class. Karen transferred to Huntington High School after Patty graduated from Marina in 1969. Karen graduated from Huntington

High in 1972.

They all drove cars so I had to have a supply on hand. Sherry was driving the Covair Monza to College and to work most of the time. Then Gale drove it part of the time. I bought a Morris Minor "Woody" Station Wagon, which Patty would be driving to school and later I would teach Karen how to drive it in Ensenada, Mexico, at our beach house. I also had the Cadillac Convertible and the Siata. It seemed that I always had enough cars to get everyone to school, etc.

While Sherry was going to Orange Coast College and working part time at the Broadway Department Store she met a nice young fellow at College in one of her classes. His name was Brandt Peterson. She did not know what he did for a living until he had the duty and did not have time to change his clothes before going to class and came in his Marine Uniform. He was a gunnery Sergeant in the Marines stationed at El Toro Marine Base. As time went by they became very fond of each other and she brought him home so we could meet him. He seemed to be a very nice young man and he was in the military. He even took Sherry to San Francisco to meet Brandt's Mother. He wanted to marry Sherry very much but Sherry told him that if he wanted to marry her he had to go to Officers Candidate School and become an officer! He also had to join the Mormon Church (LDS) and I would baptize him when it came time and what a pleasure it was. After he graduated from OCS he came back to El Toro as a 2nd Lt. They were married at the Huntington Beach Ward and had their reception at Los Alamitos Navy Base Officers Club at the time

They were immediately transferred to Quantico, Virginia, where Brant would go through Officers Leadership School for new Officers. Sherry got lonesome since this was the first time in her life she was separated from her family. She also left every thing at home since she and Brandt flew to their new assignment at Quantico, Virginia. We decided to go back and see her and Brandt and bring all her stuff she got at their wedding and shower that was held for her. We had sold the Cadillac and did not have a car big enough to pull a trailer. I had the 1952 Corvair Monza Convertible, the Morris and the Siata. Somebody told us about a Large Ford Station Wagon that was for sale for $400 it was a good buy although I had to give it a valve grind. I took the heads off and took them to school and did the job. I also found an air conditioner system at a wrecking yard and took it home and installed it in our new used Ford. By the time school was out we were ready to make the cross-country trip from Huntington Beach to Quantico, Virginia.

With all the children out of school we rented a U-Haul trailer and proceeded to load all of Sherry's stuff in it and off we went to Quantico, Virginia. Actually Sherry and Brandt would later move to Woodburn, Virginia. We took the southern route through Blythe, California, Kingman, Arizona, Winslow, Arizona, the old route 66 though Albuquerque, New Mexico and Amarillo, Texas. We stopped somewhere in Texas and bought a 50 pound watermelon! It took two for us to get it in the car. I have a picture of Karen hiding behind it. We hauled it all the way to Sherry's before we would cut it.

We stopped about every 700 miles and stayed in a Motel to rest up and sleep. We went through Memphis, Tenn., and turned northeast to Nashville, to Winston-Salem, N.C., to Richmond to Quantico, Virginia. It was quite a trip. While we were there we took a trip to Washington, D.C. with Sherry and Brandt. We had a nice trip and saw most of the sights. We all went back to Quantico for a few more days with Sherry and Brandt. Having had a nice visit so Sherry could be with her family for a short time we took off for New York City on our way home. We stayed in a Motel in Hackensack, N.J., which was much more reasonable than trying to stay in New York City. It was right across the Hudson River from New York City and was a short trip to New York though the Holland Tunnel. We went to Grand Central Park, 5th Avenue, Times Square, and saw them shooting a movie right on one of the streets in New York City. One night we were driving around looking at all the sights and finally found that we were in Harlem and got out of there immediately.

After taking in most of the sights for the children we headed for home. We took the Pennsylvania Turnpike for home. I got tired of driving and so did Fay so we let Gale drive for a while since it was a four-lane highway. Everybody was asleep including me when all of s sudden I felt like we were going real fast. I woke up and looked at the speedometer and it was reading 80mph! I told Gale to slow down a little before we got a ticket for speeding. We stopped at a Roadside park for a little lunch and relaxation. As we were eating some young fellows stopped also. It seemed they had seen Gale driving and they took a liking to her and followed us to the Rest Stop. We all had a nice visit and found out that one of the young fellow's brothers owned a Pizza Hut in St. Louis. So off we went to St. Louis to have Pizza. On the way, I think Fay was driving now, I heard a strange noise when she slowed down and a little vibration, which to me was a universal joint going out. When we got to St. Louis we went into a Shell Gas Station and they fixed it for $10.

We were off again following the young man to his brothers Pizzeria and had Pizza after being introduced to his brothers and the workers. It was such a nice jester for the young man to do. When we finished we said our "Good Byes" and were on the road again for Oklahoma City on Route 66, I-40. Not much happened on the rest of the way home. The old Ford ran like a top and so did the air-conditioner. After we were home about a month the A/C stopped working it did not matter we did not need one in Huntington Beach. It had lasted long enough just for our trip and that was enough.

I was still teaching at Manual Arts High School and disliking it more every day. There was no more discipline. Of course I kept discipline in my classrooms. We now had a woman as principal of the school. She was a liberal and did not discipline the students much at all. They were getting away with murder. Ever since they had the Watts Riots things were getting worse. One day I came from the office back through the bungalow area when I spotted a fire underneath the stairs of one of the bungalows. I immediately put it out. Fortunately it had just started but I saw no one around to blame.

The next thing that happened was seeing a student loading a .38 revolver near one of the bungalows. It was during lunchtime. The Vocational Teachers had their own recreation room where they could relax and eat their bag lunch we had window shades that you could see out but could not see in. As I looked out I saw this black student loading the .38 revolver. I immediately got on the phone and called security and told them to be careful that there was a student with a loaded .38 in back of bungalow 25. We waited and all of us were watching out the window to see what would happen. As we watched the security guard came around the bungalow and grabbed the kid and through him on the ground and took the gun away from him. We found out later that he was going to shoot another kid for stealing his girlfriend.

One day in my basic math class I had a knife fight. As I was trying to get the knife away I was knocked over my desk since they were struggling with one of the boys holding onto the arm of the other with two hands so he would not get stabbed. One of my students in the meantime called for security as the rest of the students helped me pin the knife wielder to the wall and got the knife away from him. By this time security showed up. The boy made a mistake and took a swing at the security officer the next thing he knew he was thrown up in the air and slammed to the floor and hand cuffed. The security officer was one of my old students whose father was chief of security in the L.A. school system. Now his son was following in his father's footsteps and his name was Albert Reddick. He also was and outstanding football player for manual Arts High School before he graduated.

In Auto Mechanics class one day there was an argument between a Russian white boy who was a good student and a black boy the next thing I knew was the black boy was lying on the floor. I broke it up real quick and should have sent them to the Principal's office but it was the last period of the day, which was just about over so I gave them a warning no more fighting and let them go. I found out later that the black boy and 5 of his friends beat up the Russian boy way laying him after school. He never came back to school I heard that his mother had taken him out of Manual and sent him to another school.

I was guarding the main entrance door to the school one day and thought the door was locked so nobody could come in and I kept the kids away from the door who were trying sneak out early before the bell rang at the end of the day. All of a sudden a black boy rushed in the door and I motioned him out as I held the door open. He went out only to the bottom of the outside stairs. I guessed he realized that I had put him out. As I turned to have one of the students to go get the security he rushed in as I had my back to the door and took a swing at me. Luckily for my peripheral vision I saw the punch coming just in time to rare back and felt a slight tick to my chin with the kid's fist hitting the door with a resounding blow. I had a handful of books I was holding at the time. At that the boy ran back down the stairs and yelled at me to come out "whitey" and let us "niggers" get you with that I gave my books to one of the students standing there and was just about to run down the stairs to where the kid was shouting at me, I was going to knock this kid silly, when I saw a Black and White Police car slowly passing the school. I immediately waved them in as they approached the front of the school. I was telling them what had happened when the school bell rang that school was over at 3 pm.

The students who saw the whole incident as well as the woman Principal immediately surrounded me. The police took the kid away and told me to come to the police station to file a formal complaint. After telling the Principal what had happened I went down to the Police Station, which was only a few blocks away, I went in to file my complaint. Upon talking to the arresting Officers I found out this black kid was a truant and had pulled a knife on another student in the morning class and was booked the same Police station and being a juvenile, I think he was 14 years old, they released him to the custody of his mother. Somehow he got away from his mother by noontime and was back at school looking for more trouble, which he found at 2:45 pm when the incident happened with me. The Police told me they would call his mother again and release him to her custody again since he was a juvenile. I don't know if it ever went to court since I never was called as a witness to testify against the kid.

One day on my off period I was returning from the main office by way of the bungalows I heard all this screaming and hollering in one of the bungalows. I ran up the stairs and opened the door and the students were throwing spitballs at one another and at the teacher who I found out was a substitute. I shouted at them to sit down "You Wild Africans before I beat every one of you". "What kind of animals are you to treat your substitute teacher like this?" There was complete silence in the room immediately and every one was in their seat. The Substitute teacher was almost in tears and thanked me very much and my parting word to the class was that I will be back and will check on you and it better be quite in this room! With that I gave them my meanest stare and left. I always wore a white shop coat and carried a half-inch ratchet wrench in my pocket for safety first. All Vocational teachers wore white shop coats and were known as the toughest teachers on Campus. We always got "guard duty" monitoring the closed doors, the boy's restrooms, etc.

The pilots on the formation flight. I'm the smallest pilot in the middle. I was DCO of the 68th FIS Itazure, AB Japan

One day my daughter Gale was visiting Manual Arts for something I was monitoring the tardy office as she walked by with her husband Gary. As they passed my door Gary looked in and saw me and came in without Gale seeing him do this just as the bell rang to change classes. This left Gale alone in the hallway with this surge of black students coming down the hall she looked around for Gary but he was in with me. Gale ducked into the office to miss all this humanity surging toward her. She had no idea what had happen to Gary and when found out she pounded on him for leaving her in the lurch. It was the first time that Gale had been to Manual and was surprised how many students we had. She was there for the Middle school where she was a substitute teacher that supplied all the graduates for Manual Arts. She wondered how I was able to teach such a wild bunch. I told her that you had to get their attention by any means then it was relatively easy.

Manual Arts was becoming a danger zone for me. I was thinking all the time how I could escape, since the Watts riots things were getting progressively worse and I was getting meaner by the day, which wasn't me.

I would get home exhausted both physically and mentally it was not any fun any more but the students learned in spite of themselves. I had a good program for learning and made the very best of it.

I put in for a transfer every year to no avail. I was told I was one of the few who could handle the students that they sent to my classes. I was trapped! I would look in the newspaper every day for ranches, resorts, airports that were for sale. When I thought I had a good one I would jump in my Cessna 195 usually by myself and go look at the property on a weekend or holiday.

After Brandt finished Officer's Training School at Quantico, he put in for flying training at Pensacola, Florida. Sherry had become pregnant and would have her first boy Eric at the Navy Hospital at Pensacola. Fay wanted to go see our first grandson and since I was on vacation from school teaching we decided to fly the C-195 down to Pensacola. We loaded up the C-195 and Fay, Karen and Fay's mother Gladys and off we went to Pensacola. It seemed like old times flying the route to Florida, since I had flown it so many times when I was in the Air Force in everything from a F-86D, T-33, C-47 and a C-45. Of course we were not going as fast as a jet but we were going almost as fast as a C-47 and a C-45 at 168 MPH. Our first stop was Phoenix Sky Harbor airport, Phoenix, Arizona. We would refuel here and get directions to Deer Valley airport where I was suppose to have my new radio installed for our flight. It was a new 360 channel "Skipper", which I had purchased at Long Beach Airport before we left. It did not have a VOR head so it was for communicating only but was so much better than the old radio that the C-195 came with. After landing at Deer Park airport and waiting for the radio man to install the new set it was getting dusk when we made our take off for El Paso, Texas. Referring to the map I picked up a heading and saw a highway going the general direction of our flight path, which was the highway to El Paso, Texas. I was doing pilotage as well as dead reckoning (time, distance, and heading). It was now getting dark with no moon and it was dark! I could see the car lights going down US highway I-70 and the lights of some of the little towns along the way. I finally thought I had identified Lordsburg, Arizona, and was south of town I made a correction to the north and was not sure exactly where I was until I saw a green beacon ahead and to our left and decided to land since it was getting late and I wanted to make sure that I hadn't strayed into Mexico.

We were at 9,000 feet altitude as I circled the airport to let down slowly so everyone would not have any ear problems and keep the engine from cooling too rapidly I found the "T", which gave us the direction of landing and landed into the wind with the runway lights being the only lights we had. We landed without incident and we were trying to find the parking area as a car drove up to help, when someone said, "Were in Mexico!" I looked out as we shut down and the car I saw was the New Mexico Police! They had heard us circling and came out to meet us since there was no one there to maintain the airport so the police gave us a ride to the Ramada Motel in Deming, New Mexico. It was very nice of them and we thanked them very much.

After getting our room we all "sacked out" quickly, since it had been a long day and a very apprehensive one on this very dark night with no real navigation equipment aboard. The next morning after breakfast the Motel van took us to the airport to refuel so we could take off again for San Angelo, Texas. It was daylight now, which would make it a lot easier to navigate by pilotage. We landed at San Angelo, Texas, and refueled and had lunch at the airport cafe. It took us only 2 hours and 5 minutes to get here, which was good time. After lunch we cleared for Lake Charles, Louisiana. For some reason I followed the wrong Highway out of San Angelo and the prevailing wind was from the southeast stronger than the forecast. After flying for about 3 hours I didn't recognize anything on the ground from my map and it was getting late. I told the "troops" I was going to land at the next airport I could see. I figured that I was north of my course but how much I did not know. We were looking for a strip when one came into view. I circled a few times to see which way the wind was blowing. and set up my pattern to land. Upon landing I found that it was Center, Texas, we were way north of course. As we taxied in a taxi was there to greet us. It was standard operational procedure (SOP) for the taxi to come out for all aircraft they did not recognize as being local as they flew their pattern. Our Cessna 195 was a rare bird and there were none like it in the area. The taxi took us into a home who rented rooms and we had dinner in this little town, which was in walking distance from where we were staying. After dinner I got out the maps and plotted our course to Baton Rouge. La.

The next morning the taxi driver took us to the landing strip and we took off for Baton Rouge to refuel since they had no fuel at Center. I now had very good visibility and hit the Mississippi south to Barksdale AFB, La., and headed south for Baton Rouge. Along the way the way we encountered one of the highest radio towers I had ever seen. It was 800 feet high and we were flying at 1500 feet. Luckily it was marked on our chart so I was ready for it. It was a good checkpoint. We landed at Baton Rouge and refueled and were off again to Pensacola, Florida. We landed at Pensacola Airport after 2 hours and ten minutes, called Sherry and took a taxi to her apartment. We had quite a reunion since we hadn't seen them for over a year. They lived in a nice apartment with a swimming pool, which we all enjoyed while we there.

I had bought 2 lots in Great Exuma Island in the Bahamas while we were in the Air Force at Itazuke Air Base in Japan, for an investment. Since I was so close I thought it would be a good idea to go see what we had bought "sight unseen". No one wanted to go with me through the "Bermuda Triangle" to Great Exuma so I decided to go by myself. This would be on the 25 June 1968. I left Pensacola and flew to Ft. Lauderdale, Florida, to refuel and pickup my over water flight gear. I would be flying over 300 miles down the island chain to Bimini, to Nassau to Great Exuma. After getting briefed by the local operations and customs I checked my map and radio frequencies for Miami Center and the emergency procedures and I was off. The old C-195 climbed out to 10,000 feet with no sweat since I was alone and there was not too much weight. I wanted to be high in case of an emergency I could look around for a small island to put it in. I was flying down this long string of islands so land was fairly close all the time.

The old "Shaking Jake" engine purred all the way down even over all this water. I wore a "mae west" life jacket like old times in my jet and had a one man dingy with a survival kit in it hoping that I would not have to use it. After a beautiful flight with wonderful weather I spotted Georgetown and the airstrip at Great Exuma after about two hours of flying. After I tied down in the parking area I was greeted by the customs officer who was black but spoke the "kings English" beautifully. I was amazed how well he sounded after teaching all black students at Manual Arts HS and listening to the language they used. I got a taxi and went into town to the real estate office to find out where my piece of property was located. He looked it up on a plat map and we were off. Well the property wasn't under water, like my great grand father Rankin had bought in Florida "sight unseen" when he was in Ireland. It was better than I had expected. It was about one mile from Georgetown and about a mile from the airport. It was level and about two blocks from the water. After learning that you had to generate your own electricity and dig your own well for water plus dig a septic tank for your sewer I wasn't to enthusiastic. You would have to import all your building materials from the mainland to build your house. After getting all this information on the property and all the pitfalls that went with it the real estate agent took me for a tour of the island, which was 20 miles long and 2 miles wide. The best part of the island was in the north of Georgetown, which was more expensive than where I was located in the south of Georgetown. In the north they had some very nice homes and a very nice Beach Club with and eight unit Motel, which was for sale for $120,000.

After viewing the whole island I was driven back to the airport and took off for Fort Lauderdale and climbed back out to 10,000 feet. I retraced my course up the island chain but ran into a squall line after I passed Nassau. I looked up and the clouds were higher than I could go. In the meantime I had contacted Miami Center and was told there was a small tornado over Coral Gables at the time and stay north of Miami. I then heard a pilot call Miami Center and tell them that he was going to try to get over the clouds of the squall line!

I decided I was going under the squall line and I started down until I was 500 feet over the Atlantic Ocean. As I went under it I felt like Lindbergh when he was flying to Paris he got down right over the Atlantic at about 100 feet. As I went under it was a little turbulent and it was raining like mad. I made sure I held my heading and altitude right on the money. It seemed like an hour by the time I popped out in the clear but it wasn't half that. I finally landed at Fort Lauderdale along with the pilot who was trying to get over the clouds. We were both late to go through customs so we split the cost, which was $20 a piece. After turning in my over water gear and getting my deposit back I headed for the nearest Motel.

I was bushed and ready to RON.

The next morning I was off to Pensacola back where I started. I had to land at Cross City to refuel since I had picked up a good headwind, which cut down my range. After refueling I landed at Pensacola without incident it had taken me four hours and 50 minutes from Fort Lauderdale, sure beats driving.

After having a nice visit with Sherry, Brandt, and little Erik we headed for home in the C-195. Our first stop was Montgomery County, Texas to refuel. Then to Monahan, Texas it was very hot and after take off it became a little too turbulent for my passengers so we landed at El Paso, Texas, and stayed over night (RON) and refueled. We left El Paso the next day, 28 June 1968, and headed for Deer Valley Airport near Phoenix to have my new radio checked and to have lunch. After lunch the aircraft was ready to go and we headed for home to Meadowlark Airport at Huntington Beach, Ca. It had been a long flight but we all enjoyed the convenience of flying our own aircraft to come and go as we pleased.

On the 13 July 1968 my daughter Gale and her friend wanted me to fly them up to Lake Nachiemento near Paso Robles. Her Uncle Bob Cox was there with his friends and their boats. So I decided to fly them up so they would not have to drive all that way for just one overnight stay. We flew in to Paso Robles airport where we were picked up by her Uncle Bob and driven to the lake where their camp was located. We stayed overnight and the next day I got the fasted ride in a boat I ever had we were doing 70 mph on the water and it was so rough I had to hold onto the bottom of the seat to keep from flying out.. We then started for home after being brought back to Paso Robles airport and it only took us one hour and 30 minutes to get home.

Being on school vacation I had a lot of time to go flying. On the 26 July 1968 I flew to Las Vegas, Nevada for my 68th Fighter Interceptor Reunion. It was held at the old Stardust Hotel. After three days of having a blast and meeting all the old heads I flew home. It seems I was the only one to fly my own aircraft to most of the reunions. I had flown up to Las Vegas to arrange for this reunion and they treated me very nice and I got very good rates for the troops. I think we had 50 people there from all over the US.

My mother called me and said that she had a lot of nice ripe peaches for us if I would fly up and get them. She had beautiful peach trees that produced so many peaches she could not handle them all and would give most of them away to the neighbors who wanted them. I could kill two birds with one stone by seeing and visiting with my mother and her husband Henry and get the peaches at the same time. So on the 3 August 1968 I got in the old C-195 by myself and flew up to San Jose Airport where they met me and took me home to Los Gatos where they lived. After a nice visit they had all the peaches in two huge cartons to take with me back to the airport and load them into the C-195. I took off and was home in less than 3 hours. As I landed at Meadowlark airport and taxied up to the gas pumps to get refueled by Marge Stewart who was the FBO with her husband smelled the peaches, which were giving out a beautiful aroma so I gave her some, which I had plenty to give. When I got home everybody was surprised to see how many peaches I had. I think everyone pitched in and Fay canned most of them. We had peaches for a long time and they were delicious.

Vacation was just about over and I would be flying at Long Beach in the C-150 to finish up my time to get my CFI (Certified Instructors Rating). When I finally qualified for my check ride with the FAA check pilot I wanted to spin the aircraft but he would not let me spin it because it was not required any more. I wanted to show him how proficient I was at spinning the aircraft. I passed my check ride with "no sweat". So now I was a civilian qualified flying instructor.

When I went back to school I would have the only Aeronautics class in the Los Angeles Area. They would bus the white students in and bus the black students out to white schools for special subjects a type of pseudo integration. My aeronautics class was great they were all so smart and attentive the interest was very high and it was a privilege to attend the class. It was also a pleasure to teach them.

I taught aerodynamics, theory of flight, and history of flight, during the first semester and the second semester I taught FAA regulations, navigation, map reading etc, so they could pass the ground school test to get their student license. On weekends I would take some of the most enthusiastic students flying in my C-195. This was a great event in their life especially when I would let them fly the airplane. On of these students was a black young man who was the smartest student in the class at the time his name was Don Allen. I took some more students for rides but I can't remember their names along with Don this was in November 1968. You can imagine the chattering around class on Monday after the students got to actually fly an airplane on the weekend after studying how an airplane flies. It was with great pleasure that I taught this class. They were all good students and their deportment was excellent. It was a great change from my other classes. If all my classes had been this nice I would not have retired when I did.

I was asked to teach an Aeronautics class for summer school at a High School in East Los Angeles one summer. It would be an accelerated class on the same subjects I taught at Manual Arts. They were special students who wanted to attend. They were so smart I thought they had a copy of my tests. They were all A and B students and a mixture of races from Caucasian, Latino, and Asian. After teaching for two summers I gave it up since it did not give me much of a summer vacation and I had to go right back and teach at my job at Manual Arts I wanted to spend my vacation with my family.

Having obtained my CFI I was helping out the FBO at Meadowlark airport at times flying students in the C-150. I also got a student of my own in a Mr. Alverez. He had bought a C-140 and wanted to learn how to fly it. He rode a Harley Davidson motorcycle and believed that anybody that rode a motorcycle could fly an airplane. The only trouble was getting him to fly on consecutive days in a row to learn quickly. Instead it was a hit and miss affair. Each time I took him up he had to learn all over again. He would fly for two days and then I would not see him for two weeks. This is not the way to learn to fly you must fly everyday for at least a week. I had given him 28 hours of dual time and he still did not want to solo. It took from 9 March 1969 to 1 March 1970 a whole year. I did not see him again and did not know what had happened to his Cessna 140. I did hear that a friend of his owned a Beech Bonanza who was also a student pilot and the two student pilots flew the Beech to Mexico City Airport from Fullerton, California! They said that they were treated royally when they landed! I always wondered if he ever soloed.

I was still giving my aero students rides in my C-195 and they were sure enjoying it as much as I was seeing their eagerness to learn to fly and learn all about flying in my C-195. One student in particularly was paying me $8.00 an hour to fly my plane. I taught him to everything in it but land it. It was no aircraft to for a beginner to land. This student was Dan Allen one of my best students and so enthusiastic. He wanted to be a pilot so bad I hated him to finish my class. He wanted to fly so bad I hope he realized his dream. I never heard from him again. I would be taking other students up on the weekends when they could make it.

One day at school I was notified that there would be a California Teachers Convention at Fresno, California. Another teacher wanted to go and wanted to fly with me so we split the expenses and flew to Fresno and the convention. It would be much quicker and easier than driving. We landed at Chandler Field at Fresno and rented a car for the days of the convention and had our room reservation in advance this would be on the 14 March 1969. The next day we had a special treat the Governor, Ronald Reagan, gave us a nice talk during one of the sessions. We flew home on the 16 of March 1969 after a nice convention.

With all the flying the old C-195 burned a valve so I had to have that one cylinder fixed at Meadowlark FBO. The mechanic got the cylinder off the Jacobs engine and I took it to a machinist at Long Beach Airport to have then new exhaust valve put in and new seats for both valves. All the rest of the cylinders tested strong. I got it back in a day or so and brought it to the FBO who was doing the job and was told that the mechanic had not shown up. After a few days of waiting and it was not fixed I found out that the mechanic went of a drunken spree and they did not know when he would be back! I told the FBO operator I could not wait any longer that I was going to put the engine back together myself. When I finished and gave it a good run up check I took off and gave it a test hop for 45 minutes and every thing was OK. When the mechanic finally came back to work he found that I had put the aircraft back together and finished his job he signed it off and said that I did as good a job as he could. Aircraft engines are about the same as and automobiles engine so it made it easy for me.

One day we found out that my daughter Sherry and her husband Brandt were being transferred from Quantico, Virginia to Mather Field near Sacramento, California. They rented a little house near Placerville,

California, in the Sierra foothills. After they were settled a while we decided to fly up and visit with them during Easter vacation. On the 6 April 1969 we got in the C-195 and flew up and landed at the Placerville Airport, which was close by and they picked us up. When we got there we were surprised that Brandt's Mother was visiting also from Washington State. She had driven her Buick down from Tacoma.

During our stay Brandt had to pick up their dog "Prudy" at the vet, which was in Auburn 30 miles away. Brandt and I hopped in his car to get the dog in Auburn. On arriving at the Vet I stayed in the car to wait for him and saw a real estate office across the street. I walked across the street to inquire if they had any properties that I was looking for. On talking to the man in charge he said that he had a property that had a runway on it and it was for sale at a bargain it was thirty-five acres and it was a resort at one time. I got the directions and the next day we all went to look at it. It was 30 miles to Foresthill from Auburn then another 20 miles into the mountains up a Forest Service road toward French Meadows Reservoir. We finally came to a sign that said Cedar Springs Resort after winding around mountains and going down in the American River canyon and up the other side, it was quite a drive. When we drove in the dirt road that said "Cedar Springs Resort" it climbed up a hill and finally came to a big flat where we came to a log cabin, which belonged to the Sachau's. We asked directions and were told that we were there it was just across the so called flight strip. We drove over to take a look at the place. When we got out to look we found that it was a mess. The Quonset hut had caved in from the heavy snow load an old stable had also collapsed which was made from old logs, a small duplex needed repairs and the bunkhouse needed extensive repairs. The big swimming pool was black with mud and dirt, etc. The gas station pumps looked like they might work. You had to generate your own electricity you had to pump your own water from a large spring to a 6000-gallon tank up on the upper end of the runway, which was 90 feet higher than the main buildings. The rest rooms and showers and Laundromat were burned to the ground. It was a wreck and they wanted $120,000 for it. I told the real estate man to forget it and we went home. It was a pretty setting with lots of large pine tress and firs with two very large Ponderosa Pine trees at the entrance to the place they were over 6 feet in diameter and

150 feet high. Well the price was too high so we decided against paying, off to home we went. When we got home there were many things to do. Take care of all the cars so every one would have transportation for school and work. I had to do my home teaching and vacation was just about over and I had to go back to my teaching job at Manual.

Gale had been dating a nice fellow she met at in her art class at Long Beach State named Gary Shafer and they were married at the LDS Church in Huntington Beach. She had made her own dress out of satin and with little pearls sewed in it and it was beautiful. I wore my USAF dress uniform as I gave her away. It would be a tradition to wear my dress uniform to all the marriages of all my daughters, granddaughters and grandsons weddings. I am lucky that I can still get it on after over 50 years since it was made. We had the reception at Los Alamitos Navy Station Officers Club. It was the same place that Sherry had her wedding reception. It was very nice as usual. This was before she came to Manual Arts with Gary. Now we only had Patty and Karen at home.

With Easter Vacation over I went back to the old grind of teaching at Manual Arts HS. I was now getting fed up with teaching and was trying to escape somewhere. I was still looking for a place with an airport to retire to. I continued to look in all the papers for a place that would be ideal for me and when I saw something interesting I would get in the old C-195 and fly off to see it.

Teaching at Manual was getting to be a real chore. Then one day I was giving a test in my class when one of the mothers of one of my students came into ask how her boy was doing. As we were talking I noticed through, my peripheral vision, that a student in my class was on his hands and knees and crawling around the corner of my desk and opened the drawer and take out my answer sheet for the test and to show it to the rest of the class. When the lady had left I lost my cool I ran over and grabbed the answer sheet from him and threw him up against the lockers and was going to hit him right in the nose but in a millisecond I changed my mind and hit him in the shoulder and knocked him down. He got up and called me every dirty name he could muster and I threw him out of class. The bell rang for nutrition break and all the students left and I forgot to lock my door afterwards. In came this kid and said, "Mr. Disbrow I'm going to beat your butt" He sat down on one of the chairs and started to roll up his pants leg which revealed two hardwood dowels connected by a chain taped to his leg. I was sitting at my desk when he rushed in and now stood up and grabbed my chair and said, "Kid you don't want to fight with me because I will kill you" by this time I was in a full rage. He then said, "Are you going to hit it me with that chair?" I said, "I told you I was going to kill you now if you want to fight to the death lets go!" All this time he is whirling his weapon over his head. "If not you get out of here and come back the last day of school with only your fists and let's see how tough you are". He went out without any further fuss and I was very relieved. He would have been very sorry to tangle with me I was in such a rage. I reported the incident to the office and found out that this student had been in jail for beating up a teacher and he had been out for a short time and they sent him to my class, which seem to be a dumping ground for incorrigibles, Basic Auto Mechanics. He had met the wrong teacher to try to scare. From then on I always had a ½" ratchet wrench in the pocket of my shop coat that I always wore.

We had a 12 foot chain link fence around the school and it seemed people were always cutting holes in it to sneak in. This particular day they body shop teacher caught a bunch of big apes coming through a hole in the fence and told them to get back out there at which time there was a scuffle and they knocked him down and kicked him. We had back doors to the fence, which we usually left open to get a little ventilation to the classroom. This particular day I had mine closed so did not hear what was going on or I would have been in the middle of the fight with the other teacher I have forgotten the body shop teachers name but he was quite a racer at Bonneville salt flats He had an accident and had a plate in his head so he was delirious after he was knocked down and was afraid of ill affects to his head. After this incident he armed himself with a .45 Cal automatic pistol and kept it on his person. So the next time he would be ready for anything. It happened again not too long after that. He caught some big strangers coming through a hole in the fence, which had been repaired. He told them to get out of there and when they refused he said, "You niggers are dead!" as he pulled out his .45 they then got out of there in a hurry. He was reported and he was transferred to another school. I was thinking of doing the same thing to get transferred but I decided to retire first.

I had a bad reputation for knocking kids down when they got unruly and had $10,000 worth of liability insurance on myself. They threaten to sue but never did. I would have been shot dead this day in age. Finally one day they kicked in the side of my new Javelin and jumped on the hood when I wasn't there. I always parked it in front of my classroom. When I saw it I was fit to be tied. I reported it and the school insurance fixed it but by this time I was ready to quit.

In the meantime my Stepfather had died and left my mother a widow again and she fell and broke her hip and was in the Stanford Hospital in Palo Alto, Ca. I would fly up to see her on the weekends until she got well and would eventually sell her house and move her down to Huntington Beach.

Then one day I got a letter from Mr. McClain the real estate man that he had the best deal I would have in my whole life. The Cedars Springs flight strip could be bought for half price $60,000. This got my attention immediately it was less than $18 and acre even if it was out in the "Boondocks". It had plenty of timber on it. The only catch was they wanted $30,000 down. My mind was racing on how I could swing the deal and finally escape from Manual. I now had to worry about my mother who was living in a mobile park and did not like it since she was all alone and did not have any friends like she had at Los Gatos. Her health was deteriorating and she wanted to go into a rest home. I found one for her close by to us. After a while she did not like this rest home so I found another very nice place in Leisure World in Seal Beach. It was very nice and she liked it. It was very convenient for me as I could see her everyday as I came home from teaching, it being right on the way home.

I sold the house and bought a smaller 3-bedroom home since we had only Patty and Karen at home we did not have to have a big 5-bedroom home anymore. I used the money and bought the Flite Strip Resort, which we would call it. This would be in April 1970.

THE FLITE STRIP RESORT

We had a Smith family in our LDS Ward in Huntington Beach who had three boys who wanted to help me fix up the resort during summer vacation, which was soon coming up, just for their room and board. I flew up on a weekend to make a list of all the things that would have to be done and the supplies I would have to purchase to get the job done. I think I flew the oldest boy, Russell Smith, up on a weekend to show him what I wanted to be done. Russell had an old Ford pickup truck he was fixing up and was putting dual mufflers on it at school. He would use the truck to haul supplies and his two brothers to the Flite Strip to help. It seemed that they got out of school before me for summer vacation in Huntington Beach as I was in the Los Angeles Area, which got out later. So they would leave before me in the Ford pickup with a bunch of supplies including a lot of paint to spruce things up. I would fly up later with more supplies.

They loaded up their pickup and headed for the Flite Strip. They were cruising up US 99, a four lane divided highway, with big bushes in the center divider at a speed of about 65mph when all the traffic stopped abruptly. Russell was driving and when he went to apply the brakes the brake pedal went to the floor no brakes! So rather than rear end the cars ahead of him he headed for the shoulder of the road and was doing alright weaving back and forth to slow the truck down until the shoulder ran out when a bridge showed up they went flying into a deep ravine airborne and hit on their nose on flipped over a few times. The youngest boy was sitting in the middle of the seat between his two brothers and was killed instantly as he was thrown out through to windshield and the truck rolled on top of him. The other two boys where banged up but Russell was not hurt but had bruises and contusions his other brother had a few broken bones if I remember correctly. At the time I was attending Long Beach College finishing up my degree after teaching school all day. I was in an American History class when a student came in and informed me that they wanted me in the office right away. When I got there and heard the shocking news of the accident and Mr. Curtis Smith, the boys Father, wanted to know if I could fly he and his wife to Tulare Hospital where the other two boys were being treated. I went back to class to inform the instructor that I had an emergency and would have to leave immediately. By the time I got home everyone knew about the accident. I got Curtiss Smith loaded in the C-195 at Meadowlark airport and was told that we had to pickup his wife at Van Nuys Airport where she would be waiting. It was now getting dark and the weather was getting bad. We got in the old C-195 and off we went to Van Nuys. It was easy to fly in the Los Angeles Area since there were not too many restrictions. You just made sure that we went over LAX at 7000 feet to miss the airliner pattern. We landed at Van Nuys Airport and loaded Mrs. Smith in, who was very obese, 300 pounds? I got my IFR clearance from Burbank Control since the weather now was low ceilings and raining and black as pitch.

After getting my IFR clearance and departure instructions I cranked up and taxied out for takeoff. I gave the old C-195 full throttle and off we went in the C-195 in the dark of night. I had never flown night instruments in the C-195 but I had gotten a new artificial horizon installed and it worked real well. As the radar station gave me my headings and to call passing through each 1000 feet of altitude it was like old times when I was flying in the 68th FIS but I wasn't flying a jet but an old slow tail dragger. I was using the same nomenclature I used in my jet and I knew the controller liked that. We broke out on top at 6000 feet I made very cautious turns and made sure my pitot heat was on so it would not ice up. I climbed to 6500 feet to get over the Grape Vine pass and headed up the San Joaquin Valley to Tulare. The weather was very nice in the valley you could see for miles. I followed US99 and picked up the Tulare Airport green beacon. I set up my pattern and made a poor landing, forgetting I had all that weight in the back seat. Making a good recovery we taxied into the parking area and shut down. I don't know who drove us to hospital. When we got to the hospital we found the oldest boy Russell waiting for us and showed us to the room where the other brother was in bed. After getting all the details on what happened and giving both boys a blessing we were off to a motel. I was bushed I had been up since 6am taught school all day and was in college late in the afternoon and it was about 11pm now.

The next day I flew Russell Smith back to Huntington Beach with me to take care of some family business. On the 1 June 70 I flew the C-195 back to Tulare to pickup Curtiss, his wife and his son Robin. The boys were recovering quite rapidly. We flew back to Huntington Beach without incident.

It was now time to fly back to the Flite Strip with more supplies and clean things up so we could open when summer vacation started. With the help of the two Smith boys and some other young people I had hired we cleaned up the swimming pool and got the water pipes repaired that went to it. We cleaned all the filters and got the pump working. We then had to clean all the plaster on the inside of the pool with muriatic acid with brushes. We could hardly stand the fumes that were given off from the acid but eventually got it sparkling white. When we finally filled the pool with water and got the pump working everyone got a chance to try it out since it was quite warm and it felt great. It was the first time the pool had been used in a few years.

They had delivered the big generator that I bought in Wilmington, California, which I could not haul myself in back of the pickup truck I had bought and fixed up to run like a top it was just to heavy. The generator was a 70KW and was an old standby unit for a telephone company and ran on gasoline and was a good buy at $2000. After they got it off the big truck trailer they were wondering how I was going to get into the generator house. I got a jack and raised up one end and put two large pieces of pipe under it and then began to use a pry bar to roll it along on top of the pipe I kept replacing as it inched along. I finally got it in and hooked up all the wiring and got it running. It proved to be an excellent generating plant but used too much fuel so later on I had to buy a smaller Diesel generator, which was a 30 KW and was just right for the place. It was much more economical burning only about a gallon and a half an hour. The big generator was used for standby. Fuel was only 15 cents per gallon in those days.

With electricity I now could run all my power tools to make all the repairs and make a sign out of redwood for the front of the road where it came off the Forest Service Road, which ran to French Meadows Reservoir, Norden, and Georgetown. I had to rout out all the letters on the redwood sign with my router and I made the sign look just like the Forest Service signs. Years later they decided it looked too much like their signs and they complained so I had to repaint it. The sign was big and made out of 2X10s. They would be put in three rows hooked together by chain with the letters painted in yellow on a redwood background. It was a great looking sign and no one could miss it trying to find the place.

We fixed up the duplex and cleaned up the bunkhouse and tore down the old stable that had collapsed due to heavy snow load accumulation. After cleaning the area we finally opened on the 1 July 1970. We had soft drinks, hot dogs, hamburgers, some groceries and gasoline, as a start. I had advertised our opening on the local radio station in Auburn and posted a big sign at the entrance of our road saying "Now Open". We then started to get some customers. Gladys Caples, the lady I bought the place from, came up to help me out when I wanted to leave for a few days.

It was now time to get ready to close for winter since summer vacation was about over and I had to get back to school to my teaching job. I was checking out every thing I had to do prior to closing. I had old fellow named Al Dodge for my caretaker until we came back next April when the snow melted. Al was retired and about 65 years old.

I was in the restaurant one day before we were going to leave when a tall fellow came in and asked who was the new owner of the place and I said that I was. He said that his name was Sergeant and he had a contract from the Forest Service to pave the road from our entrance to French Meadows. He needed a place for his workers to stay until the snow flew and he would guarantee us $3000 if we would stay open for them. We now had all our facilities working. I had rebuilt the shower house and the restrooms and put in a Landro-mat operated by coins and installed a 50-gallon propane water heater. We had fixed up all the trailer spaces that they all had electricity, water, and sewer hookups. We were ready for business. I immediately called Fay and told her what had happened also my cousin Georgia Lee Anderson in Antioch, California, to see if they would come up to help while I went back to teach at Manual Arts. I would be flying up every weekend bringing the supplies they needed. They would call me on the telephone and give me a list of the supplies they needed each week and I would go shopping and get them and load them in the C-195 and fly them up each weekend. This would go on each weekend until the weather got so bad I could no longer land at the Flite Strip due to snow. This was time to close up and call it a season.

I would fly to Antioch, Ca. on the 15 Nov 1970, to pickup my cousin Georgia Lee Anderson to help with cooking, etc. at the Resort. I was a little late getting there and I got off later than I wanted to. It would be dark when we got to the Flite Strip. I had no landing lights to light up the landing strip which was only 1500 feet long and 100 feet wide cut right out of the forest of big tall pine trees on each side of the runway. I told Georgia that I would make a low pass to let everyone know I had arrived and they could light up the runway with their pickup truck lights so I could see. They came out but made the mistake of getting on the wrong end of the runway and the lights were shining in my face. I buzzed them again and they got the message and came down to the landing end of the strip and shined the lights up the runway and I could now see great and landed on the next pass. Before the last pass I told Georgia that I would make one more pass and if I did not make it we would go back to Auburn and land. After we taxied back and shut down Georgia said, "That was thrilling" it was just like landing behind enemy lines in the black of night and all of a sudden the lights come on and we land and everything goes black again like in the movies". Little did she know how much I was sweating out the whole landing. I would never do that again I was right at the edge of my ability. You get away with this type operation once and luck out but I was not going to try it ever again. I would fly down to Buchanan Airport in Concord, Ca. on the 24 Nov 70 to pickup Georgia's mother Marie White to help out in the last days of the season at the Flite Strip. I would then fly her back on the 13 Dec 70 when we started to close up for the season. Our first season was not too bad since we had no liquor license and could only sell soft drinks.

On 26 Dec 1970, my daughter Karen married Paul Williamson in Las Vegas, NV at the "Sahara Hotel". Subsequently, they had two boys, Jason and Aaron who both earned their Eagle Scout Award and went on to serve 2-year honorable Church Missions for The Church of Jesus Christ of Latter-day Saints (LDS). Jason served in the Guatemala Mission and Aaron served in the Salt Lake City Mission. The Family currently resides in Huntington Beach, Ca. and I have had the pleasure for the past 15 years to spend the weekends with them to enjoy golf and family outings, what a blessing!

Following Karen's marriage I decided to take a sabbatical (In the Los Angeles School district a teacher gets to take a sabbatical leave for every 7 years of consecutive teaching, they get 1 year to enhance your experiences by travel or advancing your degree, etc.) so, Fay and I went to Europe for two months to visit some of her relatives in England and to visit all the places I bombed in WWII, also to visit my old B-24 base in Cerignola, Italy. They had a special Military flight that flew out McGuire AFB, New Jersey to Heathrow, London, England, for $180 round trip for retired personnel per person. We made reservations to take the flight. The only catch was we had to get to McGuire AFB, New Jersey. We had a Renault Dauphine at the time that we all drove. It got 40 mpg at 70mph! We would drive it straight through to New Jersey. On the way we got stopped at Las Cruses, N.M., due to a big snowstorm that covered the entire main highway US 70. The snowplows could not keep up with snowing. We were really "sweating it out" because we had to make our flight at McGuire AFB and we were cutting it short as it was and now this. After waiting for about an hour we heard that the road would be open in a few minutes and we were about first in line and when they opened the road we were off in a hurry. We rambled right a long and drove night and day taking turns at the wheel. We got to McGuire AFB on time but had to leave the Renault at a parking lot at McGuire and take a bus to Kennedy Airport in New York to catch our flight to Heathrow in England. On arriving in Heathrow Airport we got a taxicab, which took us into London. When we got to London he took us to a bed and breakfast home near Scotland Yard.

When I rang the bell a typical old world Englishman answered the door and I asked if they had any vacancy? He looked us over very carefully and said that he had and would we like to come in and look at it. It was an old mansion and it was spotless. Are room was very large and the furnishings were very nice. We stayed a week and visited most of the places of interest and also got to see one of Fay's relatives in Sussex.

One of the greatest things I saw was in the London Museum. It was one of the original S6 Super marine Seaplane Racers that won the Snider Cup races and went over 400mph in 1931! It was beautiful and it wasn't too large. It had an open cockpit with a tiny windshield and was like "putting it on" getting into the cockpit. The engine was the forerunner to the Rolls Royce Merlin and developed in excess of 2000 HP in 1931! It was a V12 engine and the pilot had to look between the V of the cylinders for straight a head vision It was a very beautiful streamline aircraft. There were no protrusions to cause drag. It was a cantilever low wing but for the safety sake it had flying wires to make sure it could stand the high speeds it was designed to reach. England won the Snider Cup 3 times and got eternal possession of the cup.

After staying a week in London we flew to Frankfurt, Germany to Rheinmain Airport. There was no Guest housing there so we had to take a taxi to town and get a pensione. It wasn't too sharp but the best we could do without a reservation. We spent a week here and I bought a movie camera at the BX. We also bought a used VW automobile for $120. I did not know at the time I bought the VW that it had to pass an inspection to get permanent license plates on it. It now had temporary plates on it until I passed the safety inspection. I bought the car from an MP enlisted man who had conveniently disappeared when I went back to get my money back when the VW would not pass the inspection. To fix it was more than the car was worth.

After wasting most of our time on the VW we left for Heidelberg in it with the temporary license. I think it was good for two weeks. When we got to Heidelberg we found a nice pensione with some nice German people. I was finding these places from the book I bought before we left the states. We had a very nice room and they served breakfast. We were surprised to find a McDonalds Hamburger place and had lunch there, just like home. We saw where the movie "The Student Prince" was filmed at the University. We went up the cable car to the top of the mountain adjoining the city, which had a wonderful view of the area but it was very cold and still had snow on the ground. When we got down we went to a castle, which was now a museum, where I saw a thermometer which read 0 degrees. The river adjoing the city was partially frozen. We watched the boats go through the locks on the river, which were large and full of cargo.

One day while having lunch at McDonalds I noticed graffiti painted on the wall across the street which read "Go home Fritz". It made us feel right at home it had invaded Germany. We had to visit all the department stores in town and do a little shopping where I bought two beautiful turtleneck ski sweaters, one red and one yellow, which I still wear skiing to this day! They wore like iron. I paid the big price of $3.00 each, which did not break our budget.

After seeing most everything in town that was interesting and our week was up we headed for Stuttgart. While driving down the Autobahn I had the old VW going as fast as it would go to keep from getting run over. The Autobahn was only two lanes each way so if you had to pass any one you had to look in the

The Stinson I got in trade for our sailboat, "the Seminole" 1 Mar 1968

rearview mirror to make sure there was no one behind you that was coming at you at better that 100mph with his lights blinking making sure you got out of his way time before he got to you. I had to pass a truck and I looked in the mirror and I did not see anyone coming but when I went to pass the truck I was horrified to see this car blinking his lights coming at me at over

100mph. I just got out of his way in time when he went by and almost blew me off the road. The old VW was wide open at 70mph.

When we got to Stuttgart we were lucky. They had an Army Camp where we could stay in the guest quarters. I think it was called Carlyle Barracks. It was very nice and was very reasonable. They had a nice Officers Club where we could eat. It was the time of the Championship fight between Casius Clay (Ali) and Joe Frazier. They had a big screen TV in the Officers Club and announced that the fight would be on at 3am the next morning. We could leave a wakeup call so we could get up and see the fight and have coffee and doughnuts as you viewed the fight. We made the fight and it was a good one and Joe Frazier won.

We went to the Mercedes factory, which was in Stuttgart; it was a big beautiful building that housed the Mercedes Auto Museum. When I walked in with Fay I was met by the curator and when I told him I had raced against Karl Kling, their driver and PR man, I got "The Red Carpet Treatment". Especially when I told him I was driving my home built "The Disbrow Special". After a guided tour of all the normal cars from the very first one to the present day, I was taken up to the top floor, which was reserved for all the racecars that had raced through the years. One beautiful car was the streamline racer that ran for the record on the Autobaum. It sure was worth the visit. They gave me the history of the Daimler Benz Automobiles and a set of colored slides when

The Cessna 195 I got in trade for the Stinson at Fox Field, Lancaster, Ca 9 April 1968

I told them I taught Auto Mechanics at High School in Los Angeles, Ca. We were treated very nicely and I will never forget the visit.

After staying for about a week we were off to Munich, Germany, to see the city where I bombed the marshalling yards and the oil supplies during WWII. This was one of the very hot targets in Europe. When we got there some snow was still on the ground and it was really chilly. We rented a pensione from some nice German people. I was still driving the old VW with the temporary plates on it and daring them to stop me. We took a city bus tour, while there, and saw all the well-known sites. The tour had mostly Americans on it and the tour guide spoke English. After the tour we went to do a little window-shopping, which was the norm in each new place we visited.

One day I found the German Aero Museum and we had a nice time looking at all the aircraft that were shooting at me in WWII. Two of the fiercest fighters were the Me-109 and the FW-190, which were displayed. I now could inspect these two aircraft close-up without being shot at. After a few days we drove to Garmische, which was the winter sports area. We got a nice room at the special services General Patton Hotel It was very nice and we hated to leave. We had dinner dancing every night to a big band which played all our good dance music. We danced up a "storm" every night.

We went to special services where I could get skis and equipment to go skiing while Fay watched and took movies of me. I wasn't much of a skier then. Just making down the beginners slope without falling was a chore. Little did I know that in ten years after moving to Lake Tahoe, Nevada, I would become a medal winning Masters Ski Racer in the US Ski Association.

We were now going to visit Venice, Italy, and stop at Innsbruck on the way but I can't get out of Germany with the VW not having permanent license plates on it. We had to find a way to sell it and get back some of our money we had paid for it. Fay found out that the OIC of the MPs belonged to our church, the Church Of Jesus Christ Of Latter Day Saints. He said that he could get $80 for it and somehow get the plates for it. We got rid of it and hopped a train for Venice not stopping at Innsbruck as we went right by it. We got to Venice after traveling through one of the longest tunnels in the world under the Alps. We got our place to stay and proceeded to see as many of the historical sites we could in a week. We road the boats everywhere since it is all canals. We did walk over many of the bridges and went to an island where all the wonderful Venetian glass comes from. We were disappointed because the unions were on strike and all the museums were closed throughout all of Italy! We were going to stop at Florence to see Leonardo's works but it was closed also so we continued on to Rome. When we arrived in Rome we proceeded to find another pensione. It had snowed in Rome for the first time in 20 years and the place where we were staying did not have any heat. We had to get extra blankets to stay warm.

We toured Rome going to all the historic spots. The Coliseum, the Forum, Etc., ending up at the Vatican on Italian Veterans Day. We got in just in time to see all the Nuns in a grandstand and before the Pope came, the Cardinals came in swinging the pots of incense. When the Pope came in the Nuns let out a shriek like a rooting section. The Pope blessed a lot of Veterans. We wanted to see the Sistine Chapel but it was closed. I had visited Rome during WWII but did not get a chance to see the Pope at that time or the Sistine Chapel.

One day coming out of our pensione I saw two Mormon Missionaries tracting on the sidewalk with an easel showing the Book of Mormon and explaining the LDS church. As I walked up to one of the Missionaries I asked, "How's business?' He replied, "Quite good". I then asked both of them if they knew a missionary named Arthur Kent. They said, "Yes, he was our head missionary and had to go home on an emergency". I then told them that he is engaged to my third daughter Patty, how about that, what a small world. We then wished them "Good Luck" and went off to see the sights.

After staying about a week we hopped the train for Naples, Italy. We found another pensione and got settled. I then rented a little Fiat car and we set out for my old WWII base in Cerignola about 100 miles east of Naples. We got up on the Autostrada, a toll road, and away we went. There was very little traffic on this road in those days and we flew as fast as the little car would go. It was sure was a change from 1944 when I had to ride in a weapons carrier from Cerignola to Naples on a two lane winding road through the mountains. When we got Cerignola I found the road that went to our old Base called San Giovanni. When we got there I could still see the old Jeep tracks going through the olive orchard where I had my tent. I met an Old Italian farmer and between my poor Italian and sign language I told him I was a pilot that flew out of here during WWII. Some of the old buildings were still standing but the runway was a big wheat field now.

After viewing the area we drove back to Cerignola and Fay did some window-shopping. Then I showed her the old church, which was a good landmark in this big plain. After trying to talk to the natives that I was a "piloto" during WWII we left for our trip back to Naples. The little Fiat buzzed right along at 100kph and was a gas miser. We made it back to Naples before dark, no sweat. When we ate out I always carried a small computer to compute the local currency to dollars. This way I always knew what they were charging me and not trying to rip me off. It was a good idea especially in Italy.

After staying our allotted time of about a week we were off to Genoa and Monte Carlo. We were going to stop at the Leaning Tower of Pisa but decided to go straight through to Monte Carlo. In Monte Carlo we stayed at a "dump" it was the only place to meet our pocket book without a reservation. We made it do since we were only going to sleep there. We made all the sites even taking a bus to Cannes. Went to the noted hotel and beach where the girls change into their swimsuits right on the beach without showing a thing! After the bus tour to Cannes we came back to Monte Carlo. The next day we visited the Castle to see if we could see Princess Grace Kelly but she was not there and neither was her husband but we did see the changing of the guard, which was very colorful. We had a chance to visit all the little souvenir shops along the way down from the Castle. The next day we had a chance to walk part of the racecourse of the Monte Carlo Grand Prix. It was quite interesting especially when they race through the tunnel to go around the harbor down the main street then up the hills and around all the houses and past the Casino then through the tunnel again.

One night we decided to go to the Casino but when we got there they would not let me in because I did not have on a shirt and tie under my sport coat. Instead I had a very nice turtle necked sweater. On top of this it was $10 per person to get in to lose your money! I told them at Las

Vegas, Nevada all the Casinos are free and much nicer than this. Of course I remember when you could not get into the Monte Carlo Casino without a tuxedo and your lady had to have an evening gown on. We also attended Jacques Costeau's Marine Museum. It was very interesting since he was the one that invented the Aqua Lung for deep sea diving. He also invented the scuba diving system. His systems did away with the heavy diving suits of old and were not restricted in your movements. He invented many other devises aboard his exploring ship the "Calypso" for the exploration of the oceans depts. By the time we were ready to leave Monte Carlo we had so much stuff we had bought we had to pack it up and send it home. This made us free from all that baggage to haul.

In the meantime we packed up to leave for Barcelona, Spain. When we got aboard the train we found a lot of young people traveling with their backpacks dressed in Levi's, which had seen a lot of wear and were a little tattered and torn. One young fellow sat next to us had on old jeans and an old tee shirt with his backpack. I forgot where he was from in the States but he was bumming through Europe. I think most of the young people were staying in Hostels.

When we got to Spain we did not have to go through Customs. I gave an agent a Silver American dollar and he handled the whole process. We were dressed up compared to the rest of the passengers. I always had on dress slacks and a shirt with tie and a sport coat or a white sheepskin parka. Fay was in dress slacks with her mink jacket. We stood out so much that we must be Americans. All the rest of the people had to go through Customs.

When we got to Barcelona I found a nice penthouse apartment for $10 a day! It was very nice with a great view of the city. Barcelona was a beautiful city with wide tree lined streets and big buildings and very clean. It also had a big seaport with many ships in the harbor from all parts of the world. It had many big department stores so we had to go shopping. In one of the department stores we were standing near the escalator when I noticed a two young men getting on the escalator and as they got off I said, "You are Mormon Missionaries". They asked, "How did we know". I said, "The Gospel books you are carrying were a dead give away and your clean cut looks". I then asked them where they were from. One was from

Utah and the other was from Auburn, California! I told him we owned the Flite Strip Resort on the road to French Meadows. He then told us that his father worked there for a short period of time and he knew where it was. I could not believe it. I got his fathers phone number and promised to call him when we got back home that we saw his boy in Barcelona, Spain and he looked good and was doing well.

We did a lot of window-shopping. On this day we were looking in the window of this ladies shop when Fay spotted a beautiful full-length leather coat. She had to go in and try it on. Of course she looked ravishing in it and I told her I would by it for her if they would take master charge, thinking no chance. They took master charge I just got stuck for $600. But she was worth it. I later went into men's leather goods and bought a leather sports coat for $39 a big bargain. I wore that leather jacket for 15 years.

We were going to Madrid but our time and money was running out so after seeing all that was interesting in Barcelona we left for Paris, France. On arriving at Paris we found another pensione, which was not the best, but we made it do since the price was right. The next day we went to the Louve, which was quite an experience. We saw all the great paintings that were painted by many renowned painters throughout the centuries. The place was huge and some of the paintings were also big. The ones painted by David for Napoleon were the largest being about 20 feet long and 10 feet high. The room where these paintings were hanging was big enough to land my C-195. We saw the statue of winged victory and Venus de Milo. We also saw the Mona Lisa and were surprised to see how small it was. We notice a lot of amateur painters copying all the old masters. It is one of the few places that this is allowed. We had a tape which when held close to your ear, would explain each painting Being a teacher I got a special low cost admission fee, which made it nice. We strolled along the river Seine and saw Notre Dame and the excursion boats plying up and down the river. We went to the French Quarters. We had lunch on the Rue Michelle and when we came out there was a big procession of official cars coming down the street from under the Arc de Triumph. I think it was the president of France going to some doings. The next day we went to Eiffel Tower Fay was afraid to go up to the top with me so watched me go up to the top. It was a magnificent view of Paris but it was hampered somewhat with the smog haze that covered the city. I could see most of the Government buildings. If I remember correctly there was a telescope for me to look through. Paris was getting smoggy just like L.A.

Riding the Metro was quite an experience it went fast and was very quite since it run on rubber-tired wheels. It also was quite reasonable to ride and was a quick and easy way to get around. You just had to remember which stop you were supposed to get off. We had map of the area, which made it fairly easy to get around. After seeing most of the sites we wanted to see we got the train to Calais, France to catch the Ferry to Dover, England, for our trip back to London. We wanted to take the Hydrofoil when we arrived in Calais but just missed it and had to take the high-speed ferry instead. Again I gave a gentleman a silver dollar and we did not have to go through customs again. Each time our passports were returned with the necessary stamps on them.

When we got to Dover we took the train to London we had just enough time to do last minute shopping before we had to catch our aircraft at Heathrow to go back home to New York. When we arrived at Kennedy Airport, New York at 9pm at night they were having a full-blown blizzard at JFK Airport and we couldn't land. The pilot was instructed to go into a holding pattern until the weather got better. This meant that he had to have at least ¼ mile visibility and at least a 200-foot ceiling. We must have been in the holding pattern for at least an hour, which is shaped like an oval racetrack and was over a fix. The entire east coast was affected by this weather so we had to sweat the weather out. The pilot finally got clearance to land but the winds were still very strong and gusty. As we broke out of the overcast we were on the final approach and it was a little bumpy but the pilot made a beautiful landing and all the passengers let out a loud cheer, as we were rolling down the runway. By the time we arrived at Customs everybody was very tired since we had been in the air for about 6 or 7 hours and sweating the weather out and by this time it must have been close to midnight. When we got to Customs he asked me what my occupation was and what I had to declare. I told him I was a schoolteacher coming back from a sabbatical leave and since we had sent most of our stuff back home already and declared it we had not much show. After showing our passports he let us go right through with no delay. Now we had to rent a car to get back to McGuire AFB in New Jersey. It was still storming out with the snow coming down quite heavy. We finally go our car and started for McGuire. After driving about half way there we decided to stop and get a motel and get some rest before going any further in the storm.

The next morning we drove to McGuire AFB to where we had parked our Renault. After I got all the snow off the car I got in and it started right up much to my surprise, since it had been sitting for 2 months. After turning our rental car in we headed for home down the Pennsylvania Turnpike. Nothing exciting happened on the way home as we toured down the "pikes". It was now Fay's turn to drive and give me a break to get a little sleep. As I was sleeping I had that old feeling we were going quite fast. I woke up and Fay was racing a VW and it was "nip and tuck". We were going in excess of 70mph at time especially going down hill. She finally got the best of the VW and left him in the dust. When we got too tired to drive any longer we got a Motel. After going down the Penn Turnpike we switched to the Will Rogers Turnpike to Oklahoma City and I-80 almost the rest of the way home to Huntington Beach. I don't know how long it took us to get home but it was less than a week.

When we got home we checked on Patty and the rest of the family and found out that Patty wanted to get married to Arthur Kent and it was time to open the Resort, 1 April 1971. Patty had known Arthur for quite a while and now was the time to get married. Fay had to stay home to make all the arrangements while I had to get up to the Flite Strip to open the place up for all the loggers and highway workers. This meant that I would have to have a supply of gasoline on hand for the gas station, propane for all the heaters, make sure the generators were in working order, fill the water tank with 6000 gallons of water, etc. I would fly up in the C-195 by myself and get everything ready and hire some temporary help so I could attend the wedding. The wedding would take place on the 25 June 1971.

When I got up to the Resort the people were already waiting for me to open the place up. There were the logging companies and the road workers who were paving the road from the Flite Strip to French Meadows Reservoir. They would bring in their trailers and park them at the Resort for a fee, which gave us a good start for the new season.

Patty and Art would be married at the Huntington Beach Ward and the reception was held in the cultural hall at the church. It was a nice wedding and everyone had a very good time. Patty was the last one to get married so now all our daughters were gone. The beauty about daughters they usually stay close to home. You don't lose a daughter but gain a son-in-law.

All the girls stayed in Huntington Beach except our oldest, Sherry Ann, who was married to Brant Peterson, who was in the USMC. They would be living mostly in the East Coast until Brandt retired then they came back to Huntington Beach where they had bought a home when Brandt was stationed at El Toro USMC base for a short time. This was a smart move, since they still live there.

So after traveling so much with me in the USAF all over the country and to Japan twice they were ready to put down roots and stay in Huntington Beach except Gale who would stay in California but would go from the Flite Strip, to Grass Valley, to Long Beach, to Huntington Beach, and finally ended up at Canyon Lake, where she resides this day with a new husband Richard Bjelland, and her beautiful and only daughter, Sarah Jane Shafer. Unfortunately Gary Shafer, Sarah Jane's Father, was killed in a trucking accident after he divorced my daughter Gale.

After the wedding Fay and I flew up to the Resort in the C-195 with all the supplies we could hold when we got there I would go into Sacramento to try to get a liquor license so we could open our bar. Fay had contracted a carpenter to build an "A" Frame building where the old Quonset hut used to be and I made a bar out of an old shuffle board that was left there. It was 20 feet wide the width of the building.

The best I could do was a Beer and Wine license but later I would qualify for a summer Resort hard liquor license, since we were only open part of the year. This was a big help and brought a lot of people in to the Resort.

I was still on my Sabbatical Leave from school and had to account for my time. I had to prepare and essay for our trip to Europe and now I had to find another subject for the final six months of the sabbatical. Then I had a great idea I would trace US Highway 49 from start to finish It was the Gold Highway since all the towns along this road had gold discoveries from Grass Valley to Death Valley. It would make a good story in my essay when I got back to school. Each week I would fly off in the C-195 to a different town that had an airstrip along the entire route of Hwy 49.

Well we were quite busy during all of the summer months with Fay doing the cooking, which was a real chore since all the loggers and highway workers ate there every night and then we would have the weekenders there. I would be doing the bar tending, gas station attendant, electrician, diesel mechanic, plumber, etc. Our best month would be in October when deer season opened up. The people flocked up and added to the customers we already had staying in our trailer park. We also had French Meadows with a big campground, which was 20 miles beyond us into the forest, which had no facilities outside a boat-launching site. The people had to come to us for any groceries, gas, or emergency repairs since the closest town from them was 40 miles of mountain roads, and that was the little town of Foresthill.

We started to close up when the snow started falling in December after a good season. We had not closed up completely when Fay got cold and wanted me to try and start the old propane forced air heater to get a little warmth in the place. It was too high to reach from the floor so I had to get a ladder to stand on. The heater was situated in the laundry room above the washer and dryer and there was not much room to spare to get to the burner and light it. After trying to light it a dozen times with no success I tried it once again and the thing exploded in my face knocking me off the ladder and I landing on the dryer which cracked a couple of ribs and I could hardly breathe. I had burned my eyebrows off and part of my eyelashes. We went off to the Doctor to get patched up. He gave me some pain pills and that was it. I was due back to school on the 2 January 1972 but I hurt so bad that I had to call the school and get an extension on my leave so I could get rid of the soreness in my side.

When I finally got back to school I had no classes. Since I was gone for a year they had put new teachers in all my classes. I then was a permanent substitute for a while until the advanced auto shop teacher transferred out and I got his job. The shop was twice as big as my old basic auto shop. I enjoyed the big shop but the students were not as sharp as they should have been but I made sure that they all caught up to my standards. They would be able to do a brake job, turn brake drums, tune-ups, valve jobs, etc. When I got through with them they would be able to overhaul an engine and do trouble shooting. In fact I was the first auto shop teacher to ever take a team to the Plymouth trouble-shooting contest from Manual Arts High School. They did not do to well but it was a great and first experience for the top students. The ones that participated got trophies and had their picture in the school newspaper.

I found that in this big shop I had to keep everyone busy or I was in trouble. In this shop the students could bring in their car and work on it under my supervision. Teachers could bring in their cars and the students would work on it Anyone bringing their car in to be worked on by the students had to sign a waiver that the students were not responsible for the

After busting up my C-195, I bought a C-182G on 13 May 1987. I flew it 10 years and sold it since Mae couldn't fly any-more. This pictures was taken at Perris Field, CA June 1996

work they did since there was no charge for the work done but only for parts. Of course I supervised all work. After a year of teaching advanced I was offered my old job back teaching Basic Auto Mechanics. I chose to go back to my old shop. It was better for me to teach basics, so when they went to advance auto shop they would be prepared a lot more than they were.

When summer vacation rolled around I went up to the Resort for the summer crowd, we had opened in April 1972 as usual. I had flown up with Fay to open up and left her there with my son-in-law Gary Shafer who had quit his job as a brakeman for the railroad in Los Angeles and wanted something to do until his wife, my daughter, Gale graduated from Long Beach College with her teachings degree.

Things were not going well for Fay, so now that all the girls were grown, on May 26, 1972 she left me. I did not get out of school for summer vacation until the 11 June 1972. I was now in a bind and had to hire someone quickly to run the resort until school got out for vacation. Gary was there but could not run the place by himself but his wife Gale would be up to help when she graduated from Long Beach State College. I immediately made an emergency fix for a cook to keep the food flowing to the loggers and road builders and any vacationers who came by.

When school got out I was on my way in the C-195 back to the Resort. I got through the summer and got some new customers from Pacifica, Ca. One of these was Sandy Sanderson who owned an Areonca Champion and when he would fly up to the resort he would let me fly it off our strip. He also owned a C-182, which I got to fly off our strip. We became very good friends and he brought a lot of his friends up to the resort on the weekends. The bar would be jumping on Fridays and Saturday nights. It helped me forget my troubles temporarily.

It was now 1974 and Fay and I have been separated for two years and I was still trying to get some one responsible to run the resort for me when I was not there. Finally one day I got a call from Gladys Caples who had sold me the Flite Strip Resort. She had a friend that had worked for her when they were running the resort when her former husband was alive. Her name was Mae Buckner a divorcee and was now working at the Soda Springs Lodge and wanted a change in jobs. She was a good cook and manager. Gladys gave me her number and I called her and we set up an interview.

I drove up the next day to Soda Springs Lodge and had an interview with her and explained my situation and what her duties would be. She was living in a big Airstream Travel trailer at the time on the Soda Springs Lodge property. We made a deal and she came to work for me. Since she worked there before she was very familiar with the place. She turned out to be very capable. She could do everything from cooking, bar tending, starting the generators to pumping gas! I had help for her when I was not there. She had set up her trailer next to the bar and lived right there on the resort. It made it very handy for her, and me. This was in 1974

After trying to run the place and teaching school at the same time for 4 years I decided to retire from school teaching and run the resort full time. What helped me make up my mind was the fact that the unruly students could not challenge me directly so they vandalized my new Javelin car. They kicked in the fenders and jumped on the hood. Fortunately the school paid for the damages.

I took a leave of absence to make sure the resort would pay enough money to support me and all the help and moved up there permanently. I rented a U-haul van and hauled all my personal goods including towing my Siata sports car behind the van. I was always going to fix the Siata but

The Flite Strip Resort in the Winter Jan 1978

it seemed I never got enough extra time to work on it.

Mae was still my manager and doing a very good job. Her grandchildren, Blaine, Blair, and sister Becky would come up during the summer vacation and help doing little jobs selling candy, pumping gas, and running errands, which helped out a lot. Even Diane, Paul Williamson's sister came up to help us. We now had almost a complete grocery supply since I could go shopping in my Ford pickup truck and load it full of everything we needed including liquor and wine for the bar. We also sold ice in the summer time, which was a boon to the campers. I froze water in milk cartons and sold it for 50 cents and it was in great demand. Summertime was a busy time so all the extra help came in handy.

I would now live at the Resort year around and we would get about four feet of snow on the runway so I would park the C-195 at the Auburn airport in the winter. So in order to get around in the winter I decided to buy 5 Yamaha snowmobiles. If you ever tried hiking through four feet of fresh snow in the wintertime it is a bear! Just going down to start the generator, which was about 50 yards from the kitchen, took about a half hour to get down and back if you walked and you were exhausted.

I contacted the Yamaha dealer in Los Angeles and made a good deal to buy five of the small one cylinder snowmobiles from a dealer in Oregon who was going out of business for $3000 and they would deliver them free of charge since I paid cash for them. Now it was no trouble to get around in the deepest snow. With the snowmobile it took about 30 seconds to get down to the generator. I could now rent them during the winter, which brought in more people and more business. Mae and I could ride around our property as well as all over the Big Oak Flat area, which was Forest Service property. It was a beautiful ride in the winter and to see all the deer that wintered there.

One winter my whole family came up since the Forest Service was keeping the road open right to our resort. We had a lot of fun riding the snowmobiles up and down the runway. We would take a night trip through the forest with our lights on through all the back roads on Big Oak Flat and back to the resort. It was quite and experience fortunately I knew my way around the area very well so nobody got lost. All of us were riding double and having a ball.

The Resort was now making money due to the fact that I could fix most anything and do most everything. This way I did not have to pay to have anything fixed, which would be very expensive since a repairman would have to travel 40 miles round trip from the closest town.

One day our deep freeze quit operating, which was very important to our business since we had all our frozen food in it besides our ice. I called the refrigerator man in Auburn to see if he could come up and fix it. He told me that it was too far, 80 miles round trip, and he would have to charge me from the time he left his shop until he got back. I asked him if he liked to fly. He said that he did. With that I told him to get himself out to Auburn airport with all his tools and I would pick him up in 15 minutes and fly him up to the resort to fix the deep freeze. I got in the C-195 and picked him up at Auburn airport and flew him up to the Resort. He had the Deepfreeze fixed in about and hour and I flew him back and he only charged me $45 because he enjoyed the flight so much. When I needed any special help I would fly them and save a lot of time and money and they always enjoyed the quick trip.

Every once in a while I would charge people to go for a scenic ride

Mae on one of our Snowmobiles, Jan 1978

around the area in the C-195. This one-day the winds were so bad at the logging area that they all shut down and came back to the resort. There was no wind at the resort at all so this fellow wanted to pay me to get a ride around the area but I told him the weather was not good for sightseeing. If we had wind farther up the mountain it would be hitting here soon and it would be very turbulent at this altitude. He insisted and against my better judgment I relented. We took off and I climbed to 10,000 feet and was making a big circle when we started to hit rough air and the dust was up there with us. . I decided that it was time to get back to the resort. I circled the strip to check the windsock for wind and direction and it was dead, no wind. I set up my pattern and came in for a landing. I was a little hot so I went around and on the second time I landed on the wheels to get a little better braking action and just as I was about to stop a gust of wind from the tail got us and over we went on our back. I could not believe it I had never had an accident in all the years flying in the USAF and had to bust my own airplane. I was sick since I had flown the old C-195 for 10 years and had almost 800 hours in it. I eventually sold it as is with a new engine that had only 50 hours on it for $2500. I took all my radio equipment out of it and I only paid $4500 for it so I did not lose a thing after flying it for 10 years. I sure liked that old airplane, though.

After running the Flite Strip Resort for about 7 years I decide it was no fun, I was beginning to get a lot of rowdy characters from the bay area and they were drinking and getting drunk and disorderly and shooting their guns at random in the air. I had to get the Sheriff up there a couple of times to warn them that they would have to leave. One day I had septic tank roped off with danger signs on it and one of these bums drove his truck through the ropes and onto the top of the septic tank, which immediately collapsed sending the truck into the muck. I had to call the AAA tow truck to get him out and then he wasn't going to pay. I thought we were going to have a big fight but after the tow truck driver threatened to go after him with a chain and me with a large limb like a ball bat he decided to pay and I told him to never set foot on the property again. Things like this took all the fun out of running the place and this type of clientele was running off my good customers.

I had the greatest urge to go to Lake Tahoe and to buy a view lot on the Nevada side to build a house on it. So Mae and I would take many trips there to see if we could find the ideal place. We were shown a number of lots but none of them were just what I wanted on both south shore and north shore.

One day I went to a realtor at South Shore and told him what I wanted. He was an ex Army Helicopter pilot. He said that he had a property his client would like to sell and he took us up to see it. It was just what we wanted and he could get it for $20,000. I put $500 down to start the proceedings. I had found just what I wanted it had a panoramic view of Lake Tahoe and was an acre of land on the down hill side of the road on Bonnie Court at Stateline, Nevada. We waited and waited for him to call that the deal had been consummated but it never came and I kept calling and could not reach him. I finally had to drive over and demand my money back, which I finally got. I later found out he was living on the deposits on properties he had no right to sell and later lost his realtor license. We were shocked that beautiful lot wasn't ours. Now we would have to start all over again. We went back to the Resort but I was determined to get that view lot at Lake Tahoe on the Nevada side.

I finally leased the Resort to a couple for $600 per month with the option of buying it for $150,000. Mae and I lived in her trailer at the Resort until we would find our lot at Lake Tahoe. The people I rented it to ran the place for about one season and found out that they could not make it pay since they could not do everything like I could. So Mae and I started to run it again until we got a real buyer. I advertised it with State Farm Realty and finally got a buyer who loved the place since they had looked all over for one at the right price and I sold it.

In the interim Mae and I went back to Lake Tahoe to look for our lot. We drove up to the place on Bonnie Court where we had put our deposit on and marveled at the view and as we were driving back on Bonnie I noticed a sign on a big pine tree "For Sale by Owner" with a telephone number to call. This lot was just down the street from the other one with the same view. We went down the hill to a telephone and called the person and bought the lot that day for $15,000, which was an acre bordering the BLM property so nobody could build in front of your view.

Having sold the Resort we moved Mae's trailer to a trailer park at the bottom of Kingsbury Grade at Stateline, Nevada. We had a professional move the trailer since it was so big. This would be in 1979. I also had my Javelin Coupe, my Ford ¾ ton pickup truck, and my Siata sports car to move. Mae had given her Toyota to her son after I fixed the timing gear, which made it run better than it ever did, in fact her grandson got going too fast and rolled it over after all my work. After we got settled in the trailer park I asked my son-in-law, Arthur Kent, who was an architect, to draw up some plans for a house to match the lot. He came up to take a look at the lot and plan the house for the tremendous view. After two drawings I redrew them and modified them to meet my desires. I then took them down the building department in Minden, Nevada and had them approved.

Before I sold the Resort I cut down 21 large Douglas fir trees to trade for finished lumber to build our new home. As it turned out the logger also had a small saw mill and beat me out of quite a lot of lumber. I heard later that his house burned to the ground! I did have enough lumber to

Mae Disbrow at work on our home at 680 Bonnie Court, Stateline, Nevada (South shore Lake Tahoe) Dec 1978

start the house.

I had to have the foundation built and got the best down hill foundation man in the business named Ed. I first had to hire a bulldozer to push some huge boulders out of the way and make the lot ready for the foundation. I was surprised as I watched him drive the bulldozer over the side of the steep incline and land on his blade I thought he was a goner until he spun around and started to level portions of the lot for the foundation. He also pushed the big boulders over the side and let roll them all the way down into the canyon. He was wild. When he got through he could not climb out the way he went in and had to go to the bottom of the lot and take a road out of there and get loaded on a large trailer.

Ed, the foundation man, put in a real foundation for $5000. I got a full perimeter foundation with two backbone foundations all concrete block with reinforced steel and filled with concrete. It was the only one on the block with this type of foundation with no piers like the other houses.

The years were passing fast and I had fallen away from the Church and was not living righteously and I knew it. Then one day I got a call from Salt Lake City verifying my name and my church records. They had tracked me down and I was ashamed of not living worthy. The next thing that happened I got a visit from the Church hometeachers. I knew I had to get back in Church and get my life in order. I started to attend Church on Sunday and finally had a talk with the Bishop. He told me that I had two choices, either stop living with the woman (Mae), or marry her. So I finally married Mae on the 8 May 1981 at Reno, Nevada, by the Justice of the Peace.

Mae and I were working on the big house and people would come by and ask us if we were building the house ourselves and when we would say, yes, they could not believe it. While were building the big house we were living in Mae's travel trailer at the bottom Kingsbury Grade. One day we got word from the owner that the park was being sold for a Seniors Center and we had to move! All the trailer parks in the area were full and we had no place to go. We had the house enclosed but the interior walls were raw dry wall and only the plywood on the floors. We had no bathrooms finished but the plumbing was roughed in. I had a small travel trailer which was not self contained but had living quarters and a sink. Everybody had moved out of the trailer park but us and the owner was after us daily begging us to get out so he could sell the property. I finally moved the small travel trailer up to the big house and parked in the driveway. Mae and I worked feverishly to finish one bedroom and a bath so we could move into the big house with all the facilities. She gave the big trailer to her grandson to live in at Auburn.

I had volunteered to stage the reunion for my 68th Fighter Interceptor

Squadron at Harvey's Casino and a gang tried to rob the Casino with a bomb, which would go off if they did not pay the money they wanted, in the millions. They had all the experts trying to defuse the bomb but had no luck and after they evacuated all the people at the Casino and away from the area the bomb went off and destroyed a lot of the Casino. I finally got into see the manager, after the FBI verified me, to see where we were going to hold our reunion. Fortunately they owned a small Casino at the bottom of Kingsbury grade, which had a nice motel. I made arrangements to stay in the motel so Mae and I could take a shower since I had not quiet finished the bathroom at the big house.

Of course all my friends of the 68th FIS saw the explosion on the TV all over the US and I began to get a lot of phone calls if we were still going to have the reunion. I assured everyone that we were. I would be responsible for three reunions at Lake Tahoe, two in Reno, and one in Las Vegas. I seemed to get the best deal when I put the reunions on so we always had a good turn out.

After the reunion we really started to work on the interior to make the house livable. When we got tired working and needed a break we would go to Arkansas to see Mae's family at Blytheville. During the winter we would go to Mexico to visit my relatives. We would visit my Aunt Mary Villaran and her husband Trino to try to get information on my Father's family for my genealogy. On one trip we went to Colima, Mexico, where my Uncle Ignacio Leyva owned a small store that sold children's clothes, which was called El Negro. I asked him, "Where was your mother born, he said, "In Acaponeta". Which was a small town north of Tepic and between Mazatlan on the west coast of Mexico. So off we went in the Javelin to Manzanillo and up the Pacific Coast on a highway that was not finished as yet but I enquired and found out that VW Campers were driving it so if they could I certainly could but I did not take into account how low the Javelin was. Mae and I proceeded up this road, which was only paved about 100 miles out of Manzanillo. Luckily we left on a weekend when they were not working on the road with the big earthmovers but we had to go slowly to avoid big boulders and keep from scraping the bottom of the car in the deep ruts. Of course there were no bridges and we had to cross the rivers. I was told before I left that we would be in good shape as long as there were no thunderstorms in the mountains to fill up the rivers.

Everything went well getting across the rivers, which were no less than five until we came to a very wide river with a lot of Mexicans ready to help you get across. The river did not appear to be very deep but the water was flowing quite fast. I eased the Javelin into the water and gave it the gas and went about forty feet and it drowned the engine out. Now the water was pilling up on Mae's side and started to come in through the door. I took off my shoes and rolled up my pants and got out and took the fan belt off and dried out the distributor got in and it started right up and with the Mexicans pushing I flew across the river and up the other side like a motorboat.

We made it to Puerto Vallarta and stayed in a beautiful old Mexican Hotel right on the beach. We stayed a few days and saw all the sights and then off to Acapaneta. In Acapaneta I found the old Catholic Church and asked the Priest if they had a Herlinda Mondragon in their files, my father's mother, and my grandmother, after searching his files he had no such name. He could not find any of the family names so we left for Mazatlan and home to Lake Tahoe.

The next year we went down to Guadalajara to visit my Aunt Mary and her husband Trino. While there I would ask her, "Where was your Mother born?" And she replied, "In Colima". So after our visit we headed for Colima again. We went to Acapulco first and stated in a lovely Mexican Hotel with swimming pool and right close to the beach. We also went to see the divers that dive off the cliff at Acapulco. It was very spectacular to see. We had seen it in the movies now we were seeing first hand.

After seeing all the sights we proceeded to Colima and checked into the same hotel we had stayed in before. The next day I found the old Catholic Church that had been built in the 1870's. I found the secretary and told her what I wanted so we started to look through all the old record books. We were looking for my Grandmother, Herlinda Mondragon. All the old records were lined up in a large bookcase that covered the whole wall about 20 feet long and about eight feet high. We started in the morning and by 3pm we had found nothing. The Priest wrote all the records in long hand at the time. The secretary said that they might be in the illegitimate books. It seems if one is not married in the Catholic Church you are illegitimate.

We found my Grandmother Herlinda Mondragon in the illegitimate book plus my Father Luis Gomez, Jr. my Grandfather, Luis Gomez, Sr. and Great Grandfather, Christobal Gomez, my Uncle Ignacio Leyva and my Aunt Guadalupe Leyva and a lot of the other members of the family. I finally found my roots. The secretary typed all the information up in Spanish and the Priest put his stamp on each one and signed that they were official. This would be on the 9 January 1975, at the Parochial Church of Saguario de Colima, Colima, Mexico.

When we got home I had the records translated to English and

Our home under construction South Shore Lake Tahoe 1979

showed them to my daughter Gale who was going to genealogy class in Sacramento. Her teacher was Mexican and Irish and Gale told her about my experience and where I got the information where upon she notified Salt Lake Church Headquarters and they sent some people to Colima to microfilm the entire library for the Church's Genealogy Library located in Salt Lake City, Utah.

As the years passed and the house was made livable I met a nice older member of the Church who was the Patriarch of the South Tahoe Ward.

Our living reoom with rock fireplace and 8 foot watertfall

At the time I was not attending Church regularly like I should. His name was Tony Clark and he was an avid snow skier and about 7 years older than me. I was catching on to the fine points of good skiing at the time. So Tony and I became fast friends and went skiing a lot together. I had bought some used skis at a garage sale with boots and poles so I had the basic equipment to get me down the hill. They were old Salomon skis but were in good condition. I had a friend in Reno, Robin Cridelich that had been a ski instructor at Alpine Meadows at one time so we went skiing together and he gave me a few good tips on good technique when skiing. I managed to ski quite well with them.

Our new home was just around the corner from Heavenly Valley North ski run, which made it very convenient for me but I found out I could ski at Alpine Meadows free because I was over 65 years old, a senior citizen. At the time Heavenly Valley was charging me $14 per day so Tony and I would go to Alpine Meadows and ski free. We found that seniors would not pay over $5 per day at any of the other ski resorts so we had quite a variety of slopes to try.

One day at Church Tony told me that they were going to have a senior's ski race at Sierra Ski Ranch and they gave great prizes and I should enter. He had won his class the year before and got a lot of good stuff. He finally talked me into entering; I was 69 years old at the time and figured if Tony could do it I certainly could. This would be in 1984. When we got there on a Saturday morning there were 13 senior citizens ready to race. I had never raced the gates before and I would be "on the edge again". When I got in the starting gate and looked down the hill with at least 25 gates I said to myself "You have done it now". Then the starter said, "10 seconds" I planted my poles ahead of the timing wand and the next thing was the count down, 5,4,3,2,1 I was away going down this hill and trying not to fall and make every gate, what a thrill. Fortunately I made all the gates and did not fall and placed six after two runs. That did it, I was "hooked". The following week I joined the US Ski Association and became a Masters Ski Racer attached to the Far West Ski Club. They had classes for all ages so I had a good chance of placing if I did not fall or miss a gate. Winter became my ski racing time. I began to race at least twice a week I would race any place there was a race. The Far West Ski Club had scheduled races every weekend during the winter season and gave every member a racing schedule so you could plan your racing days. Every Thursday they had racing at Alpine Meadows Ski Resort where I would race almost every Thursday for 15 years, which helped my skiing very much. Of course I had my spills and wipeouts but fortunately only cracked a couple of ribs a couple of times by landing on my pole with my chest. I always was wearing my crash helmet; in fact I was the only one wearing a crash helmet when I started to ski now everybody wears them. It is a good safety factor.

When I first started to race at Alpine Meadows Thursday races they charged $5.00 for two runs counting the fastest run, only. After everybody had their turn they would award prizes to all the contestants who had their name drawn. Once you signed up for the race they automatically put your name in a hat for the drawing. The local merchants donated the prizes. You also got points for finishing the race, 25 points for first place, 15 for second place, 10 for third place, and 5 points for fourth place. At the end of the racing season they would add up your points and you got so many extra tickets to draw for the big prizes, which included a trip to Jamaica in 1991. I would win almost every time including the trip to Jamaica for one week but got an extra week from a friend, Bill Thomas, who had a time-share there. You had to present to win the prizes and one time I went home early after doing poorly in the race. They called my name for a pair of racing skis and I was not there to claim them. From then on I would always be present for the drawings.

The trip to Jamaica was an all expense paid vacation and we stayed in a beautiful hotel at Morro Bay for a week and the second week at Rio Ocho at the Ramada Hotel. The first night we got there they had entertainment for all the new people that checked in that day it was fabulous. We had a rental car and toured all over the island except for Kingston. They were having trouble there at the time and assassinated the Vice President. I had a great time but poor Mae was having trouble with her Parkinson's disease and too tired at times to do anything. She had been diagnosed at Stanford Hospital in Palo Alto, California in 1988 and the stuff was getting

Our finished home after 10 years of work

progressing worse with no cure in sight. At the airport terminals I got her a wheel chair so she did not have to walk when changing airplanes.

When we got home she complained about the cold and the high altitude since it was hard for her to breathe. We belonged to the Experimental Aviation Association with its clubhouse at Carson City Airport. We would attend their meetings and go to their pancake breakfasts on Saturday. I told Mae that the only way I would move out of the big house was to a place where I had my own airport and hanger for our airplane.

Across the street from the airport was a large mobile home park. I asked Mae if she would like to live in Carson City, which was 3000 feet lower in elevation than the big house. She thought it would be all right. So every Saturday we would go to the mobile home park to look for a good home for sale. After many weeks we finally found one that was suitable for us and bought it. We would move from a 5000 square foot home to a 1400 square foot mobile home. After ten years of hard work on the big house, which was my dream home, I had to move. Fortunately all the family had come up on a Thanksgiving Holidays and got a chance to see our handiwork and enjoy the marvelous view. Some of Mae's family would come to visit to enjoy the view and the warmth of the house with its spacious surroundings. My old friend Don Disbrow and his wife Eleanor would visit us many times even when the house was barely livable. We had many visitors while we lived there who would marvel at our work

I had bought another airplane in May 1997, a C-182 at Brookings, Oregon. It was a bargain a friend told me about so we drove up to see it and the price was right, $12,000 but it needed TLC; it was a "dog". The fellow who made the deal for me told me of a place in Banden, Oregon, that would paint the C-182G for $2500 so he flew it up there for me. When I went back up to pick it up I could not believe it was the same airplane. It was beautiful with the late model Imron paint job in white trimmed in orange and brown. I kept it at Douglas County Airport in Minden. Now I would have my house across the street from the Carson City Airport where I bought a hangar to put the C-182G in to protect that beautiful paint job. I would only have to go across the street to my airport and take off to any place we wanted to go. It was very convenient. It almost made up for the pain for selling the big house. We also were right across the street from the

Racing at the National Masters Ski Meet at Breckenridge, CO

EAA clubhouse. After we got settled and sold the big house I got all my excess stuff in the hanger with the C-182G. We became quite active and would attend the Reno Air Races every year for 20 years. The Club would handle the security on the pit area of the races and it was a good income for our other activities.

We moved down to Carson City in 1990 and Mae was getting worse gradually. We did fly back to see her family every year in Arkansas and Tennessee in the C-182G. One time we were visiting one of her sisters Lou Ellen in Gurdon, Arkansas, we were supposed to stay a week but after three days she wanted to go home she did not feel well. The weather was bad but she insisted. I told her it would be a rough ride since there were thunderstorms all over the route home. Luckily I had a loran in the airplane, which made navigation easy. We skirted all the thunderstorms and made it home safe and sound. Mae never flew with me again in the C-182G since the altitude and sitting so long in one place without being able to move around bothered her.

Mae was getting worse so we decided to take a trip to Hong Kong

Racing at Mammoth, Ca in the local Far West Races
Dec 2003

before she would not enjoy it. We spent two weeks there and I had a great time since I had not been there for years. Hong Kong had changed so much I could hardly believe it. There were so many high-rise buildings and modern changes it was hard to believe. We visited all my old places I used to go when I was on active duty in the USAF and stationed in Japan. After a while Mae would want to sleep a lot so I would go out by myself to take pictures. When we got home she was not getting any better and she was tiring quickly. In fact I had to ride her in the car to the EAA meeting just across the street. She could not walk that far. I thought living in Carson City would be better for her but it was just as cold as Lake Tahoe at times and much hotter in the summer. Finally her only son Eddie Aud died so there was nothing to keep her in this part of the country. We had lived in Carson City for 5 years now and I was 500 miles from all my family. I would periodic fly down to Huntington Beach to see them in the C-182G by myself now I was thinking of moving down to Southern California where the weather would be much better for Mae and down at sea level where she could breathe easier. I would be close to all my family, which was growing fast and I could enjoy them more often. I would miss my skiing, which was so close that I could ski any day I wanted to and the conditions were usually excellent in the winter. I did have Big Bear to practice my skiing in the winter, which was relatively close to the L.A. Basin.

My daughter Gale was living at Canyon Lake, near Lake Elsinore, California, at the time and had remarried to Richard Bjelland. I contacted her to see if there were any homes in her area that we could buy. After discussing it on the telephone I decided to fly down and check the place out. After a couple of flights down there I went around the place with my son-in-law Paul Williamson the husband of my youngest daughter Karen. We finally found a mobile home that was ideal and it was better than the one we had in Carson City. The price was right so we bought it for cash since we had sold our old one in Carson City. I rented a U-Haul truck and trailer and loaded all our stuff aboard with the help of the EAA members and moved to Canyon Lake, California. After getting settled I checked to see if I could get help for Mae, which was beginning to be a real chore. I hired a housekeeper, Mary Padilla, and a caregiver Bea Hayes so I could go skiing in the wintertime. I now had good equipment and was skiing much better. I also got help from the Care Department of Riverside County. A lady would come in from SCAN and HMO I belonged to. I now was covered in the time for 9am to 5 pm but the worst part was from 5pm to 9am.

With all this help I could take off and go skiing in the winter and not have to worry that Mae was not having good care. I would get special help when I would go for the weekend or longer. I would practice my skiing at Snow Valley in the San Bernardino Mountains. I started to race all over the United States from California to Maine in all the USSA Masters races plus a lot of the Far West races. I would race in the Western Regional races, the Nationals, and the International races and winning or at least placing.
Mae was getting worse and was keeping me up at night. One day I asked

her if she expected me to do this the rest of my life. She was now in a wheel chair but could walk a little with a walker. She said that she did not expect me to do this forever so she agreed to go to a rest home after taking care of her for 12 years. I made arrangements to put her in the Stanley Healthcare Center in Westminster, California. It was right close to Huntington Beach and all my family. I could now see her and see all the family at the same time. They would take care of her at the rest home 24 hours a day and give her much better care than I could ever give her.

I visit her regularly at least once a week. It is heart rending to see her gradually going down hill and I can't do a thing about it. She is still taking her medication that only slows the process down but no cure as yet. I feel so sorry for her and also for the old ladies that are in the same fix. Some are worse than Mae. Mae can hardly talk and when she does try I can't understand her. She can't feed herself and all her food has to be pureed

since she can hardly swallow. She can't walk and is in her wheelchair or in bed. I ask the Lord every night how long does she have to suffer?

I am still skiing at 88 years old and still winning since the competition is getting sparse in the 85+ class. There are three of us still racing in this class, John Woodward, Rodney Alard, and Me. I heard that there was a new skier that just came into our class at the National Races at Aspen, Colorado this year and he beat John Woodward. I have never heard of him because I heard that he only skis in Colorado. I did not go since it was too expensive to win a 50-cent medal and the place is overrated and overpriced my ego wasn't that big. It was a good thing since the weather was too hot and the snow was not good and they had canceled some of the races.

When I go to the first race of the season everyone asks me how I stay in shape in the off-season. I tell them that I am a ballroom dancer and I get as much exercise as they do riding bicycles and climbing mountains and having much more fun. I dance at least three times a week. They also wanted to know how I look so young for my age and have so much energy, what was my secret. My testimony is the Lord said that if I kept his commandments I would be blessed and if I did not I had no promise. I try to live his commandments daily and he has blessed me beyond my fondest dreams. I have had a wonderful life even with all the adversity I have had to endure. But the Lord didn't say this life would be easy. This adversity is to make one stronger so we can endure all things to return to the presence of the Lord.

One night I stayed at the San Diego Marine Corp Recruiting Depot in their BOQ and was hungry so I went to the old Officers Club and found that they were having a dinner dance. As I was eating my dinner I noticed this one fellow was with two women and was dancing with them alternately. He would dance with one then she would sit and he would dance with the other one and she would sit. I said to myself, "I'm going to help this guy out", so I asked the nice lady if she would like to dance. She consented and she was a very good dancer. I found out that her name was "Pirry" Petrich and the fellow with her and her friend Ava was her dance instructor and a professional escort named Tom. This was how I started to dance again after many years and at least 3 times a week, which was wonderful exercise and kept me in shape for skiing. I am still dancing with Peroska "Pirry" Petrich who became my wonderful friend and dance partner. We dance all over San Diego and enter contests when the opportunity arises. Our specialty is the Tango and the Waltz but we can dance anything including all the Latin

Bill Disbrow, Helena & Stanley Timoshek at the top of Heavenly Valley Ski Lift, CA 1989

American dances. We have now been dancing together for three years and getting better all the time.

Well winter is here again and I'm at Mammoth Mountain for the first race of the season. I am now 89 years old at the end of my 80+ class wondering if anybody in my class will show up. There may be a new skier coming into this class now but it is harder for me since I have to race against 80+ in the Far West Ski meets and in the 85+ in the championship meets. My ambition is to make it to 90 years old and they will have to make a new class for me 90+. When I turned 85 they had to make a new class for me since they never had an 85-year old racer before. I got a standing ovation after winning three medals. Well here I am waiting at the starting gate again for my first race of the new season and they call my number "407". I take my place in the starting gate. I hear the starter call "Ten seconds" I plant my poles beyond the starting wand as I have done for the past 20 years of ski racing, then the count down starts - five, four, three, two, one.

THE END

MY WWII COMBAT RECORD

Date	Hours	Target
5-06-44	7:00	Campina, Rumania Ploesti Area
5-12-44	6:25	La Spezia, Italy
5-18-44	7:30	Ploesti **
5-23-44	4:15	Nemi, Italy
5-27-44	8:10	Montpelier, France
5-28-44	6:20	Genoa, Italy
5-29-44	4:05	Bos Krupa, Yugoslavia
5-30-45	4:00	Banja Luka, Yugoslavia
5-31-44	7:10	Unirea Spiranza, Rumania, Ploesti Area**
6-02-44	6:35	Miscolc, Hungary
6-04-44	6:20	Genoa, Italy**
6-07-44	5:50	Sestri, Italy
6-10-44	6:10	Ferrarb, Italy
6-11-44	6:50	Giurgi, Rumania, Ploesti Area, **
6-13-44	6:40	Munich, Germany**
6-22-44	6:30	Chiavassa, Italy
6-24-44	6:10	Craivoa, Italy
6-26-44	6:15	**Moosebierbaum, Austria****
6-28-44	6:10	Karlovo, Bulgaria
7-02-44	6:20	Budapest, Hungary**
7-07-44	7:40	Odertal, Germany**
7-12-44	8:00	Miramas, France
7-15-44	7:00	Ploesti, Rumania**
7-16-44	6:00	Munchendorf, Austria**
7-17-44	7:30	Avignon, France
7-20-44	6:40	Freidrichafen, Germany**
8-06-44	8:00	Lyon, France
8-07-44	7:10	Blechhammer, Germany**
8-10-44	7:00	Campina, Rumania, Ploesti Area
8-12-44	6:35	So. France Invasion Gun Positions
8-13-44	7:25	Avignon, France

7-03-44	7:00	Bucharest, Rumania
8-17-44	7:10	Ploesti, Rumania **
8-20-44	6:35	Du Bova, Czechoslavakia
8-21-44	6:20	Hadu Boszorment, Rumania
8-23-44	5:35	**Ferrarb, Italy**
8-26-44	7:10	Bucharest, Rumania
8-28-44	5:25	Bridges, Northern Italy, Last Mission

Almost Got Shot Down On These Missions

** Double Sortie

TYPES AND MODELS OF MILITARY AIRCRAFT FLOWN

TRAINERS: RYAN, PT-22, STEARMAN, PT-17, FAIRCHILD, PT-19, VULTEE, BT-13, NORTH AMERICAN, AT-6D AND AT-6F, BEECH, AT-7, AT-7G, AND AT-11, CESSNA, AT-17A AND AT-17B, LOCKHEED, T-33 JET.

FIGHTERS: LOCKHEED, P-38L, NORTH AMERICAN, P-51D, RF P-51D, AND THE F-82G. FIGHTER JETS; LOCKHEED, F-80A, F-80B, F80C, REPUBLIC, F-84E, NORTH AMERICAN, F-86A, F-86D, F-86E, F-86F. F86L AND THE F-100C, CONVAIR, F-102 AND THE TF-102, NORTHROP, P-61 AND THE RF-61C

BOMBERS: BOEING, B-17E, B-17G AND THE VB-17E, CONSOLIDATED, B-24D, B-24J, B-24G, B-24 H, NORTH AMERICAN, B-25, B-25K, B-25N, B-26B, AND THE B-26C, BOEING, B-29 AND THE RB-29

CARGO: BEECH, C-45B, C-45F AND THE C-45G, CURTISS, C-46, DOUGLASS, C-47A, C-47B, C-47D, C-54G, AND THE VC-54, FAIRCHILD, C-119G.

LIASON: L-4J, L-5B, L-5G, L-13A, L-16A, L-17G, L-19, AND THE L-20.

HELICOPTERS: H-4, H-6A, H19, AND THE H-23.

MISC: Q-14 AND THE AO-10A (PBY)

A total of 68 makes and models

CIVILIAN AIRCRAFT FLOWN

CESSNA: C-140, C-150, C-172, C-182G, C-195A, C-206, C-320
PIPER: CHEROKEE "6", CHEROKEE 180, CAMANCHE 260, TRI-PACER
BEECH: SKIPPER, BONANZA, AND A-36
AERONCA: CHAMPION
STINSON: VOYAGER
GRUMAN: TIGER
HOMEBUILT: TAILWIND, TURNER, AND PIENTOL

A total of 20 makes and models

MILITARY AWARDS

The Distinguished Flying Cross
Air Medal With 5 Oak Leaf Clusters
ETO Medal With Two Battle Stars,
American Defense Medal
Victory Medal
Japanese Occupation Medal
National Defense Medal
Korean Service Medal
United Nations Medal
Longevity Ribbon With Silver Oak Leaf Cluster
The Republic Of Korea Medal
The Distinguished Unit Citation With One Oak Leaf Cluster.

KOREAN FLIGHT RECORD

30 June 1950, C-47B Loaded With 5000lbs Of Howitzer Shells For Delivery To Taegue, Korea, For Combat

30 June 1950, Called In At Itazuke, Japan, to Change Combat Load For Suwon, Korea And To Evacuate All Personel Wanting To Escape Back To Itazuke, Japan

1 July 1950, C-47B Went To Taejon, Korea To Pick Up Wounded And All Personel Escaping To Itazuke, Japan.

3 July 1950, C-47B Loaded With Supplies For The Troops At K-1 Korea.

3 July 1950, C-47B Loaded With General Timberlakes Jeep For K -1 Korea, Runway Collaped Taxiing To Park.

3 July 1950, C-47B Loaded With More Supplies For The Troops, Tire Blew After Landing. After Repair Flew Back To Itazuke To Fly Back To Feamcom In Generals VB-17E. A New Crew Took Over My Job. I Was Needed Back At Flight Test To Greet 150 P-51Dds To Get Ready For Combat

Mar 1951 Assigned To The 101st Fmu At Puson, Korea As Commander. Flew 14 Recon And Recovery Missions With Some Under Fire Until Being Reassigned Back To Japan On 20 April 1951 To Return To The US After My 3 Year Tour Of Duty Was Up.

Printed in the United States
27798LVS00001B/1-36